Misfits of Avalon™

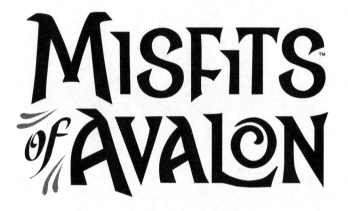

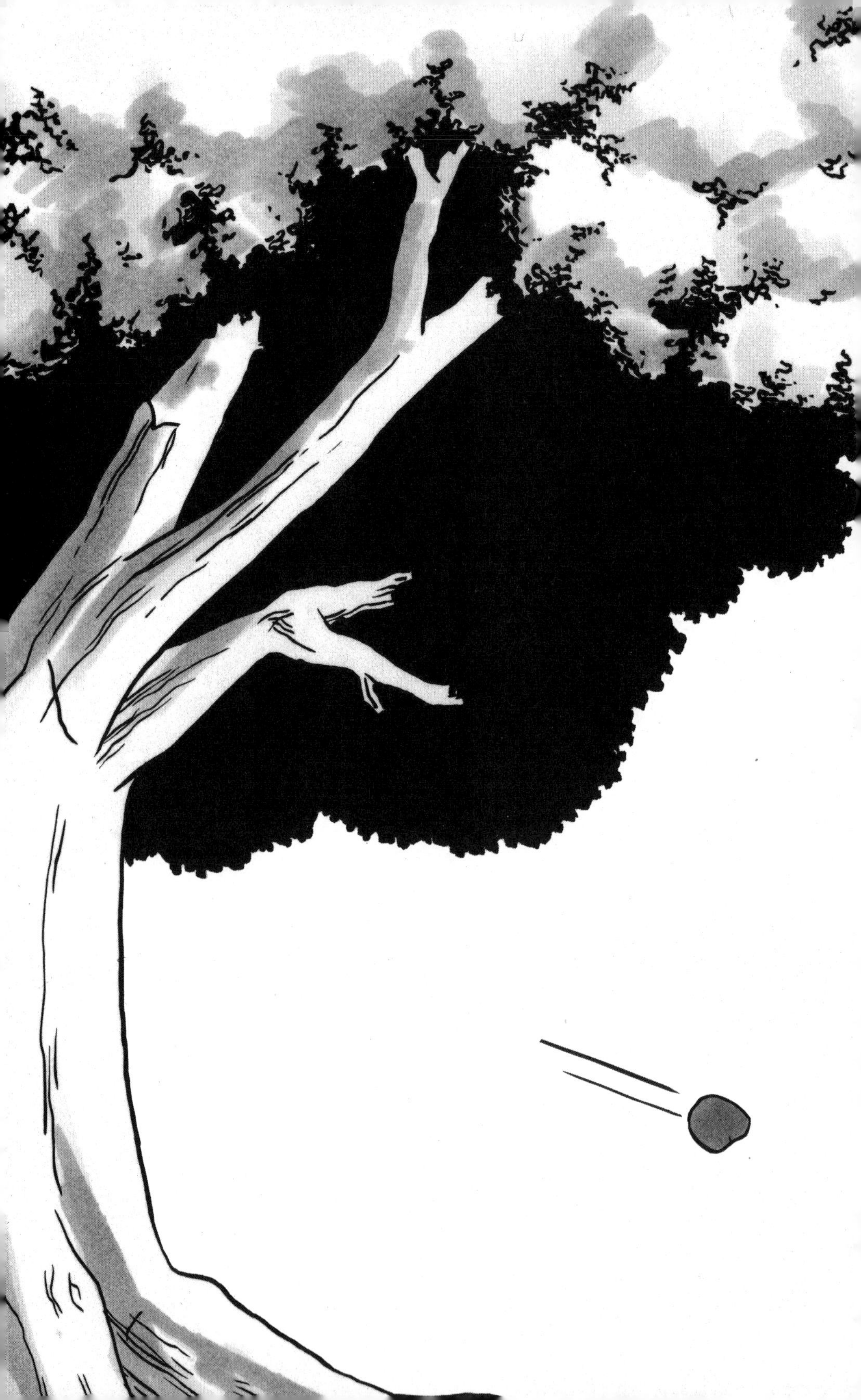

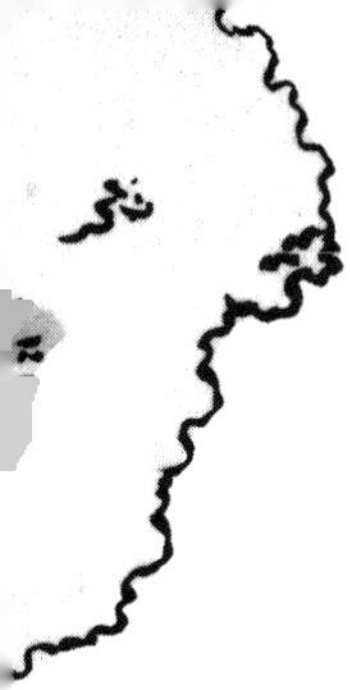

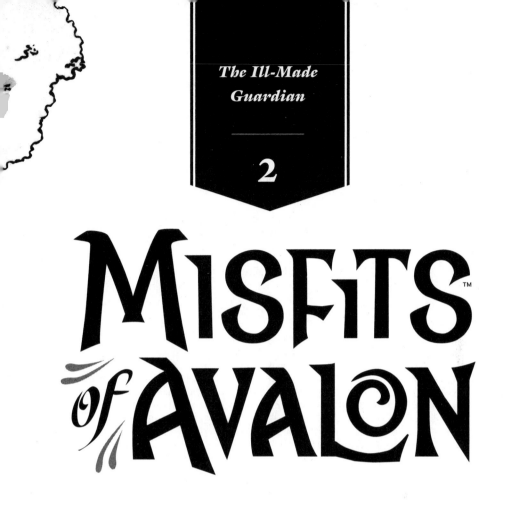

The Ill-Made Guardian

2

MISFITS™ of AVALON

Written & Illustrated by

Kel McDonald

DARK HORSE BOOKS

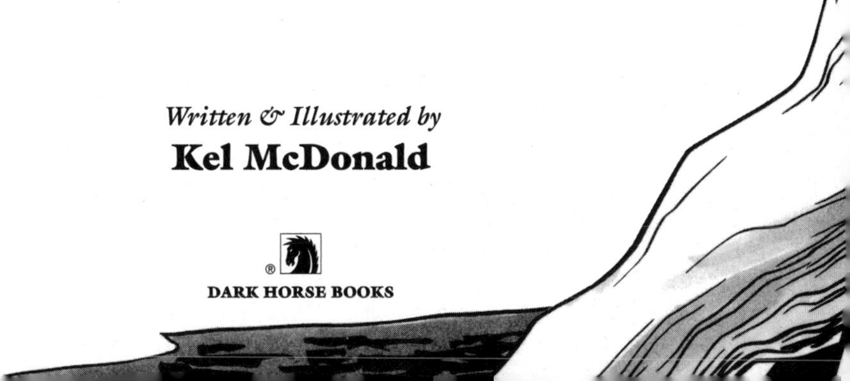

president and publisher
Mike Richardson

editors
Shantel LaRocque and Sierra Hahn

assistant editors
Katii O'Brien and Freddye Miller

collection designer
Sarah Terry

digital art technician
Christina McKenzie

Special thanks to Jay Rachel Edidin.

Neil Hankerson Executive Vice President · **Tom Weddle** Chief Financial Officer · **Randy Stradley** Vice President of Publishing · **Michael Martens** Vice President of Book Trade Sales · **Matt Parkinson** Vice President of Marketing · **David Scroggy** Vice President of Product Development · **Dale LaFountain** Vice President of Information Technology · **Cara Niece** Vice President of Production and Scheduling **Ken Lizzi** General Counsel · **Davey Estrada** Editorial Director · **Dave Marshall** Editor in Chief **Scott Allie** Executive Senior Editor · **Chris Warner** Senior Books Editor · **Cary Grazzini** Director of Print and Development · **Lia Ribacchi** Art Director · **Mark Bernardi** Director of Digital Publishing

MISFITS OF AVALON VOLUME 2: The Ill-Made Guardian

This volume collects comics originally published online at KelMcDonald.com.

Published by Dark Horse Books
A division of Dark Horse Comics, Inc.
10956 SE Main Street
Milwaukie, OR 97222

DarkHorse.com · KelMcDonald.com

International Licensing: 503-905-2377
To find a comics shop in your area, call the Comic Shop
Locator Service toll-free at 1-888-266-4226.

First edition: March 2016
ISBN 978-1-61655-748-5

1 3 5 7 9 10 8 6 4 2
Printed in the United States of America

Contents

CHAPTER 1:
The Loveless and Faithless Ones

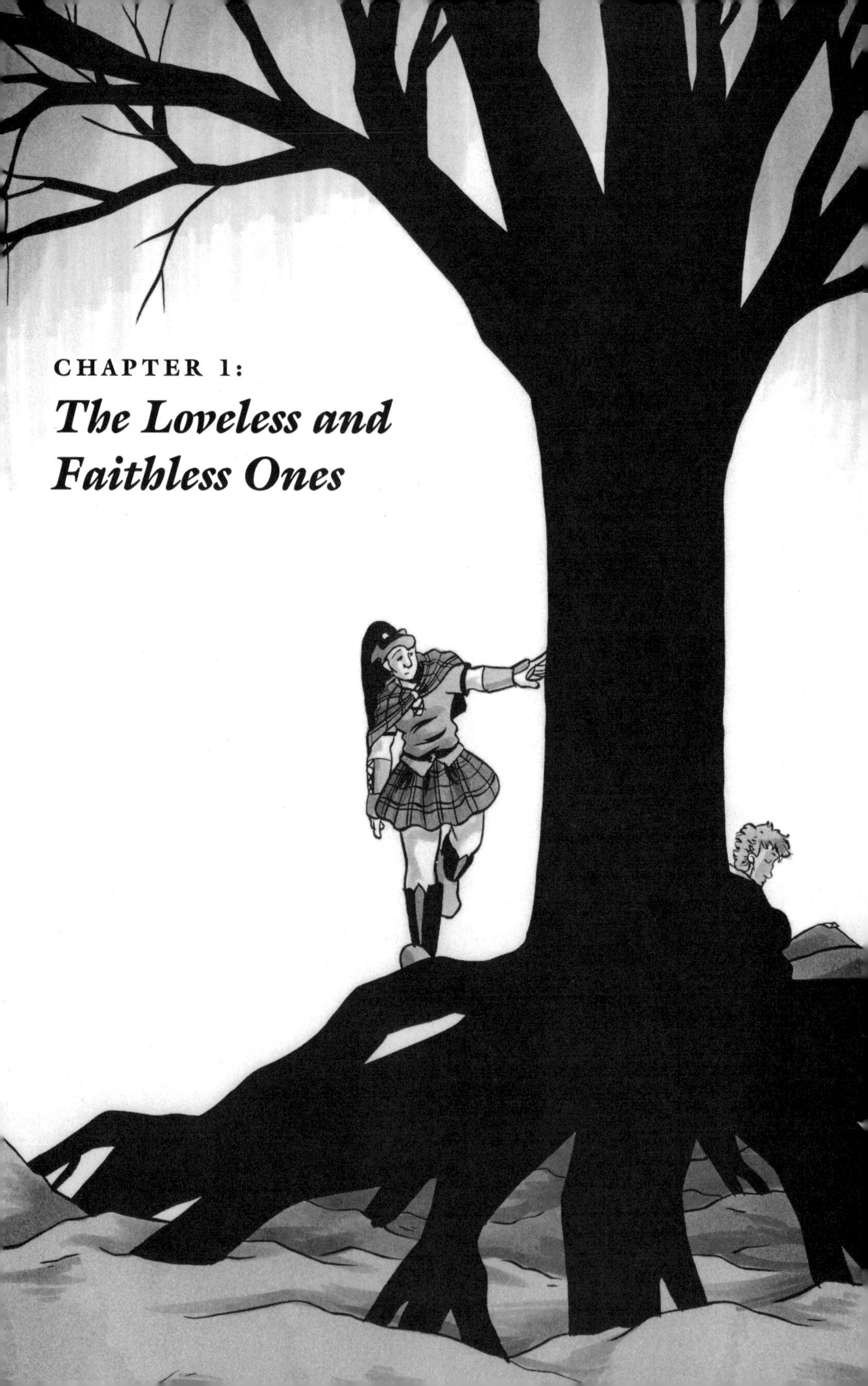

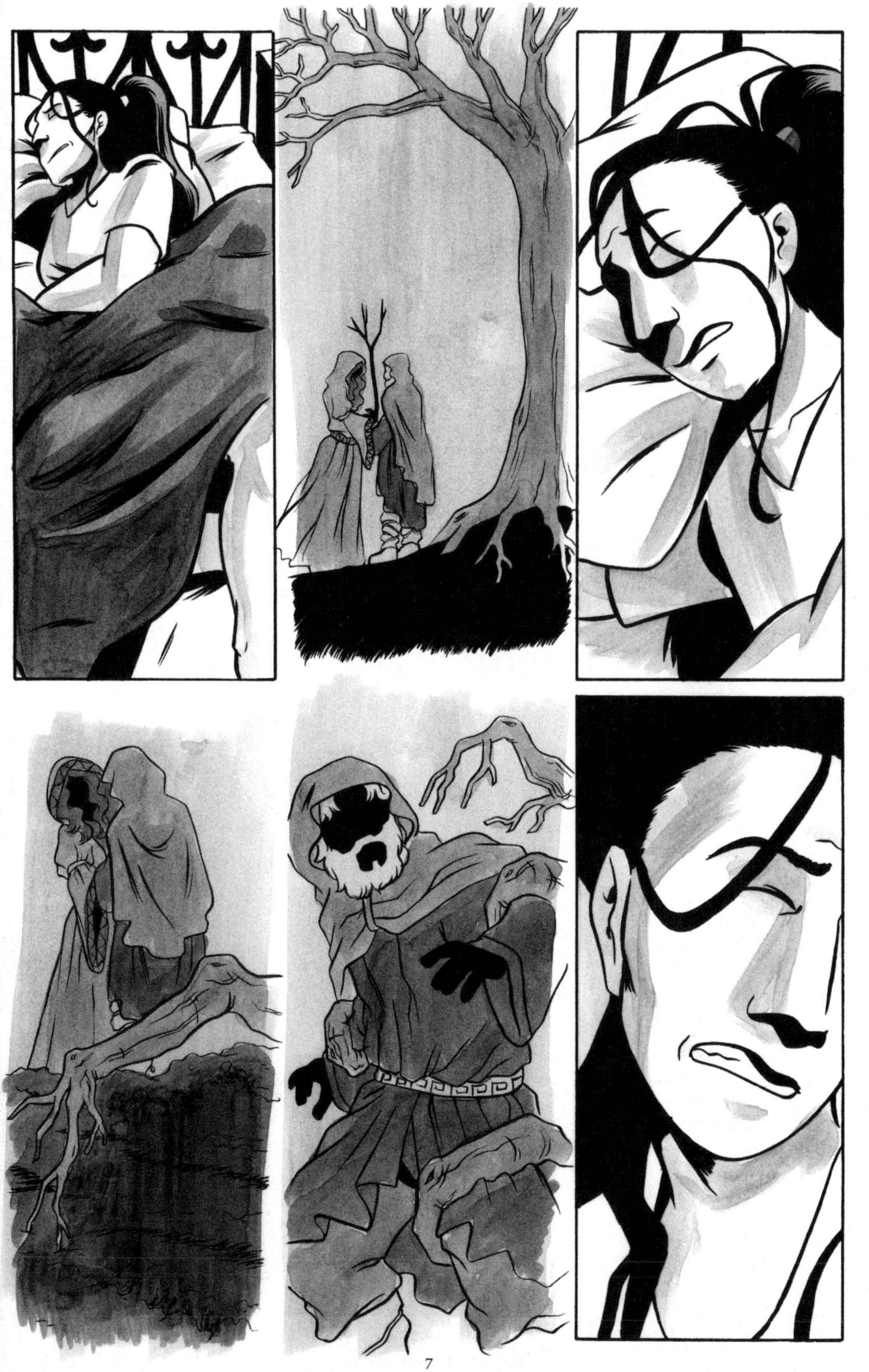

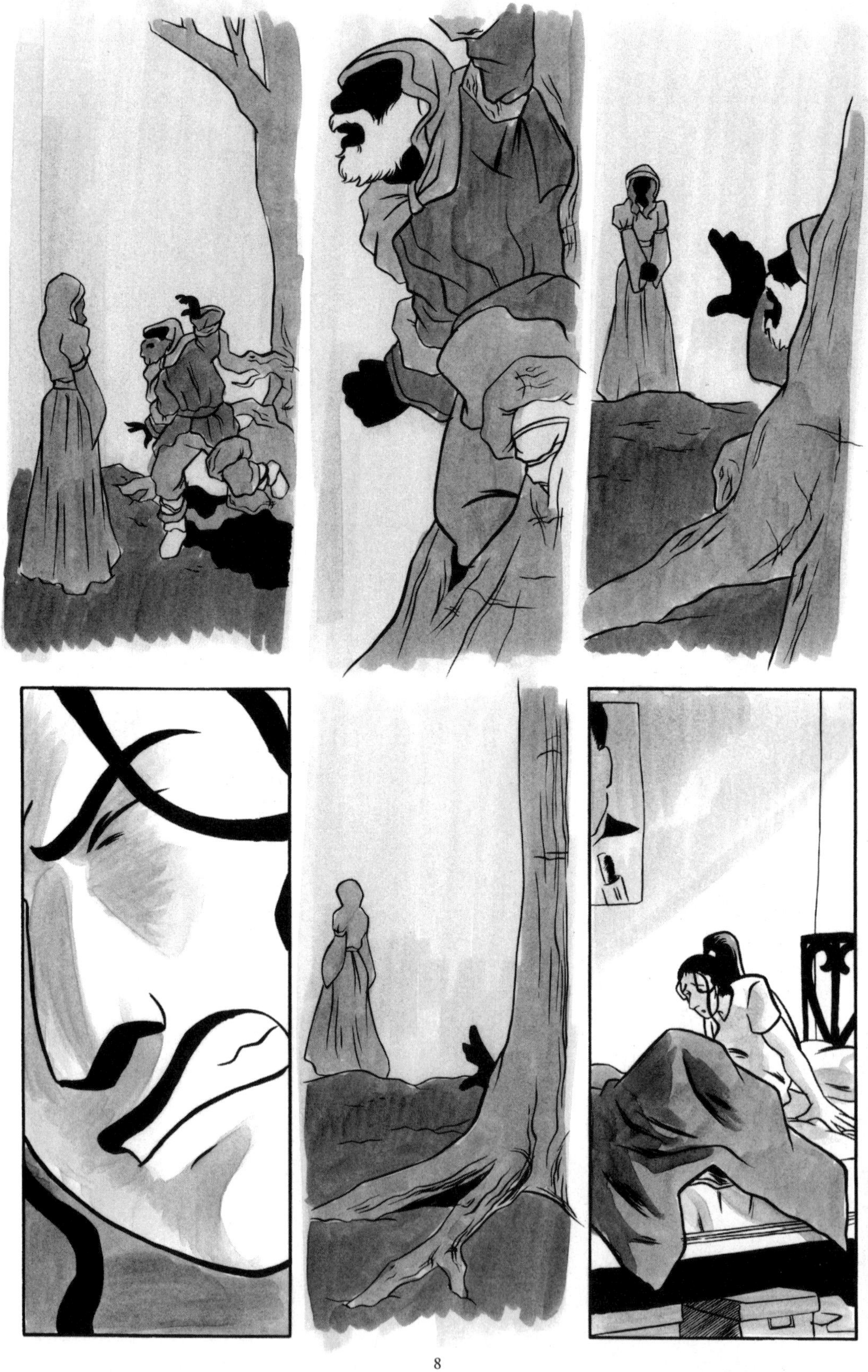

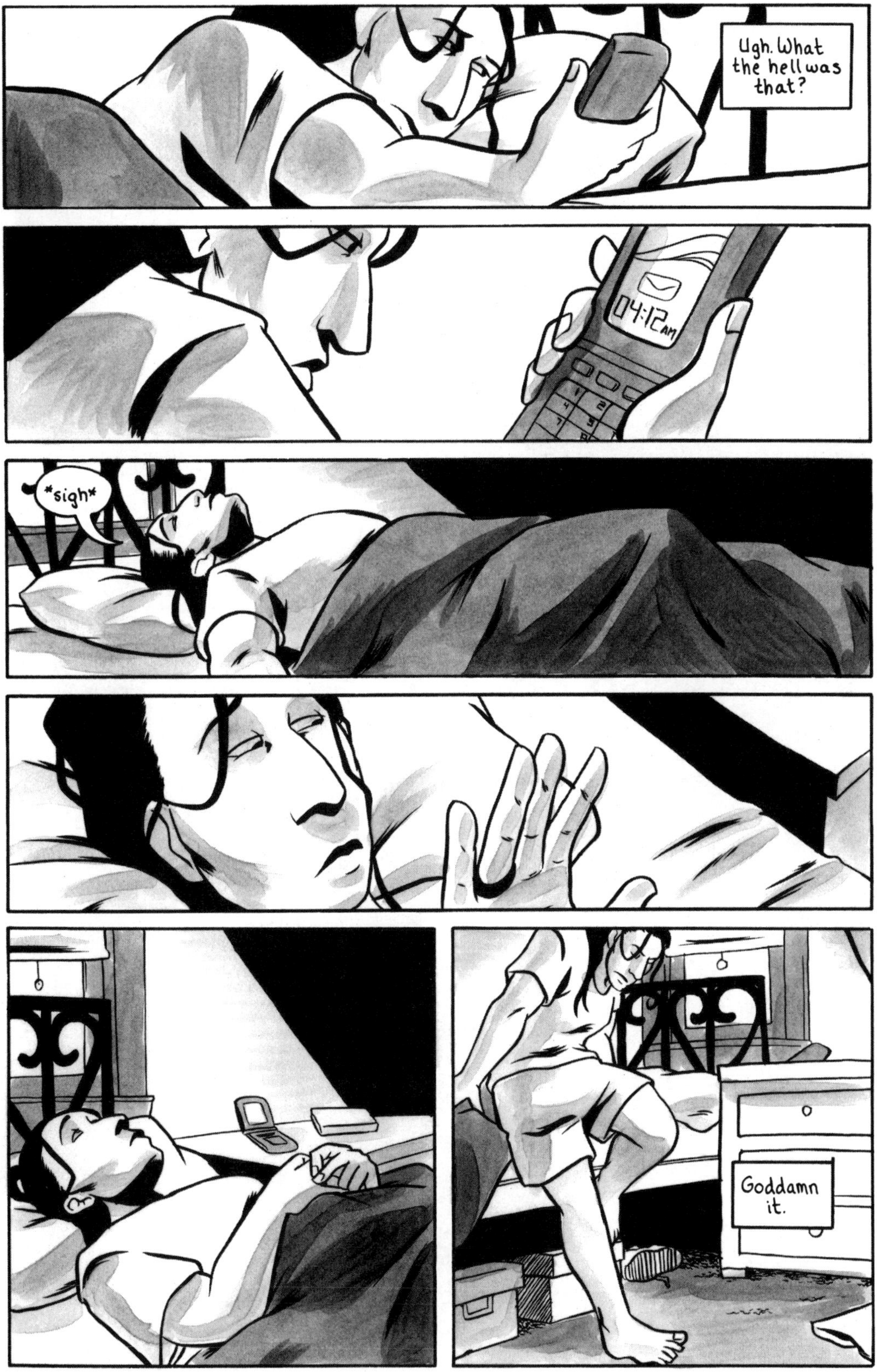
Ugh. What the hell was that?
04:12AM
sigh
Goddamn it.

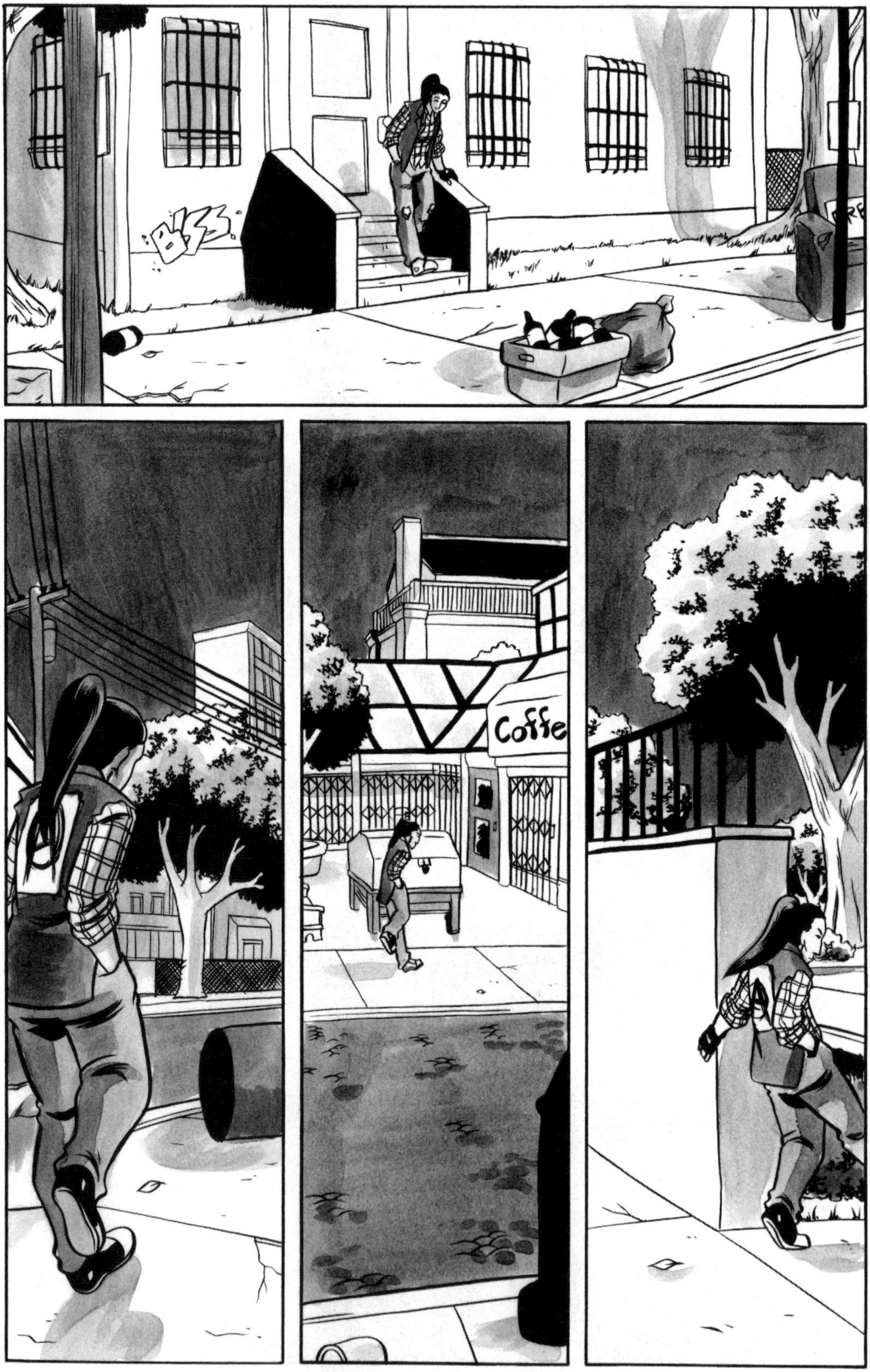
Coffe

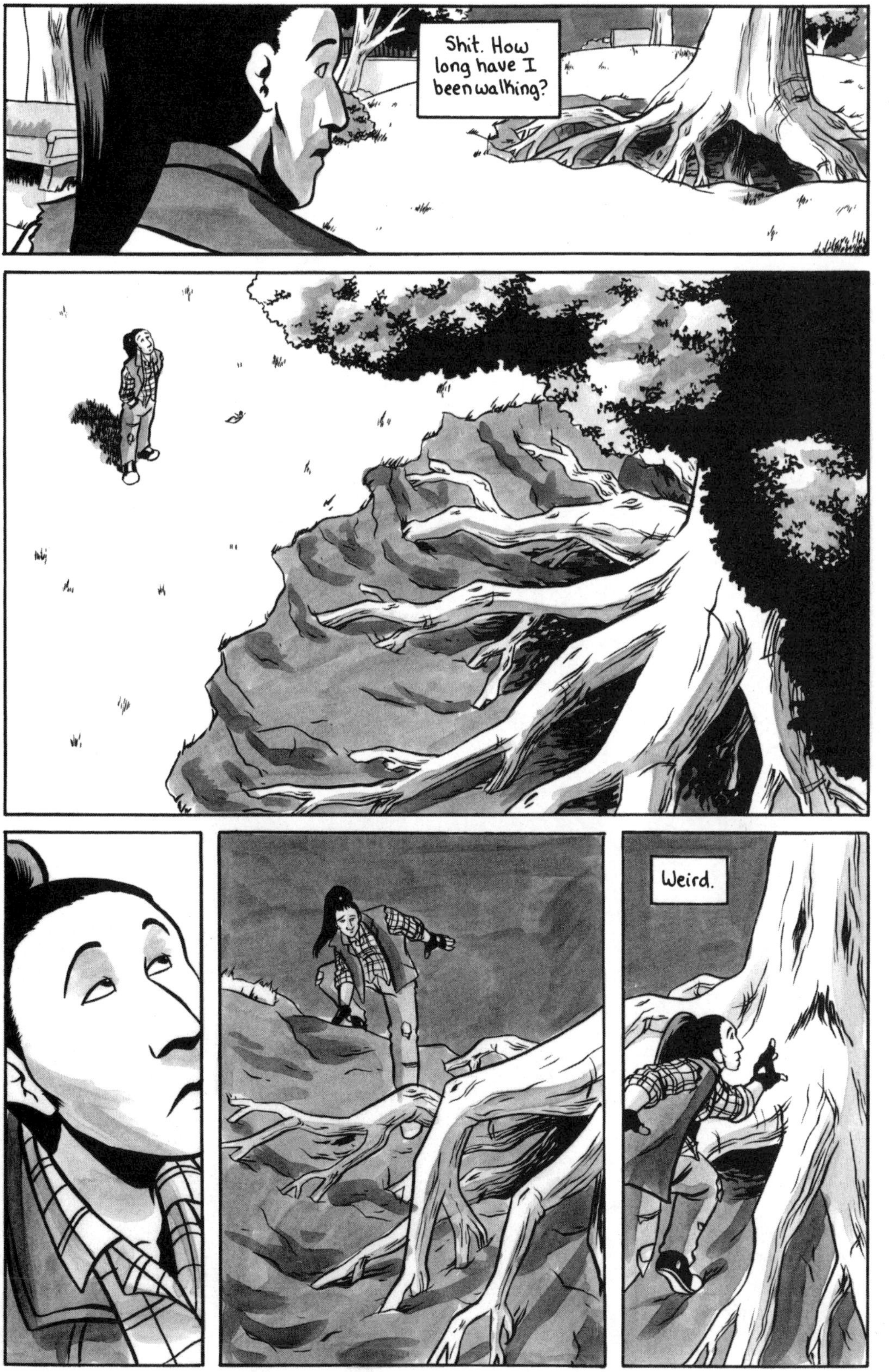
Shit. How long have I been walking?
Weird.

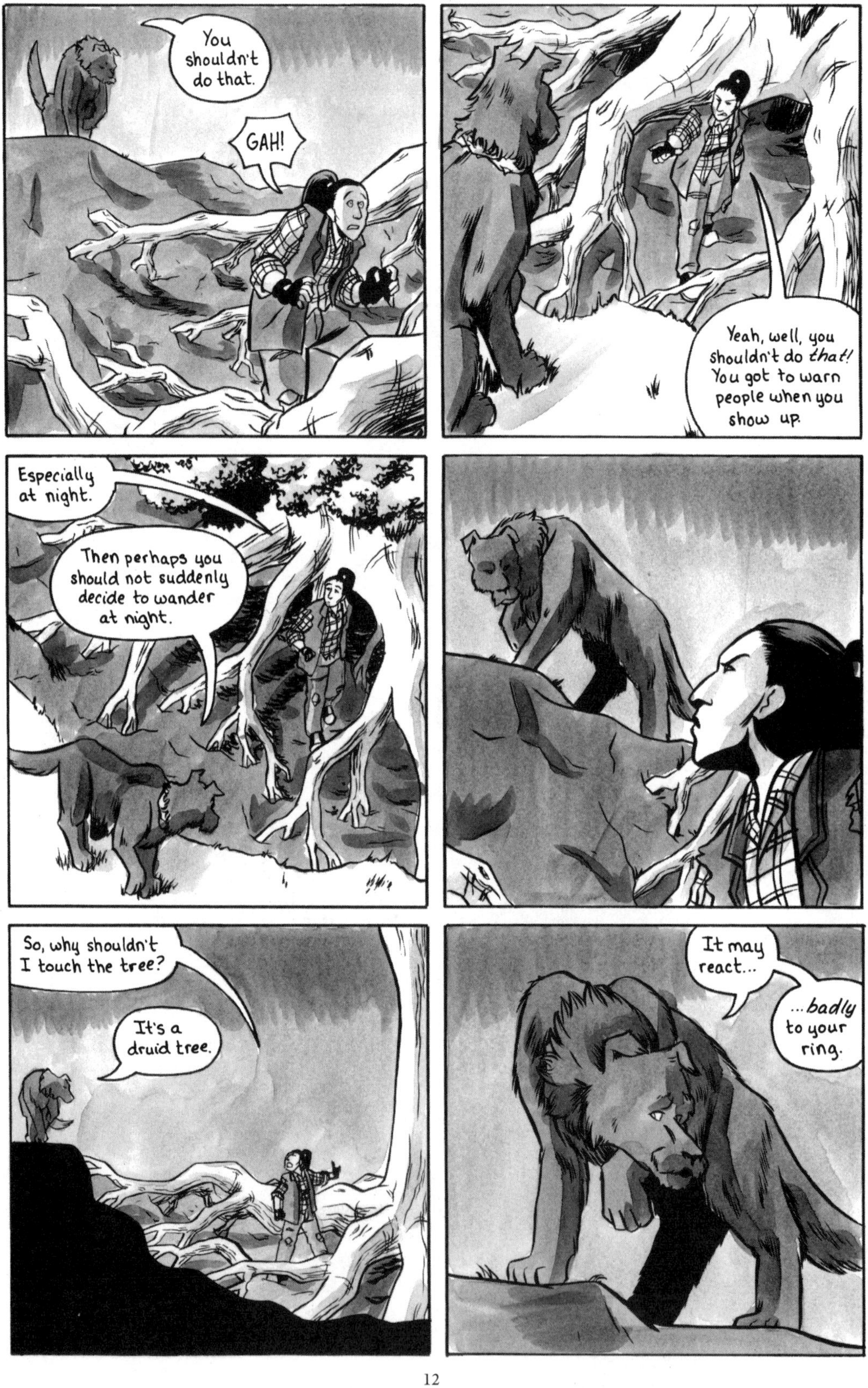
You shouldn't do that.
GAH!
Yeah, well, you shouldn't do *that!* You got to warn people when you show up.
Especially at night.
Then perhaps you should not suddenly decide to wander at night.
So, why shouldn't I touch the tree?
It's a druid tree.
It may react...
...*badly* to your ring.

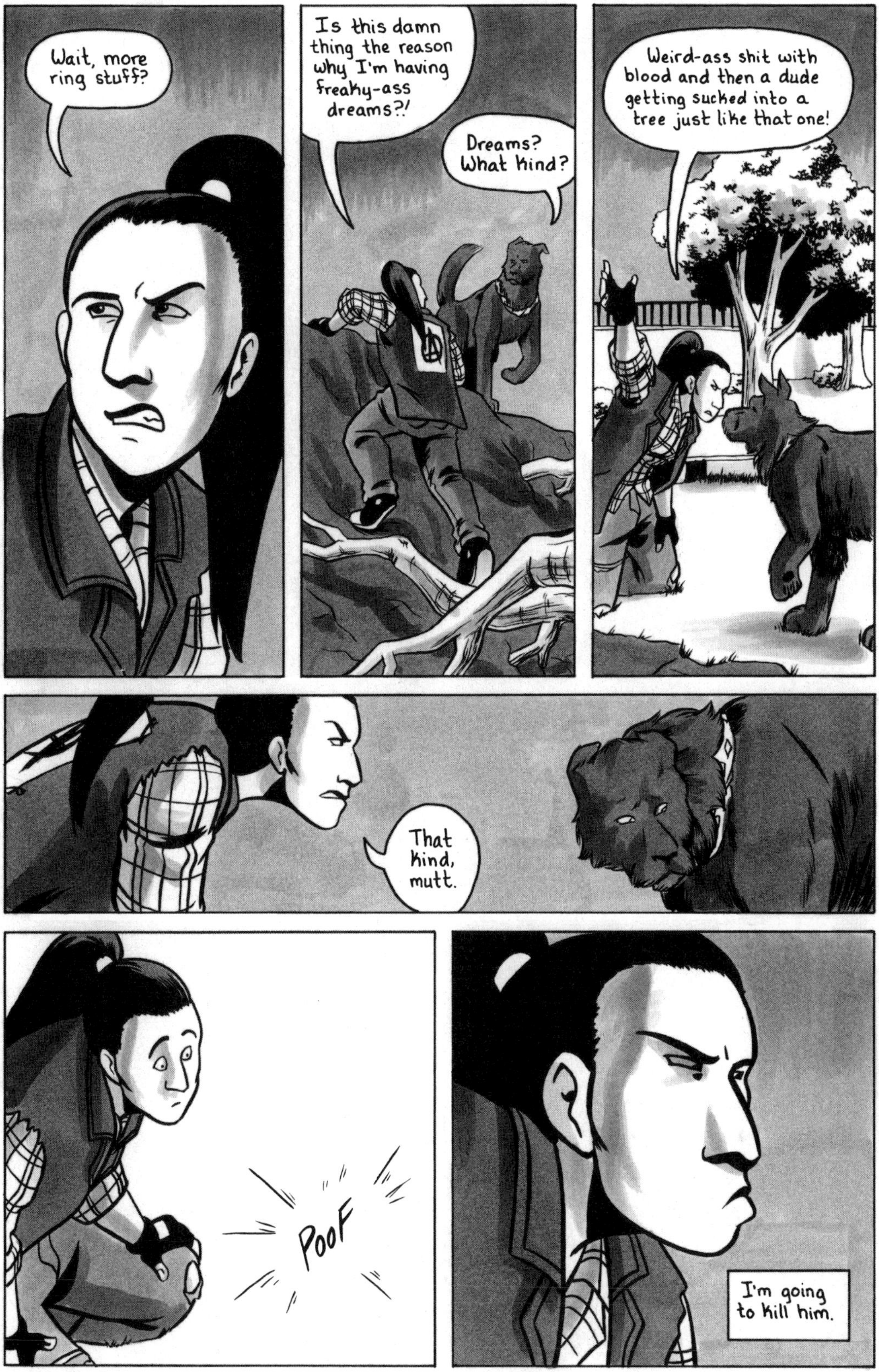

Wait, more ring stuff?
Is this damn thing the reason why I'm having freaky-ass dreams?!
Dreams? What kind?
Weird-ass shit with blood and then a dude getting sucked into a tree just like that one!
That kind, mutt.
POOF
I'm going to kill him.

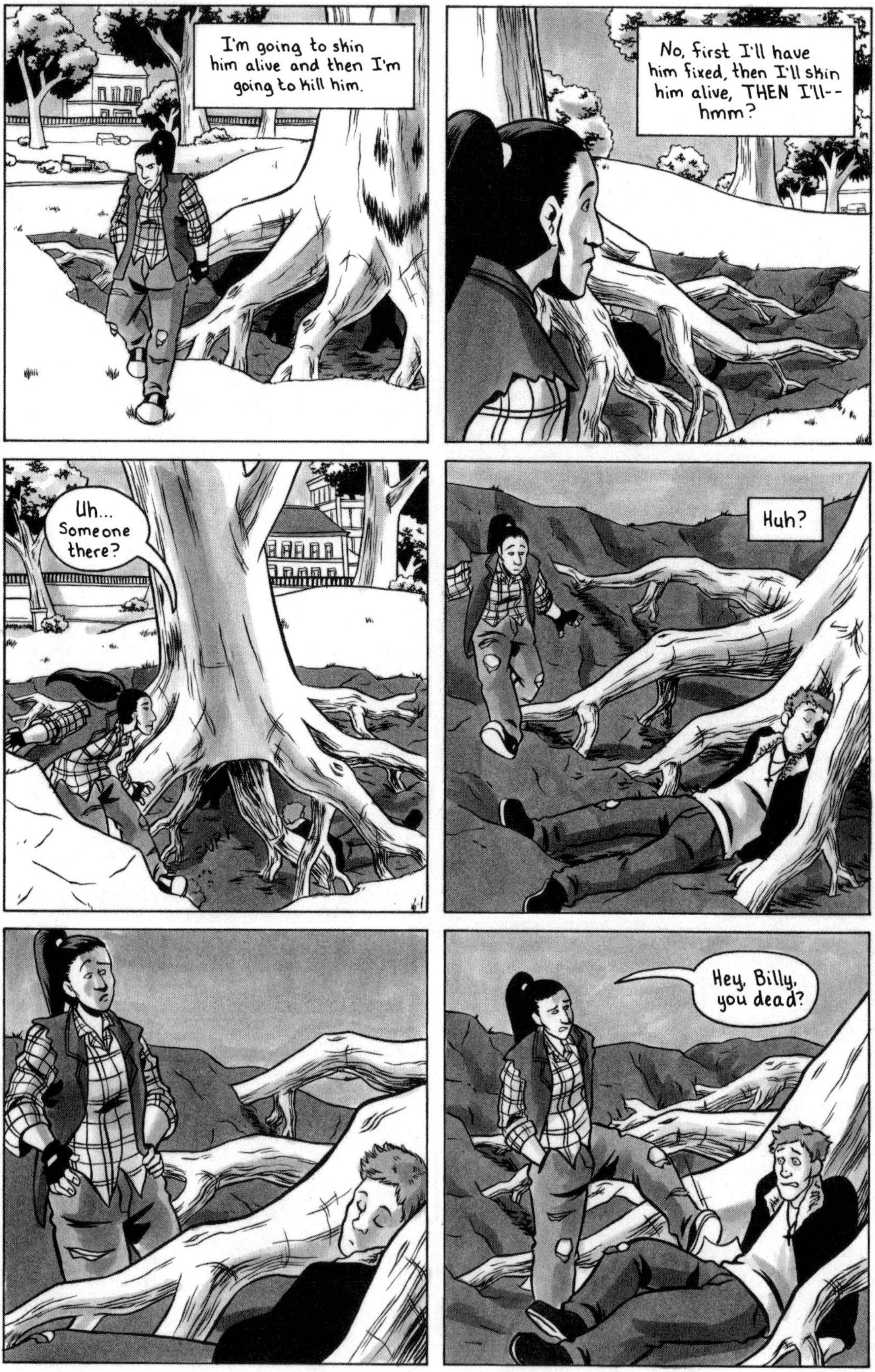
I'm going to skin him alive and then I'm going to kill him.
No, first I'll have him fixed, then I'll skin him alive, THEN I'll-- hmm?
Uh... Someone there?
Huh?
Hey, Billy, you dead?

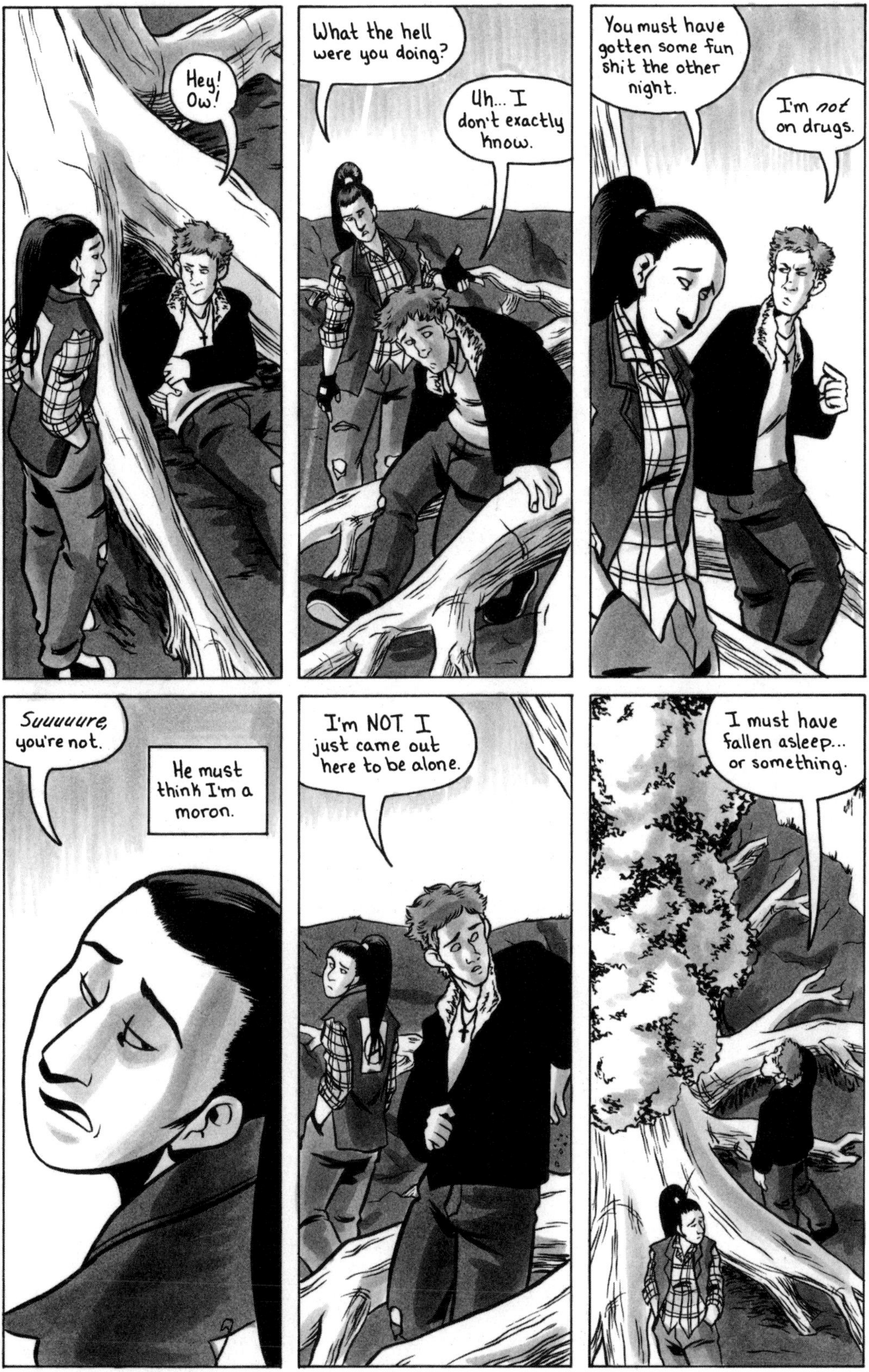
Hey! Ow!
What the hell were you doing?
Uh... I don't exactly know.
You must have gotten some fun shit the other night.
I'm *not* on drugs.
Suuuuure, you're not.
He must think I'm a moron.
I'm NOT. I just came out here to be alone.
I must have fallen asleep... or something.

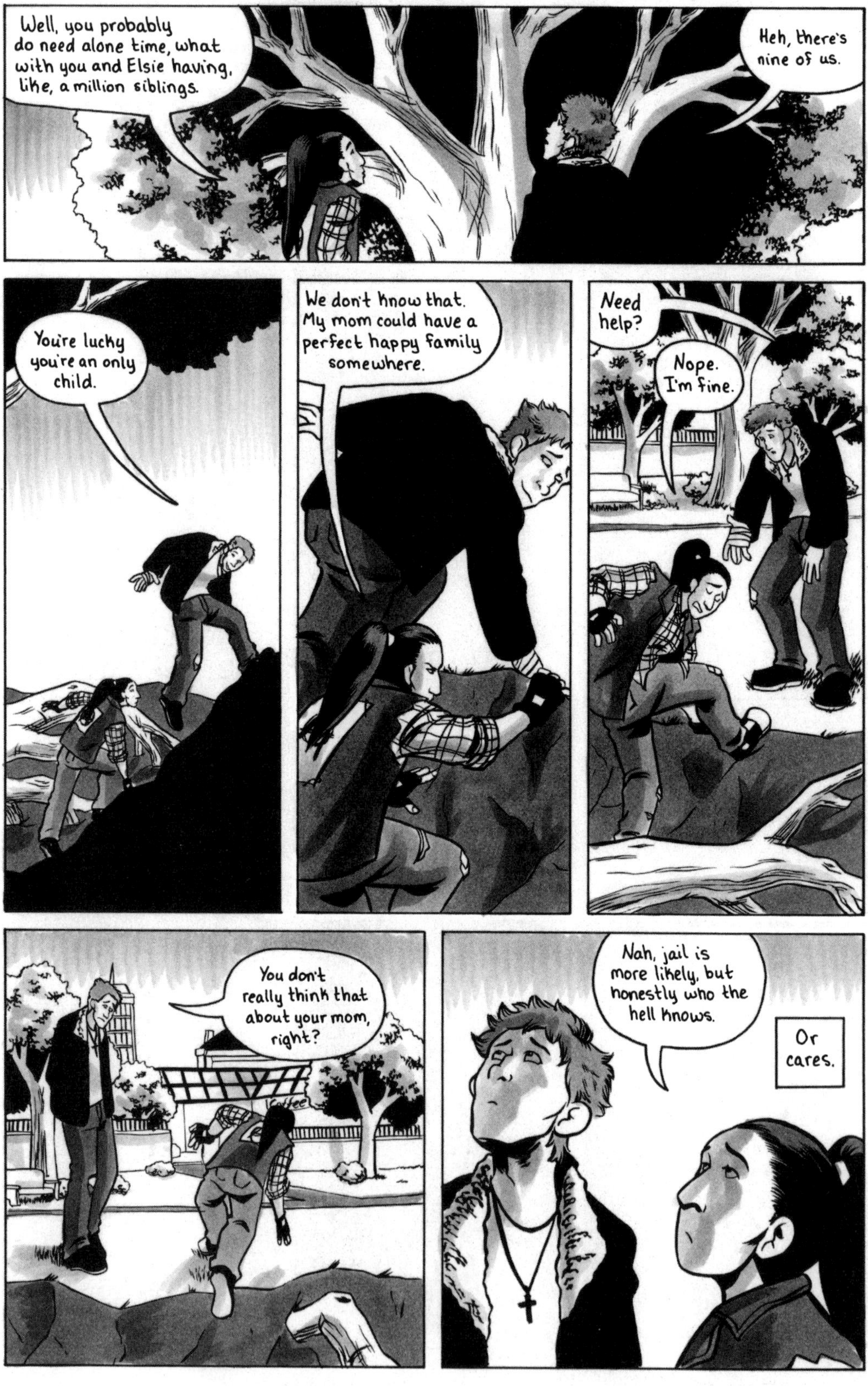
Well, you probably do need alone time, what with you and Elsie having, like, a million siblings.
Heh, there's nine of us.
You're lucky you're an only child.
We don't know that. My mom could have a perfect happy family somewhere.
Need help?
Nope. I'm fine.
You don't really think that about your mom, right?
Coffee
Nah, jail is more likely, but honestly who the hell knows.
Or cares.

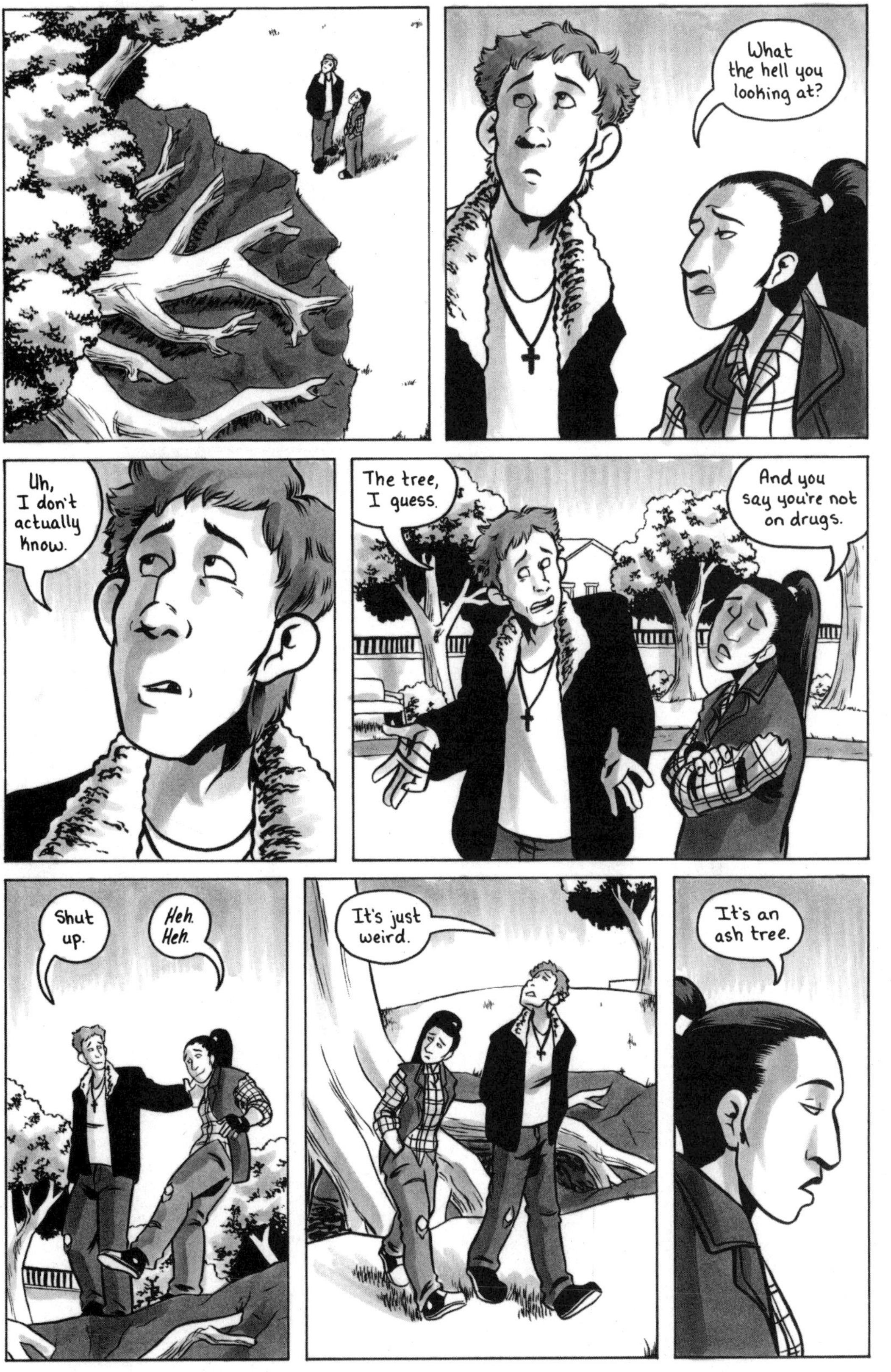
What the hell you looking at?
Uh, I don't actually know.
The tree, I guess.
And you say you're not on drugs.
Shut up.
Heh. Heh.
It's just weird.
It's an ash tree.

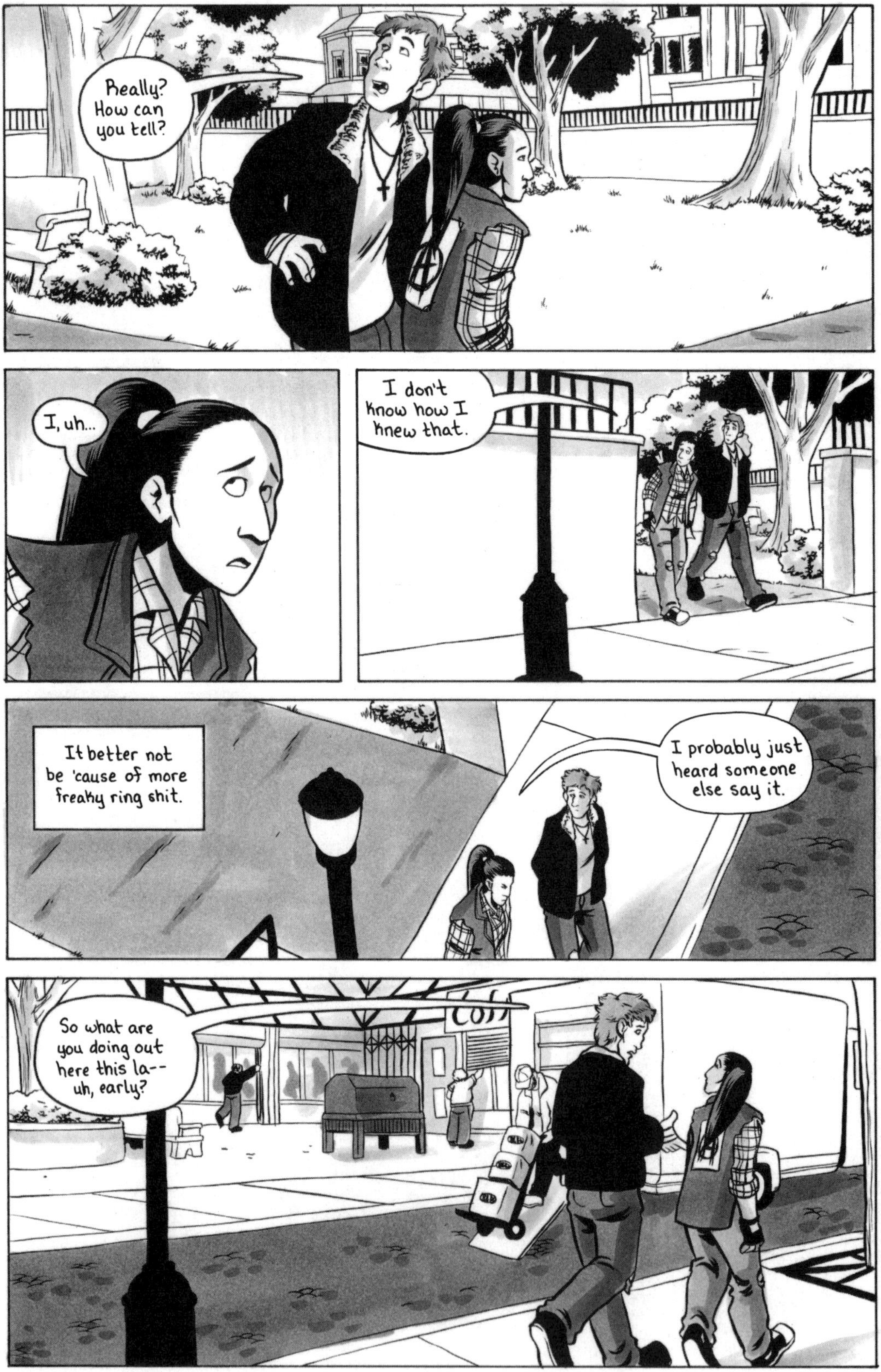
Really? How can you tell?
I, uh...
I don't know how I knew that.
It better not be 'cause of more freaky ring shit.
I probably just heard someone else say it.
So what are you doing out here this la-- uh, early?
Coff

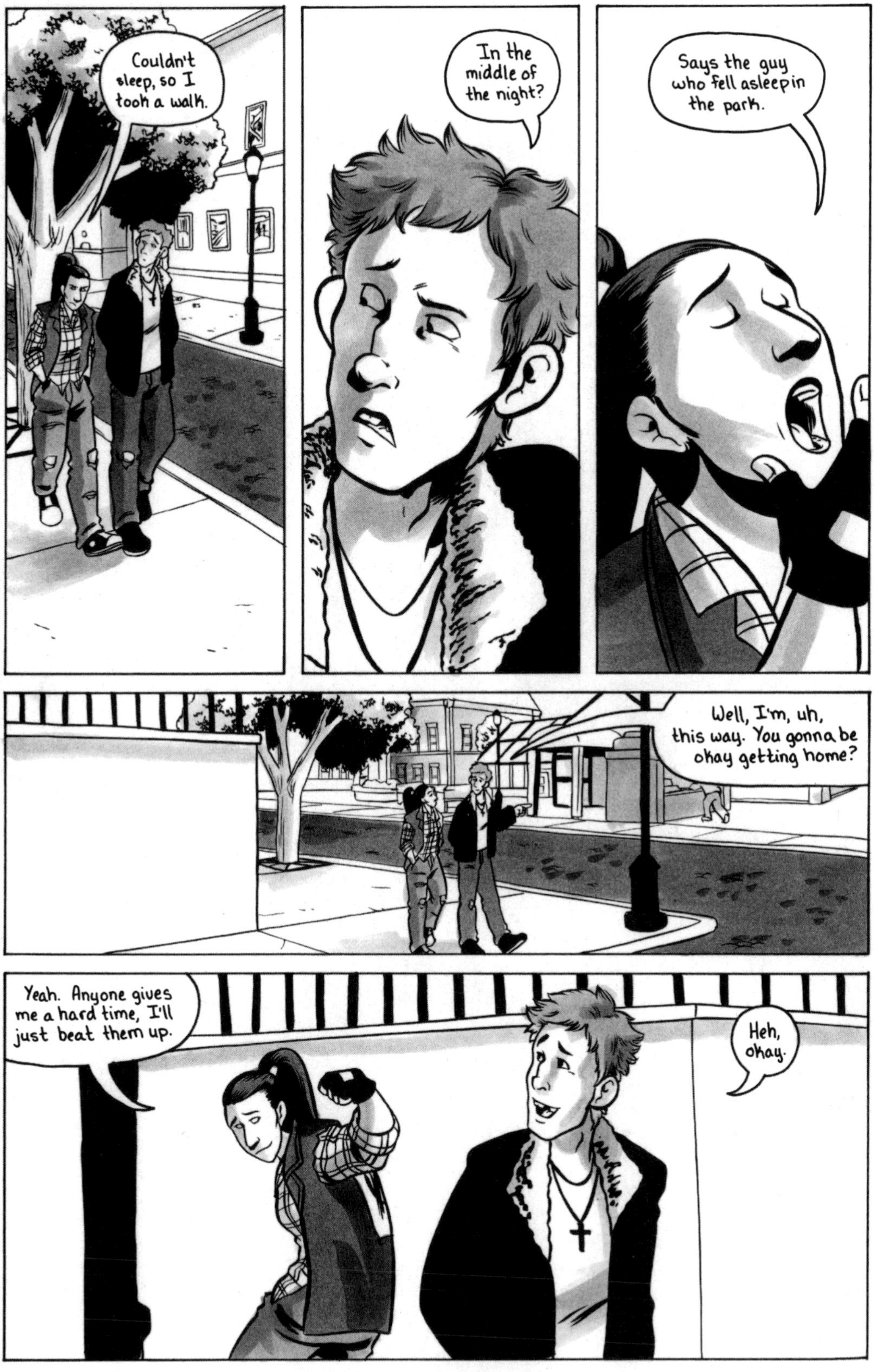
Couldn't sleep, so I took a walk.
In the middle of the night?
Says the guy who fell asleep in the park.
Well, I'm, uh, this way. You gonna be okay getting home?
Yeah. Anyone gives me a hard time, I'll just beat them up.
Heh, okay.

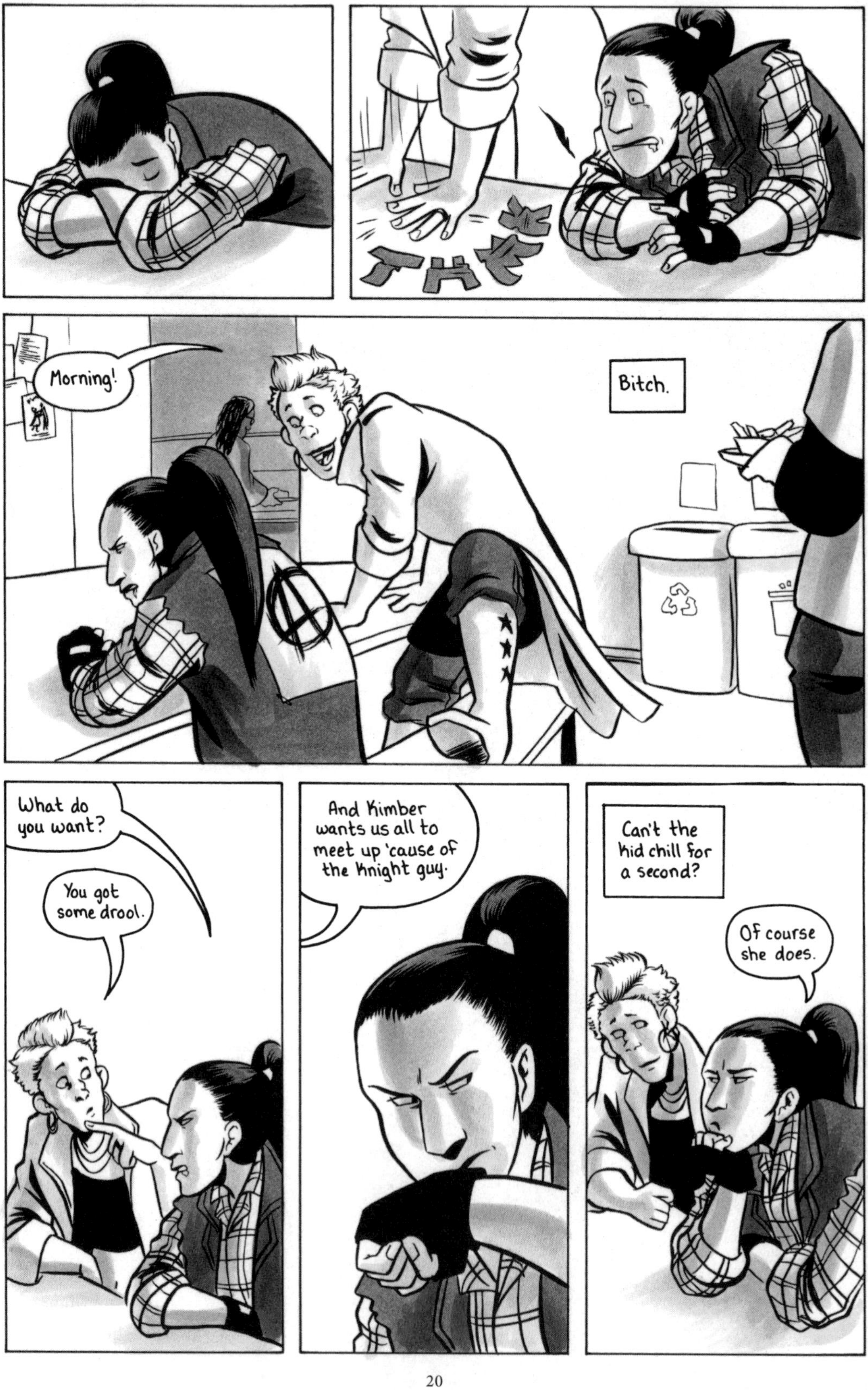
Morning!
Bitch.
What do you want?
You got some drool.
And Kimber wants us all to meet up 'cause of the knight guy.
Can't the kid chill for a second?
Of course she does.

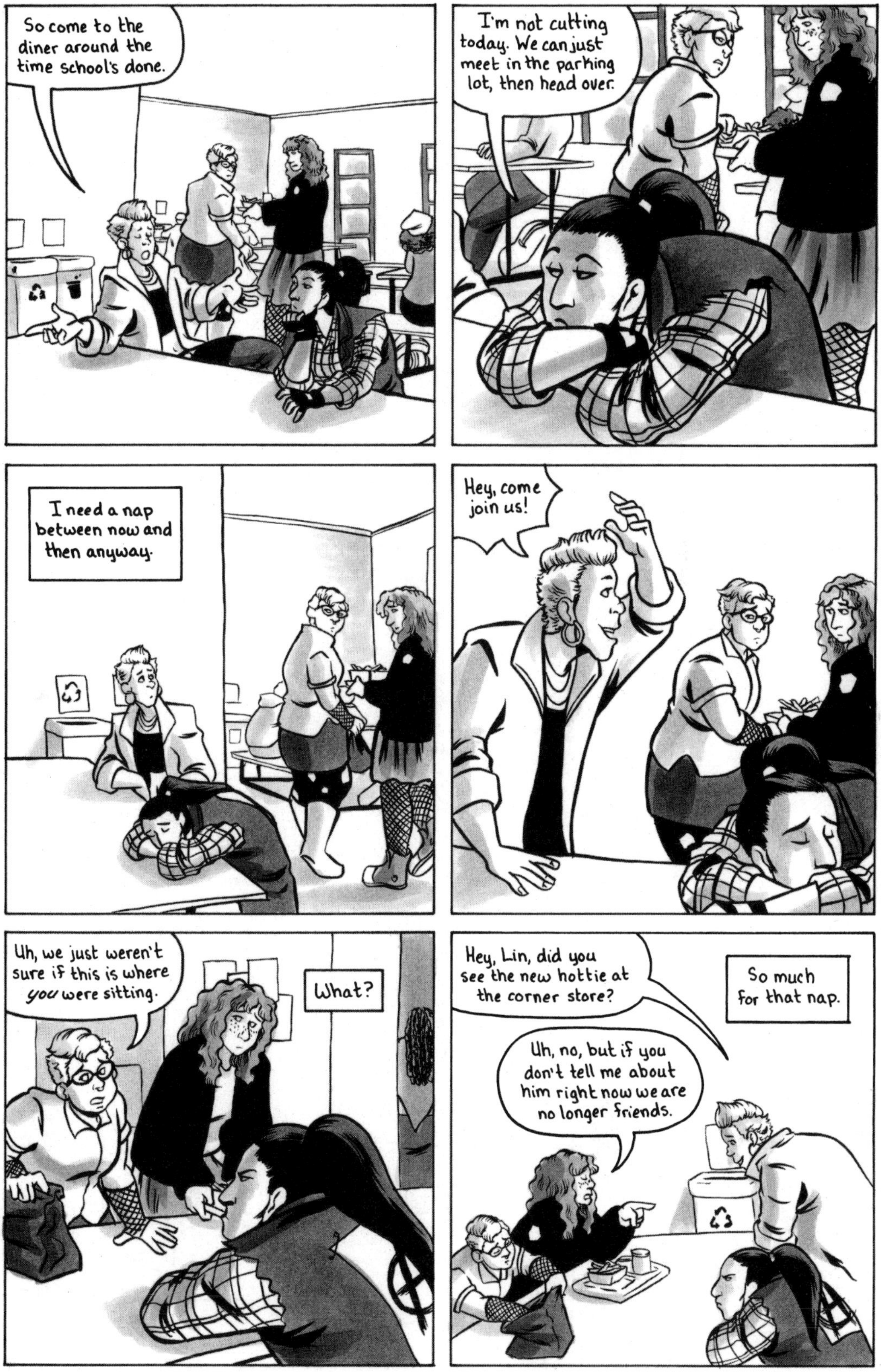

So come to the diner around the time school's done.
I'm not cutting today. We can just meet in the parking lot, then head over.
I need a nap between now and then anyway.
Hey, come join us!
Uh, we just weren't sure if this is where *you* were sitting.
What?
Hey, Lin, did you see the new hottie at the corner store?
Uh, no, but if you don't tell me about him right now we are no longer friends.
So much for that nap.

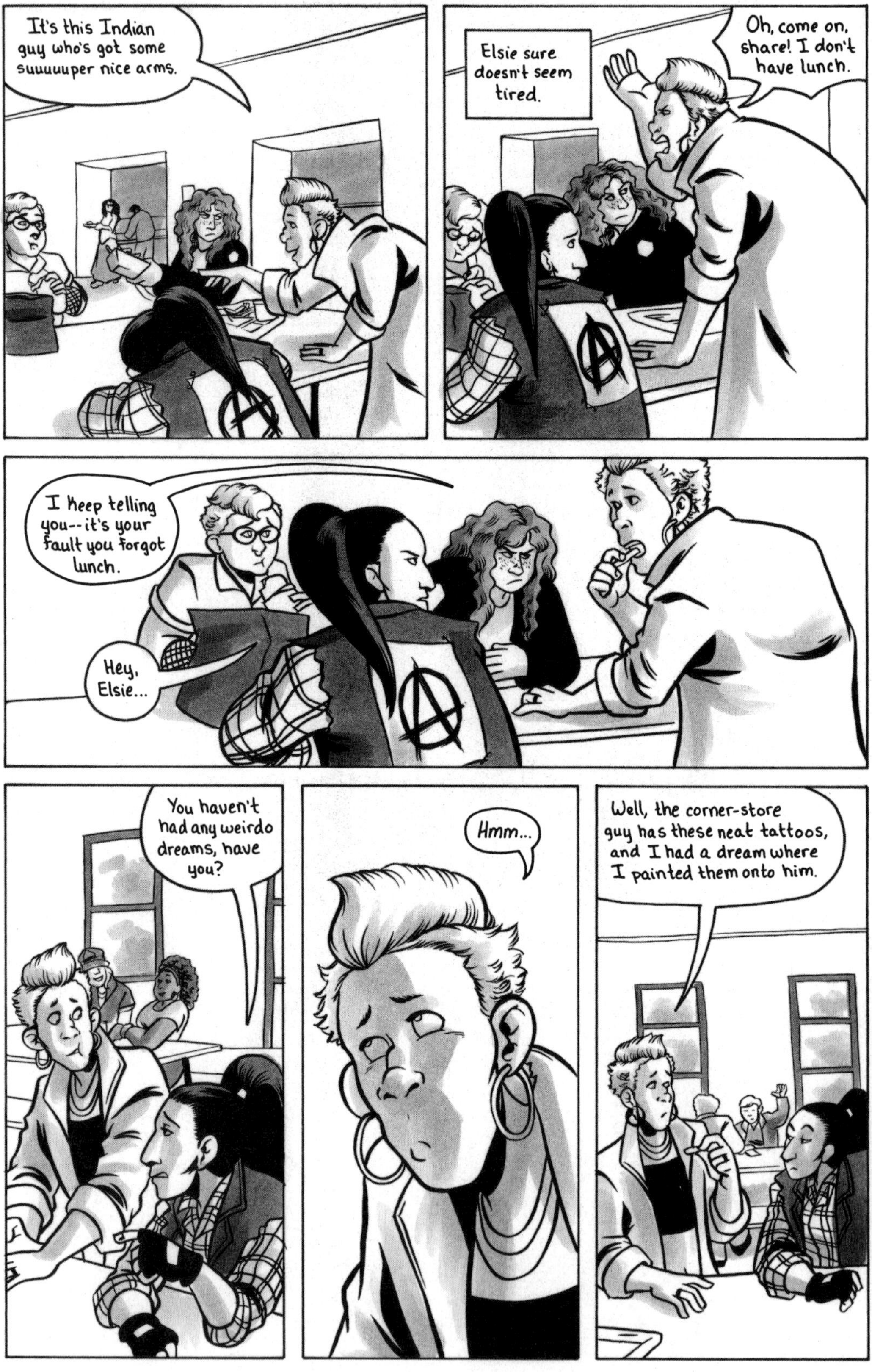
It's this Indian guy who's got some suuuuuper nice arms.
Elsie sure doesn't seem tired.
Oh, come on, share! I don't have lunch.
I keep telling you--it's your fault you forgot lunch.
Hey, Elsie...
You haven't had any weirdo dreams, have you?
Hmm...
Well, the corner-store guy has these neat tattoos, and I had a dream where I painted them onto him.

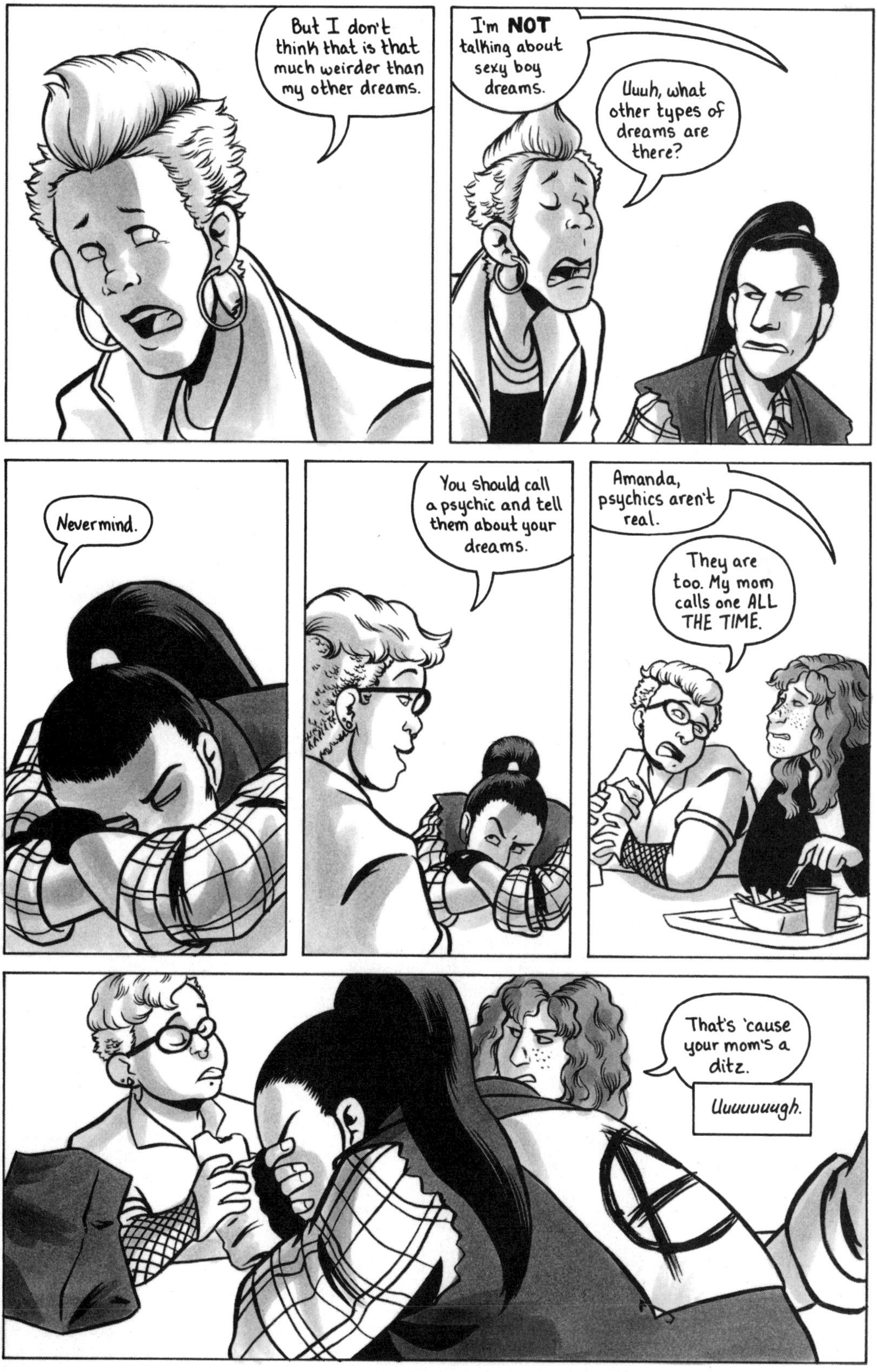
But I don't think that is that much weirder than my other dreams.
I'm **NOT** talking about sexy boy dreams.
Uuuh, what other types of dreams are there?
Nevermind.
You should call a psychic and tell them about your dreams.
Amanda, psychics aren't real.
They are too. My mom calls one ALL THE TIME.
That's 'cause your mom's a ditz.
Uuuuuuugh.

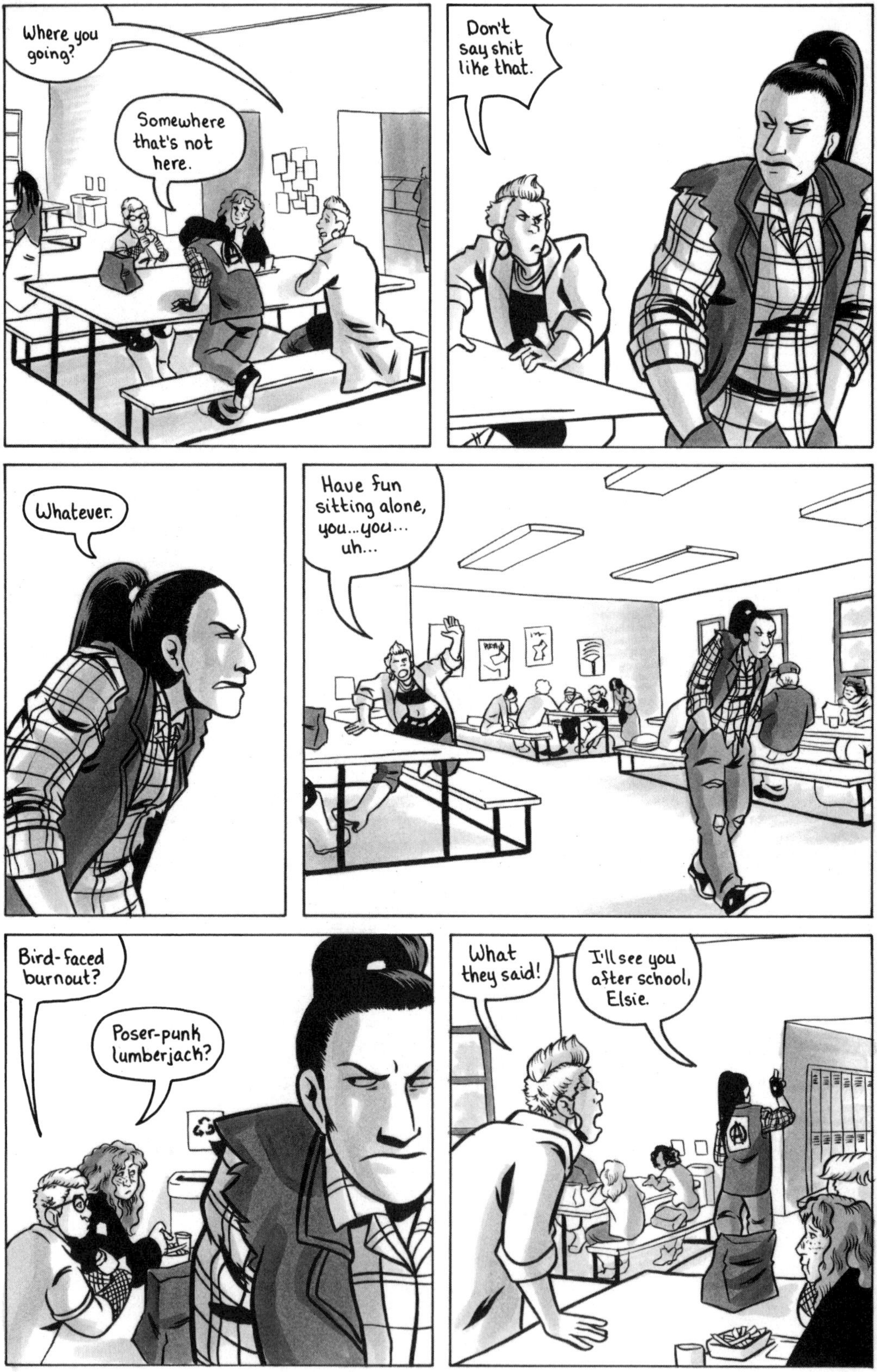
Where you going?
Somewhere that's not here.
Don't say shit like that.
Whatever.
Have fun sitting alone, you...you... uh...
Bird-faced burnout?
Poser-punk lumberjack?
What they said!
I'll see you after school, Elsie.

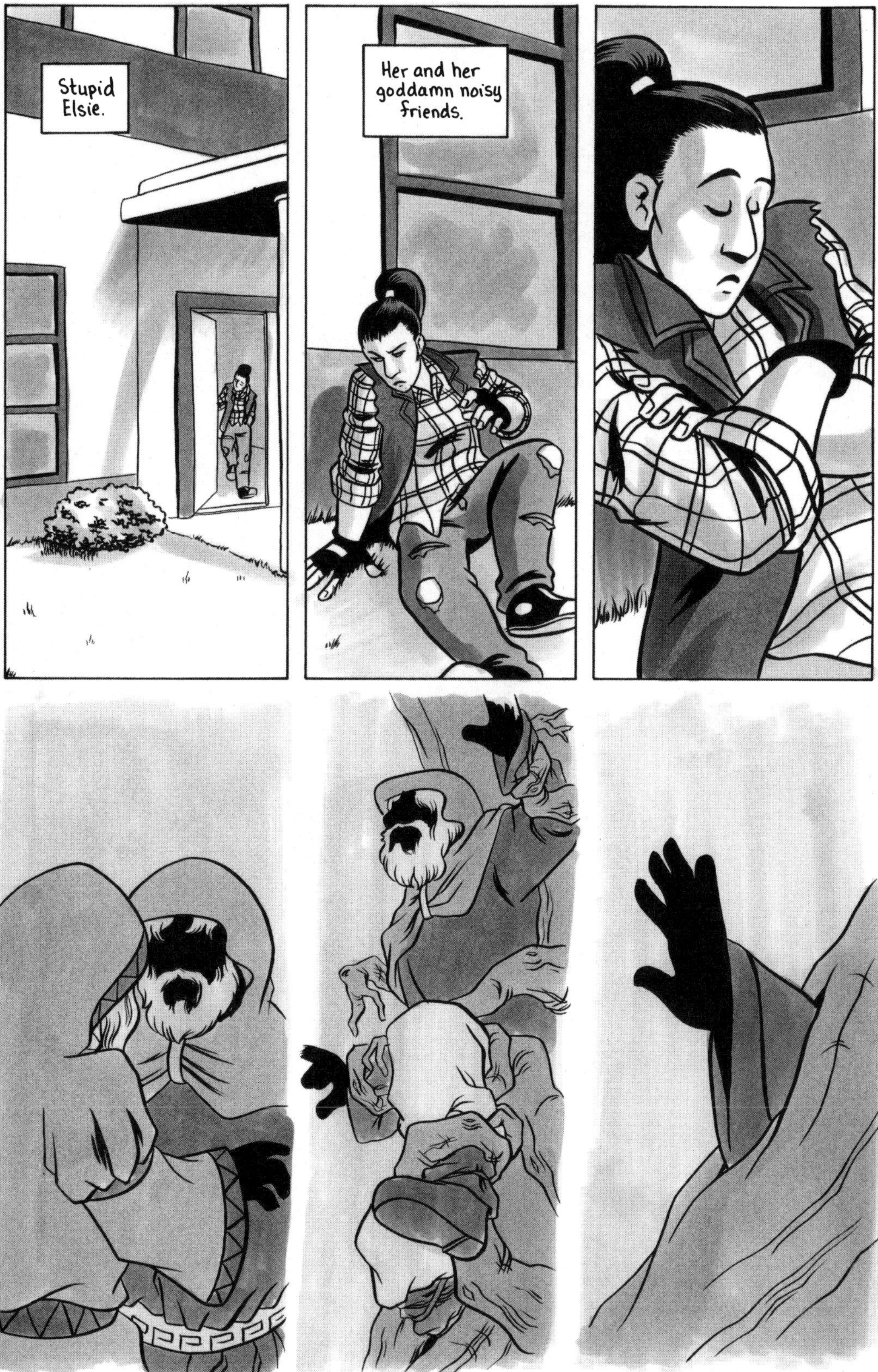
Stupid Elsie.
Her and her goddamn noisy friends.

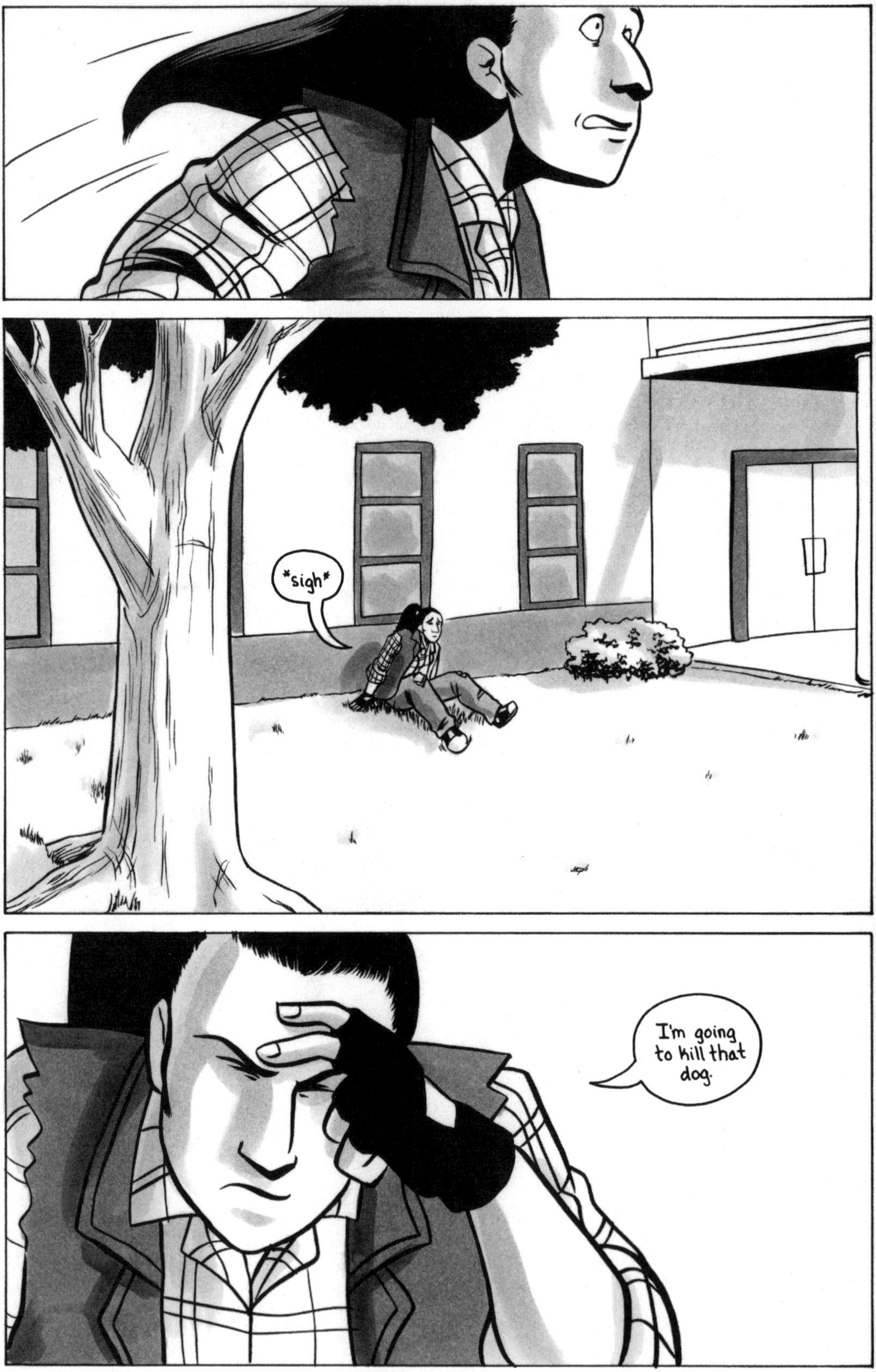
sigh
I'm going to kill that dog.

CHAPTER 2:
Pretending That Children Are Childish

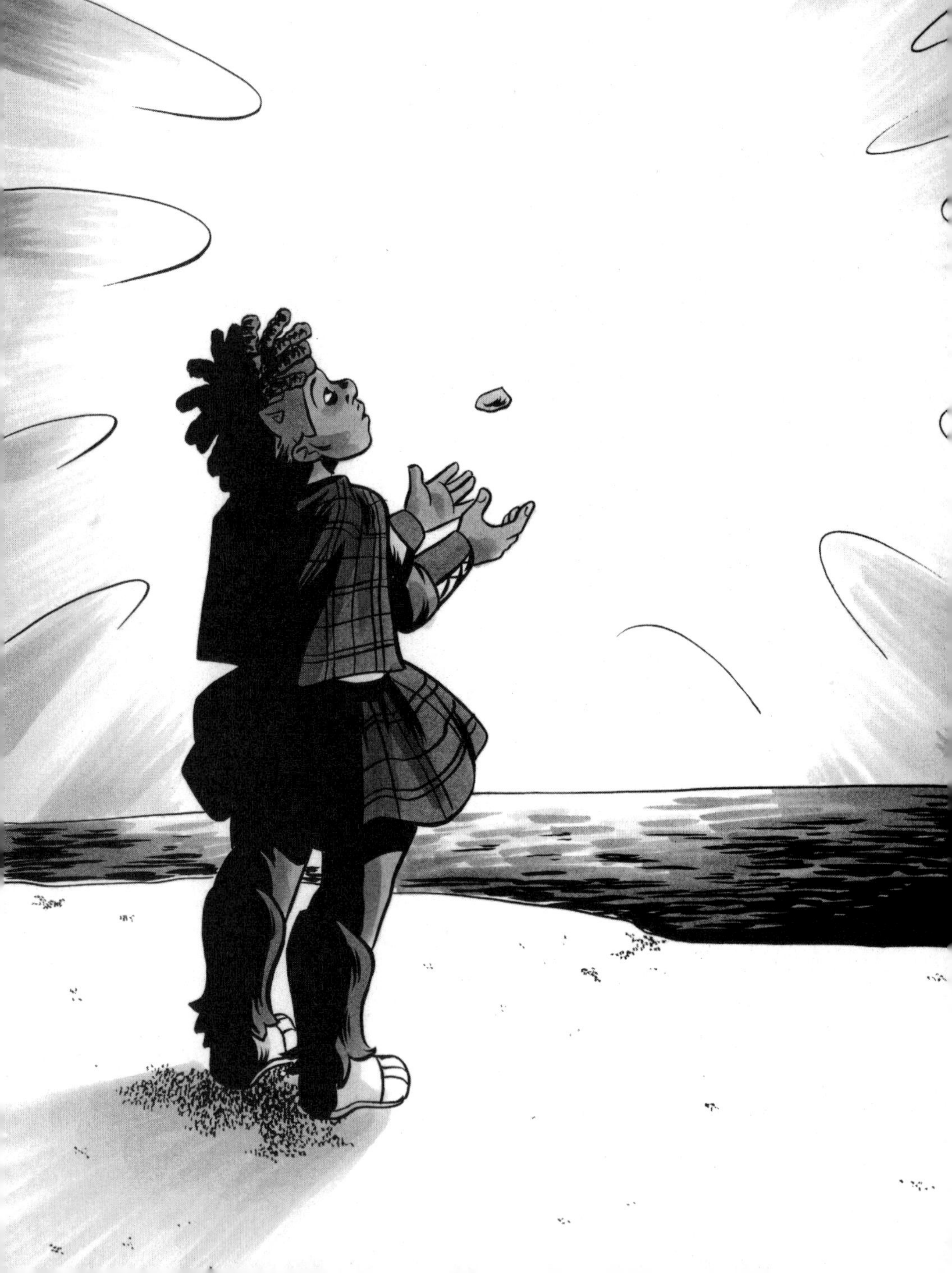

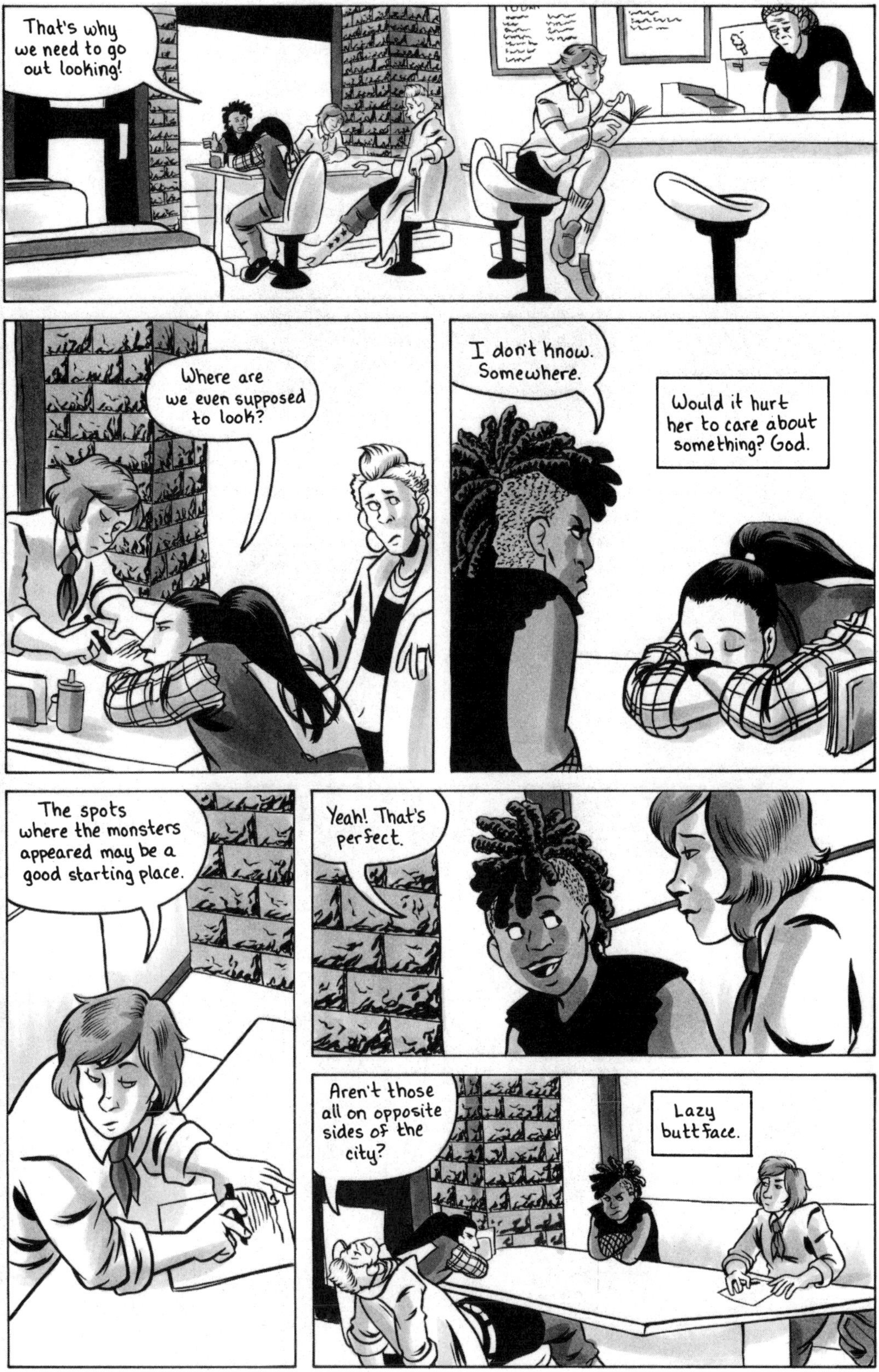
That's why we need to go out looking!
Where are we even supposed to look?
I don't know. Somewhere.
Would it hurt her to care about something? God.
The spots where the monsters appeared may be a good starting place.
Yeah! That's perfect.
Aren't those all on opposite sides of the city?
Lazy buttface.

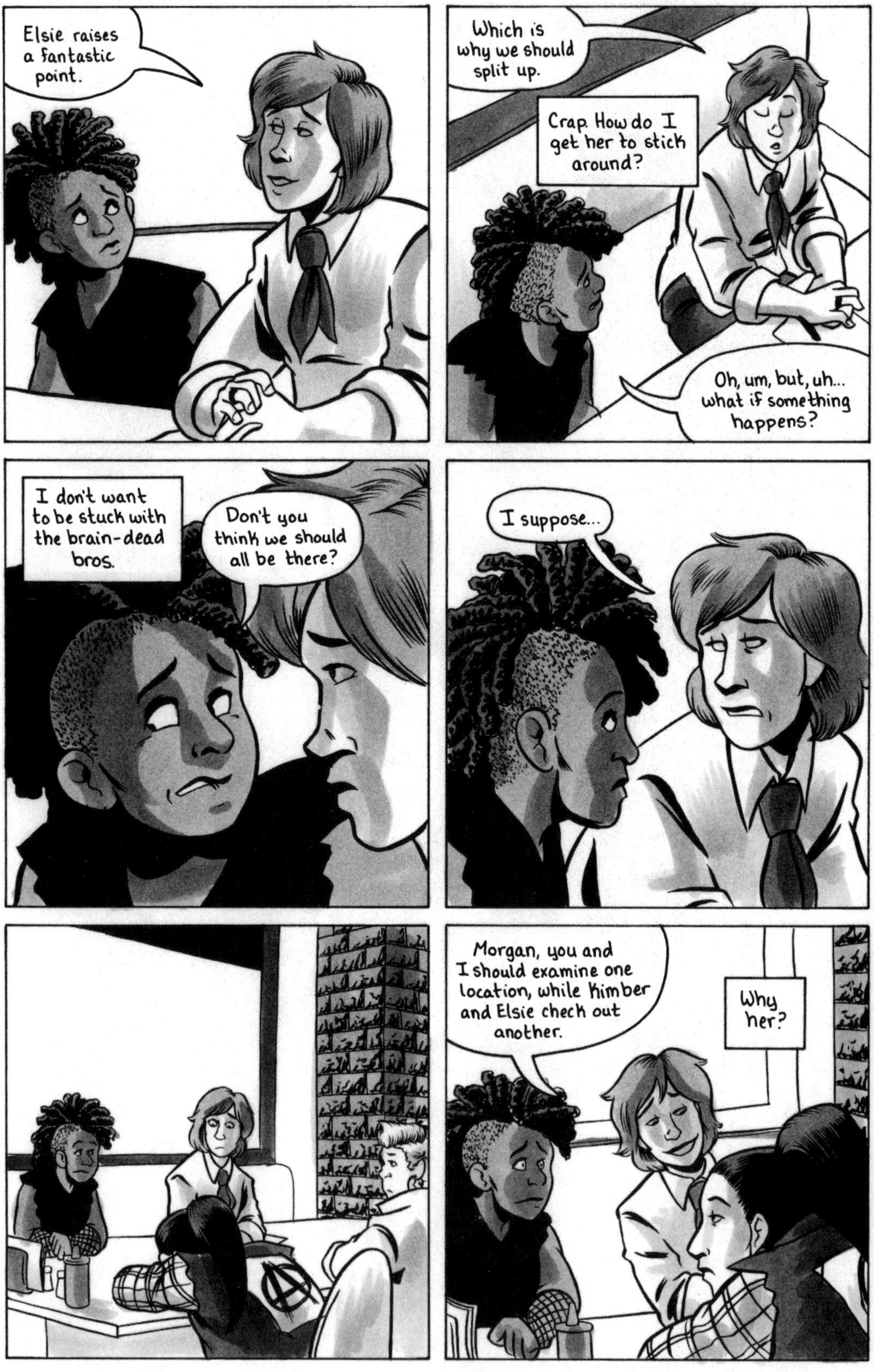
Elsie raises a fantastic point.
Which is why we should split up.
Crap. How do I get her to stick around?
Oh, um, but, uh... what if something happens?
I don't want to be stuck with the brain-dead bros.
Don't you think we should all be there?
I suppose...
Morgan, you and I should examine one location, while Kimber and Elsie check out another.
Why her?

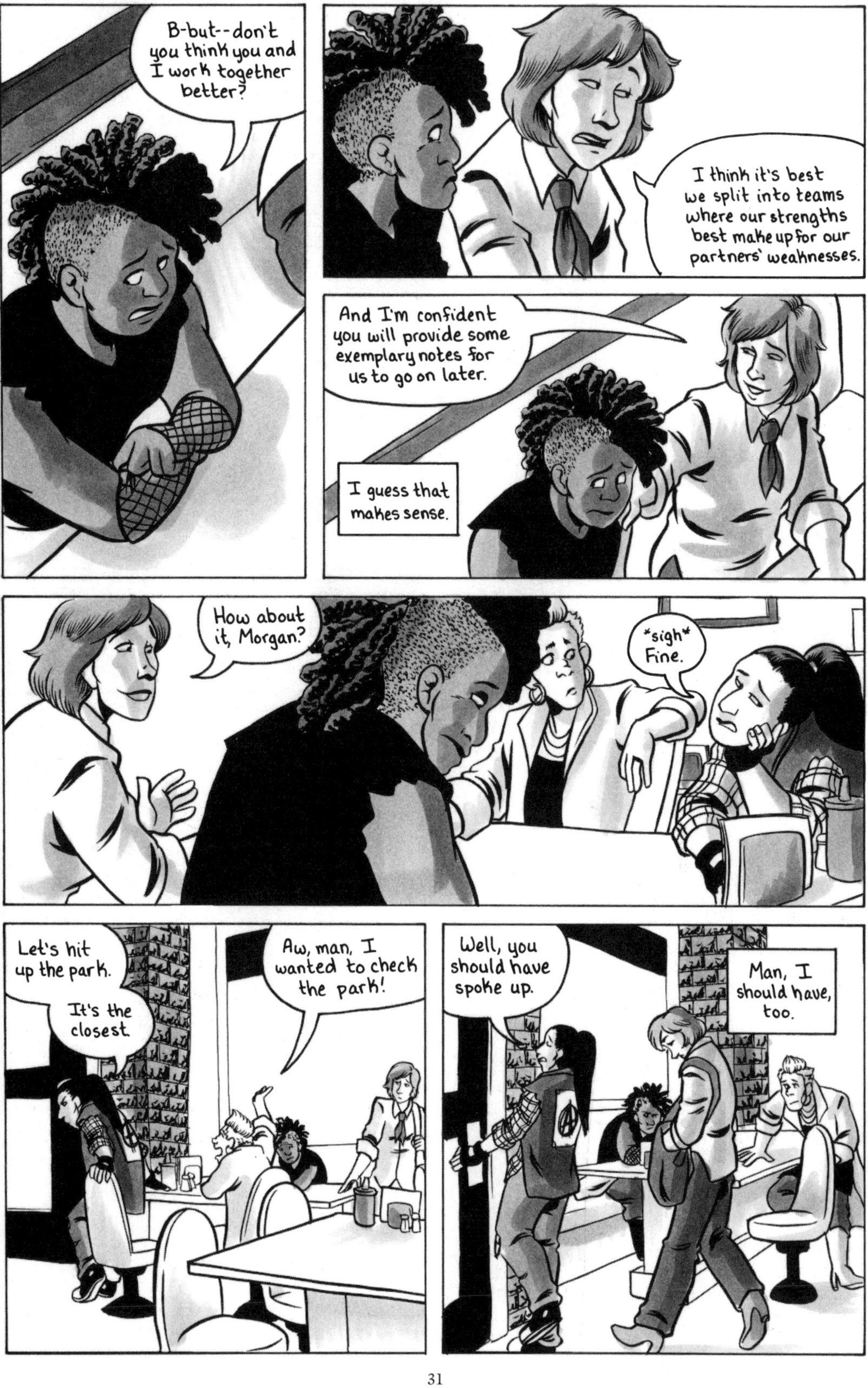

B-but--don't you think you and I work together better?
I think it's best we split into teams where our strengths best make up for our partners' weaknesses.
And I'm confident you will provide some exemplary notes for us to go on later.
I guess that makes sense.
How about it, Morgan?
sigh Fine.
Let's hit up the park.
It's the closest.
Aw, man, I wanted to check the park!
Well, you should have spoke up.
Man, I should have, too.

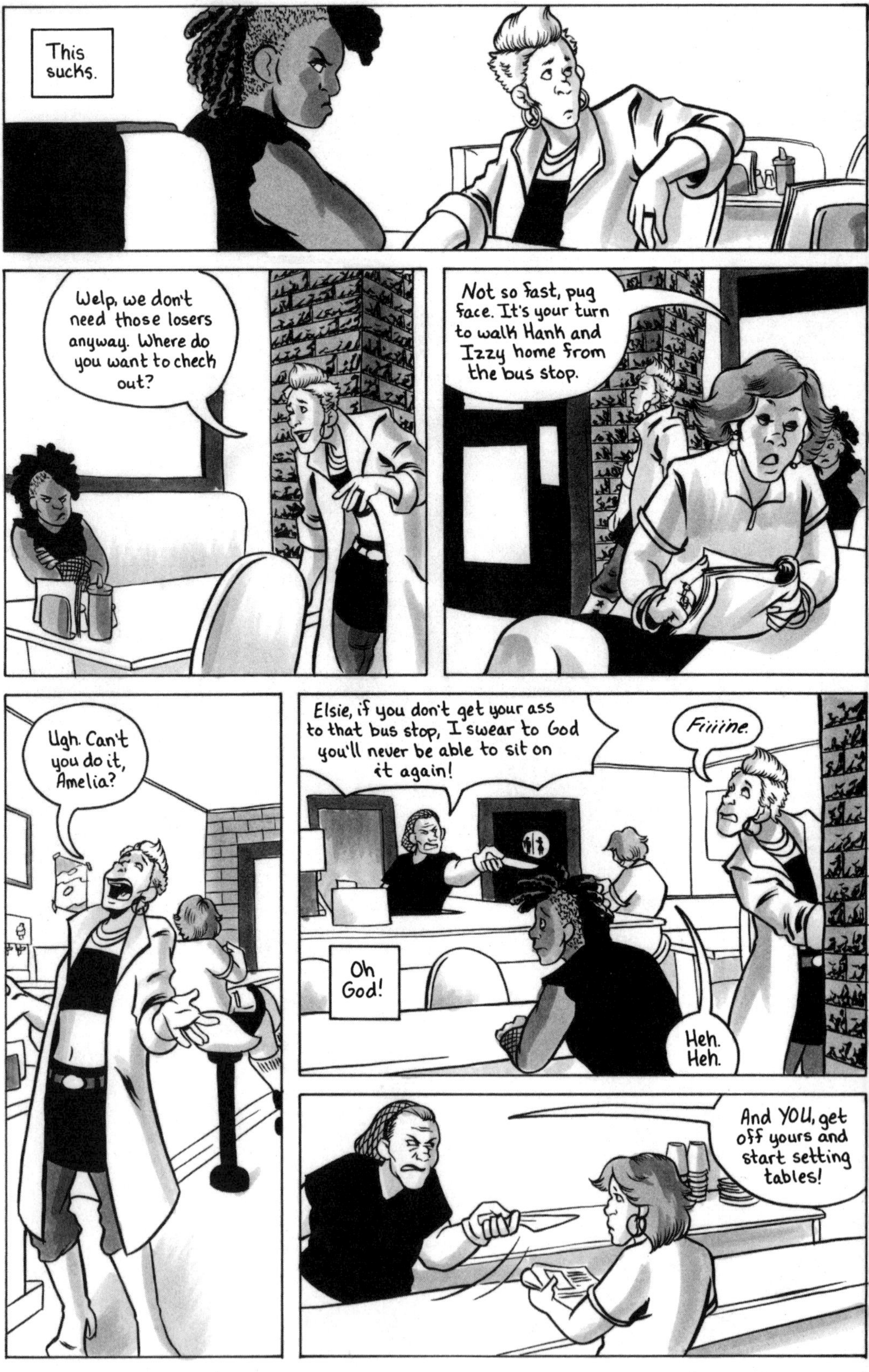
This sucks.
Welp, we don't need those losers anyway. Where do you want to check out?
Not so fast, pug face. It's your turn to walk Hank and Izzy home from the bus stop.
Ugh. Can't you do it, Amelia?
Elsie, if you don't get your ass to that bus stop, I swear to God you'll never be able to sit on it again!
Fiiiine.
Oh God!
Heh. Heh.
And YOU, get off yours and start setting tables!

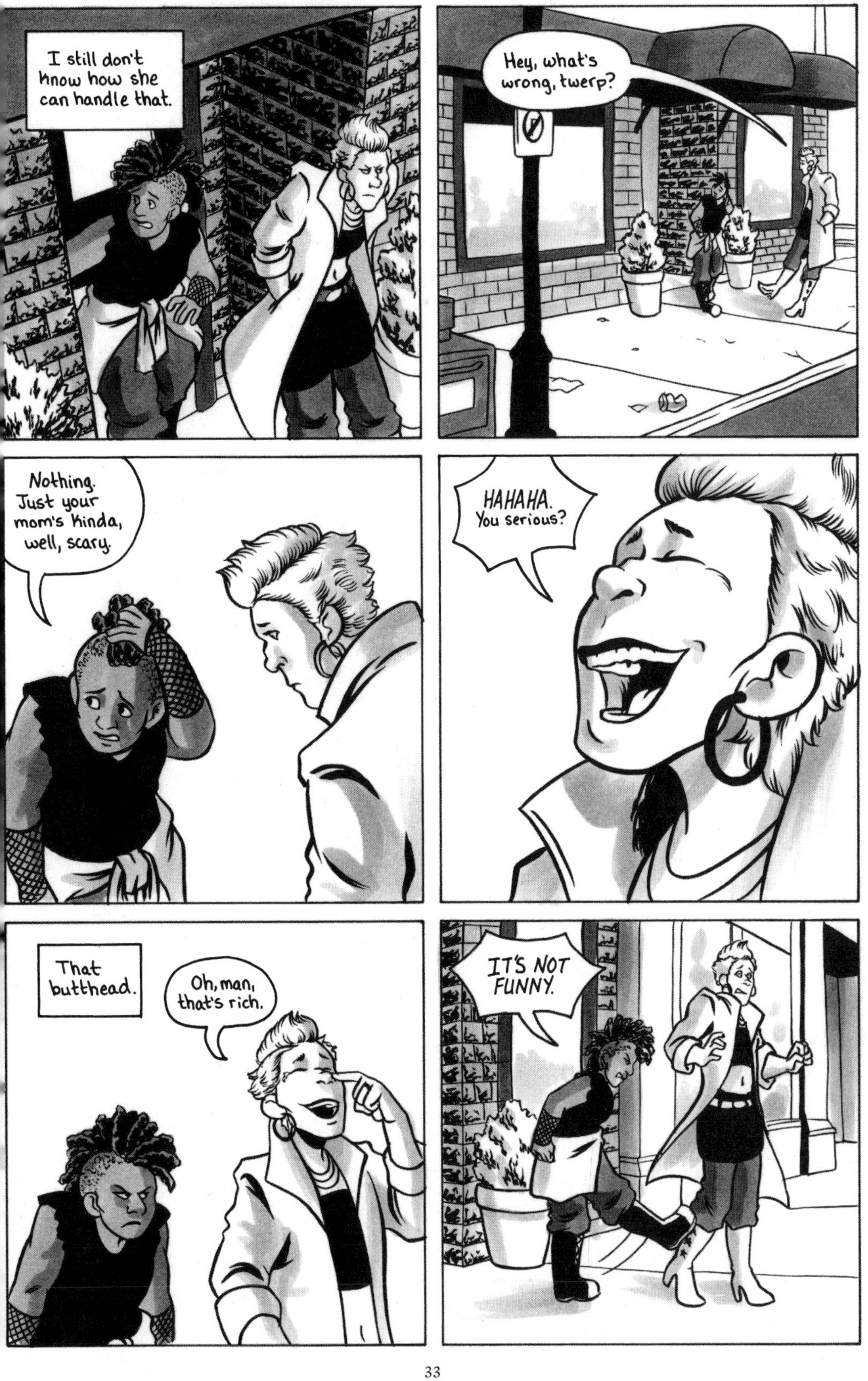

I still don't know how she can handle that.
Hey, what's wrong, twerp?
Nothing. Just your mom's kinda, well, scary.
HAHAHA. You serious?
That butthead.
Oh, man, that's rich.
IT'S NOT FUNNY.

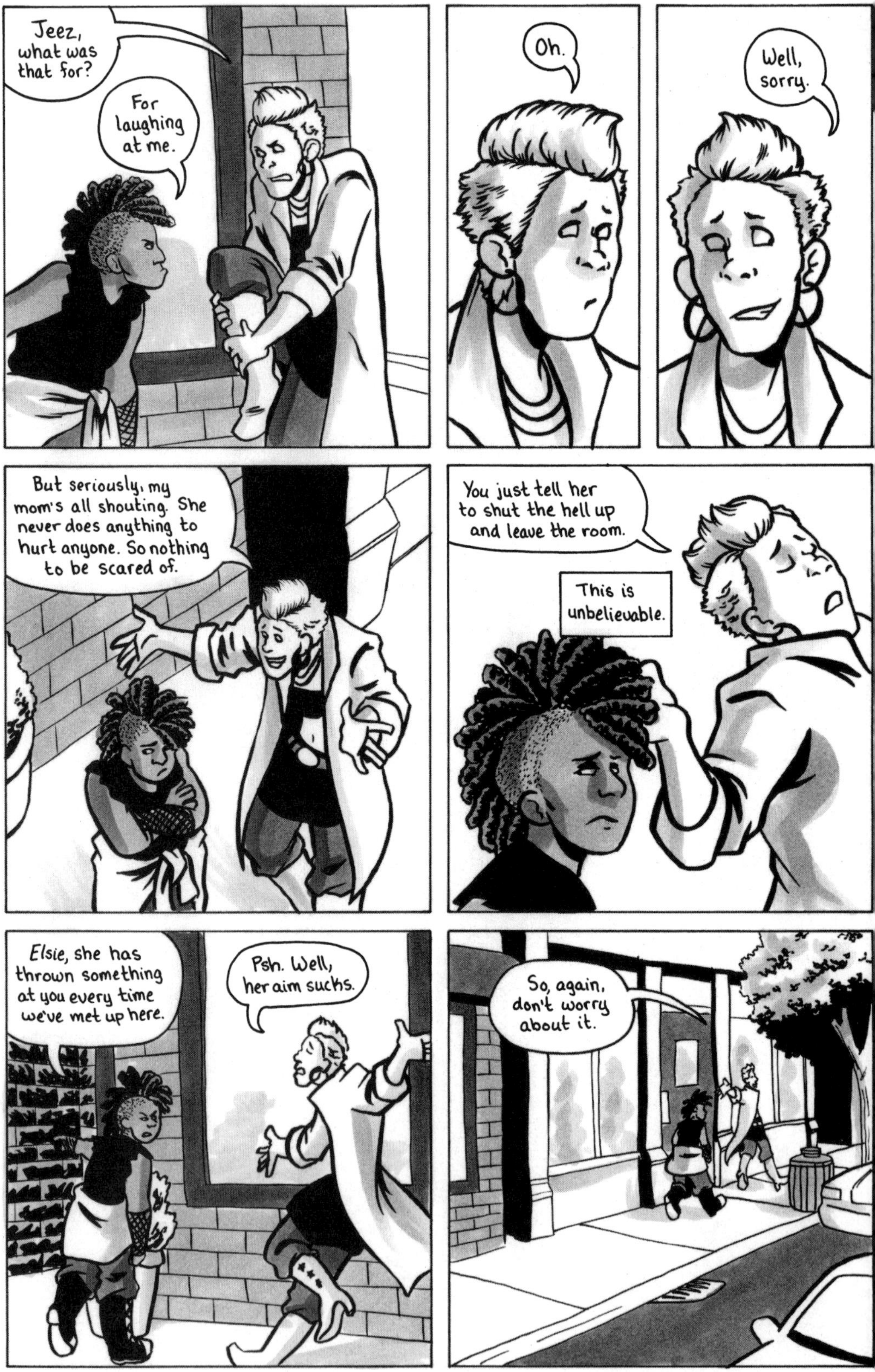
Jeez, what was that for?
For laughing at me.
Oh.
Well, sorry.
But seriously, my mom's all shouting. She never does anything to hurt anyone. So nothing to be scared of.
You just tell her to shut the hell up and leave the room.
This is unbelievable.
Elsie, she has thrown something at you every time we've met up here.
Psh. Well, her aim sucks.
So, again, don't worry about it.

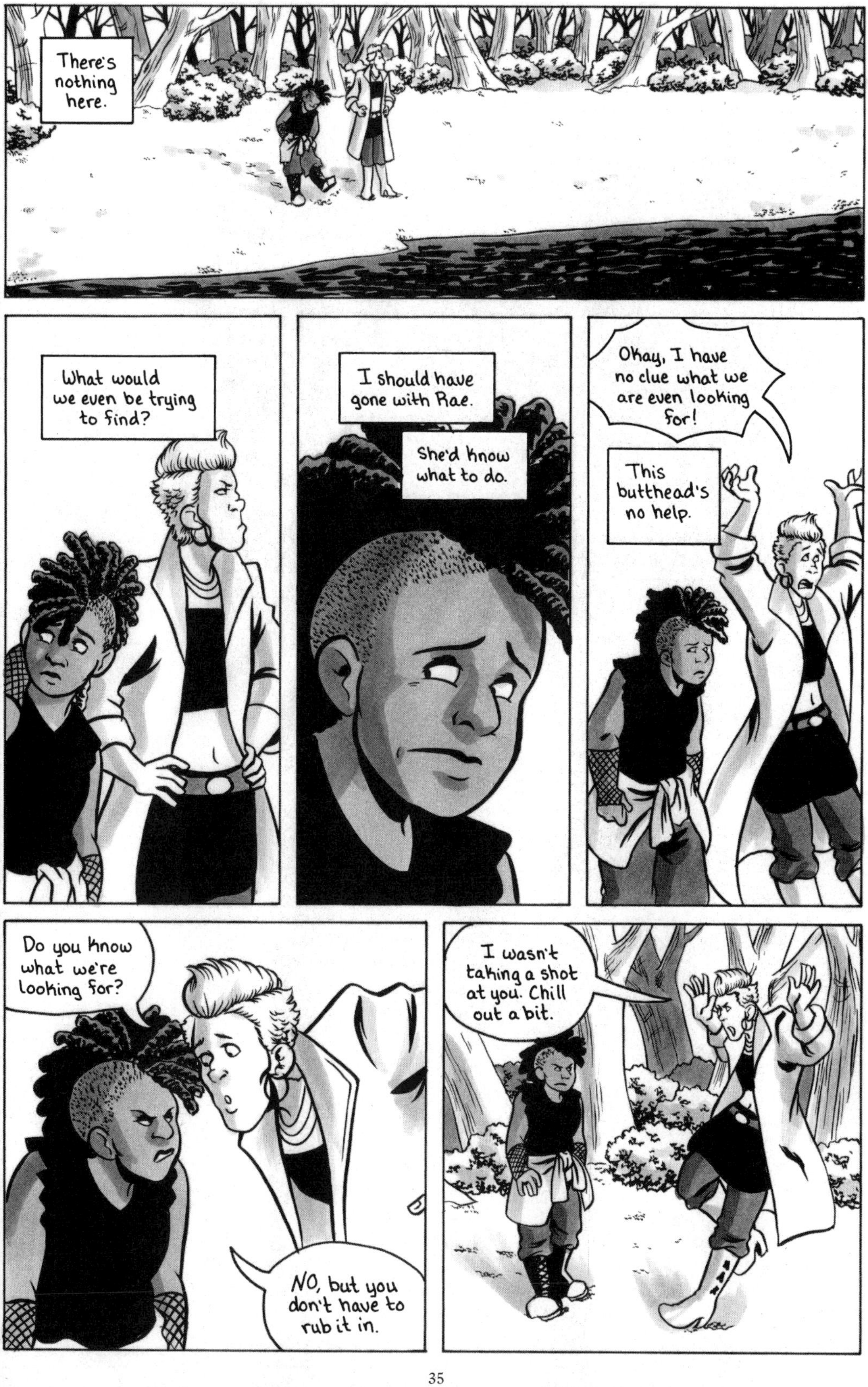
There's nothing here.
What would we even be trying to find?
I should have gone with Rae.
She'd know what to do.
Okay, I have no clue what we are even looking for!
This butthead's no help.
Do you know what we're looking for?
NO, but you don't have to rub it in.
I wasn't taking a shot at you. Chill out a bit.

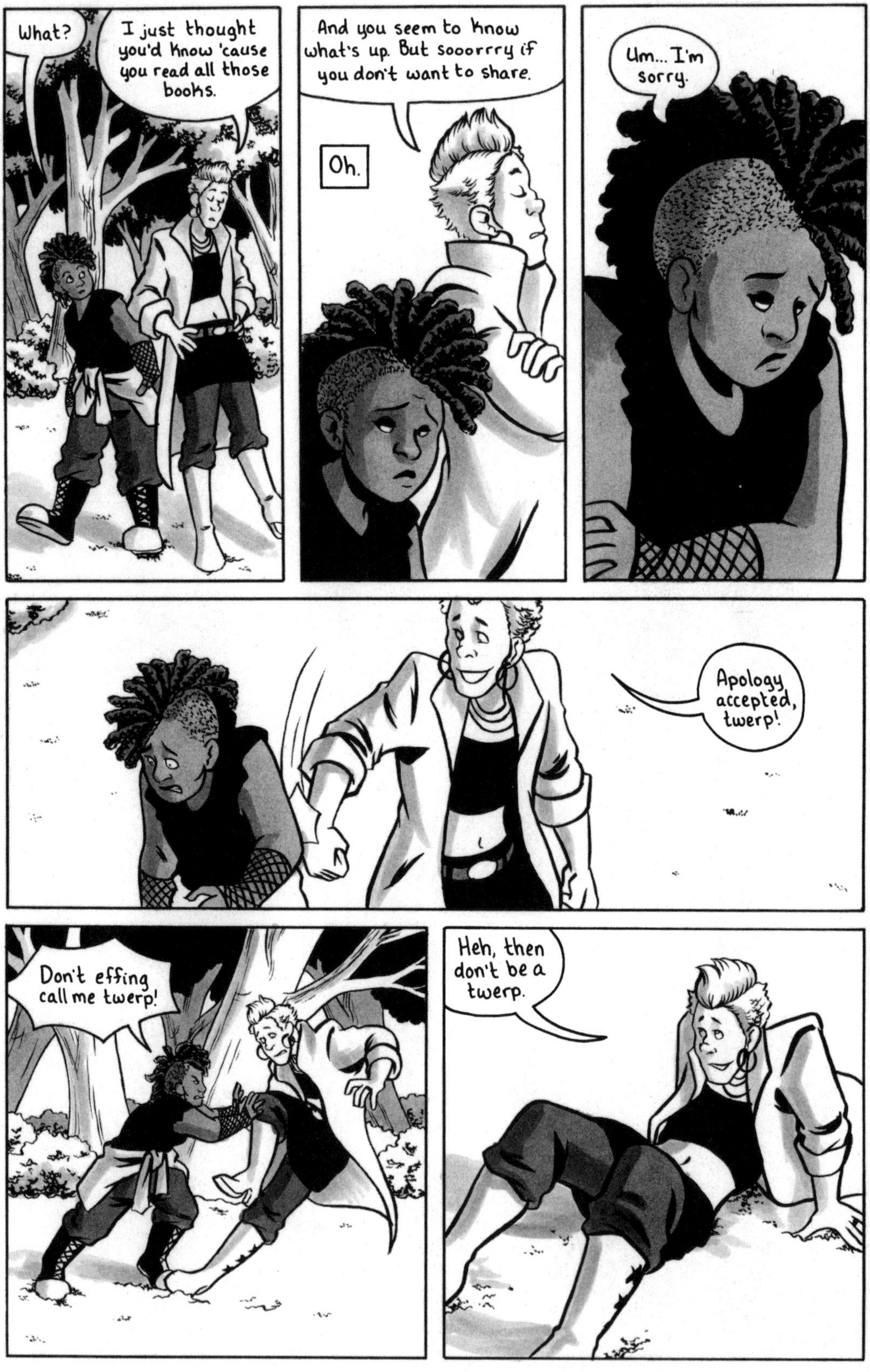
What?
I just thought you'd know 'cause you read all those books.
And you seem to know what's up. But sooorrry if you don't want to share.
Oh.
Um... I'm sorry.
Apology accepted, twerp!
Don't effing call me twerp!
Heh, then don't be a twerp.

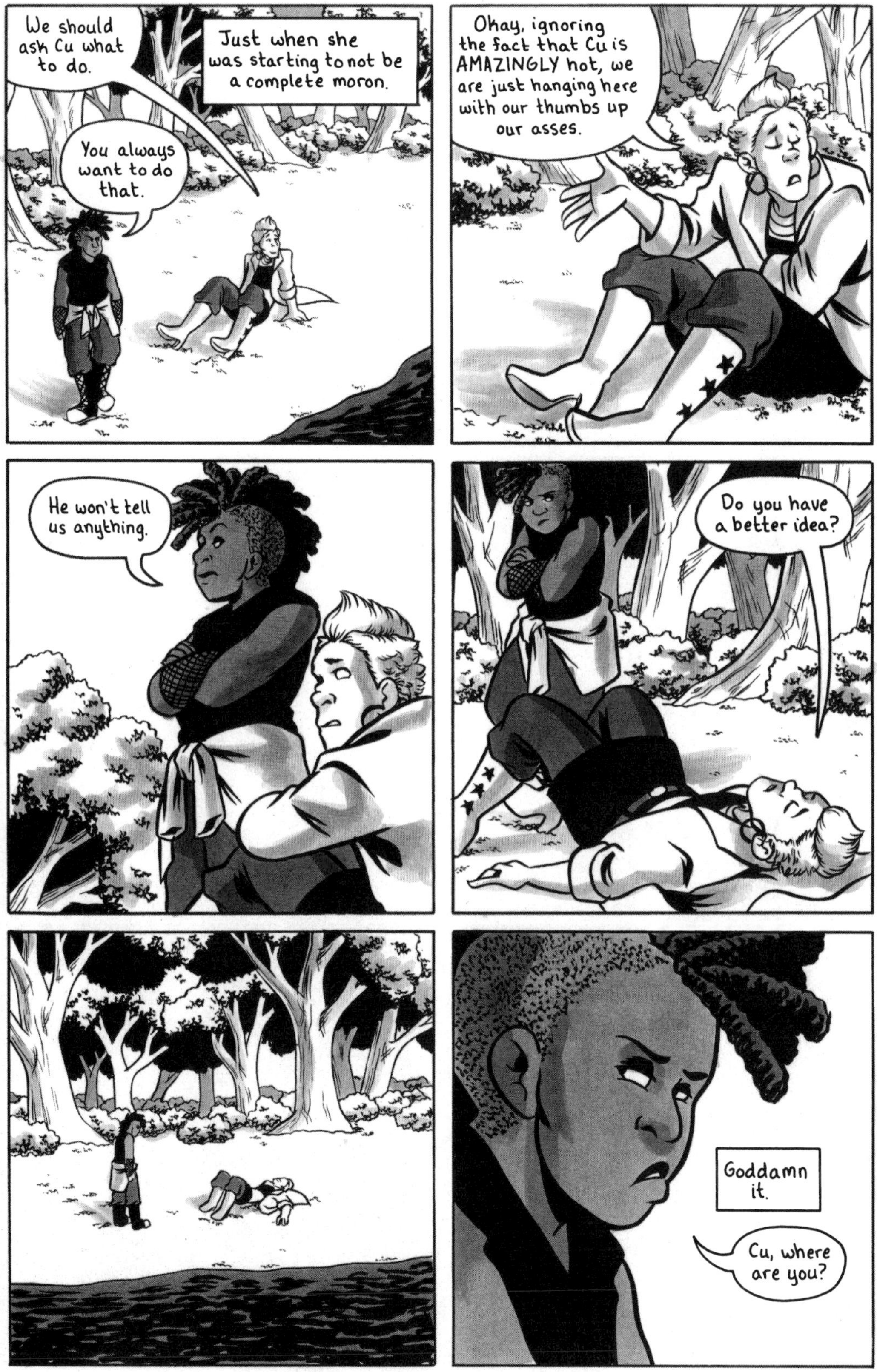
We should ask Cu what to do.
Just when she was starting to not be a complete moron.
You always want to do that.
Okay, ignoring the fact that Cu is AMAZINGLY hot, we are just hanging here with our thumbs up our asses.
He won't tell us anything.
Do you have a better idea?
Goddamn it.
Cu, where are you?

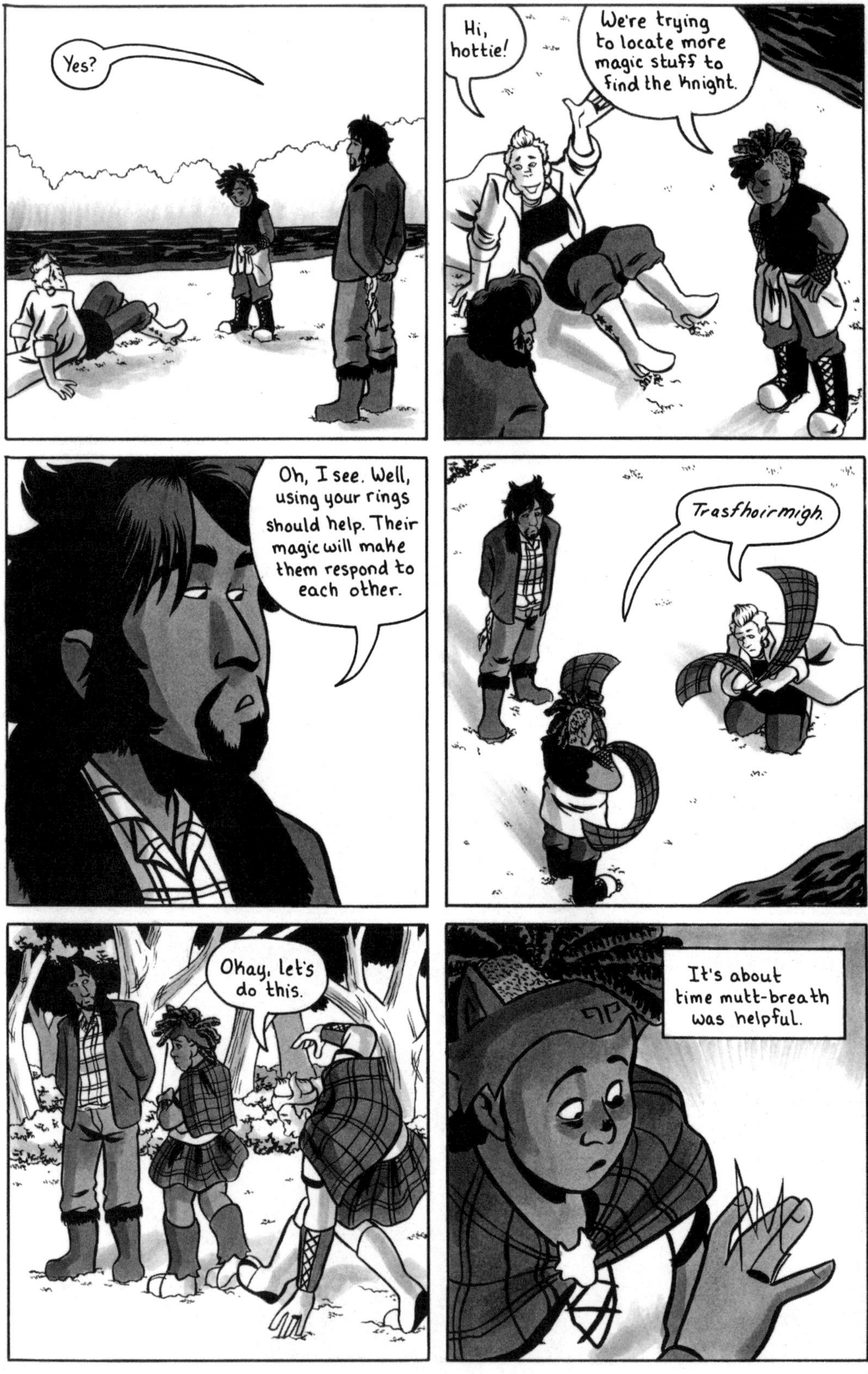
Yes?
Hi, hottie!
We're trying to locate more magic stuff to find the knight.
Oh, I see. Well, using your rings should help. Their magic will make them respond to each other.
Trasfhoirmigh.
Okay, let's do this.
It's about time mutt-breath was helpful.

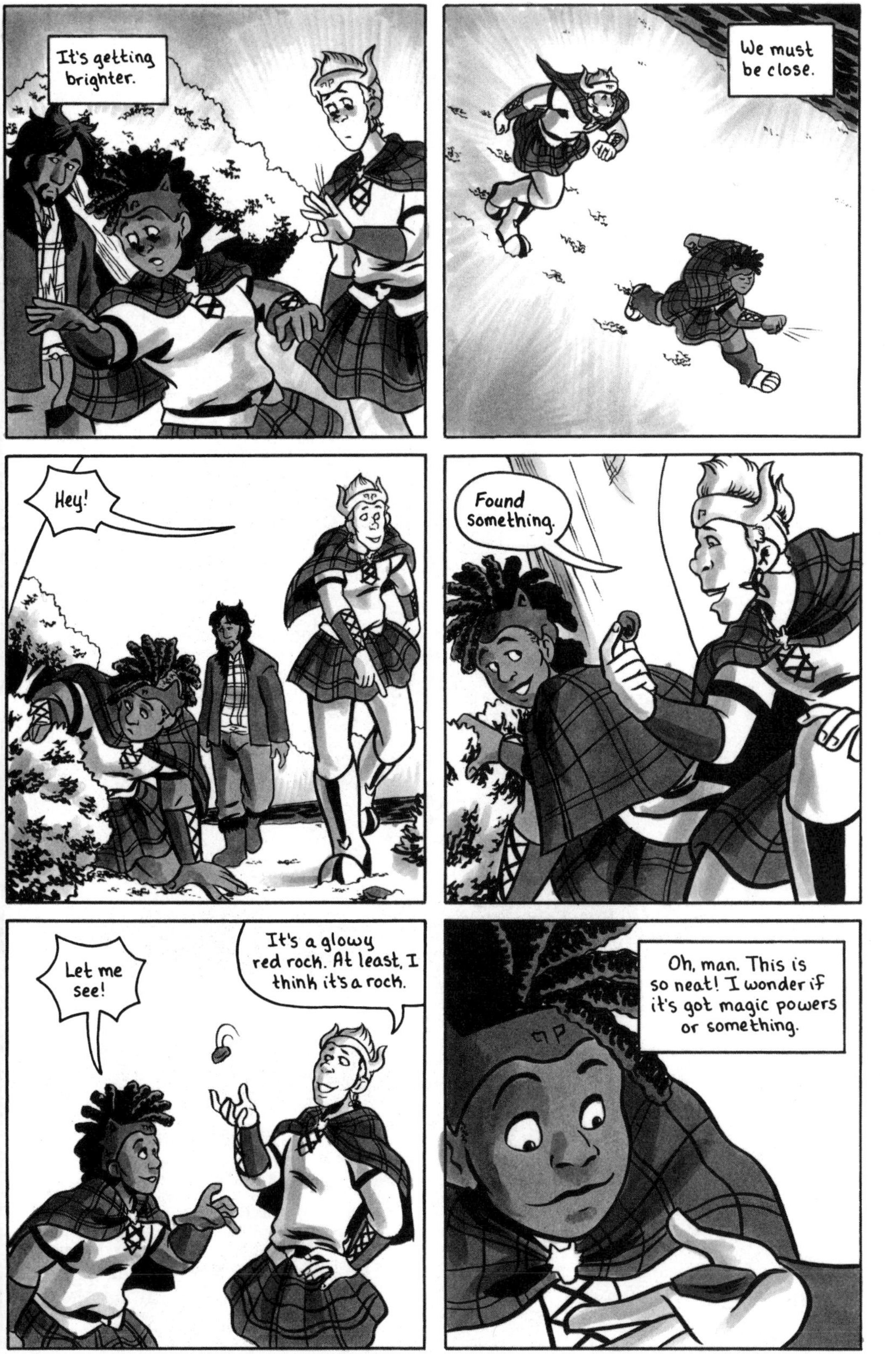
It's getting brighter.
We must be close.
Hey!
Found something.
Let me see!
It's a glowy red rock. At least, I think it's a rock.
Oh, man. This is so neat! I wonder if it's got magic powers or something.

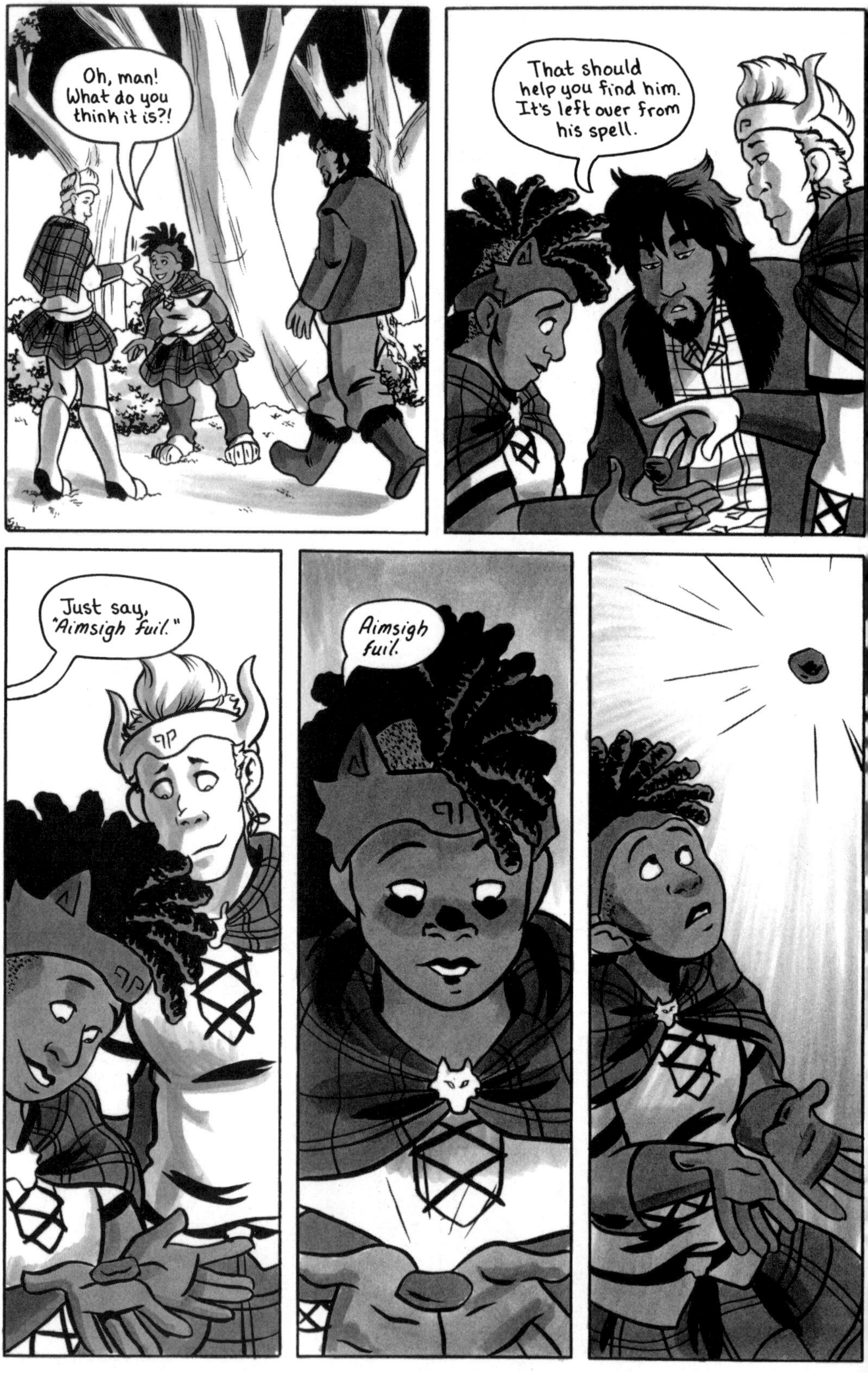
Oh, man! What do you think it is?!
That should help you find him. It's left over from his spell.
Just say, "Aimsigh fuil."
Aimsigh fuil.

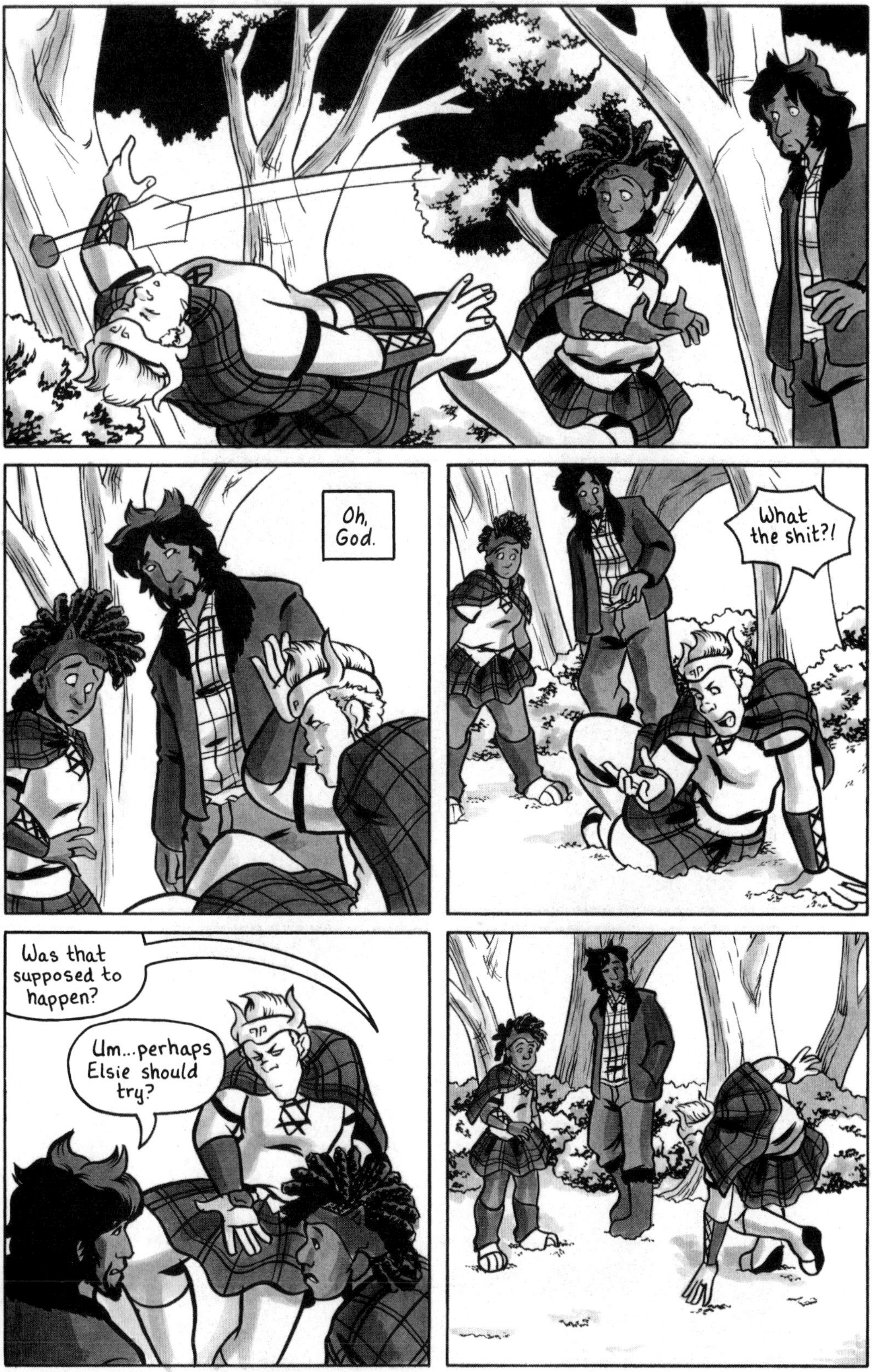
Oh, God.
What the shit?!
Was that supposed to happen?
Um...perhaps Elsie should try?

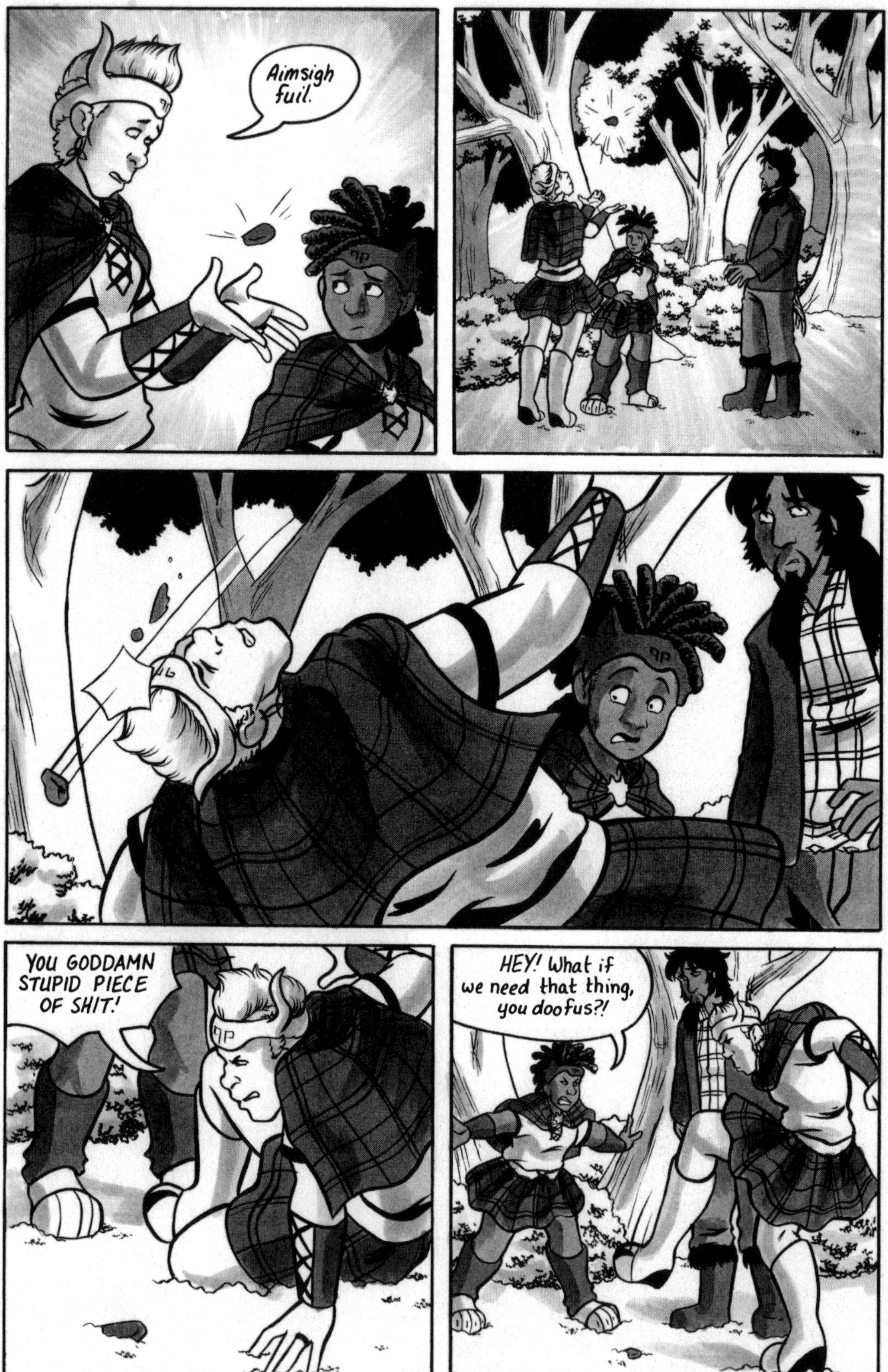
Aimsigh fuil.
YOU GODDAMN STUPID PIECE OF SHIT!
HEY! What if we need that thing, you doofus?!

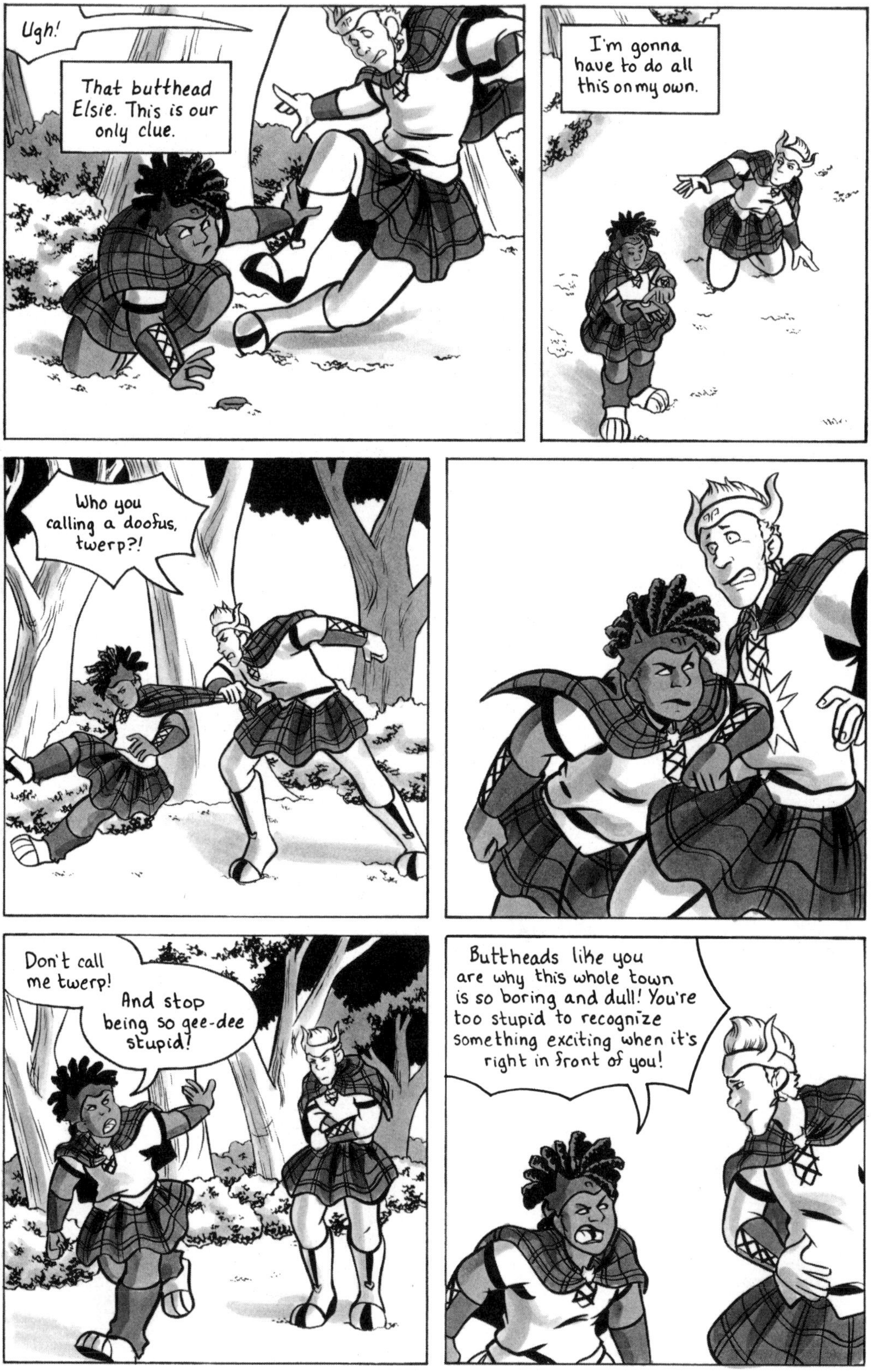

Ugh!
That butthead Elsie. This is our only clue.
I'm gonna have to do all this on my own.
Who you calling a doofus, twerp?!
Don't call me twerp!
And stop being so gee-dee stupid!
Buttheads like you are why this whole town is so boring and dull! You're too stupid to recognize something exciting when it's right in front of you!

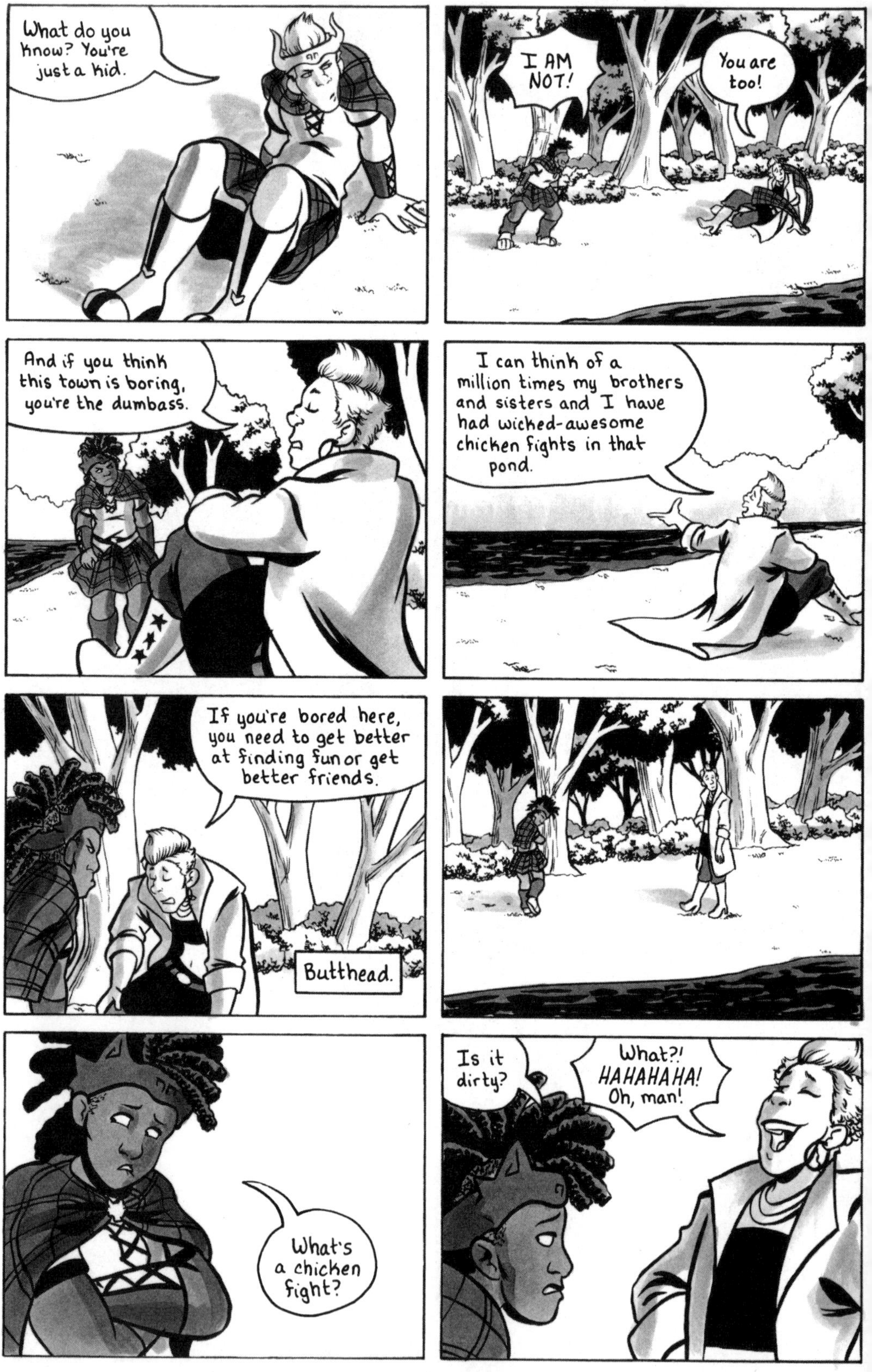
What do you know? You're just a kid.
I AM NOT!
You are too!
And if you think this town is boring, you're the dumbass.
I can think of a million times my brothers and sisters and I have had wicked-awesome chicken fights in that pond.
If you're bored here, you need to get better at finding fun or get better friends.
Butthead.
What's a chicken fight?
Is it dirty?
What?! HAHAHAHA! Oh, man!

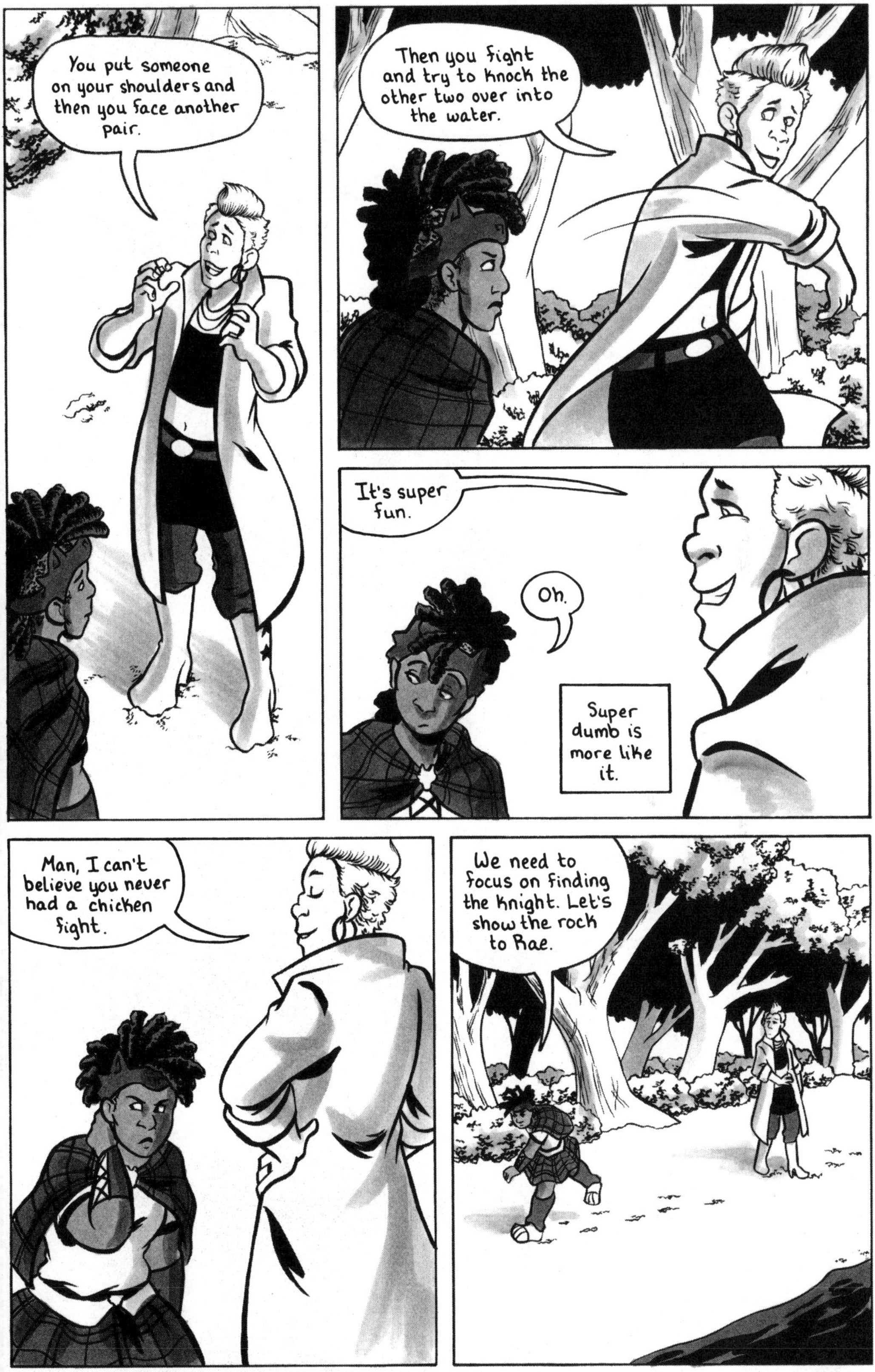
You put someone on your shoulders and then you face another pair.
Then you fight and try to knock the other two over into the water.
It's super fun.
Oh.
Super dumb is more like it.
Man, I can't believe you never had a chicken fight.
We need to focus on finding the knight. Let's show the rock to Rae.

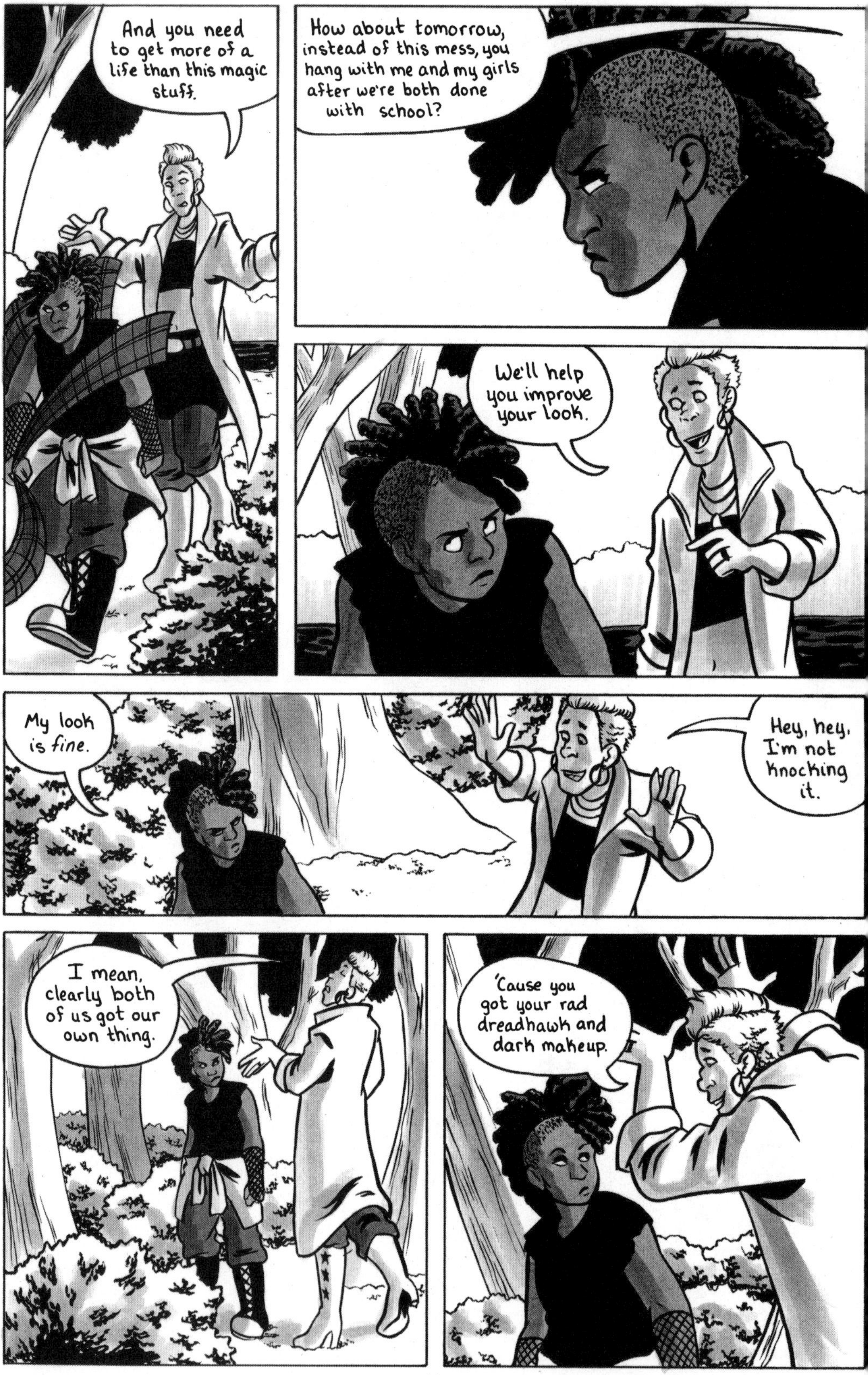
And you need to get more of a life than this magic stuff.
How about tomorrow, instead of this mess, you hang with me and my girls after we're both done with school?
We'll help you improve your look.
My look is fine.
Hey, hey, I'm not knocking it.
I mean, clearly both of us got our own thing.
'Cause you got your rad dreadhawk and dark makeup.

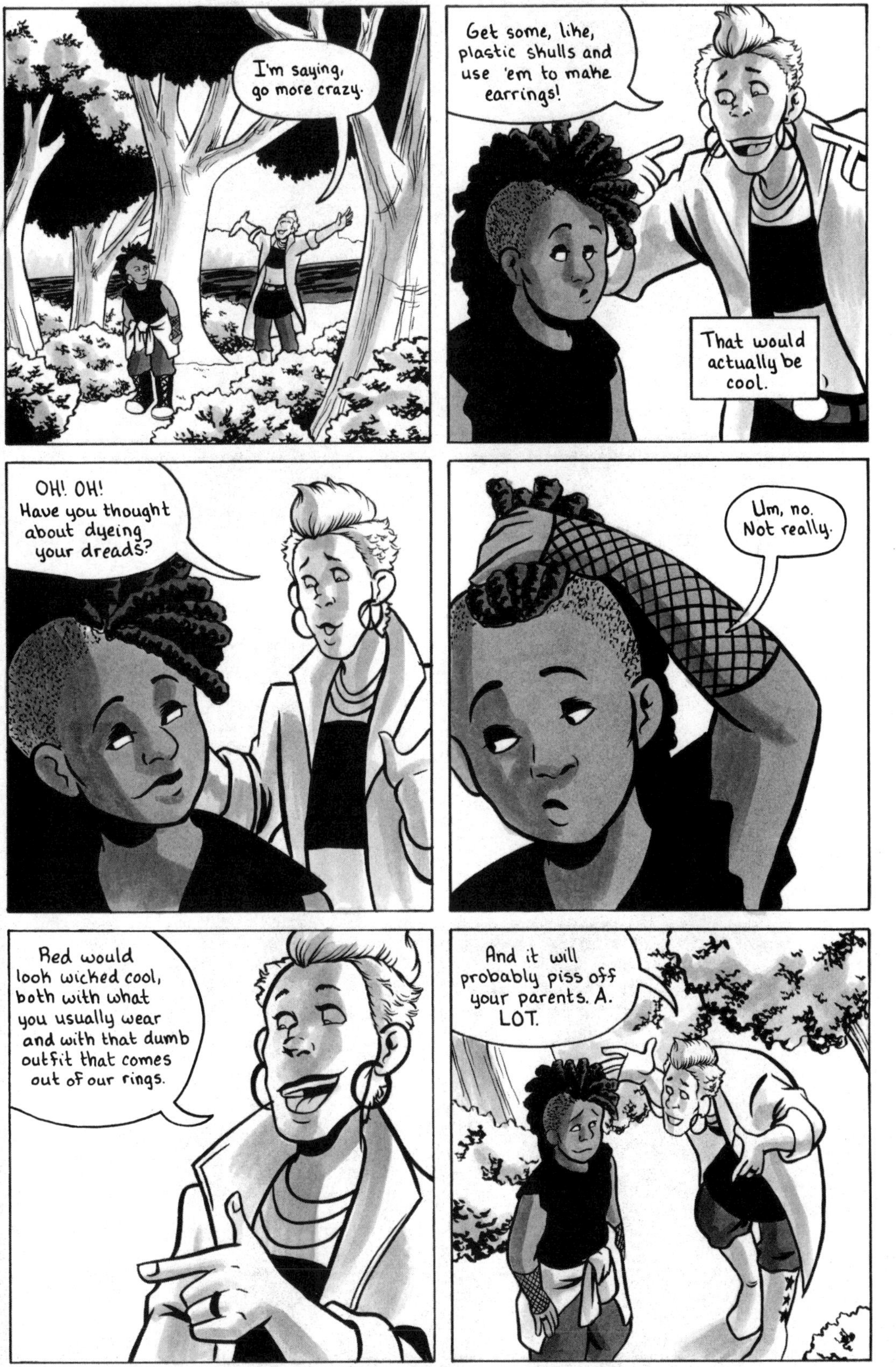
I'm saying, go more crazy.
Get some, like, plastic skulls and use 'em to make earrings!
That would actually be cool.
OH! OH! Have you thought about dyeing your dreads?
Um, no. Not really.
Red would look wicked cool, both with what you usually wear and with that dumb outfit that comes out of our rings.
And it will probably piss off your parents. A. LOT.

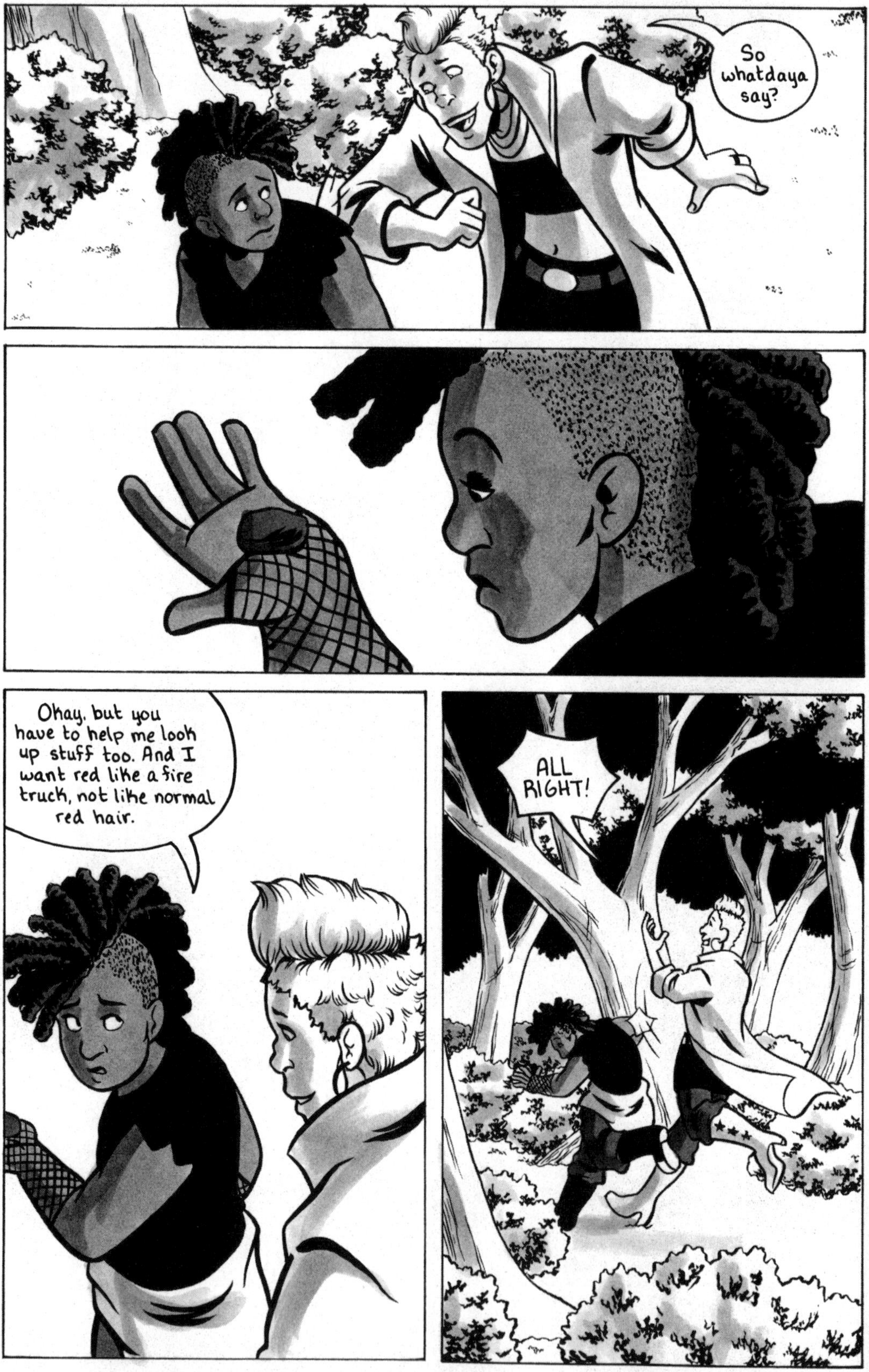
So whatdaya say?
Okay, but you have to help me look up stuff too. And I want red like a fire truck, not like normal red hair.
ALL RIGHT!

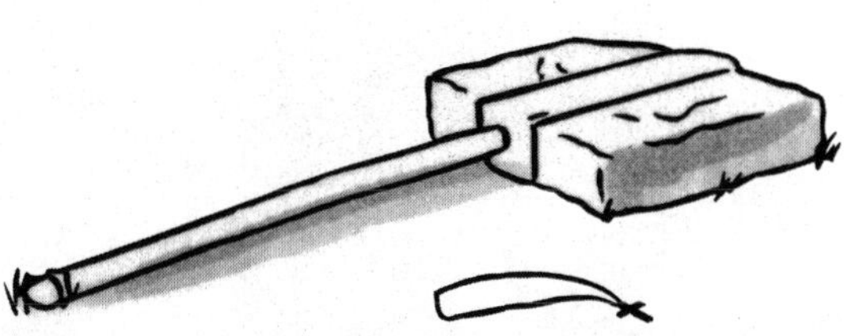

CHAPTER 3:

Watch Someone Else Do It Wrong without Comment

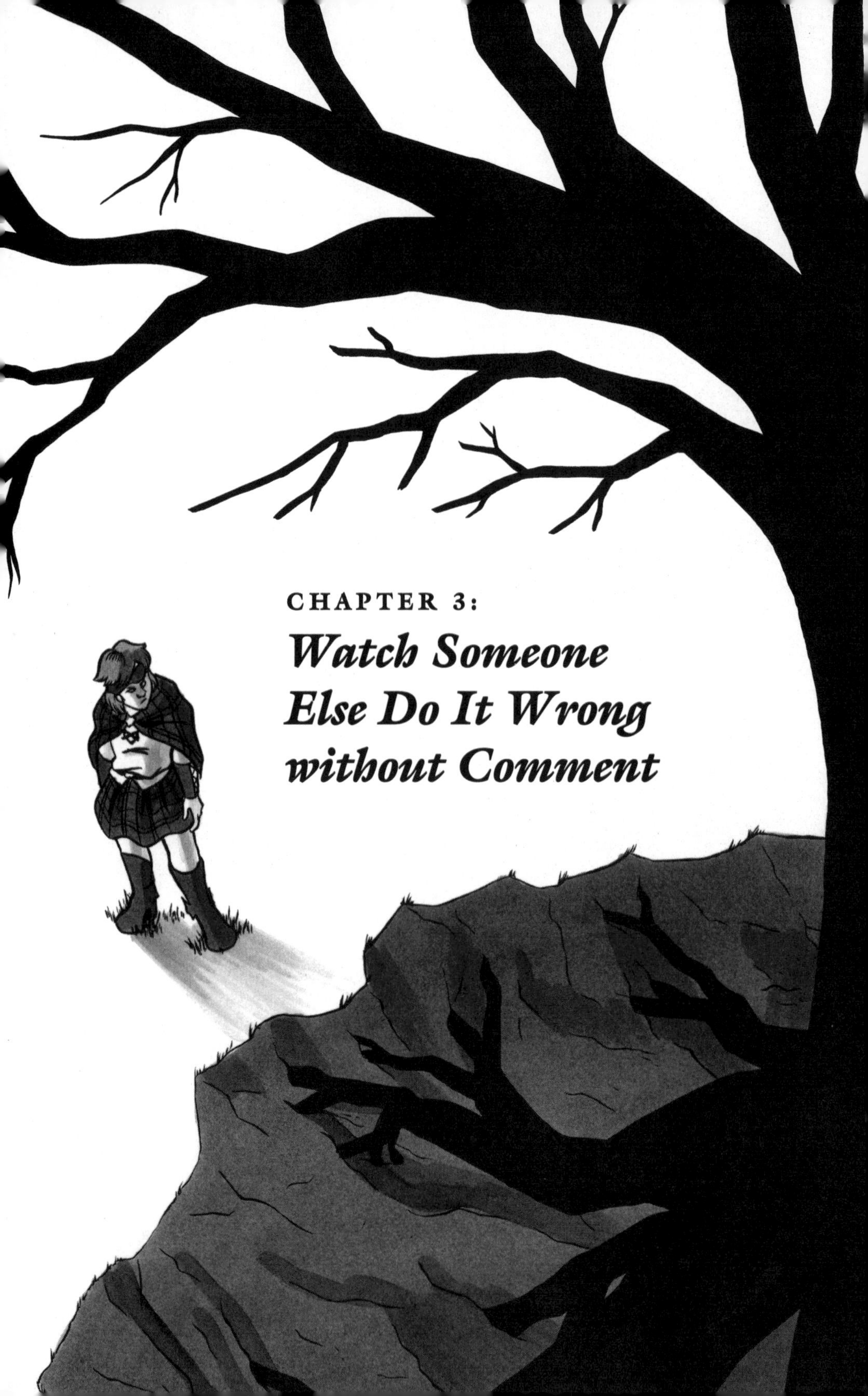

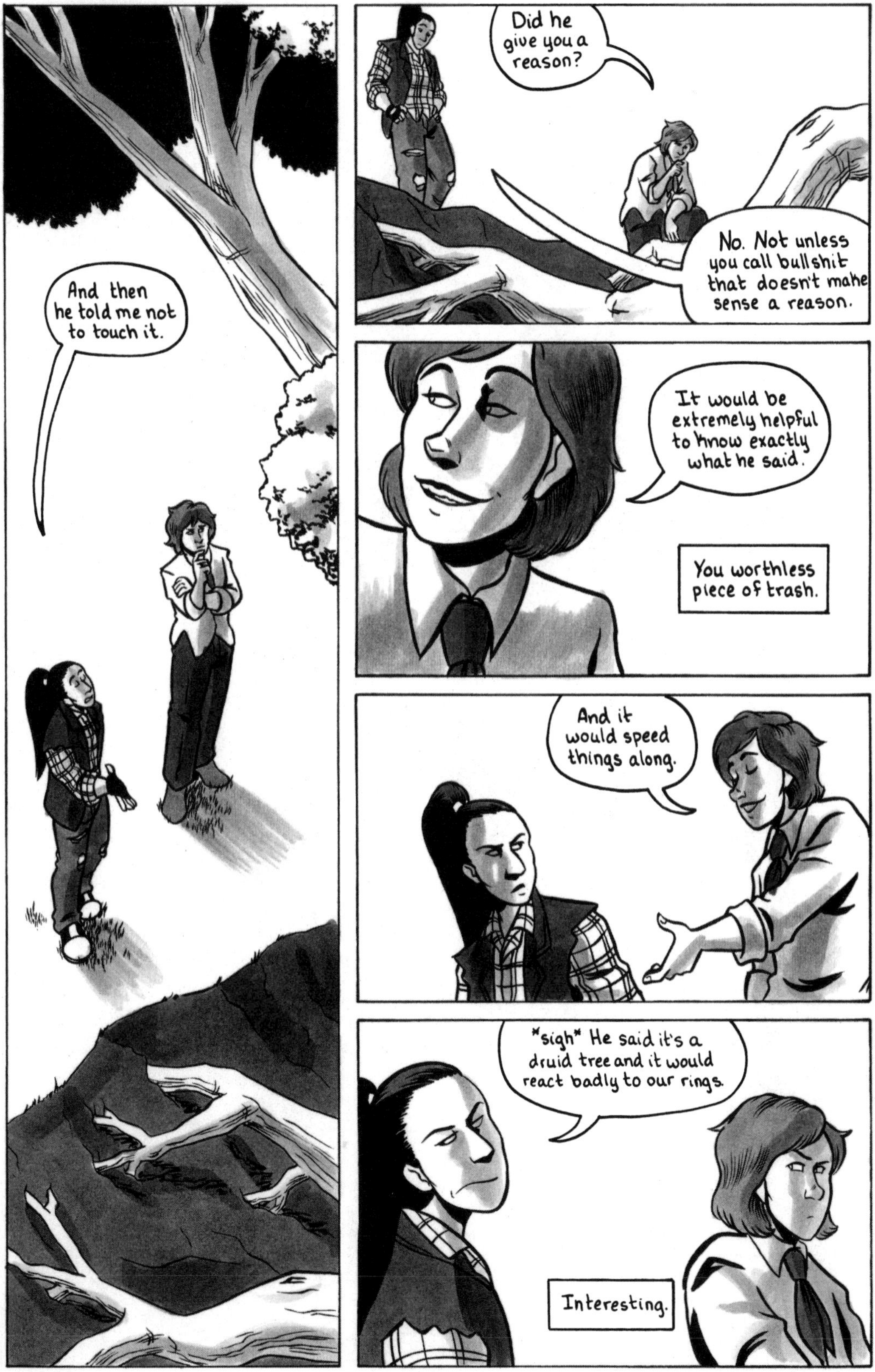
And then he told me not to touch it.
Did he give you a reason?
No. Not unless you call bullshit that doesn't make sense a reason.
It would be extremely helpful to know exactly what he said.
You worthless piece of trash.
And it would speed things along.
sigh He said it's a druid tree and it would react badly to our rings.
Interesting.

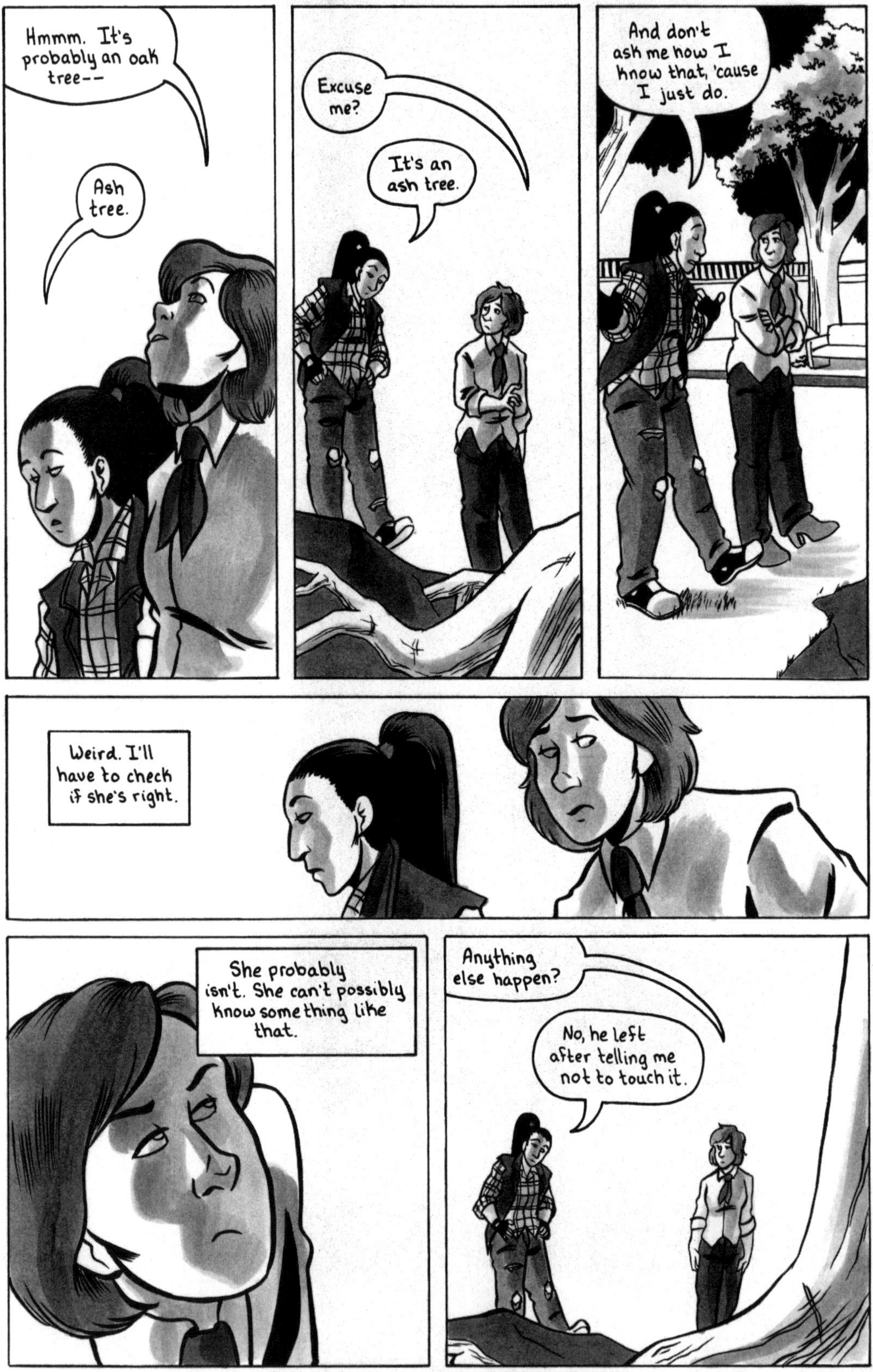

Hmmm. It's probably an oak tree--
Ash tree.
Excuse me?
It's an ash tree.
And don't ask me how I know that, 'cause I just do.
Weird. I'll have to check if she's right.
She probably isn't. She can't possibly know something like that.
Anything else happen?
No, he left after telling me not to touch it.

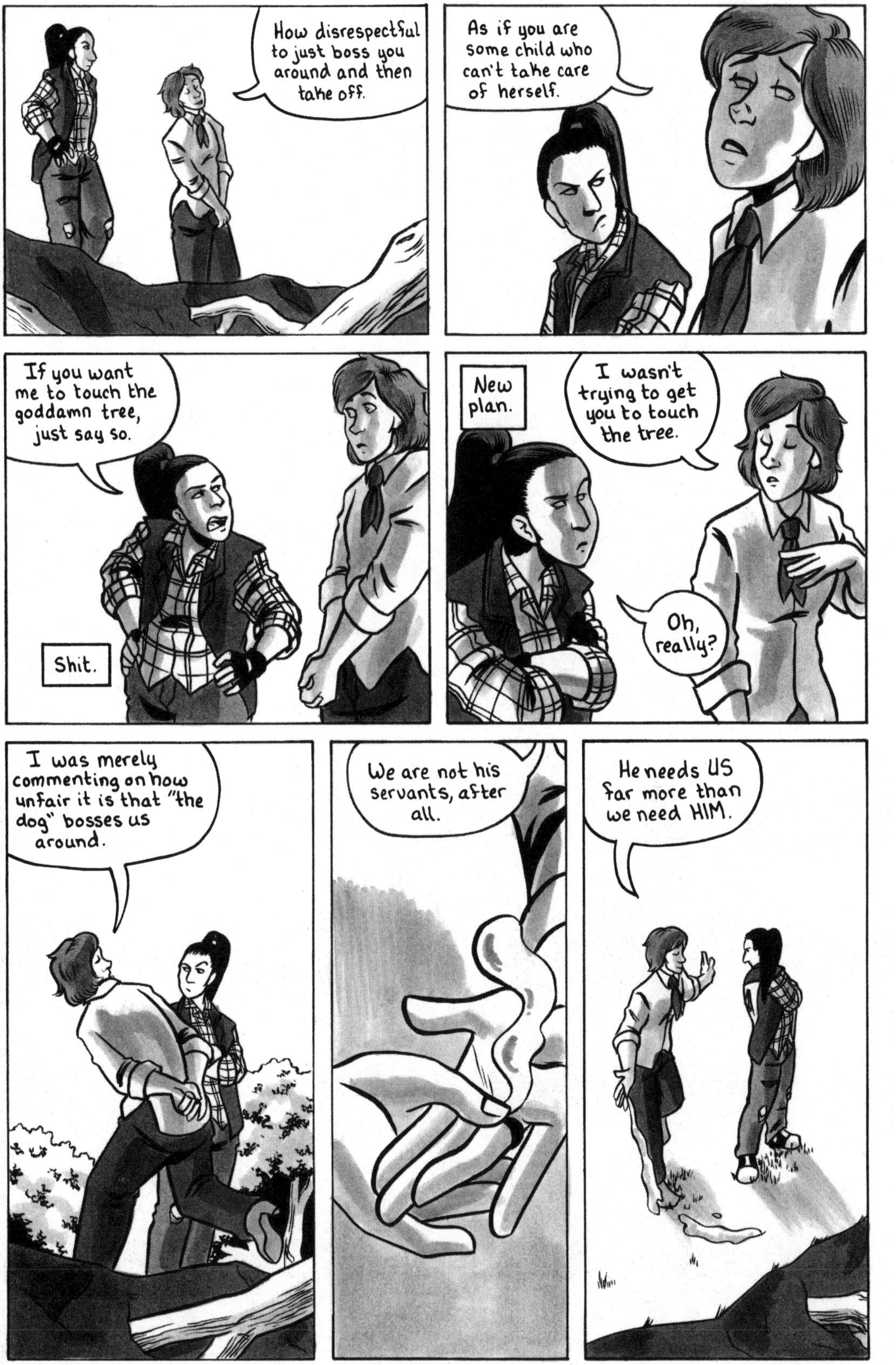
How disrespectful to just boss you around and then take off.
As if you are some child who can't take care of herself.
If you want me to touch the goddamn tree, just say so.
Shit.
New plan.
I wasn't trying to get you to touch the tree.
Oh, really?
I was merely commenting on how unfair it is that "the dog" bosses us around.
We are not his servants, after all.
He needs US far more than we need HIM.

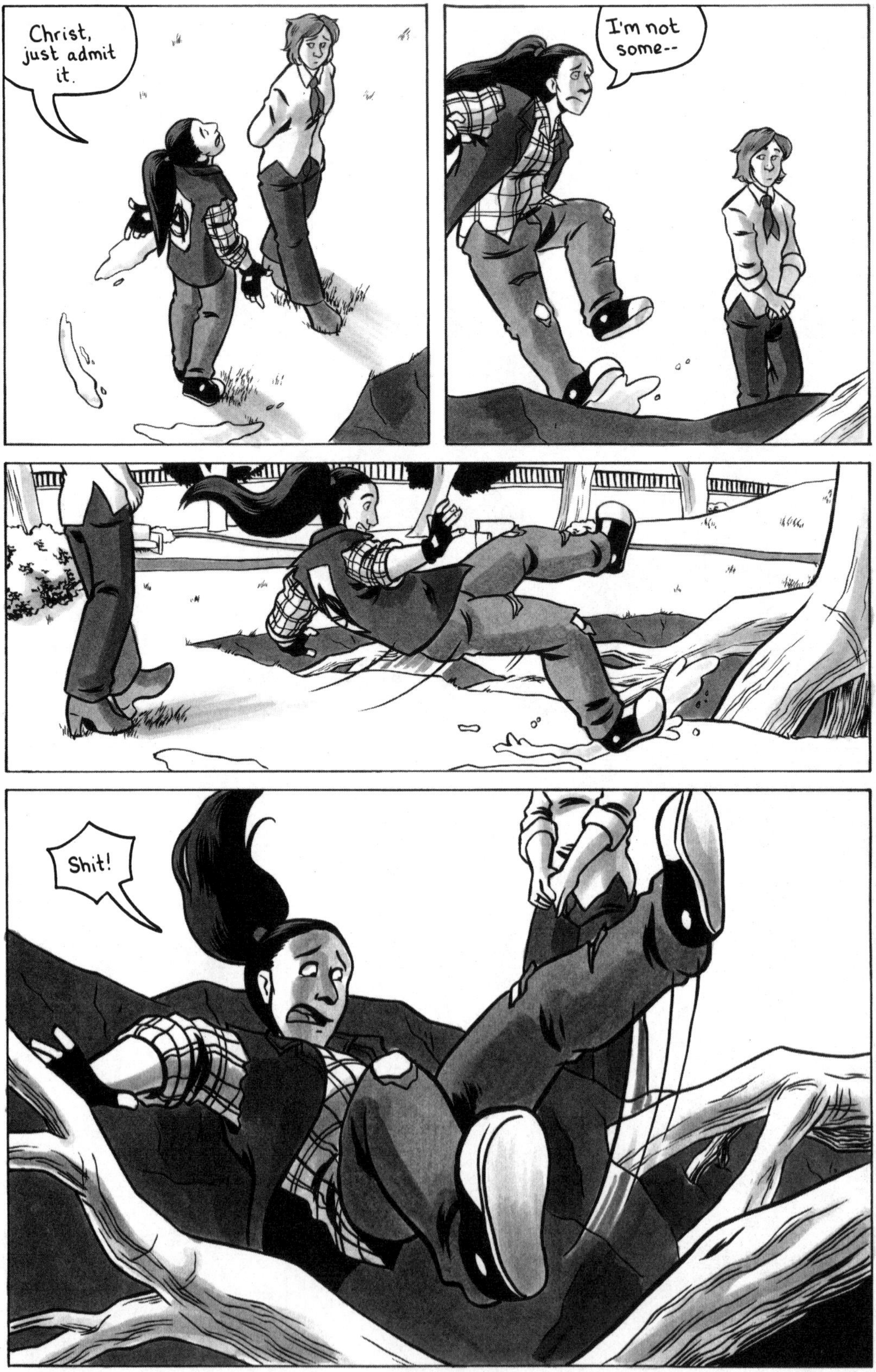
Christ, just admit it.
I'm not some--
Shit!

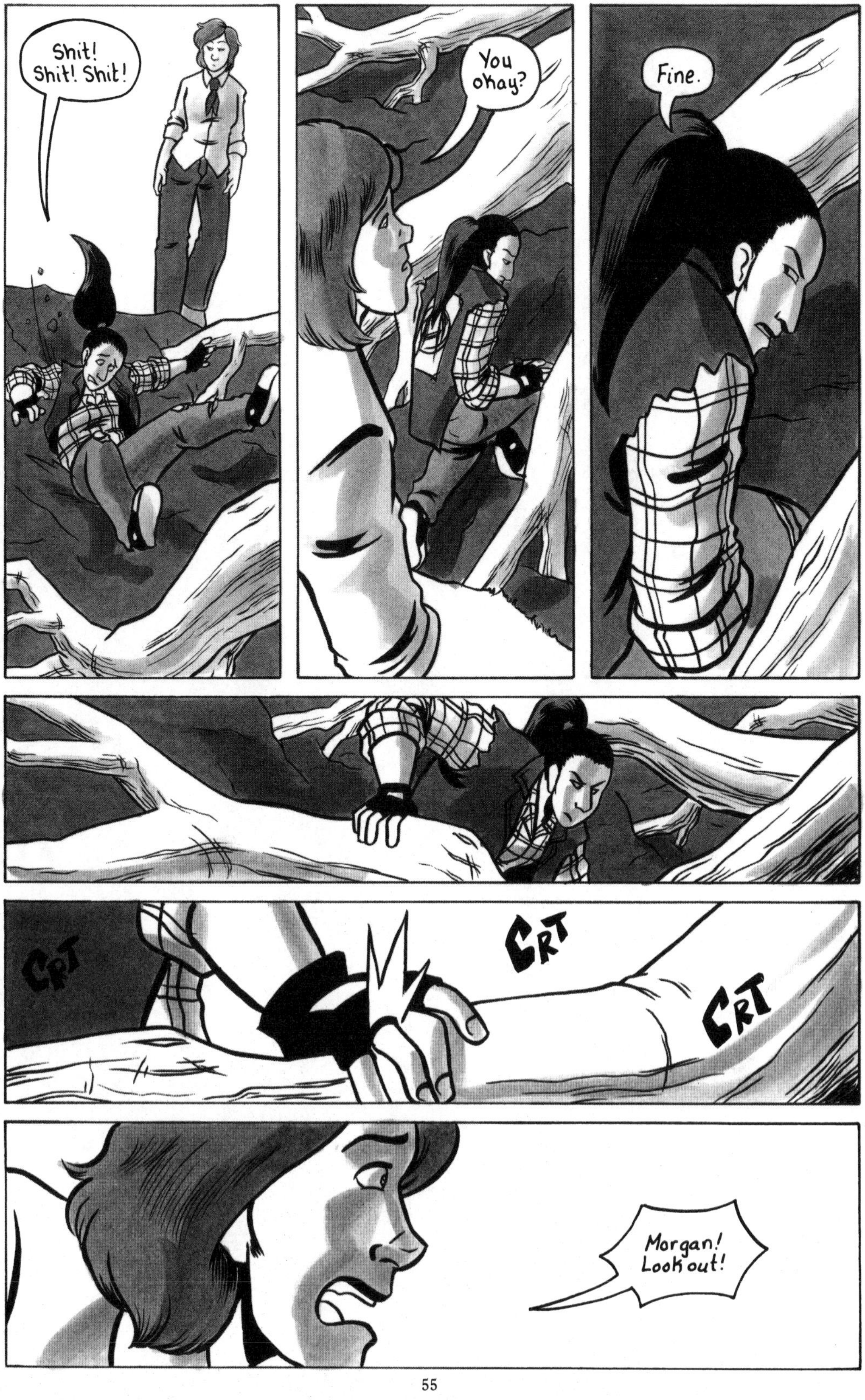
Shit! Shit! Shit!
You okay?
Fine.
CRT
CRT
CRT
Morgan! Lookout!

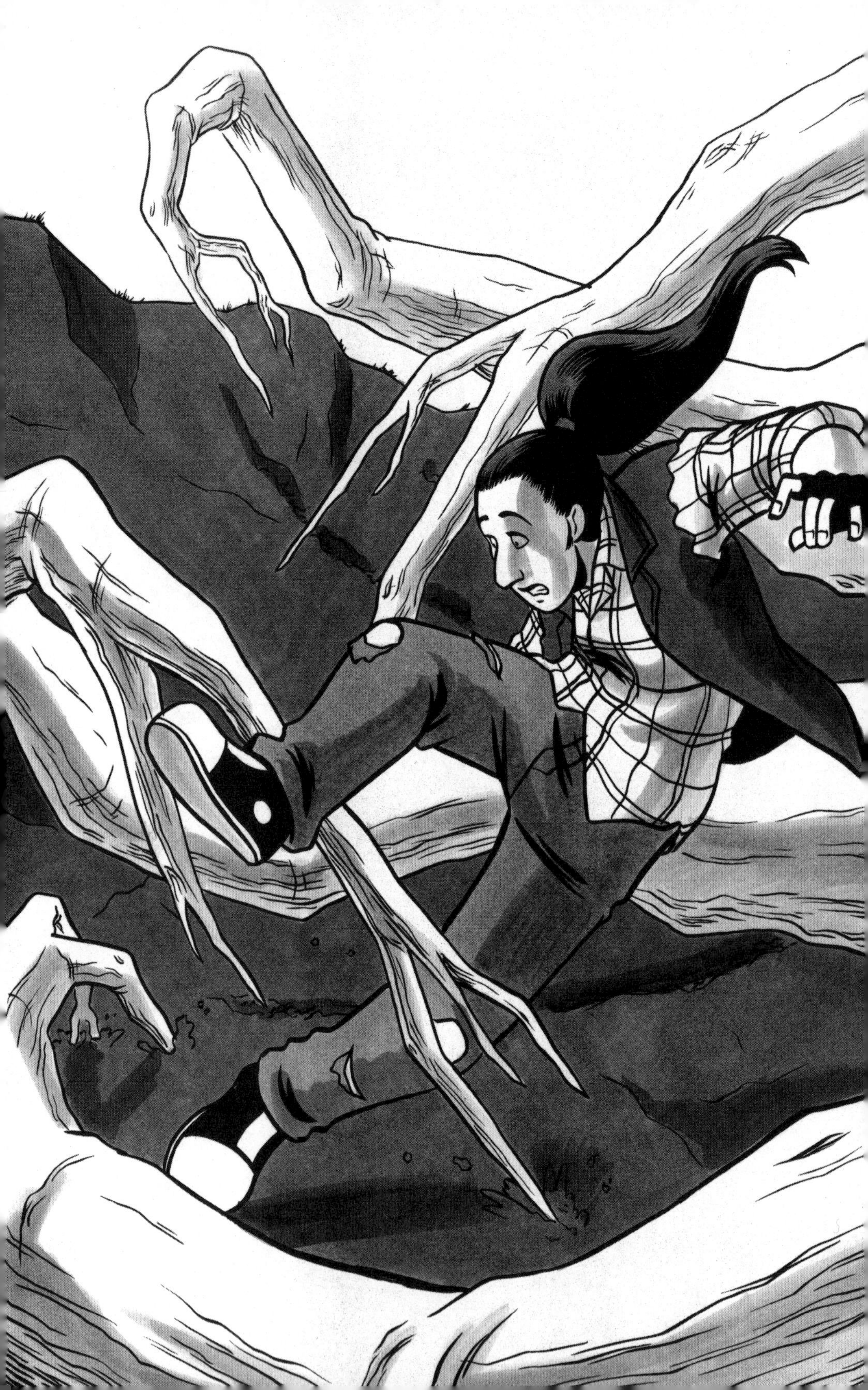

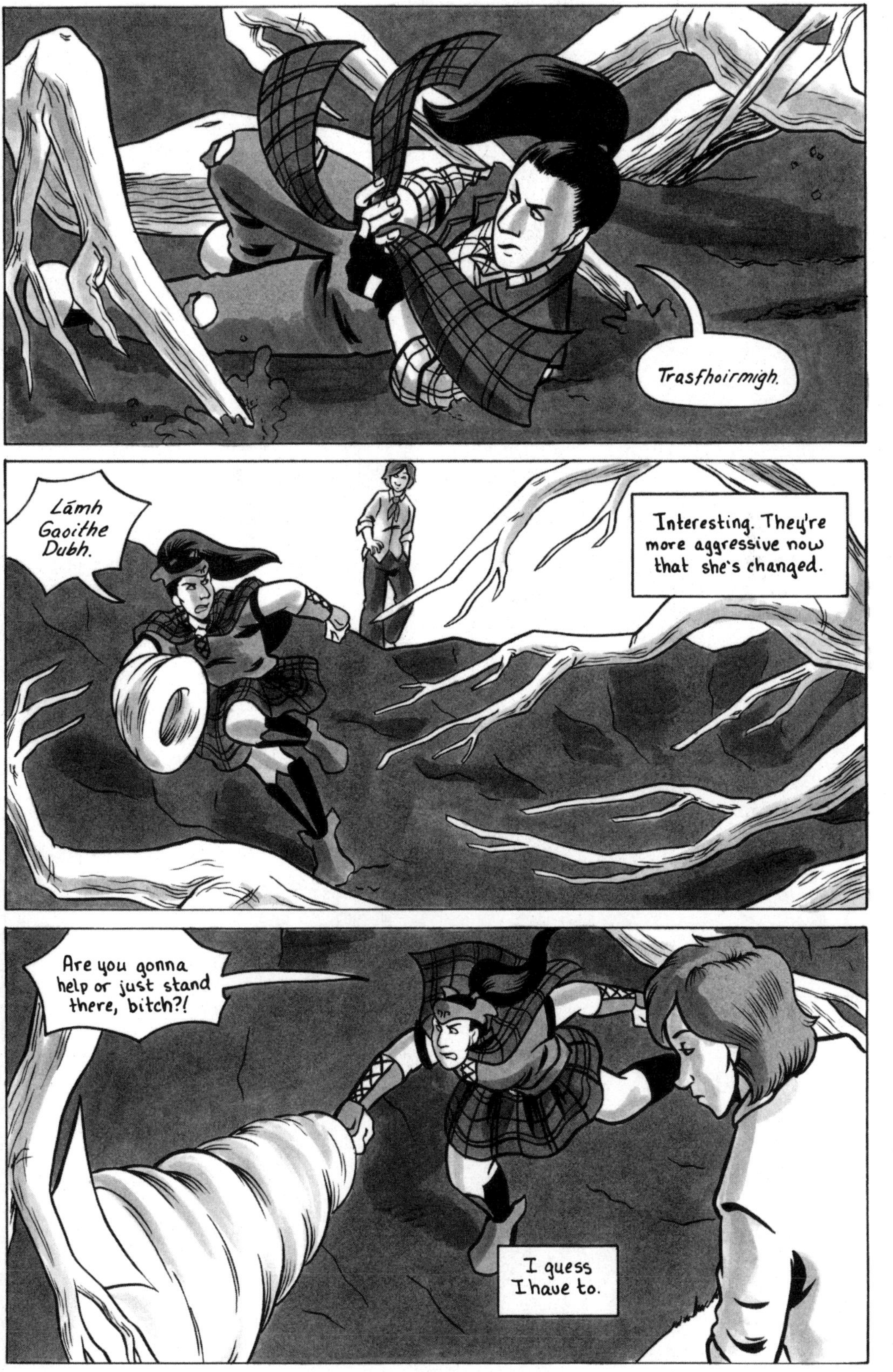
Trasfhoirmigh.
Lámh Gaoithe Dubh.
Interesting. They're more aggressive now that she's changed.
Are you gonna help or just stand there, bitch?!
I guess I have to.

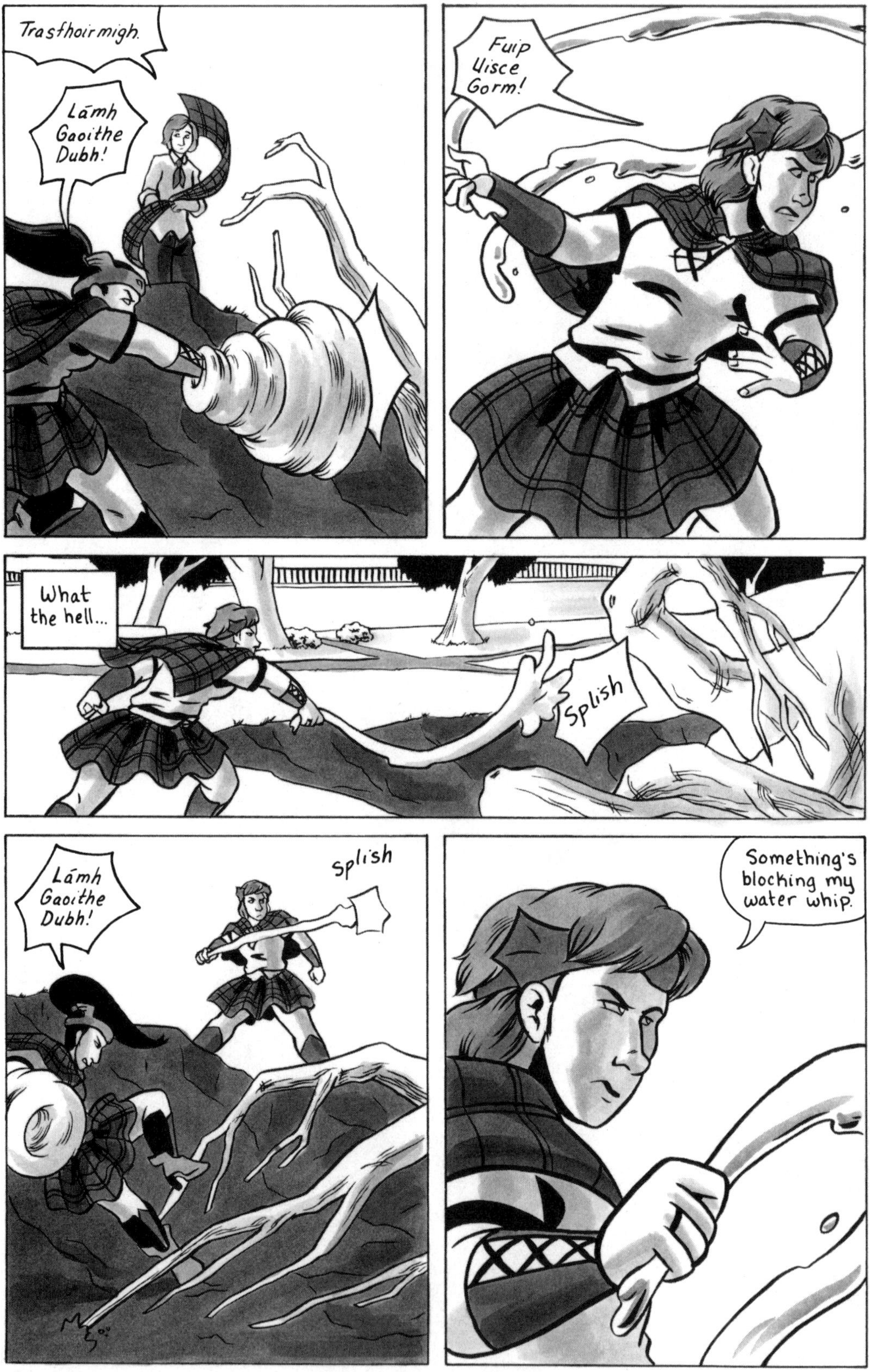
Trasfhoirmigh.
Lámh Gaoithe Dubh!
Fuip Uisce Gorm!
What the hell...
Splish
Lámh Gaoithe Dubh!
Splish
Something's blocking my water whip.

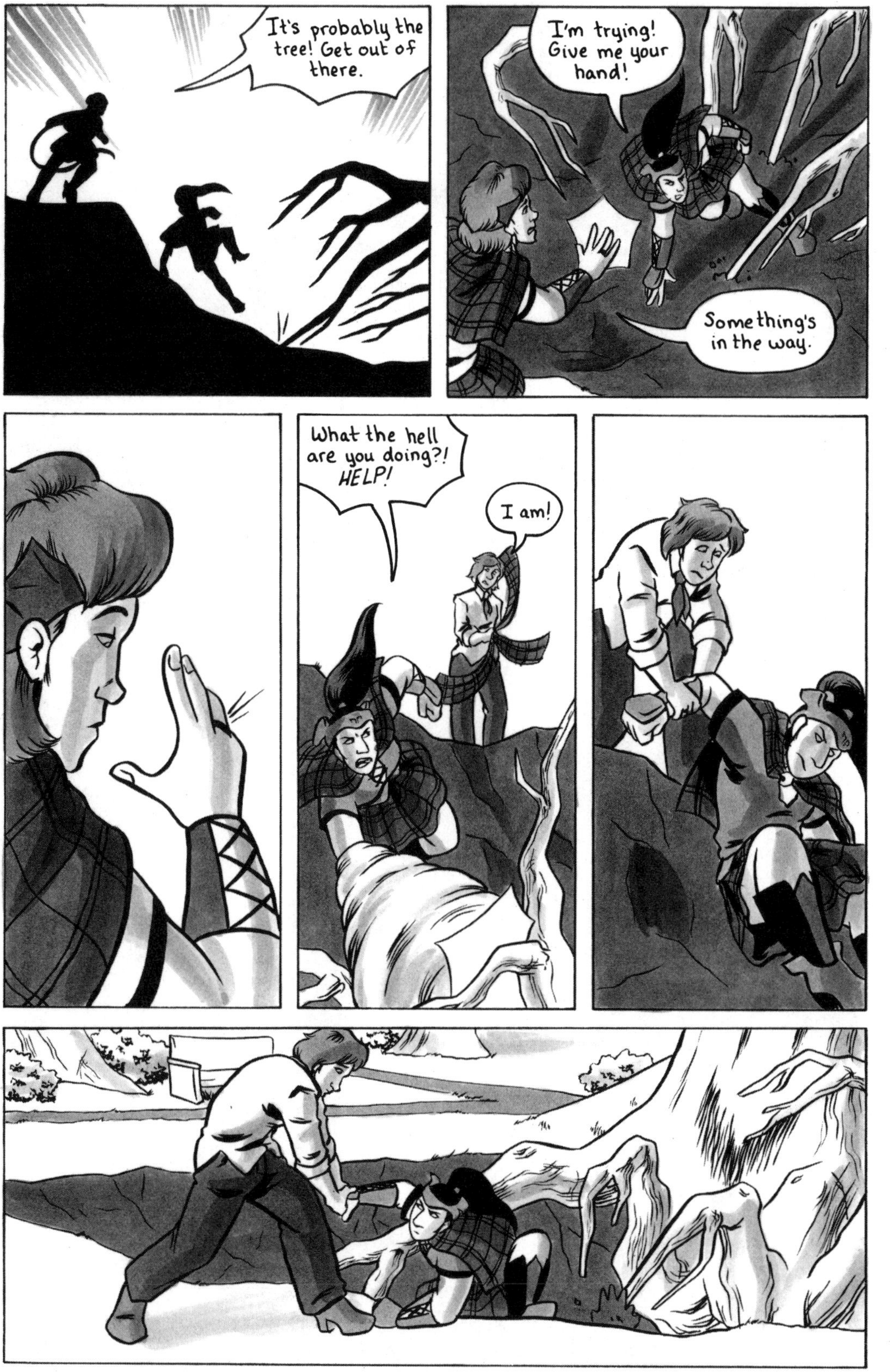
It's probably the tree! Get out of there.
I'm trying! Give me your hand!
Something's in the way.
What the hell are you doing?! HELP!
I am!

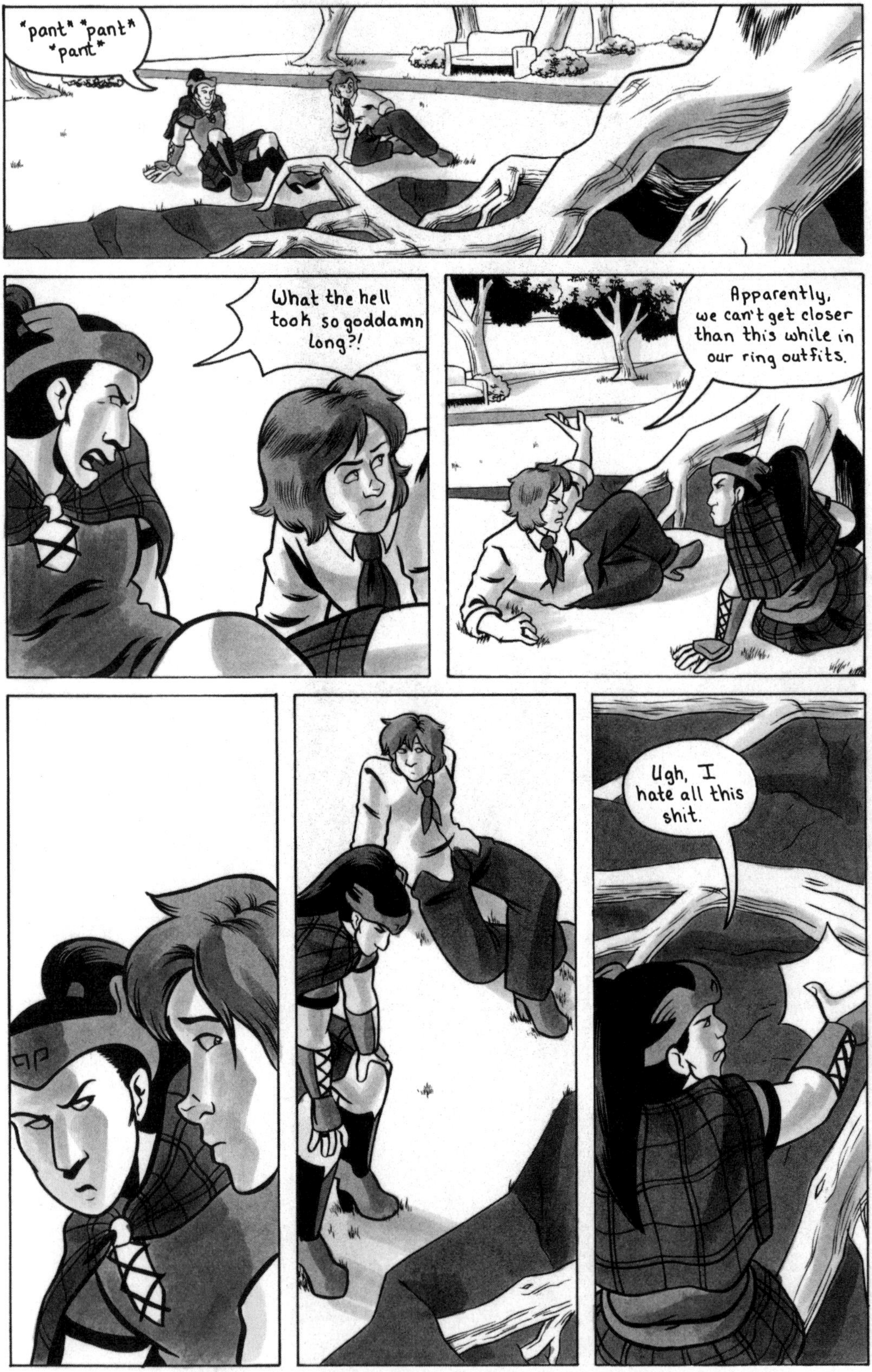
pant *pant* *pant*
What the hell took so goddamn long?!
Apparently, we can't get closer than this while in our ring outfits.
Ugh, I hate all this shit.

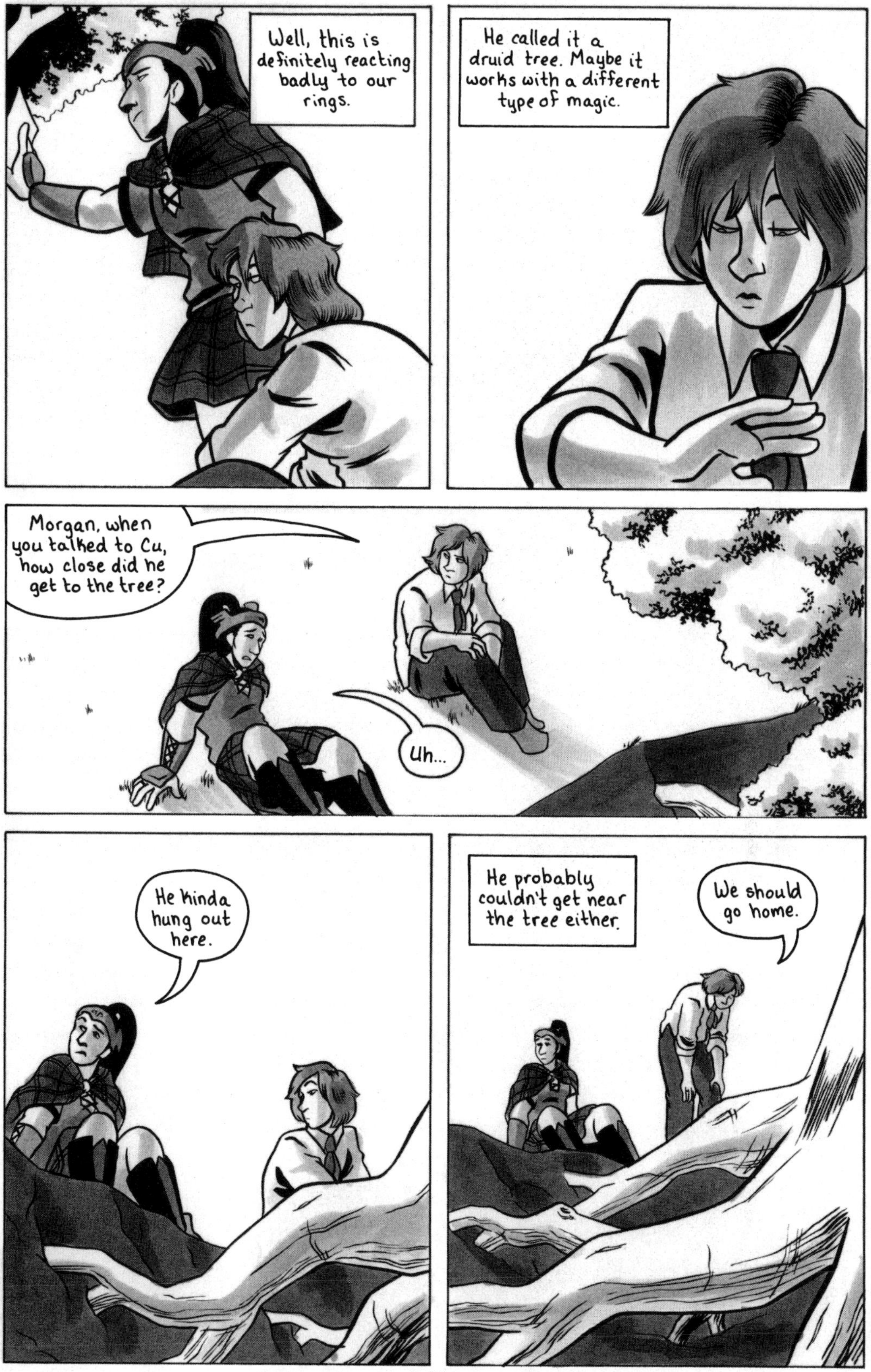

Well, this is definitely reacting badly to our rings.
He called it a druid tree. Maybe it works with a different type of magic.
Morgan, when you talked to Cu, how close did he get to the tree?
Uh...
He kinda hung out here.
He probably couldn't get near the tree either.
We should go home.

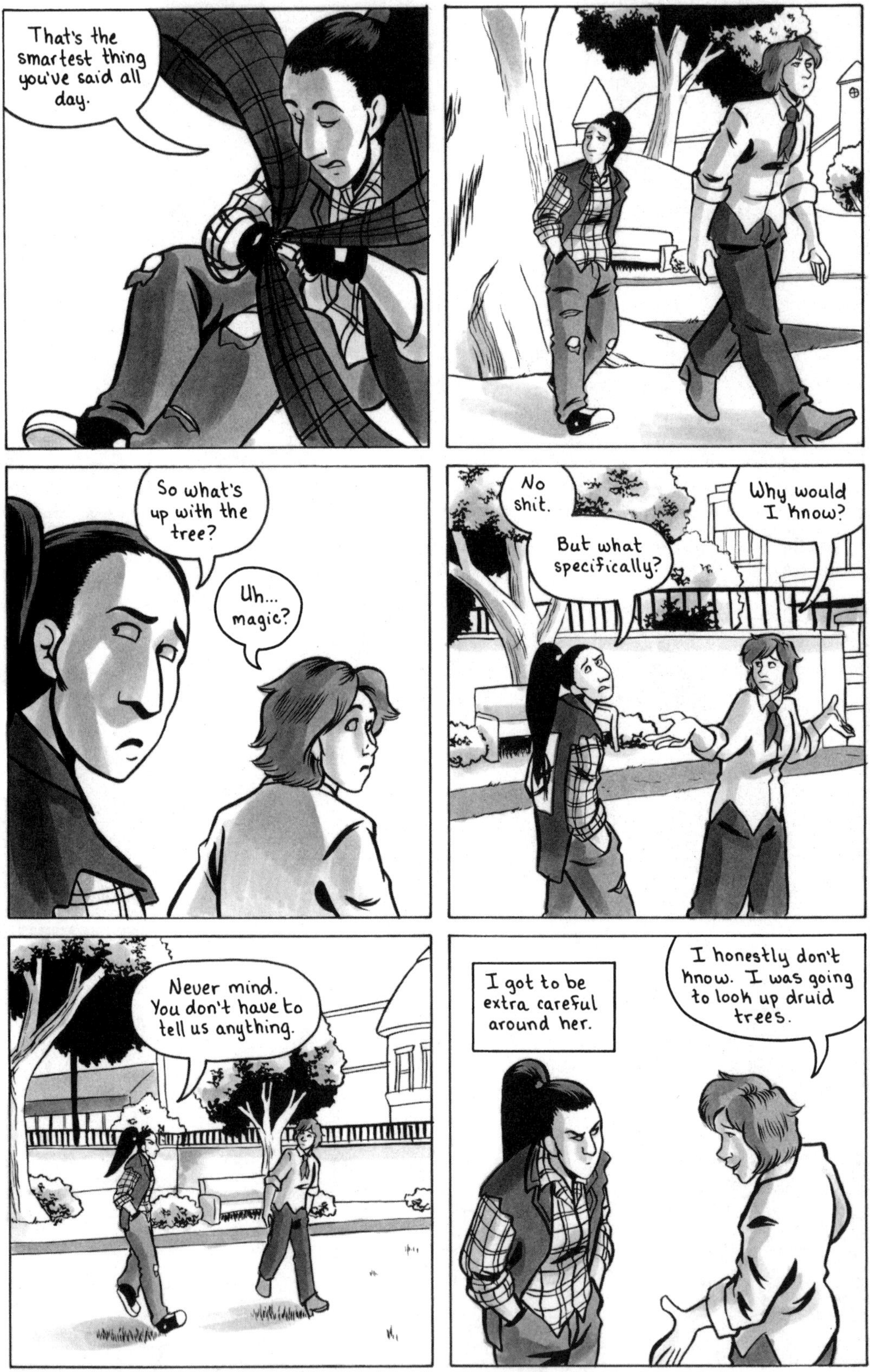
That's the smartest thing you've said all day.
So what's up with the tree?
Uh... magic?
No shit.
But what specifically?
Why would I know?
Never mind. You don't have to tell us anything.
I got to be extra careful around her.
I honestly don't know. I was going to look up druid trees.

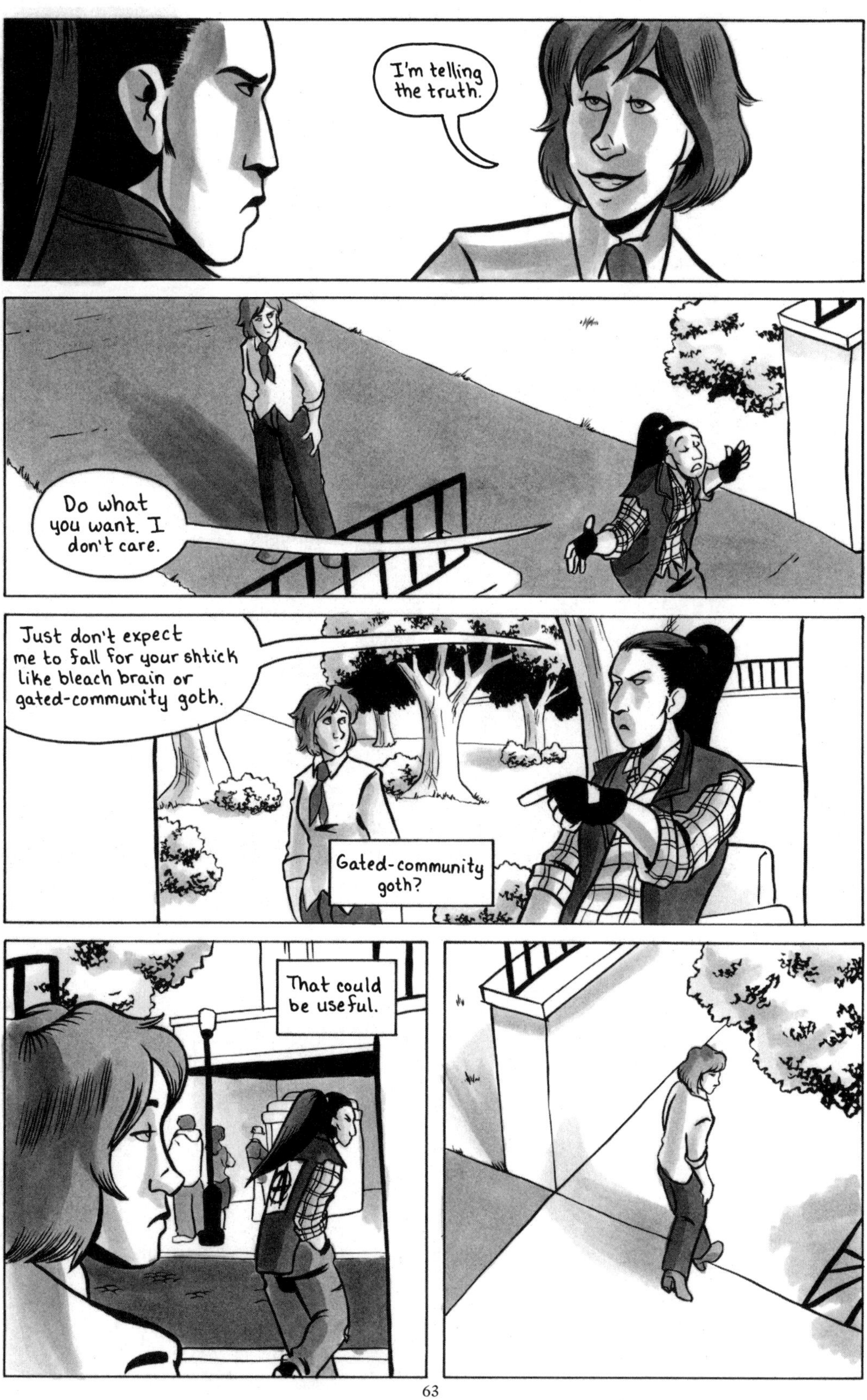

I'm telling the truth.
Do what you want. I don't care.
Just don't expect me to fall for your shtick like bleach brain or gated-community goth.
Gated-community goth?
That could be useful.

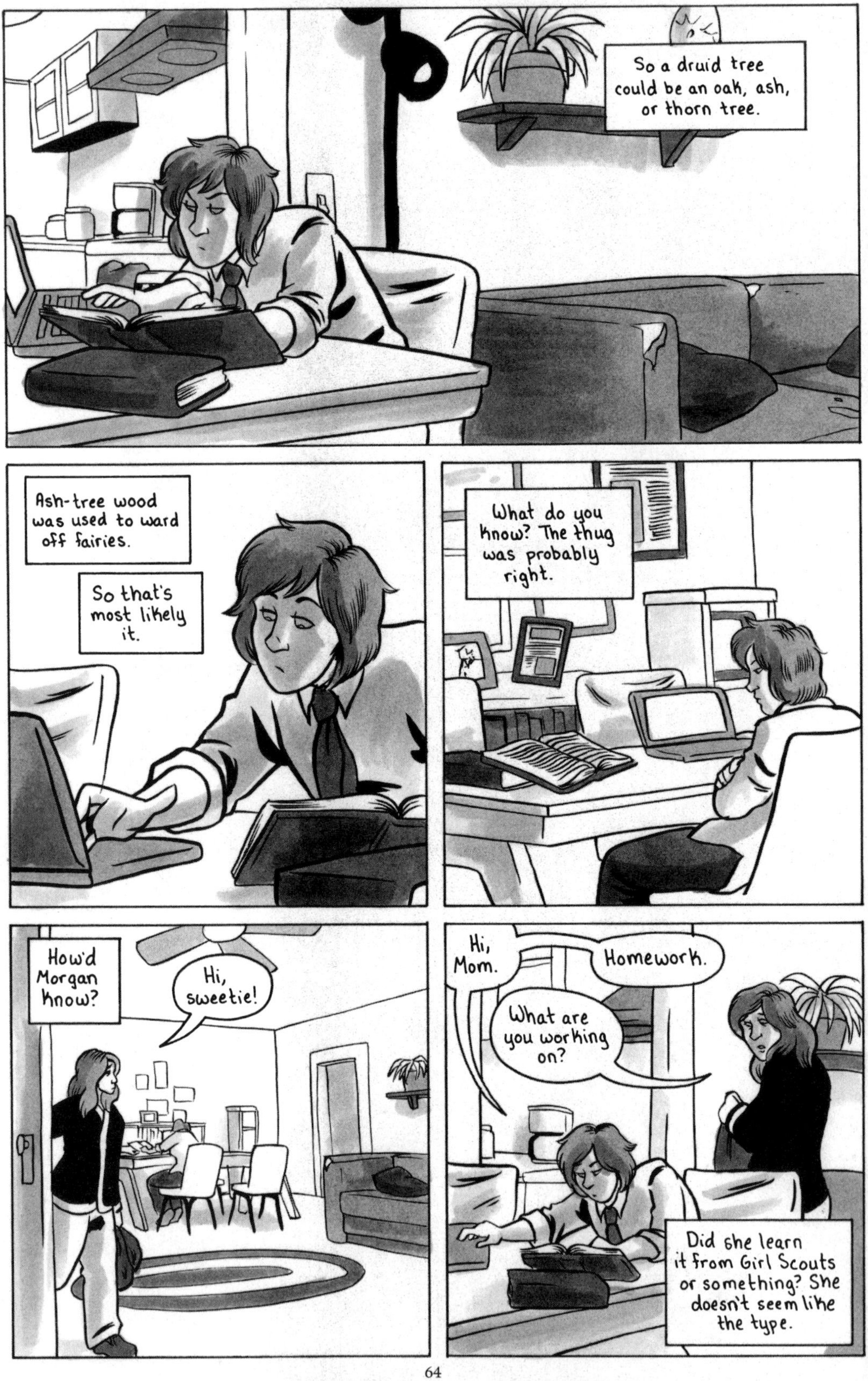

So a druid tree could be an oak, ash, or thorn tree.
Ash-tree wood was used to ward off fairies.
So that's most likely it.
What do you know? The thug was probably right.
How'd Morgan know?
Hi, sweetie!
Hi, Mom.
Homework.
What are you working on?
Did she learn it from Girl Scouts or something? She doesn't seem like the type.

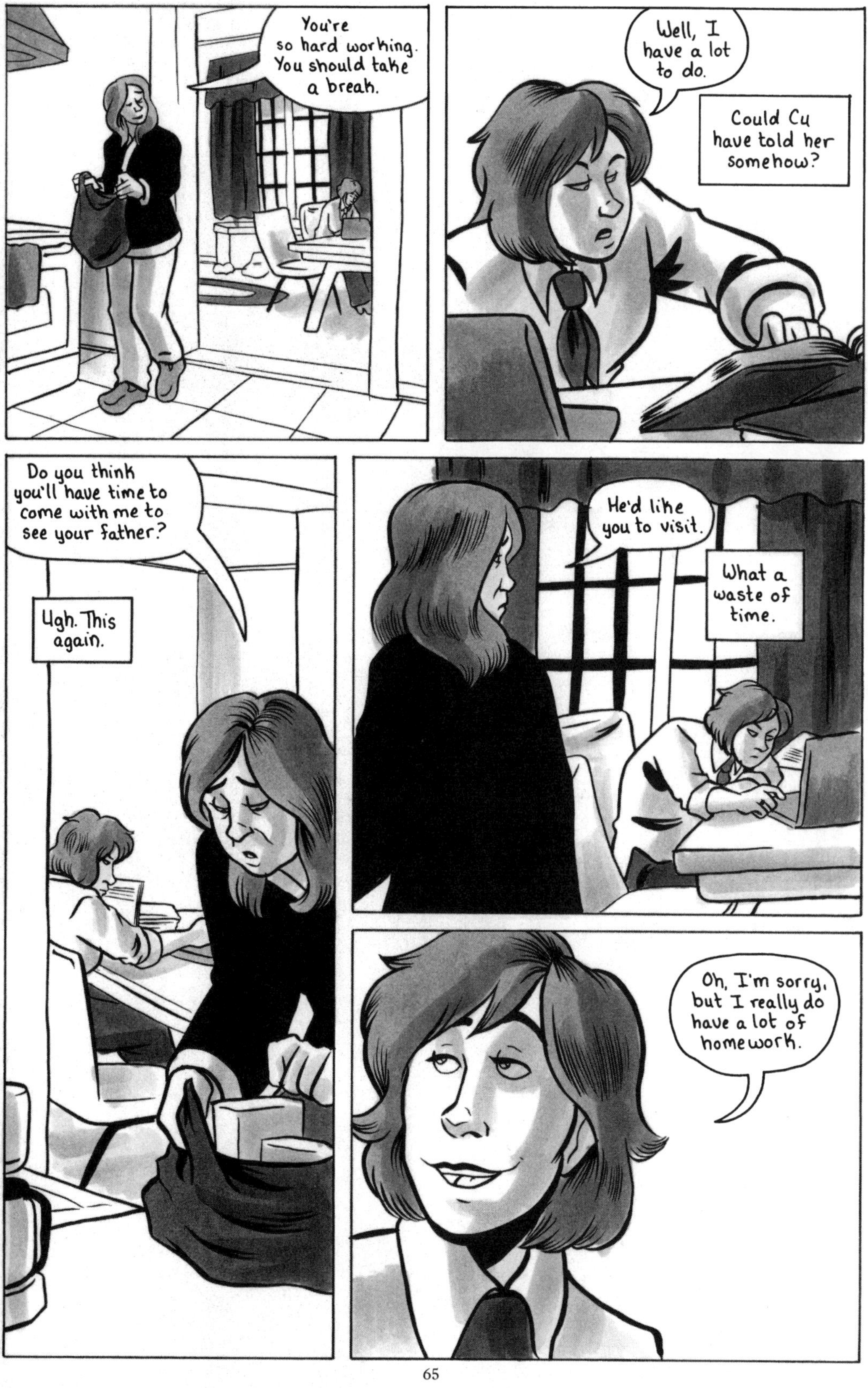
You're so hard working. You should take a break.
Well, I have a lot to do.
Could Cu have told her somehow?
Do you think you'll have time to come with me to see your father?
Ugh. This again.
He'd like you to visit.
What a waste of time.
Oh, I'm sorry, but I really do have a lot of homework.

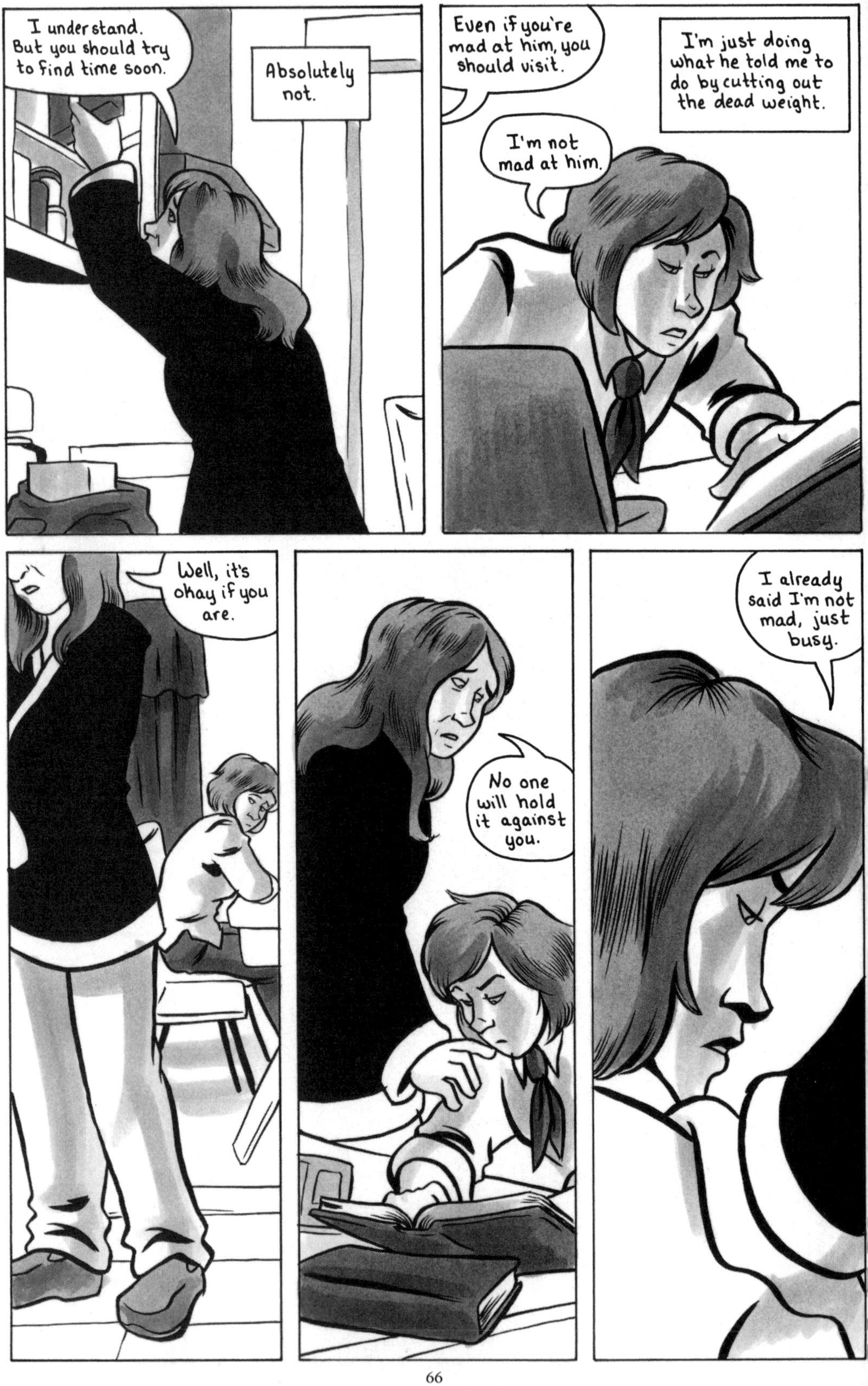
I understand. But you should try to find time soon.
Absolutely not.
Even if you're mad at him, you should visit.
I'm just doing what he told me to do by cutting out the dead weight.
I'm not mad at him.
Well, it's okay if you are.
No one will hold it against you.
I already said I'm not mad, just busy.

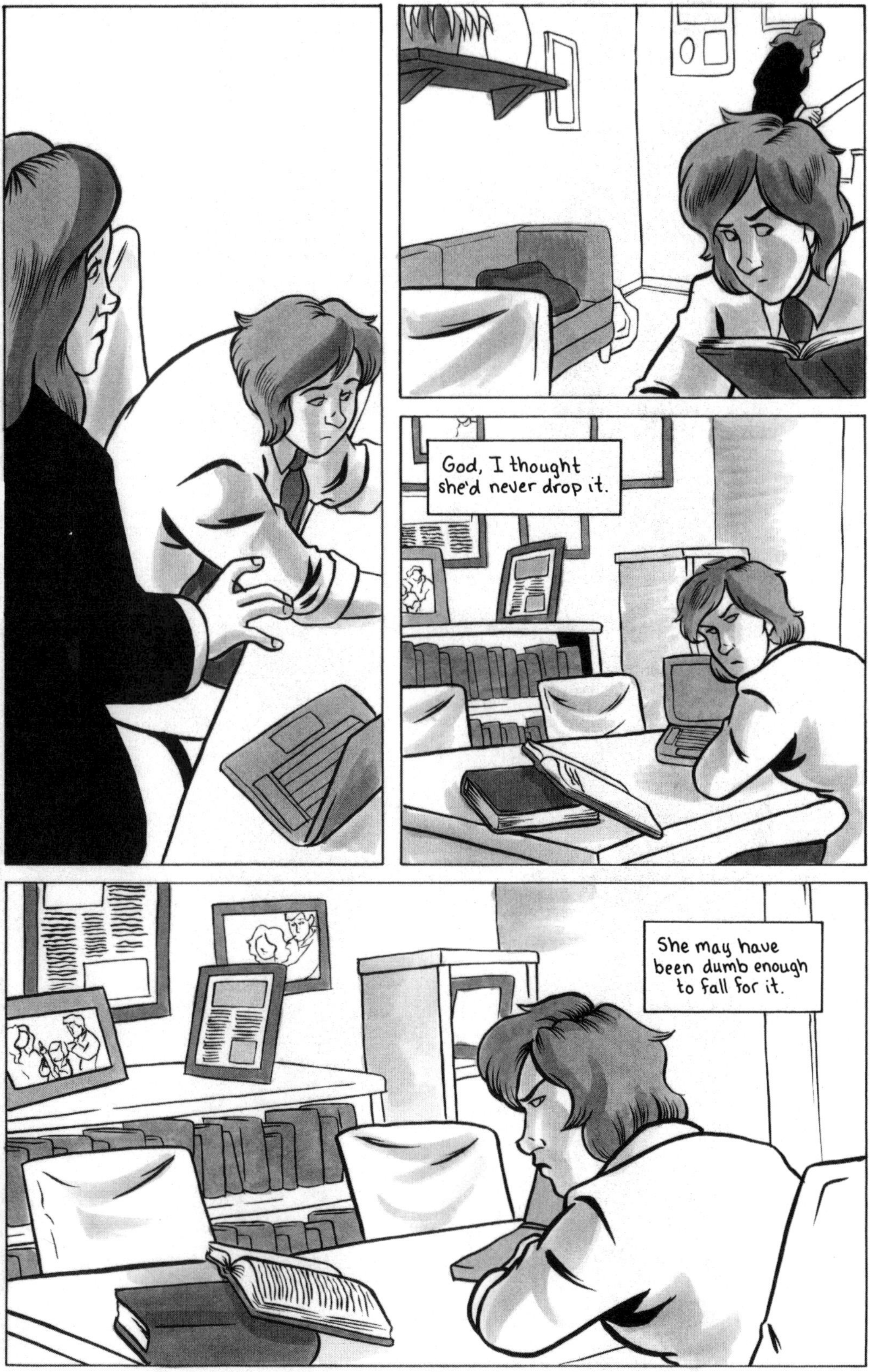
God, I thought she'd never drop it.
She may have been dumb enough to fall for it.

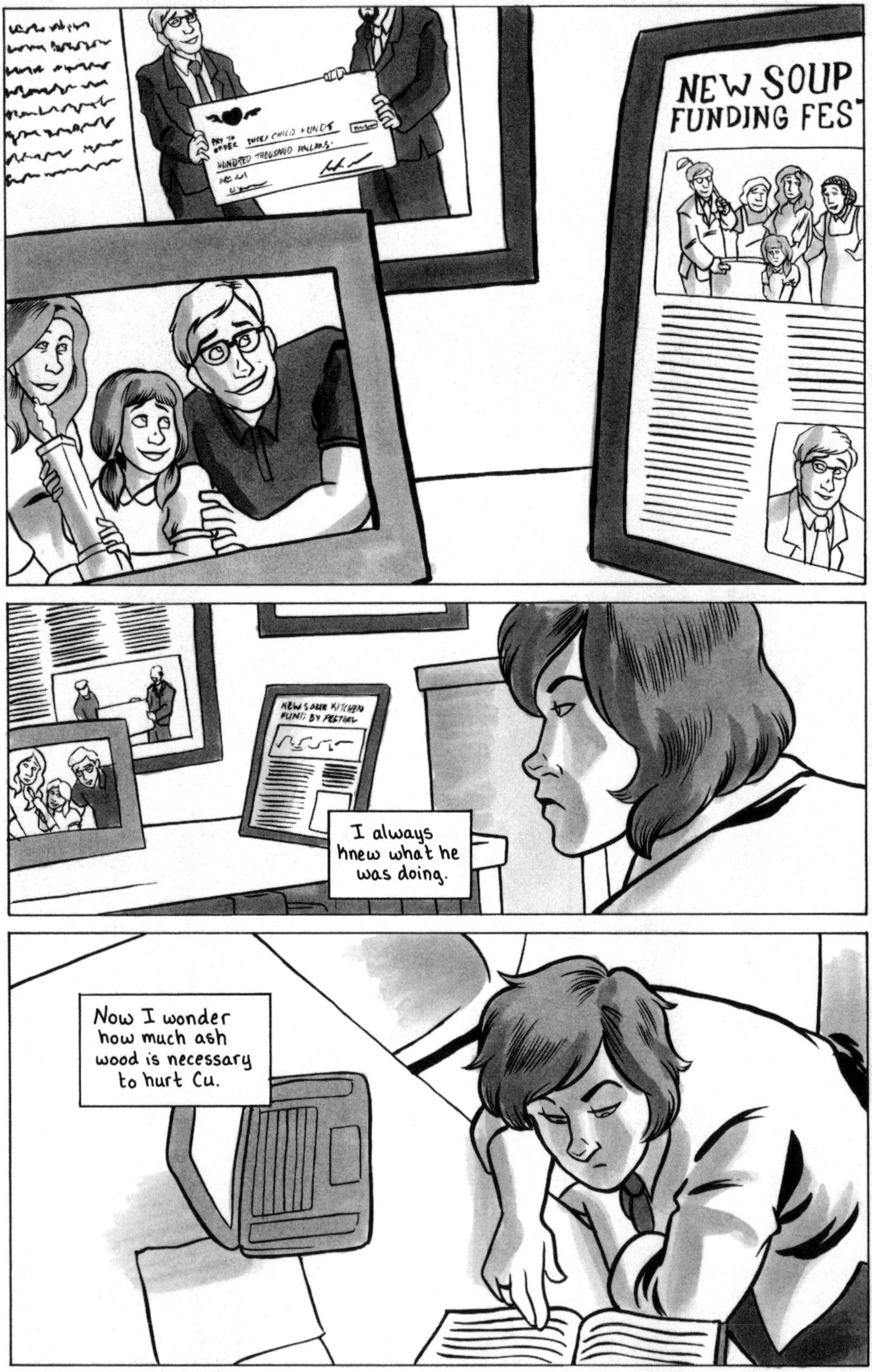
NEW SOUP FUNDING FEST
I always knew what he was doing.
Now I wonder how much ash wood is necessary to hurt Cu.

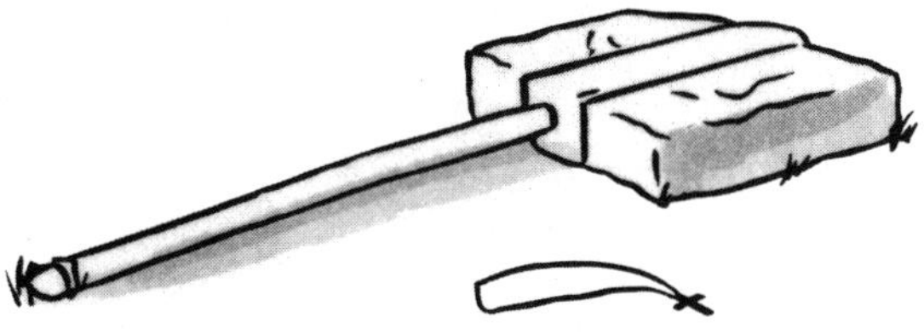

CHAPTER 4:

Only Fools Want to Be Great

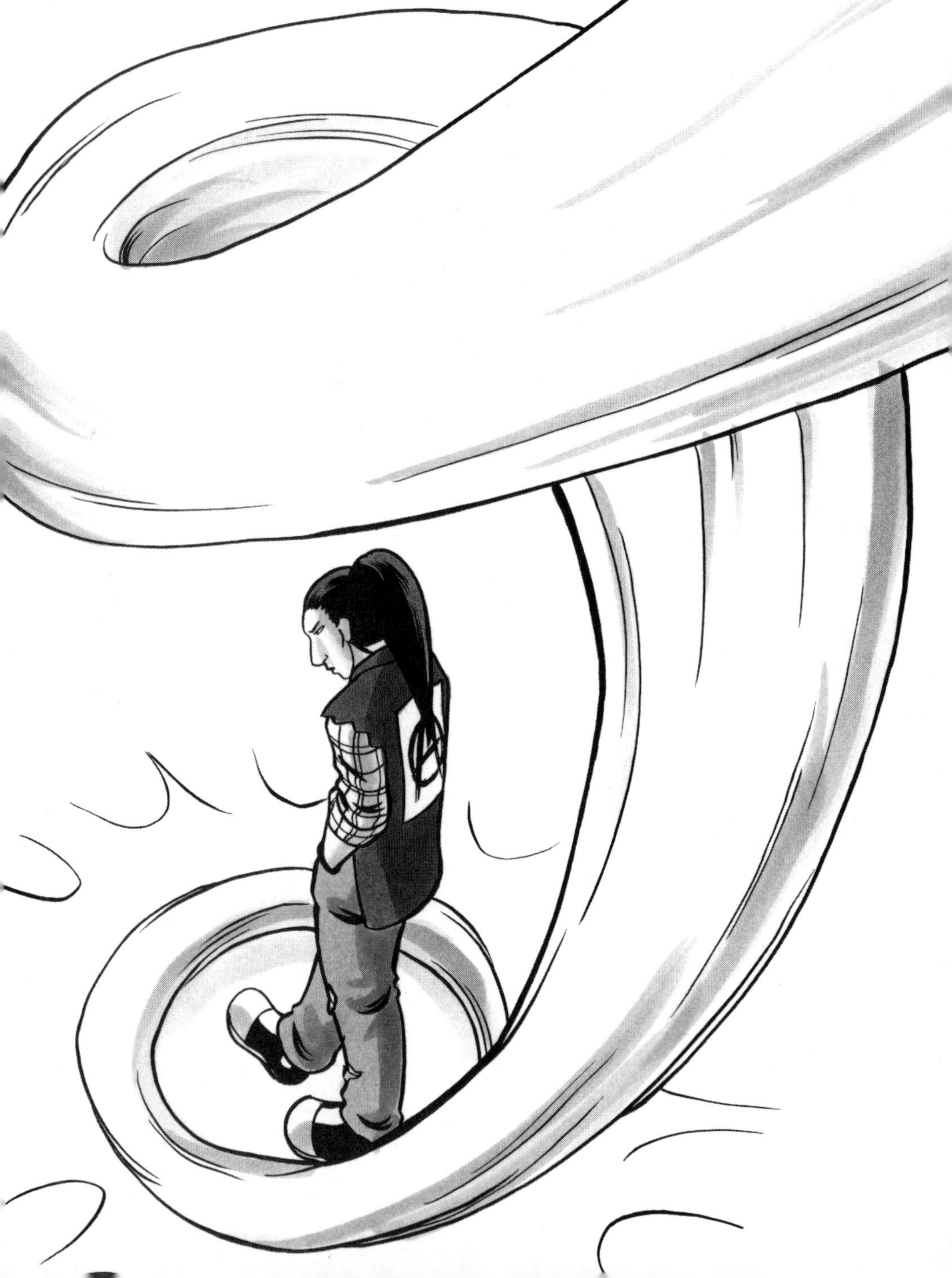

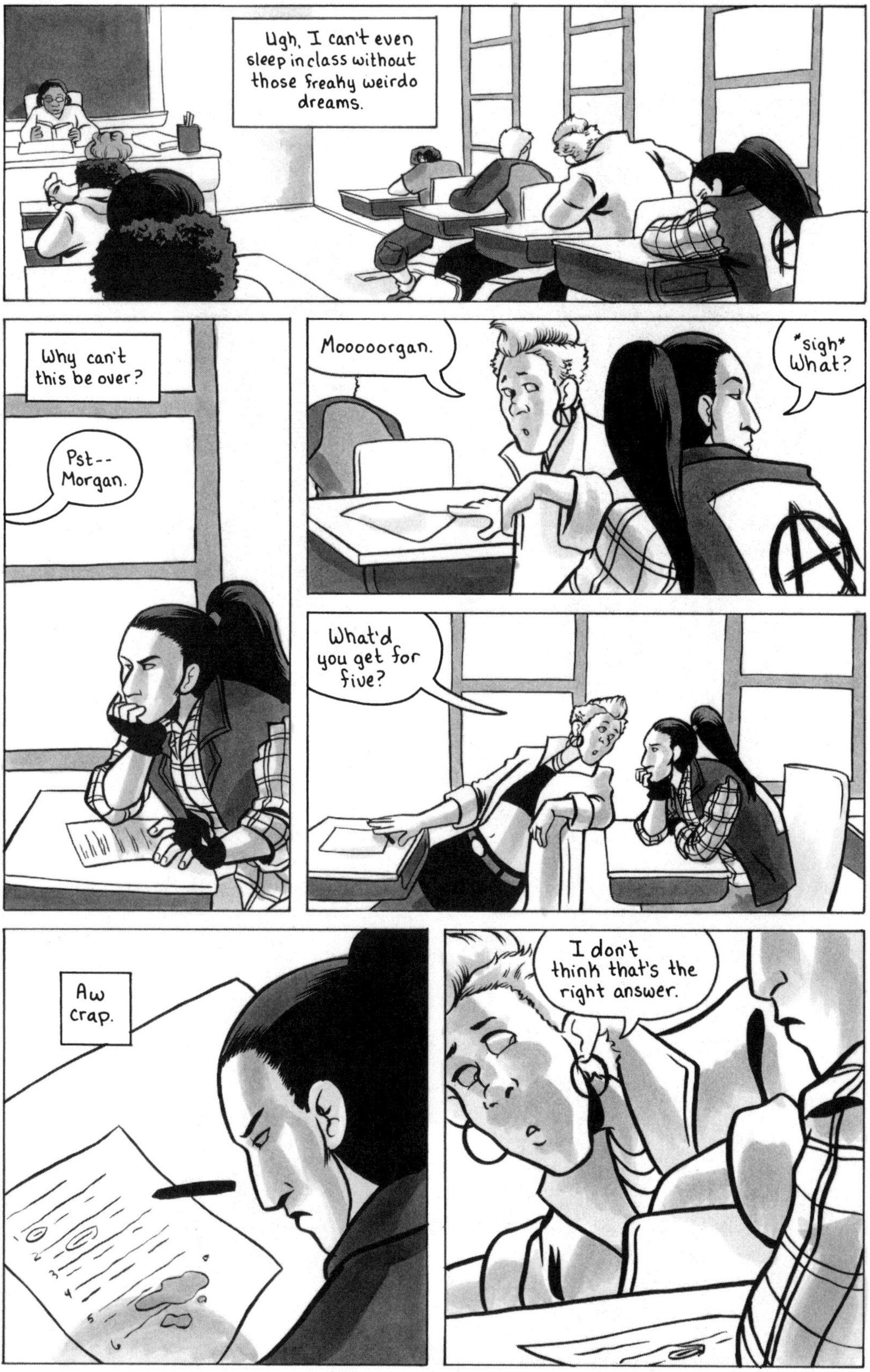

Ugh, I can't even sleep in class without those freaky weirdo dreams.
Why can't this be over?
Pst-- Morgan.
Moooorgan.
sigh What?
What'd you get for five?
Aw crap.
I don't think that's the right answer.

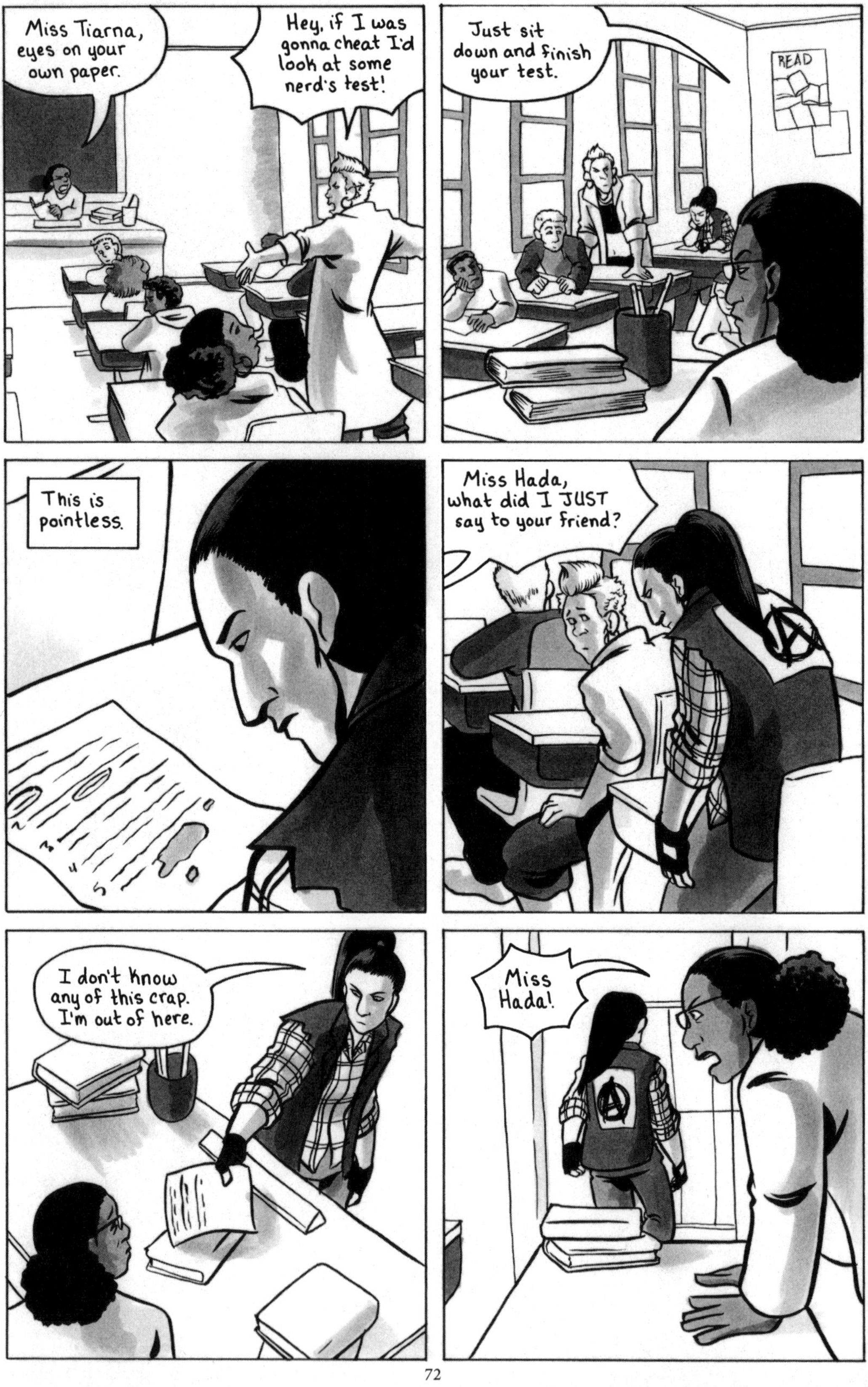
Miss Tiarna, eyes on your own paper.
Hey, if I was gonna cheat I'd look at some nerd's test!
Just sit down and finish your test.
READ
This is pointless.
Miss Hada, what did I JUST say to your friend?
I don't know any of this crap. I'm out of here.
Miss Hada!

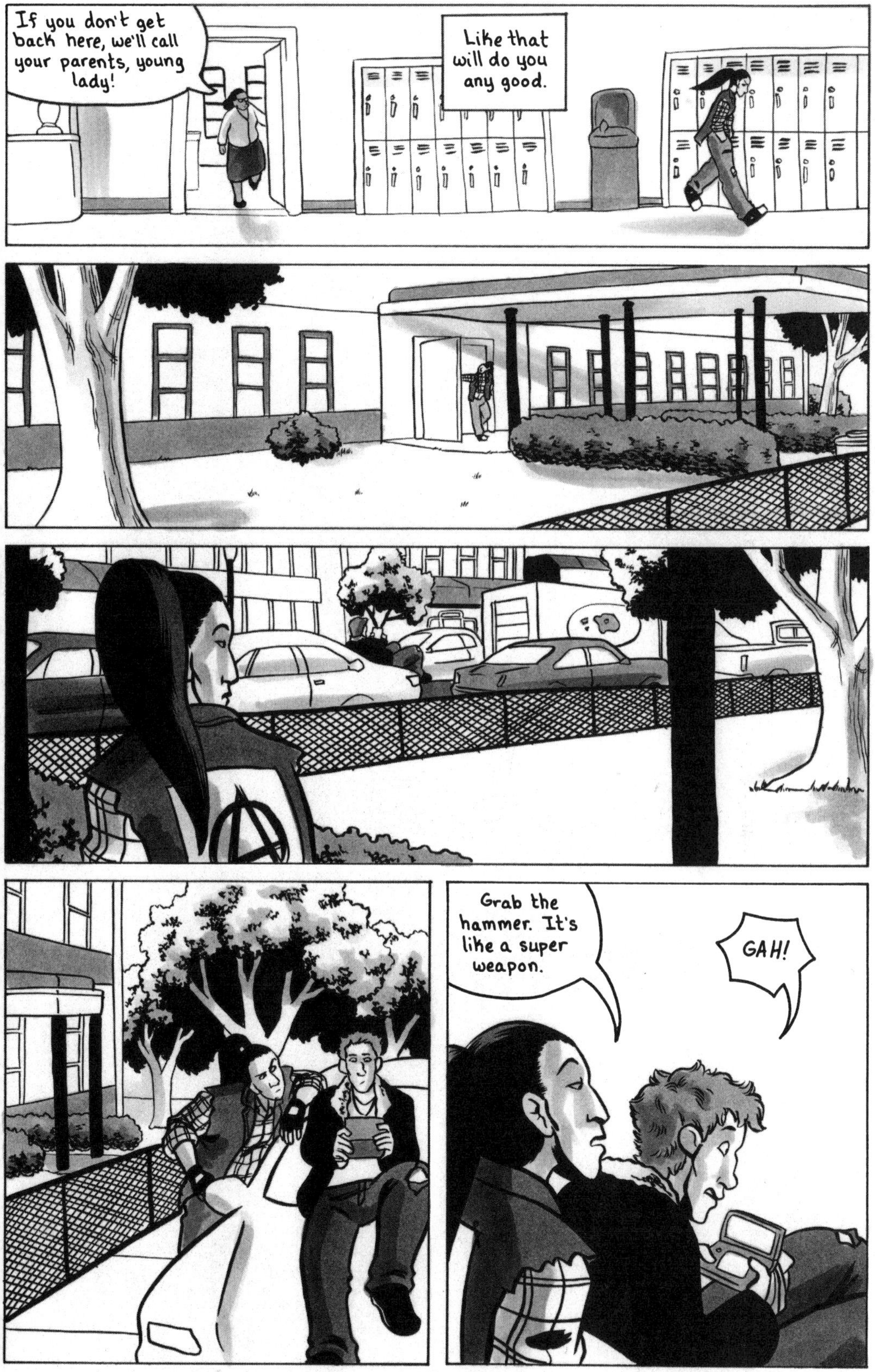
If you don't get back here, we'll call your parents, young lady!
Like that will do you any good.
Grab the hammer. It's like a super weapon.
GAH!

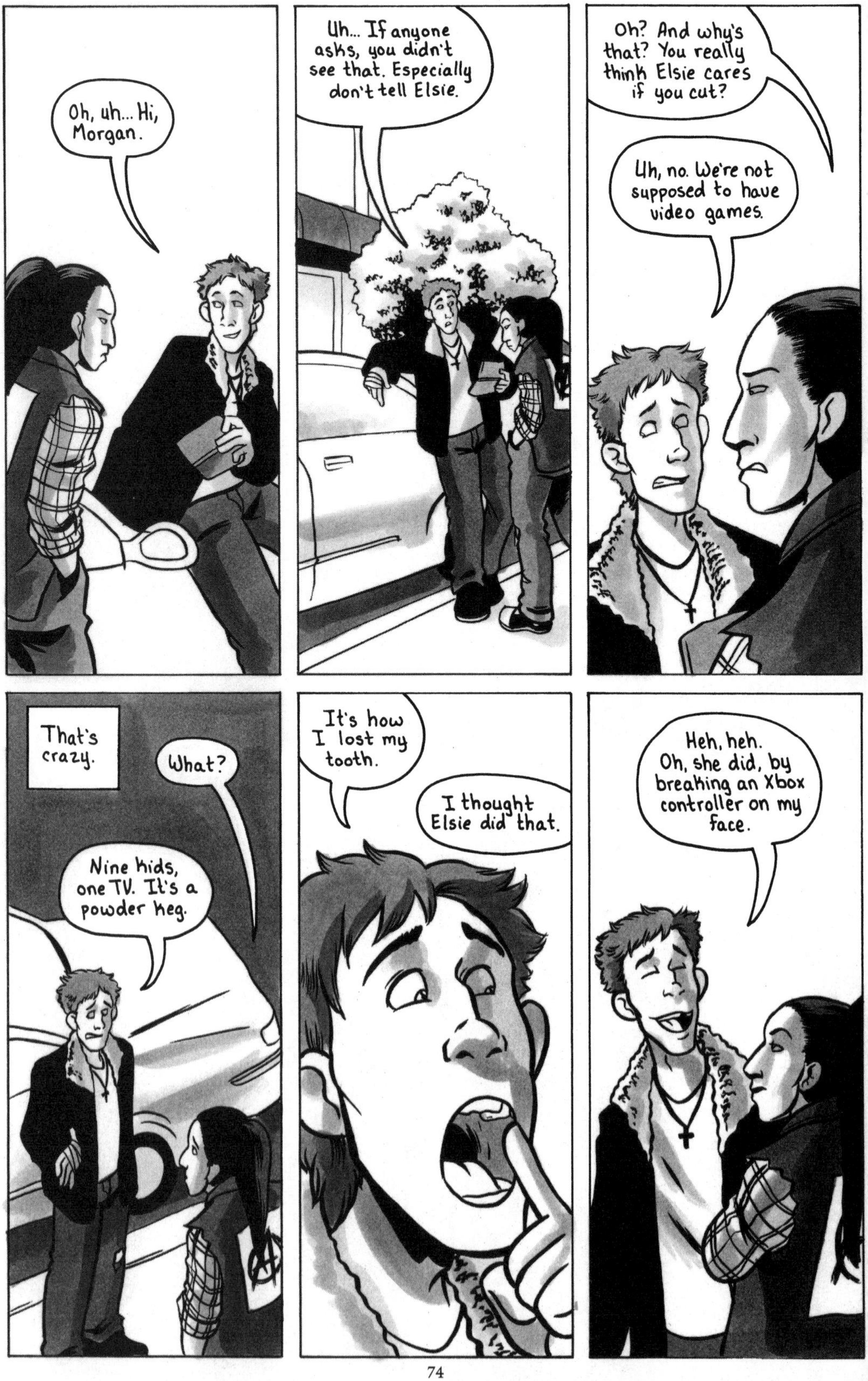
Oh, uh... Hi, Morgan.
Uh... If anyone asks, you didn't see that. Especially don't tell Elsie.
Oh? And why's that? You really think Elsie cares if you cut?
Uh, no. We're not supposed to have video games.
That's crazy.
What?
Nine kids, one TV. It's a powder keg.
It's how I lost my tooth.
I thought Elsie did that.
Heh, heh. Oh, she did, by breaking an Xbox controller on my face.

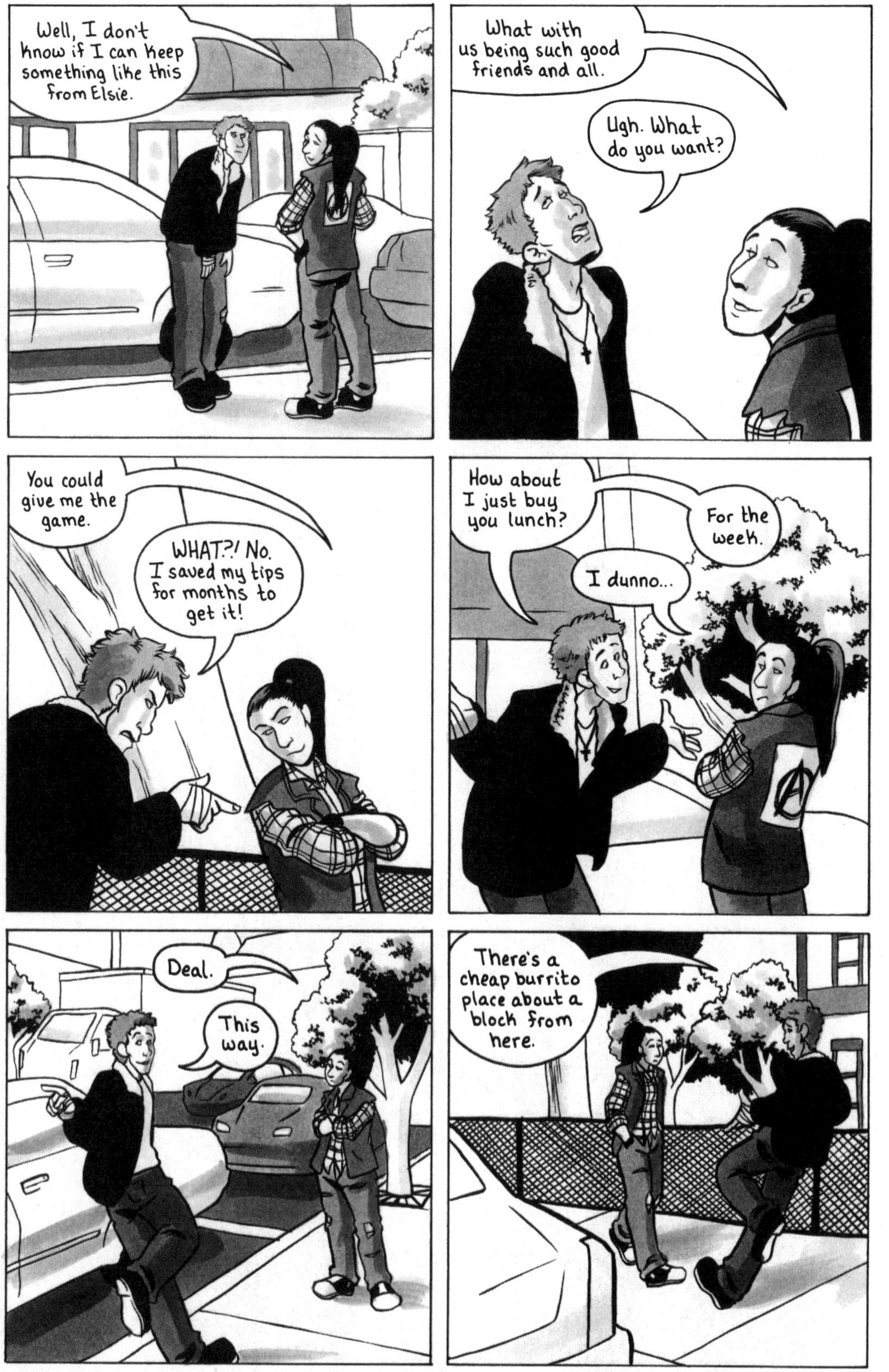
Well, I don't know if I can keep something like this from Elsie.
What with us being such good friends and all.
Ugh. What do you want?
You could give me the game.
WHAT?! No. I saved my tips for months to get it!
How about I just buy you lunch?
I dunno...
For the week.
Deal.
This way.
There's a cheap burrito place about a block from here.

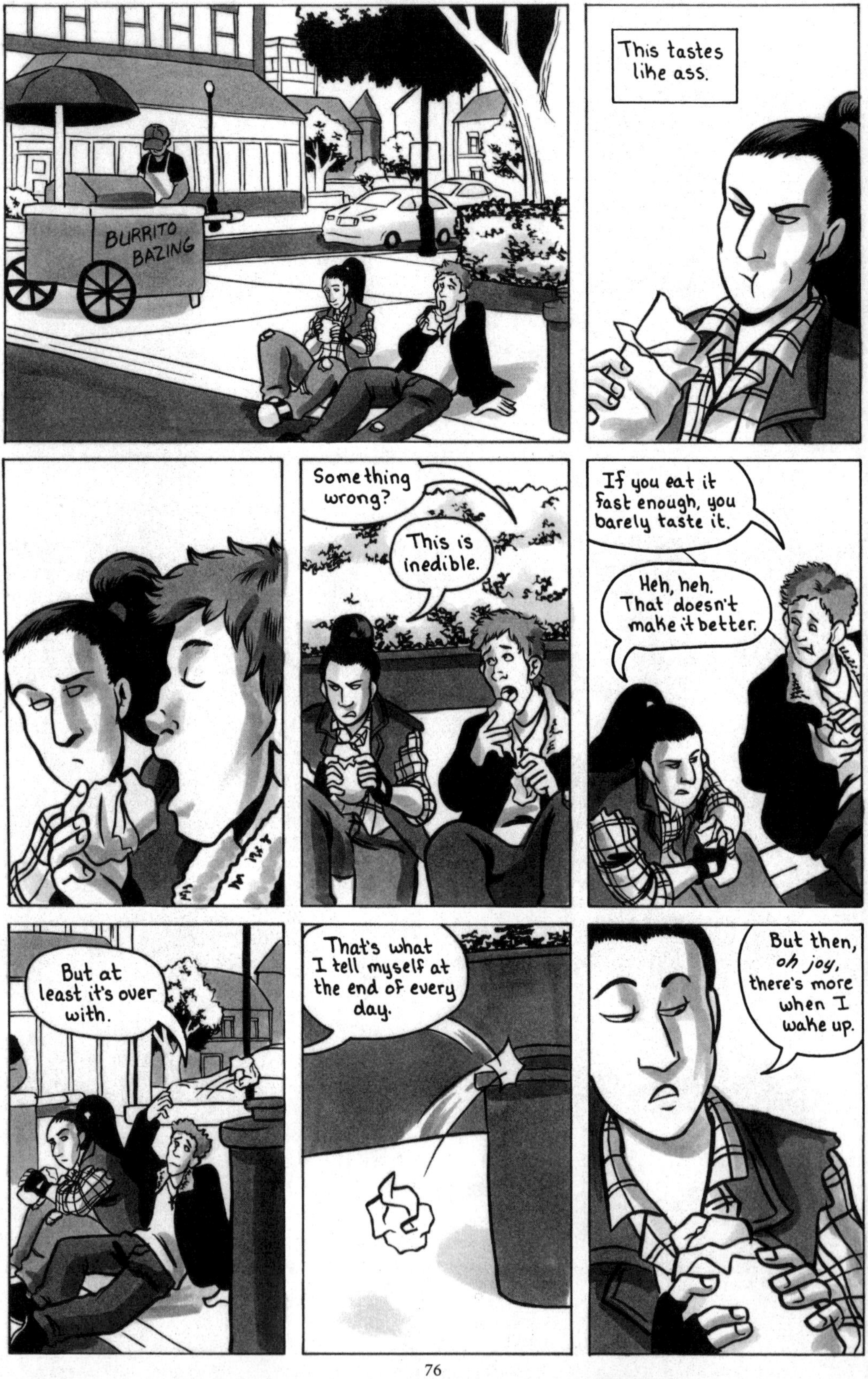
BURRITO BAZING
This tastes like ass.
Something wrong?
This is inedible.
If you eat it fast enough, you barely taste it.
Heh, heh. That doesn't make it better.
But at least it's over with.
That's what I tell myself at the end of every day.
But then, *oh joy*, there's more when I wake up.

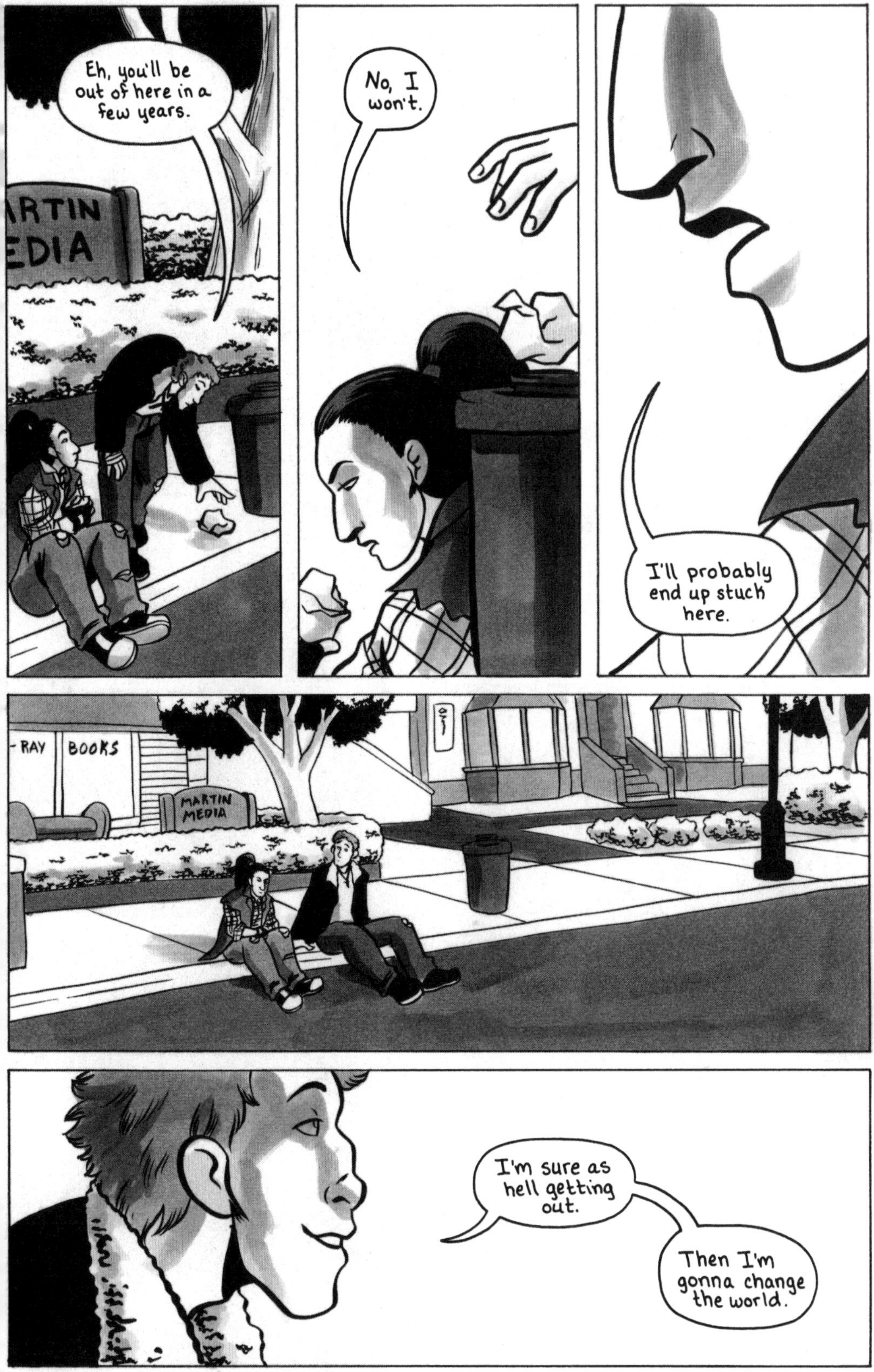
Eh, you'll be out of here in a few years.
ARTIN
EDIA
No, I won't.
I'll probably end up stuck here.
-RAY
BOOKS
MARTIN MEDIA
I'm sure as hell getting out.
Then I'm gonna change the world.

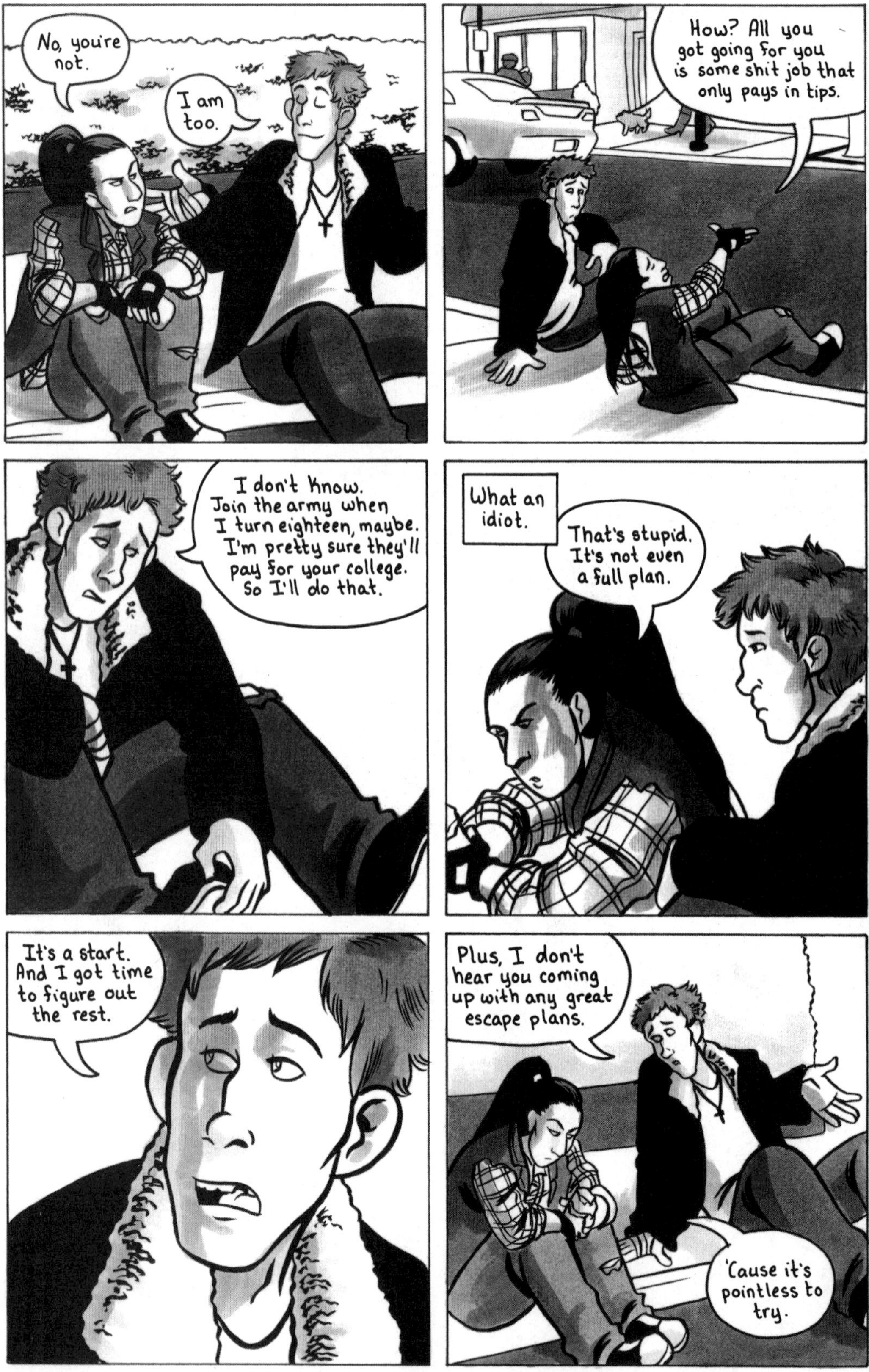
No, you're not.
I am too.
How? All you got going for you is some shit job that only pays in tips.
I don't know. Join the army when I turn eighteen, maybe. I'm pretty sure they'll pay for your college. So I'll do that.
What an idiot.
That's stupid. It's not even a full plan.
It's a start. And I got time to figure out the rest.
Plus, I don't hear you coming up with any great escape plans.
'Cause it's pointless to try.

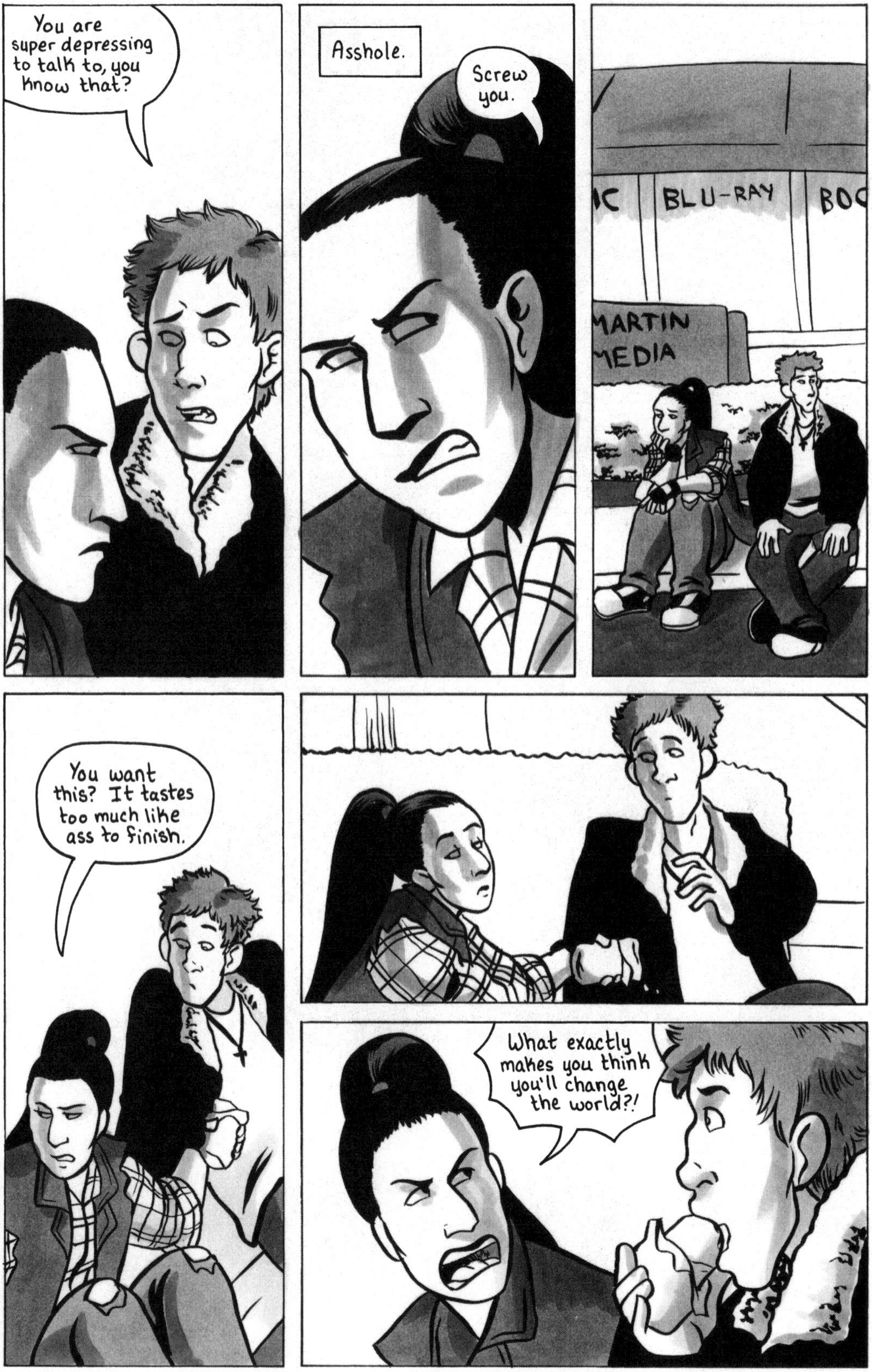

You are super depressing to talk to, you know that?
Asshole.
Screw you.
BLU-RAY
MARTIN MEDIA
You want this? It tastes too much like ass to finish.
What exactly makes you think you'll change the world?!

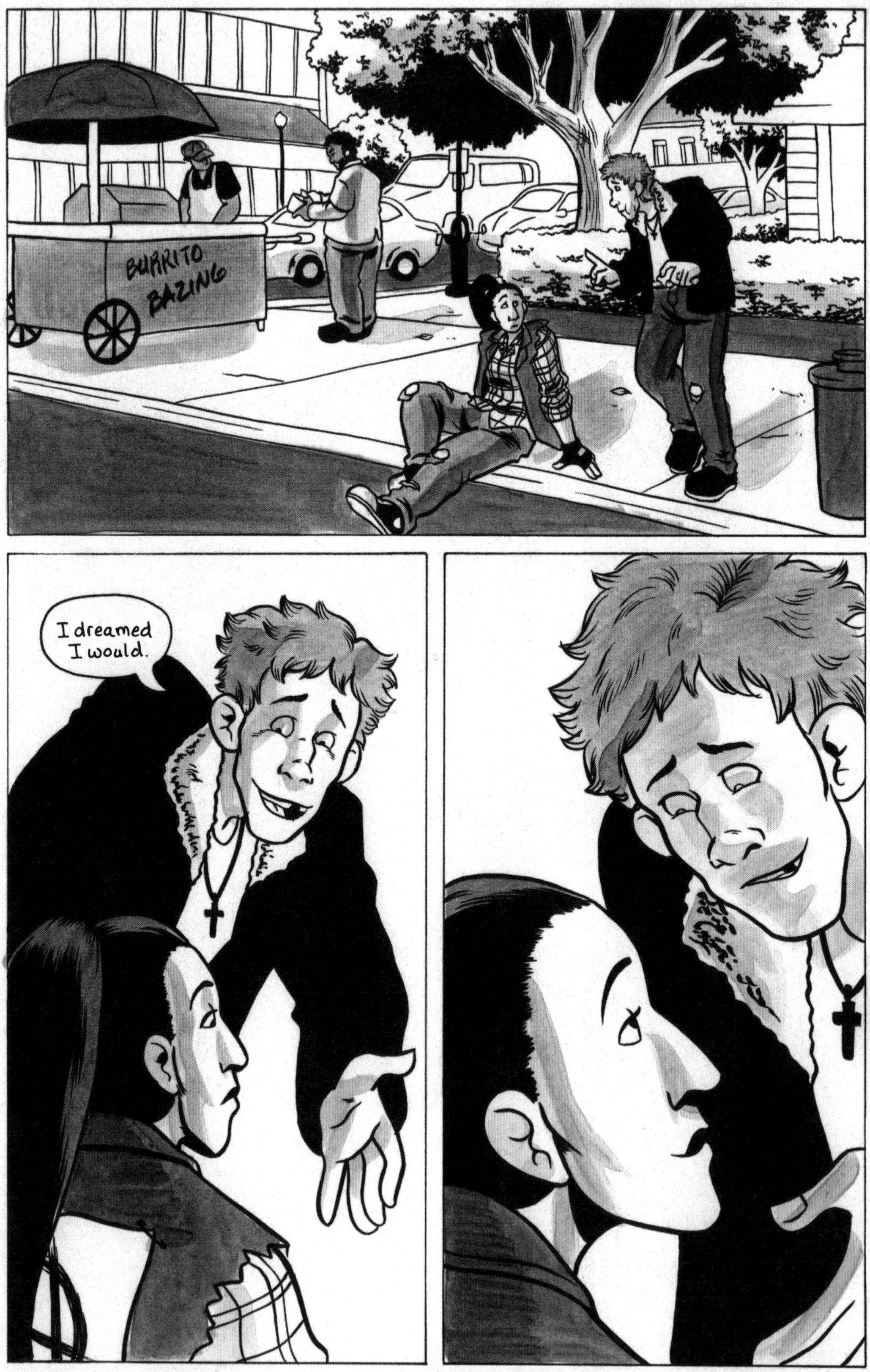
BURRITO BAZING
I dreamed I would.

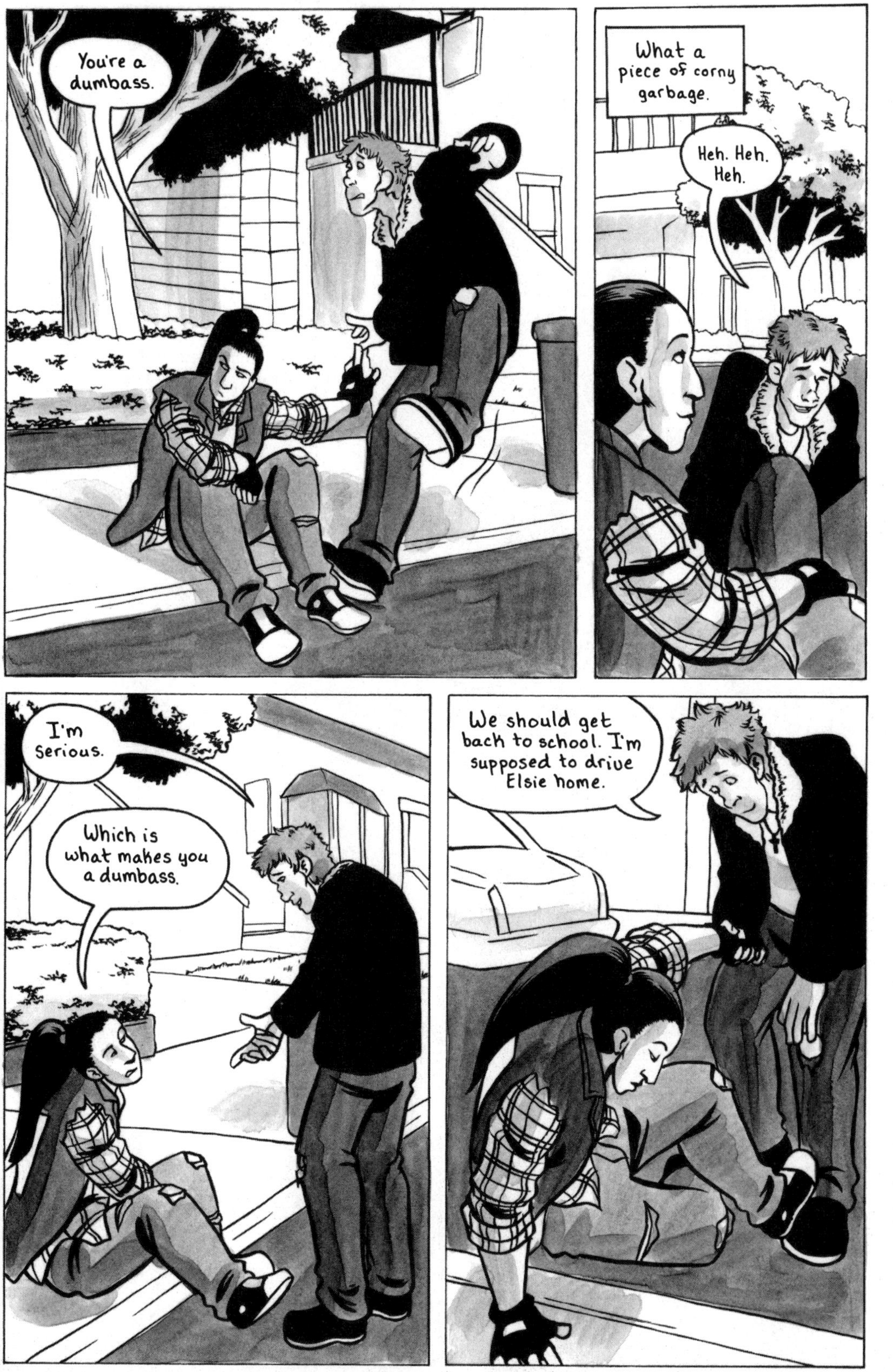
You're a dumbass.
What a piece of corny garbage.
Heh. Heh. Heh.
I'm serious.
Which is what makes you a dumbass.
We should get back to school. I'm supposed to drive Elsie home.

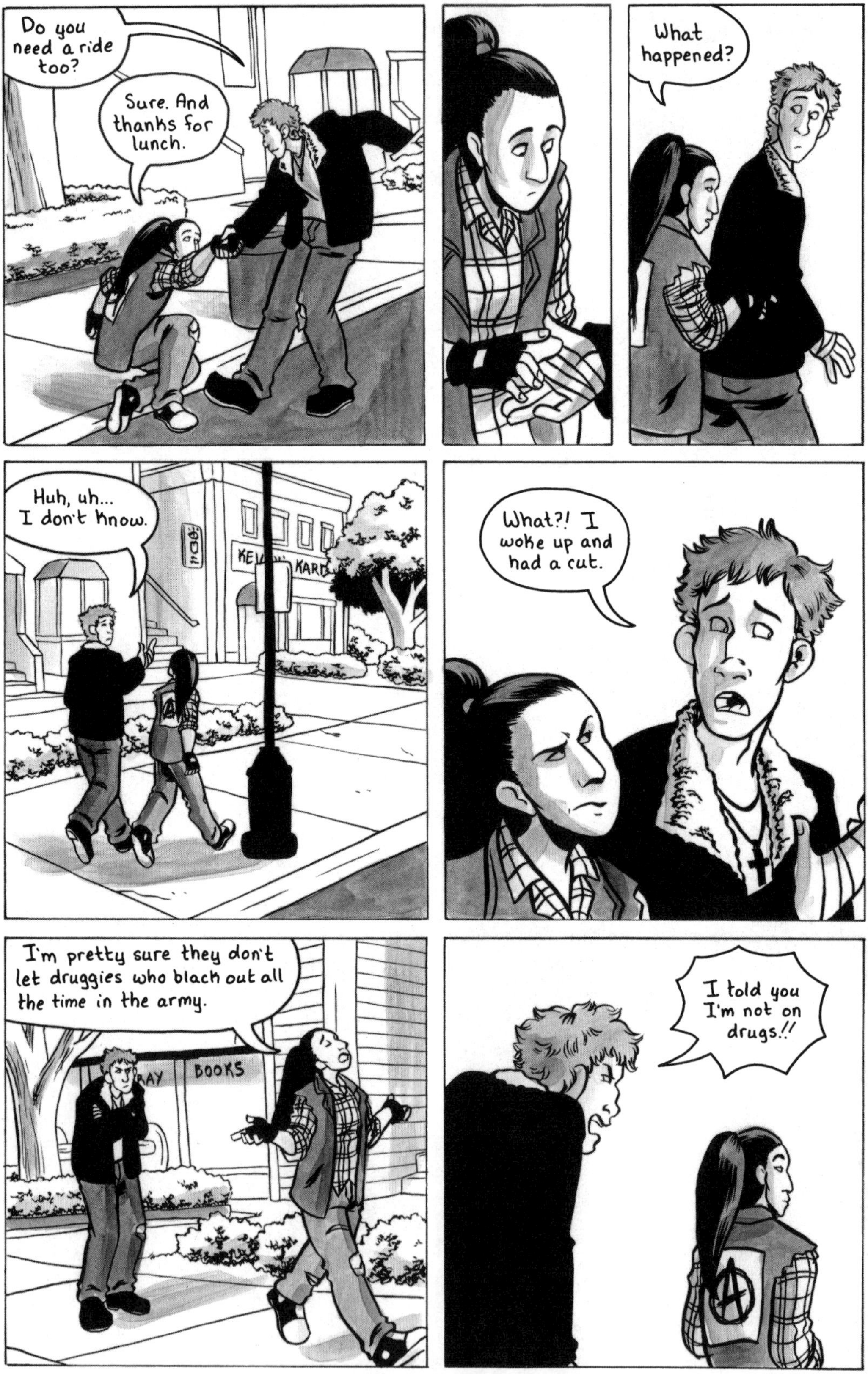
Do you need a ride too?
Sure. And thanks for lunch.
What happened?
Huh, uh... I don't know.
KARD
What?! I woke up and had a cut.
I'm pretty sure they don't let druggies who black out all the time in the army.
BOOKS
I told you I'm not on drugs!!

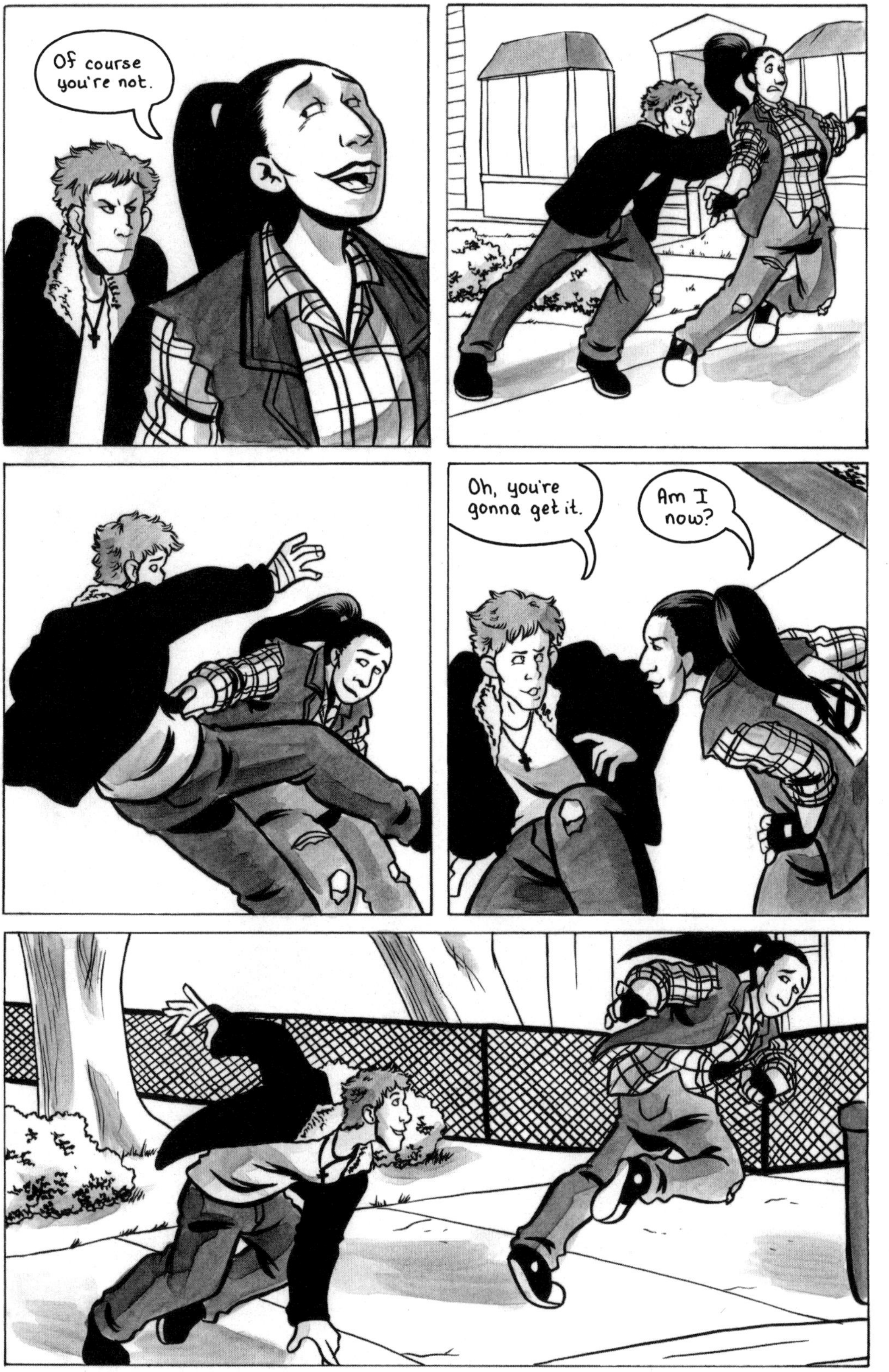
Of course you're not.
Oh, you're gonna get it.
Am I now?

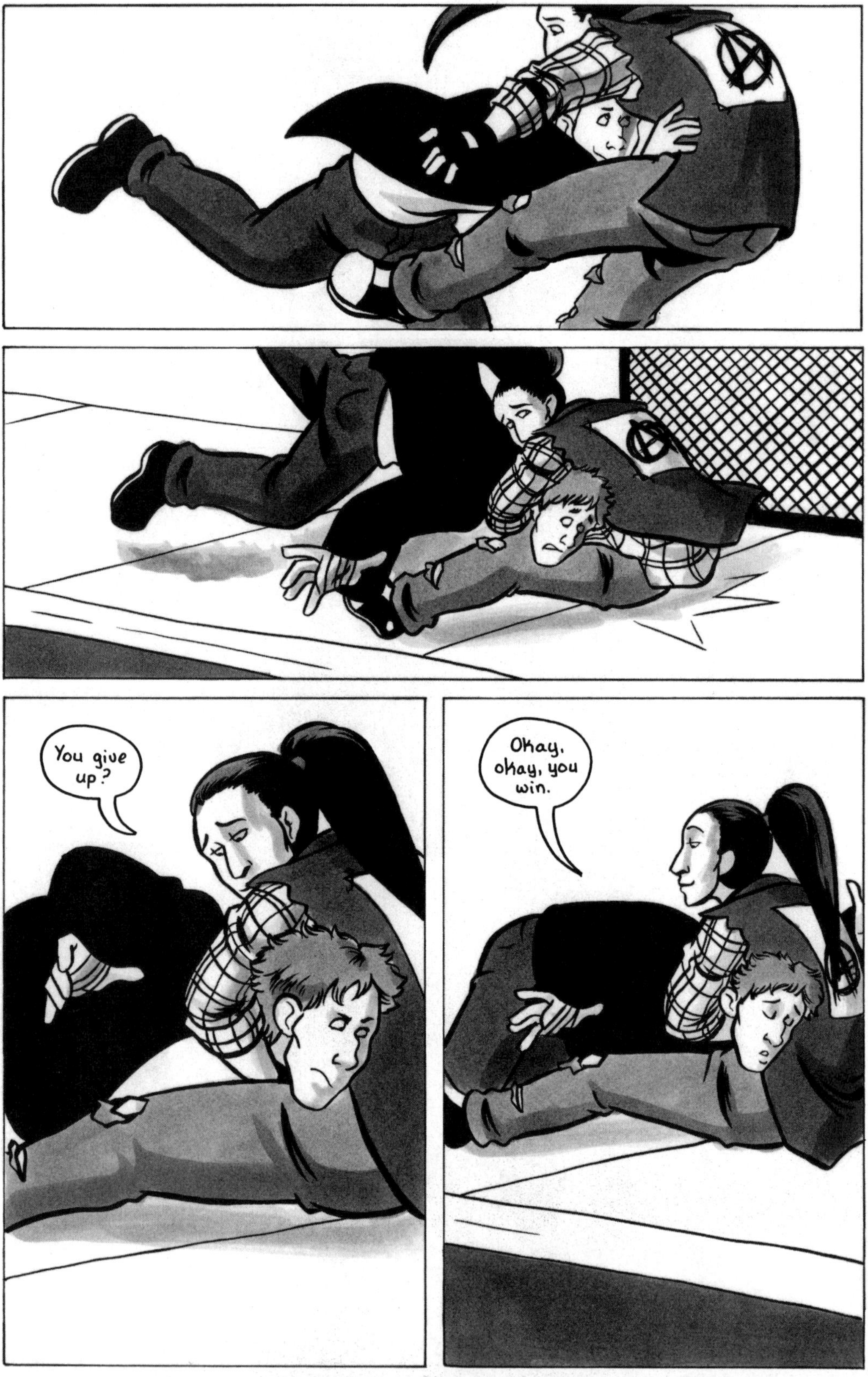
You give up?
Okay, okay, you win.

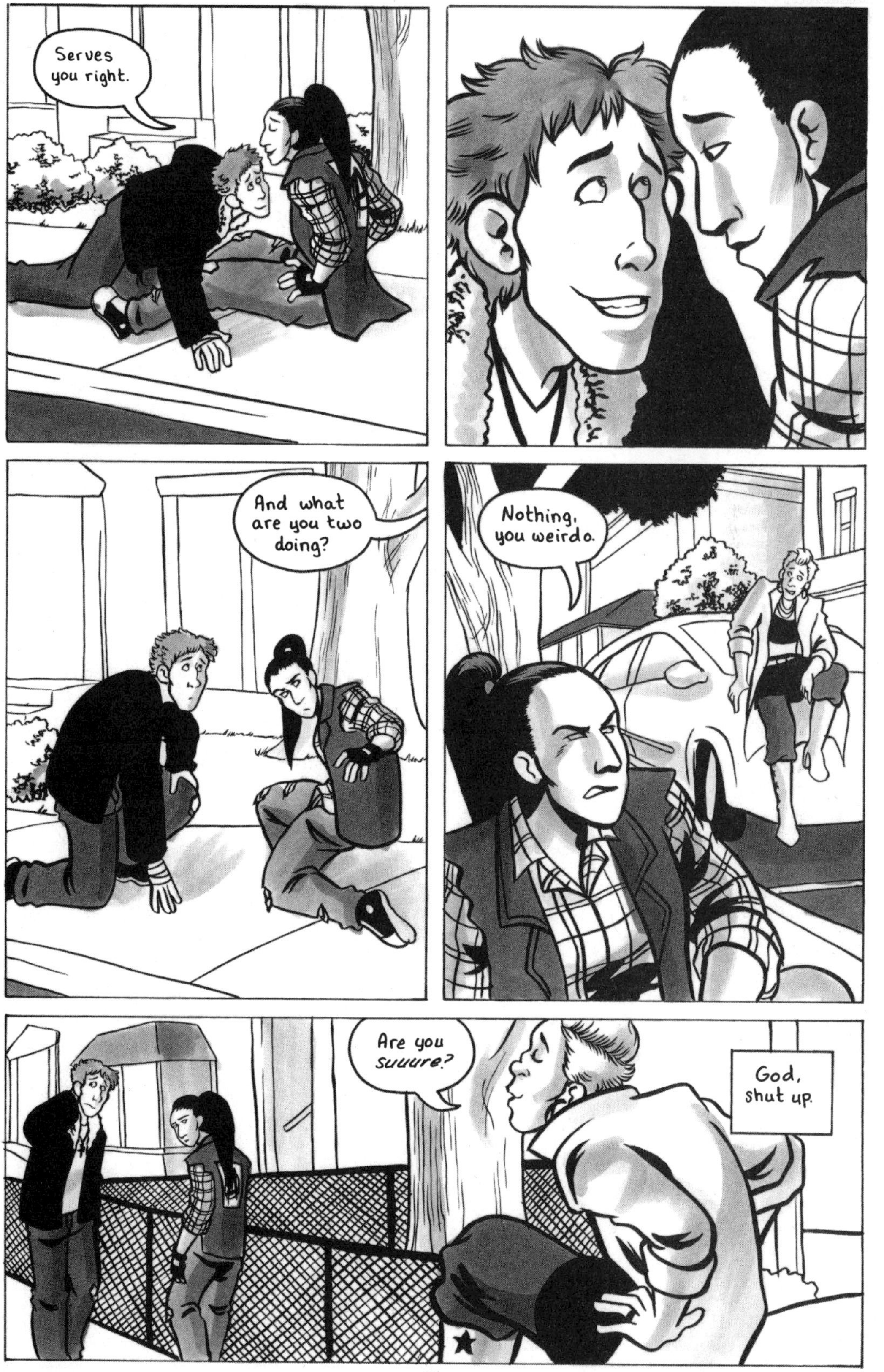

Serves you right.
And what are you two doing?
Nothing, you weirdo.
Are you suuure?
God, shut up.

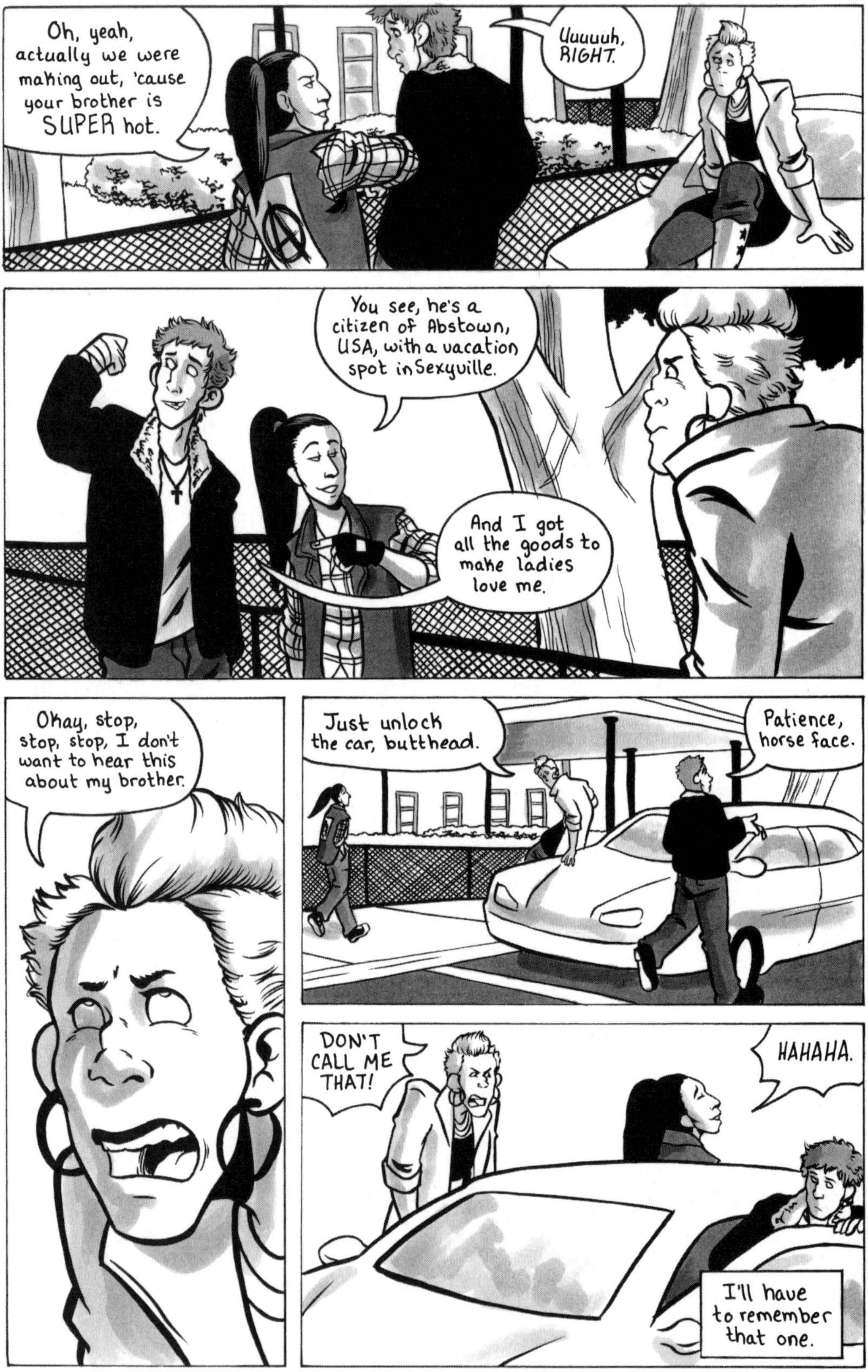
Oh, yeah, actually we were making out, 'cause your brother is SUPER hot.
Uuuuuh, RIGHT.
You see, he's a citizen of Abstown, USA, with a vacation spot in Sexyville.
And I got all the goods to make ladies love me.
Okay, stop, stop, stop, I don't want to hear this about my brother.
Just unlock the car, butthead.
Patience, horse face.
DON'T CALL ME THAT!
HAHAHA.
I'll have to remember that one.

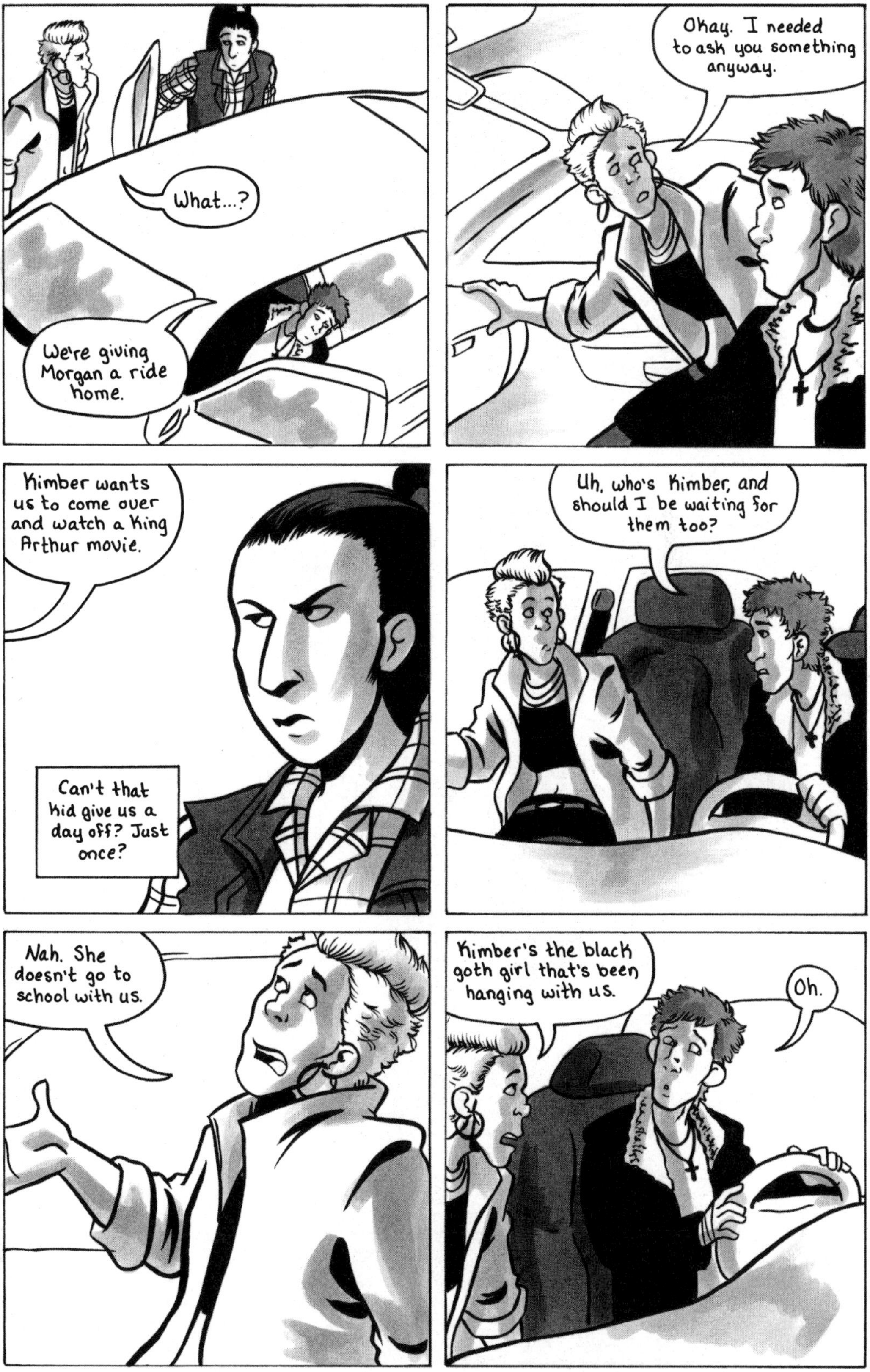
What...?
We're giving Morgan a ride home.
Okay. I needed to ask you something anyway.
Kimber wants us to come over and watch a King Arthur movie.
Can't that kid give us a day off? Just once?
Uh, who's Kimber, and should I be waiting for them too?
Nah. She doesn't go to school with us.
Kimber's the black goth girl that's been hanging with us.
Oh.

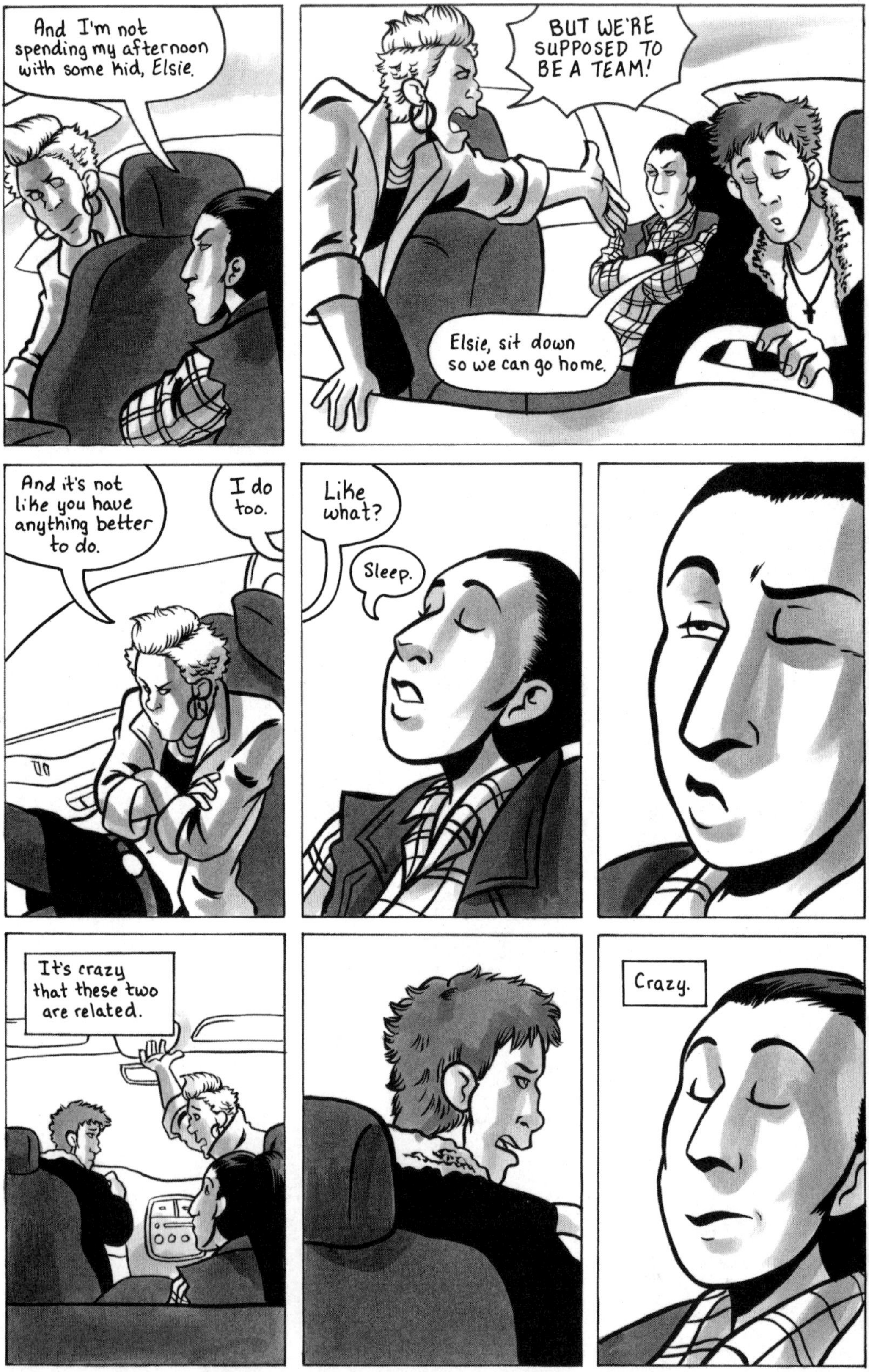
And I'm not spending my afternoon with some kid, Elsie.
BUT WE'RE SUPPOSED TO BE A TEAM!
Elsie, sit down so we can go home.
And it's not like you have anything better to do.
I do too.
Like what?
Sleep.
It's crazy that these two are related.
Crazy.

CHAPTER 5:

Only Disguised as Themselves

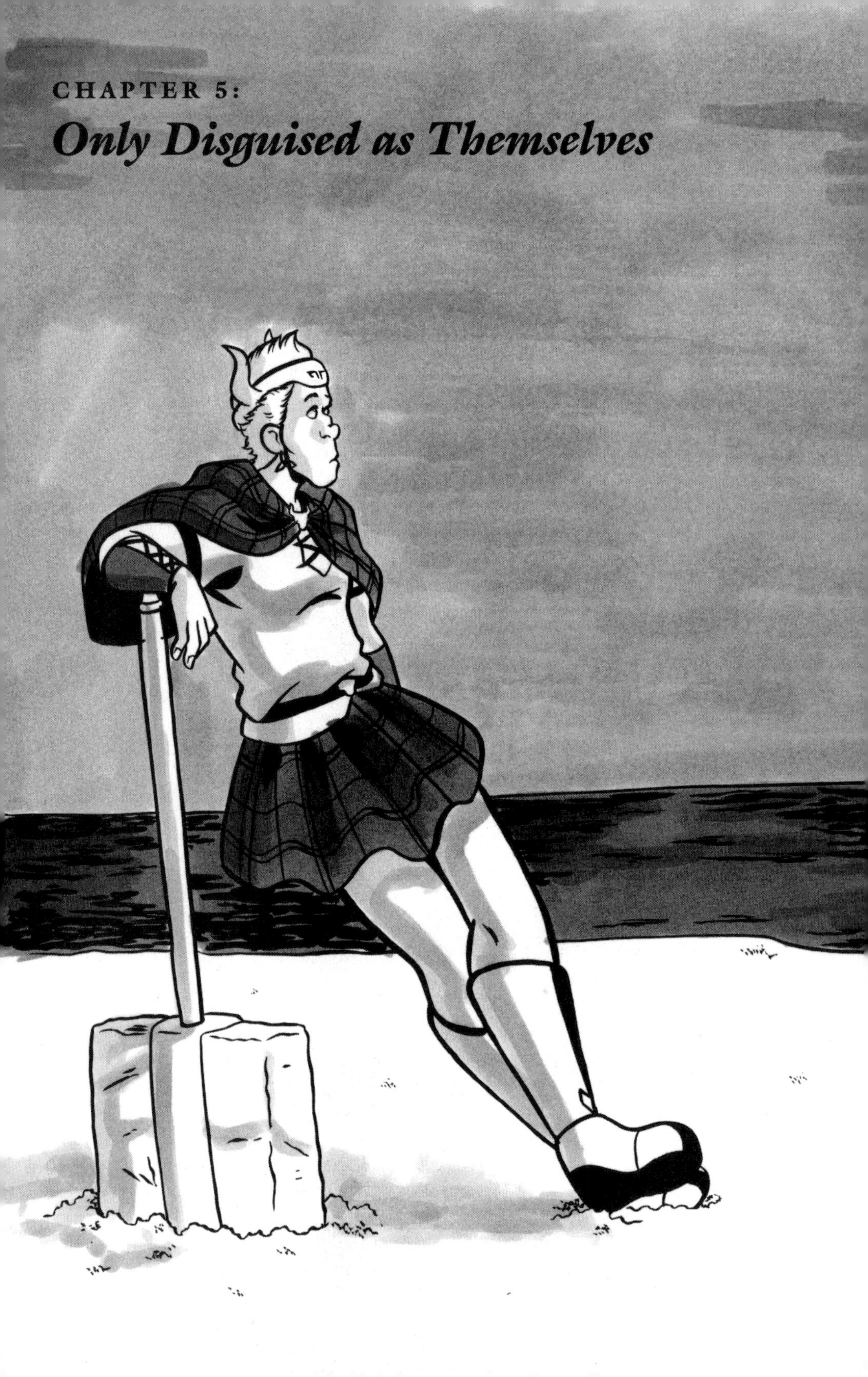

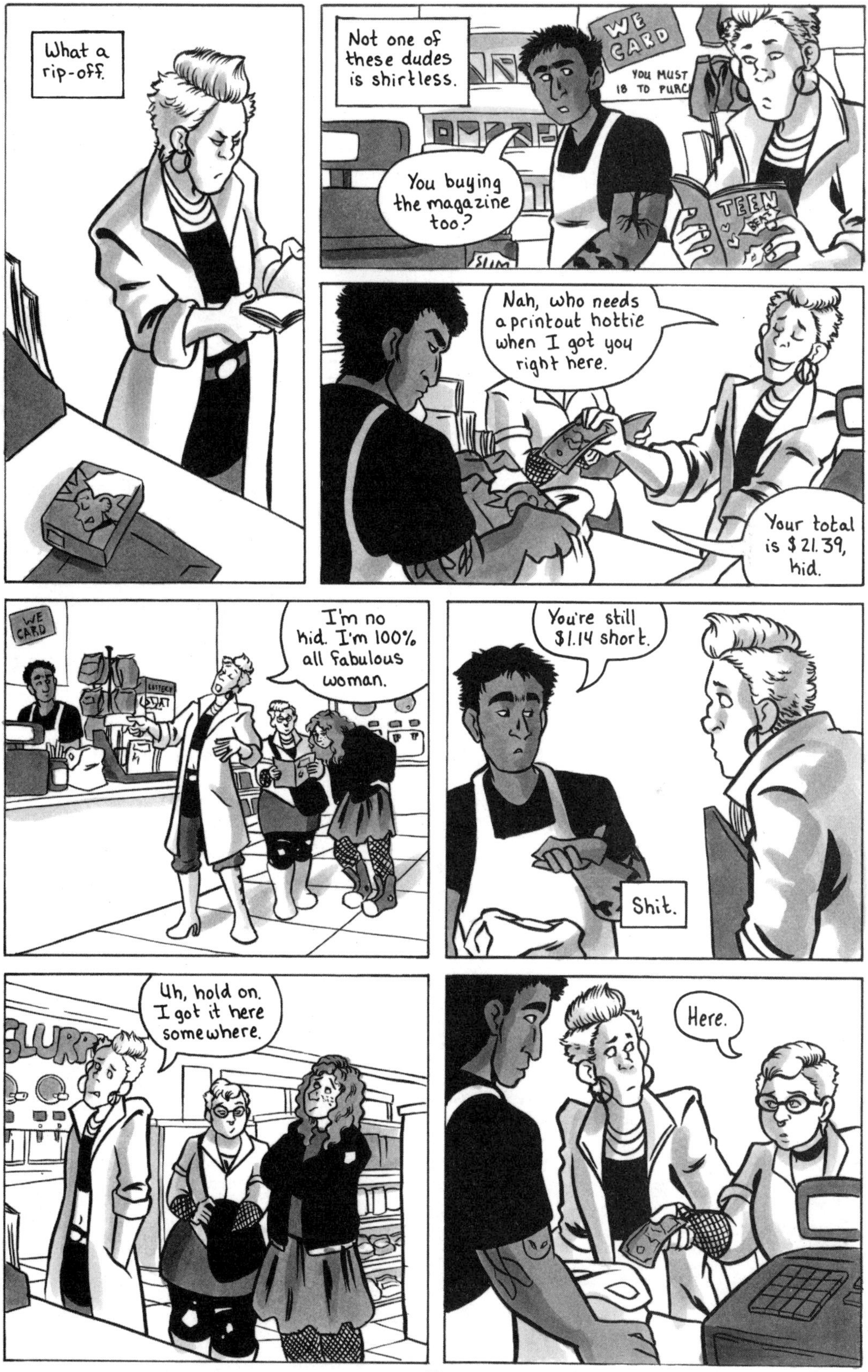
What a rip-off.
Not one of these dudes is shirtless.
WE CARD
YOU MUST 18 TO PURC
You buying the magazine too?
TEEN BEAT
Nah, who needs a printout hottie when I got you right here.
Your total is $21.39, kid.
WE CARD
I'm no kid. I'm 100% all fabulous woman.
You're still $1.14 short.
Shit.
Uh, hold on. I got it here somewhere.
Here.

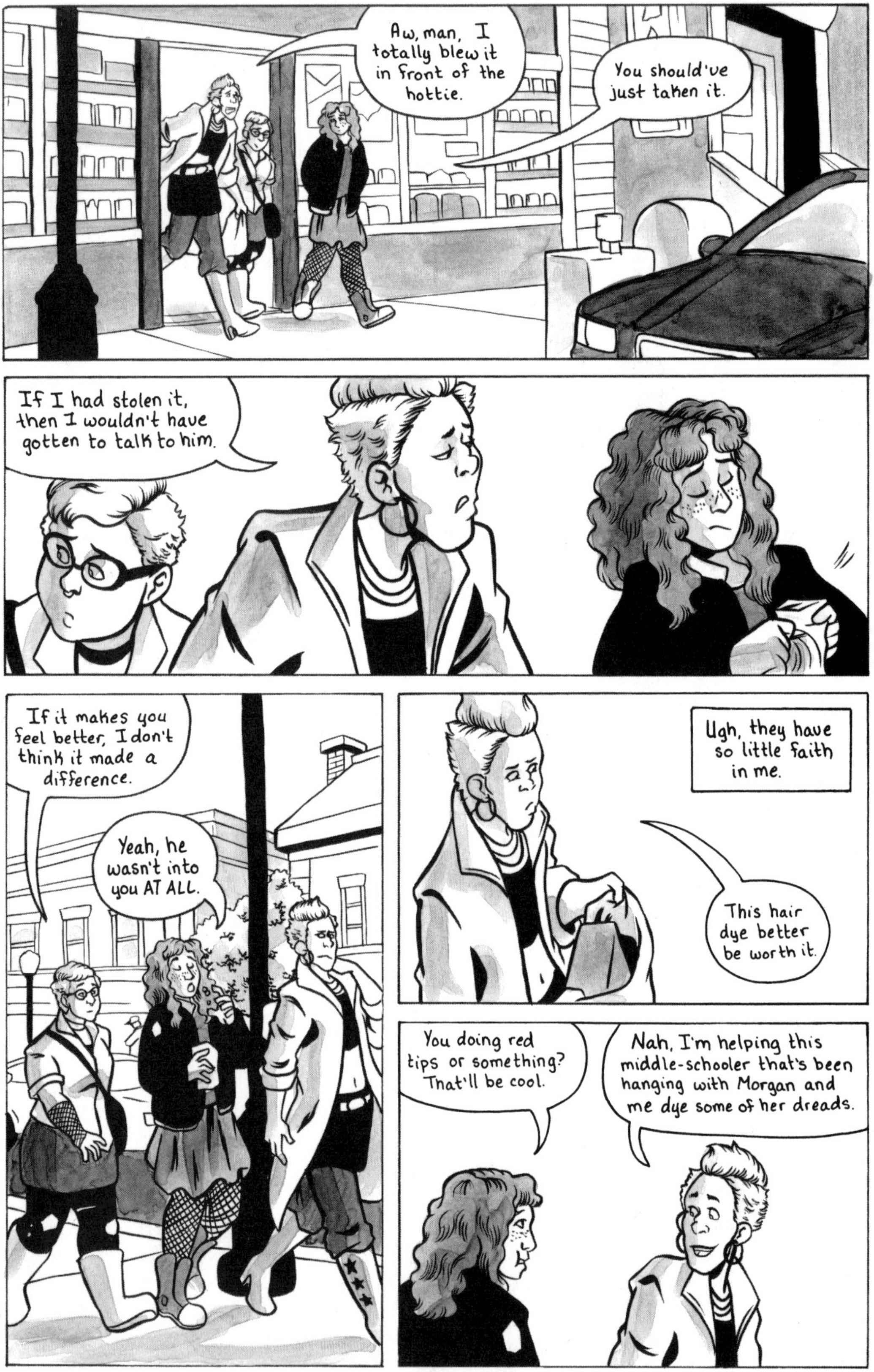
Aw, man, I totally blew it in front of the hottie.
You should've just taken it.
If I had stolen it, then I wouldn't have gotten to talk to him.
If it makes you feel better, I don't think it made a difference.
Yeah, he wasn't into you AT ALL.
Ugh, they have so little faith in me.
This hair dye better be worth it.
You doing red tips or something? That'll be cool.
Nah, I'm helping this middle-schooler that's been hanging with Morgan and me dye some of her dreads.

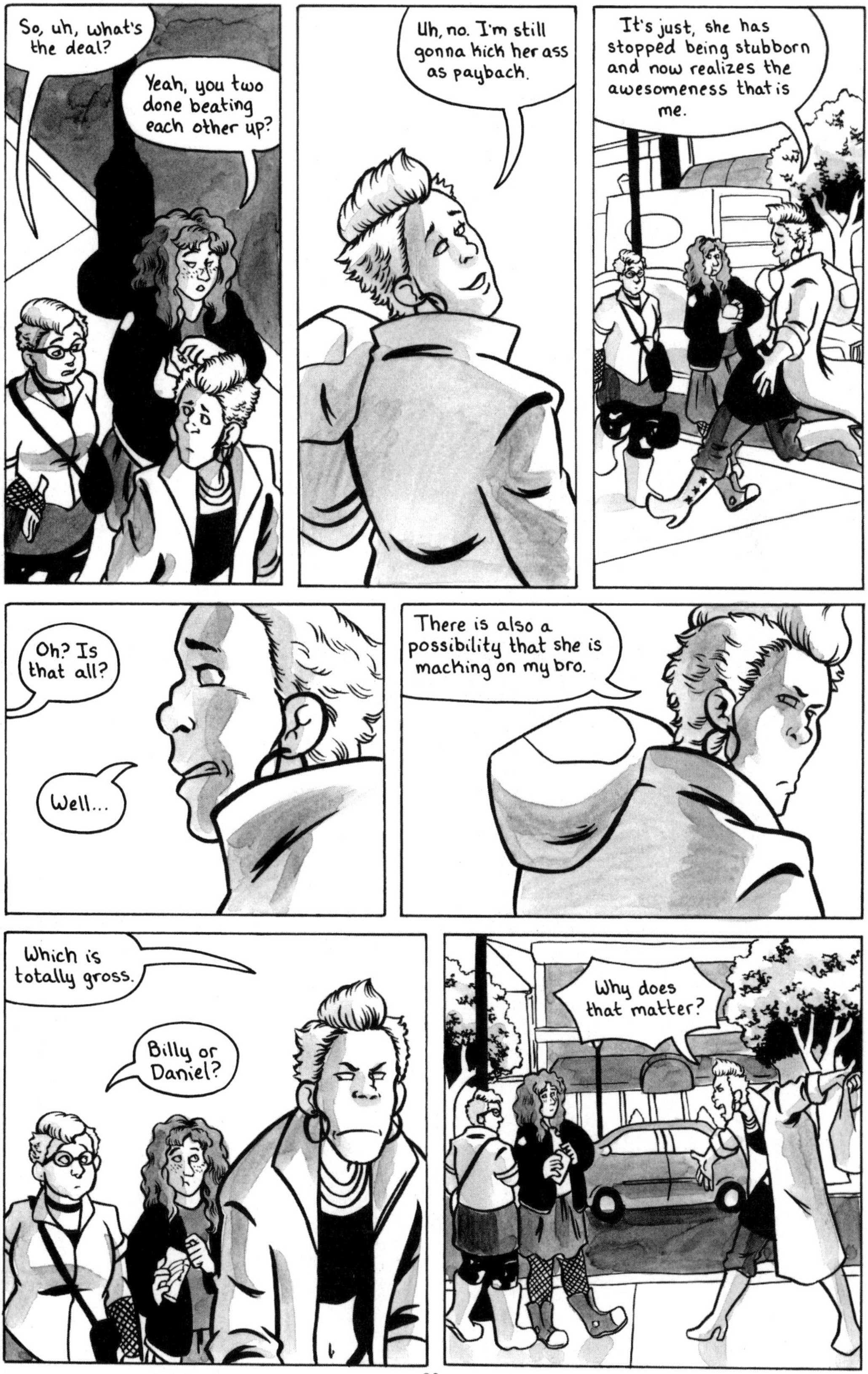
So, uh, what's the deal?
Yeah, you two done beating each other up?
Uh, no. I'm still gonna kick her ass as payback.
It's just, she has stopped being stubborn and now realizes the awesomeness that is me.
Oh? Is that all?
Well...
There is also a possibility that she is macking on my bro.
Which is totally gross.
Billy or Daniel?
Why does that matter?

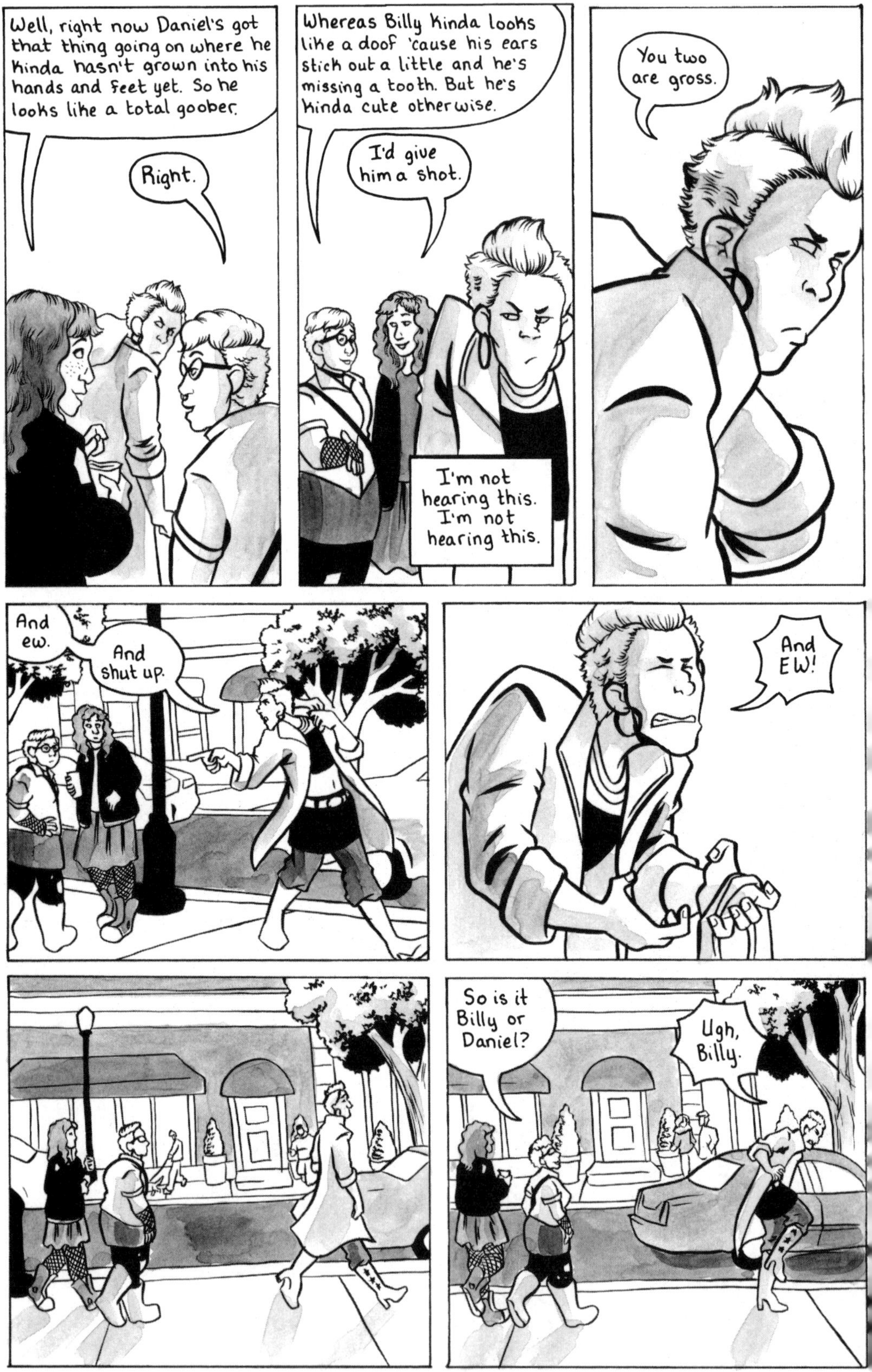
Well, right now Daniel's got that thing going on where he kinda hasn't grown into his hands and feet yet. So he looks like a total goober.
Right.
Whereas Billy kinda looks like a doof 'cause his ears stick out a little and he's missing a tooth. But he's kinda cute otherwise.
I'd give him a shot.
I'm not hearing this. I'm not hearing this.
You two are gross.
And ew.
And shut up.
And EW!
So is it Billy or Daniel?
Ugh, Billy.

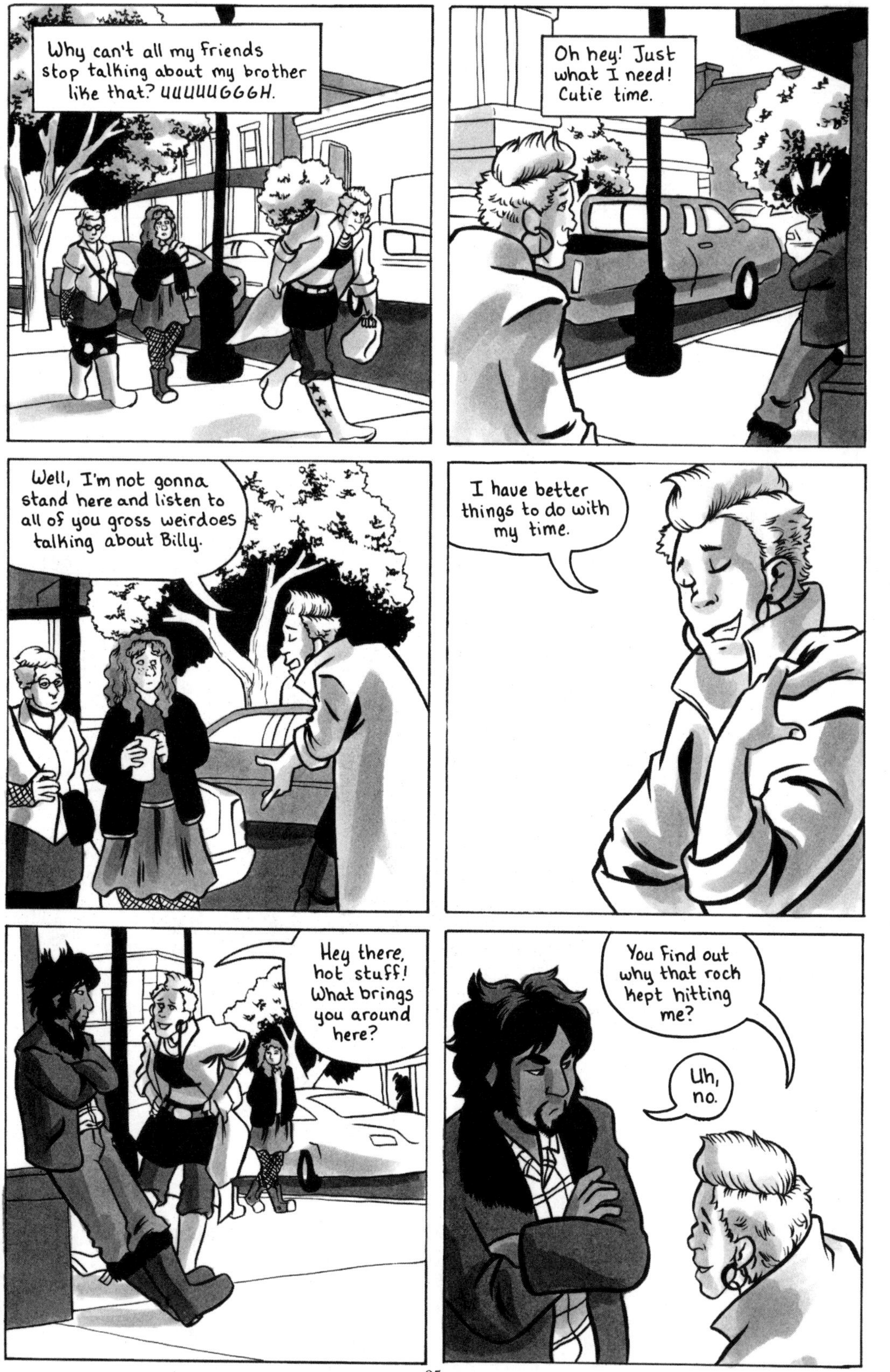
Why can't all my friends stop talking about my brother like that? UUUUUGGGH.
Oh hey! Just what I need! Cutie time.
Well, I'm not gonna stand here and listen to all of you gross weirdoes talking about Billy.
I have better things to do with my time.
Hey there, hot stuff! What brings you around here?
You find out why that rock kept hitting me?
Uh, no.

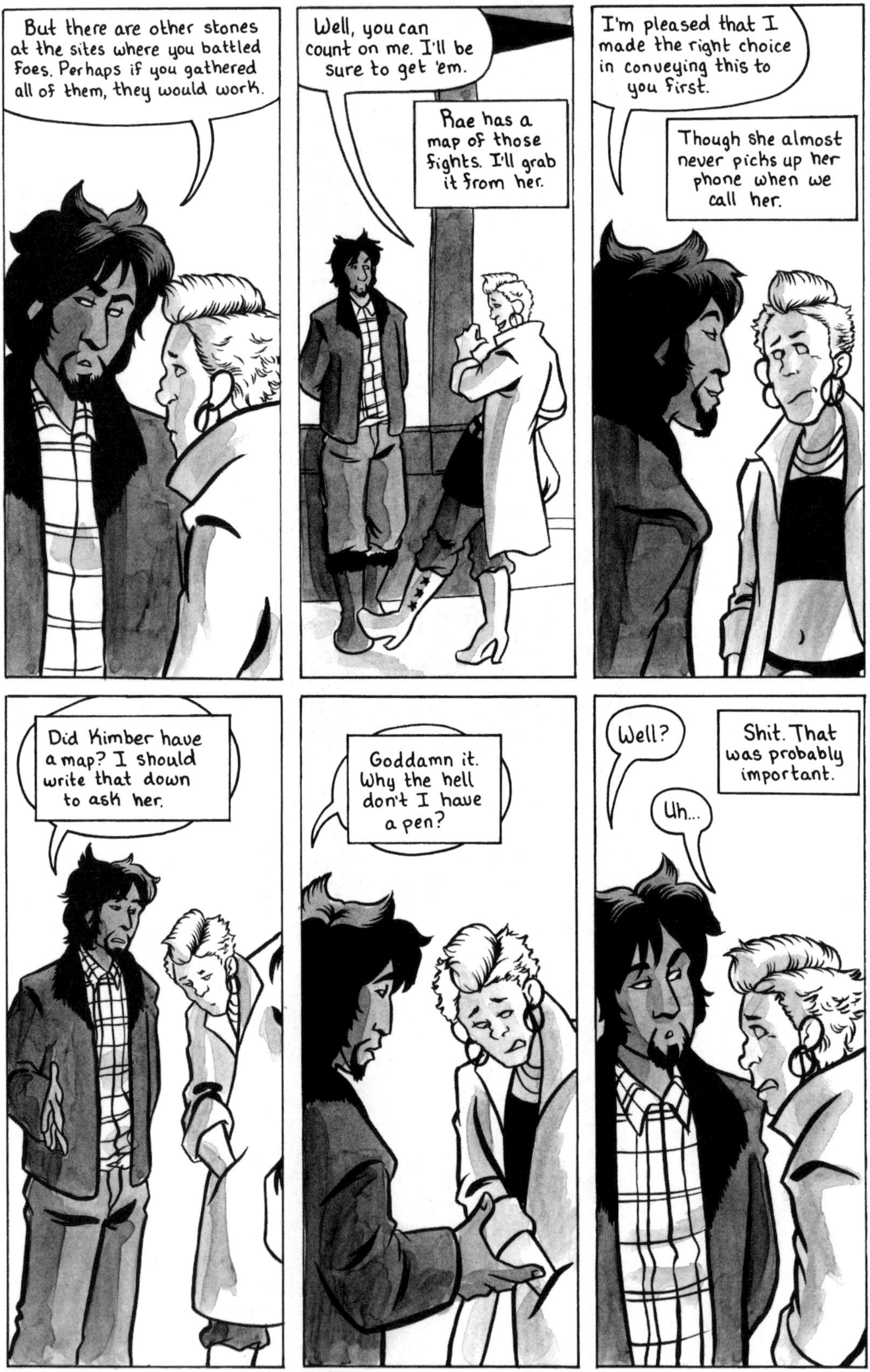
But there are other stones at the sites where you battled foes. Perhaps if you gathered all of them, they would work.
Well, you can count on me. I'll be sure to get 'em.
Rae has a map of those fights. I'll grab it from her.
I'm pleased that I made the right choice in conveying this to you first.
Though she almost never picks up her phone when we call her.
Did Kimber have a map? I should write that down to ask her.
Goddamn it. Why the hell don't I have a pen?
Well?
Uh...
Shit. That was probably important.

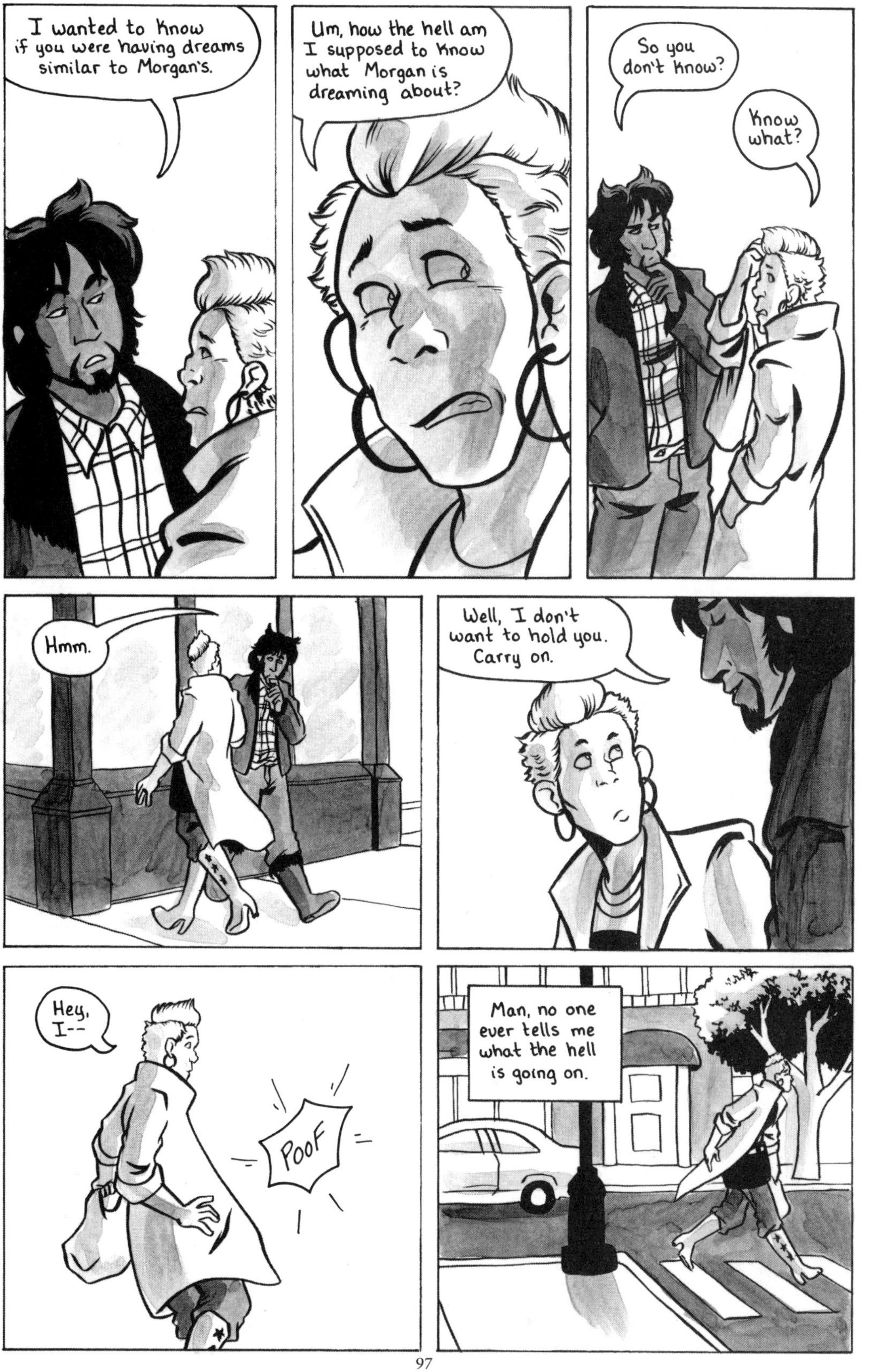
I wanted to know if you were having dreams similar to Morgan's.
Um, how the hell am I supposed to know what Morgan is dreaming about?
So you don't know?
Know what?
Hmm.
Well, I don't want to hold you. Carry on.
Hey, I--
POOF
Man, no one ever tells me what the hell is going on.

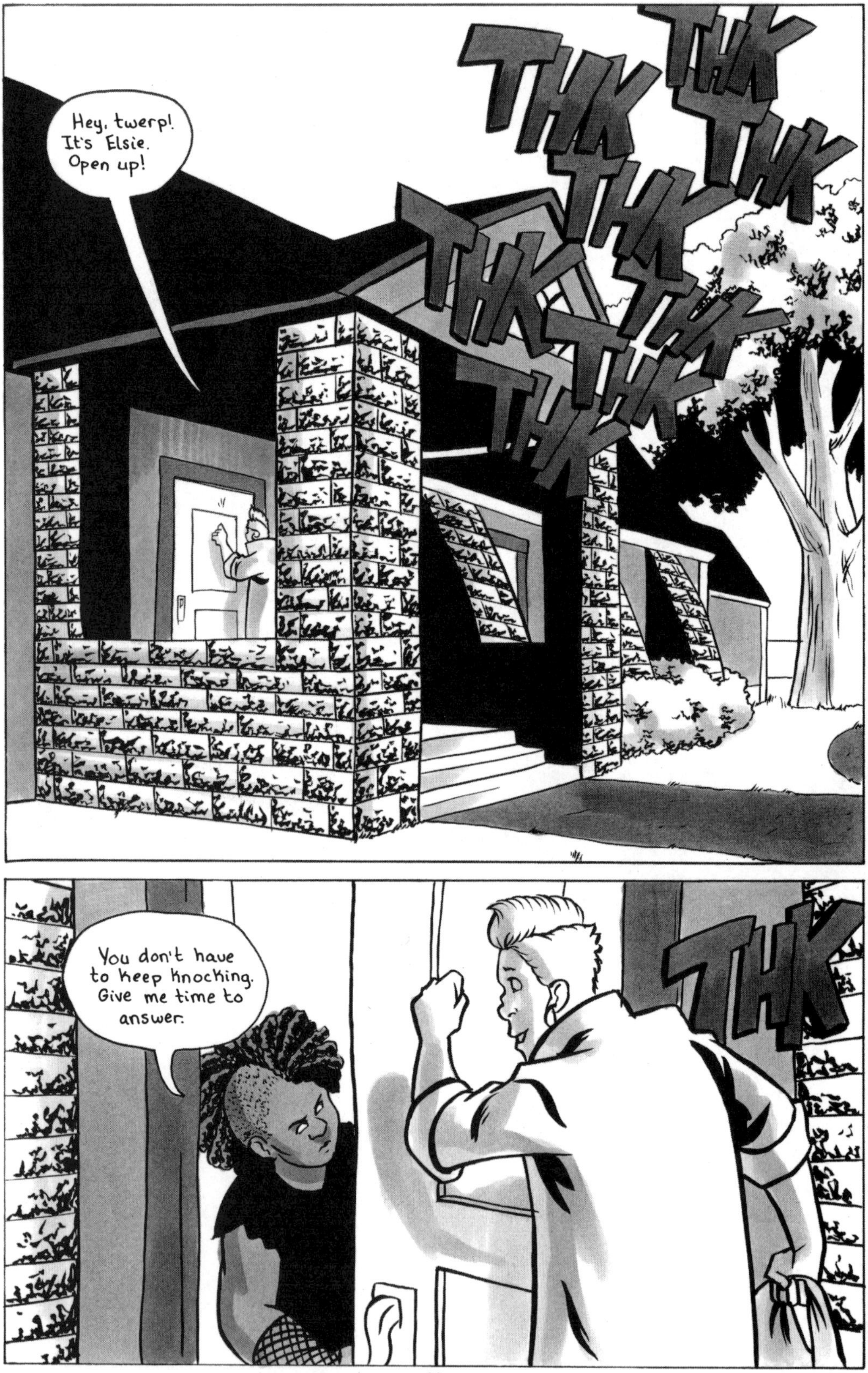
Hey, twerp! It's Elsie. Open up!
THK THK THK THK THK THK THK THK THK
You don't have to keep knocking. Give me time to answer.
THK

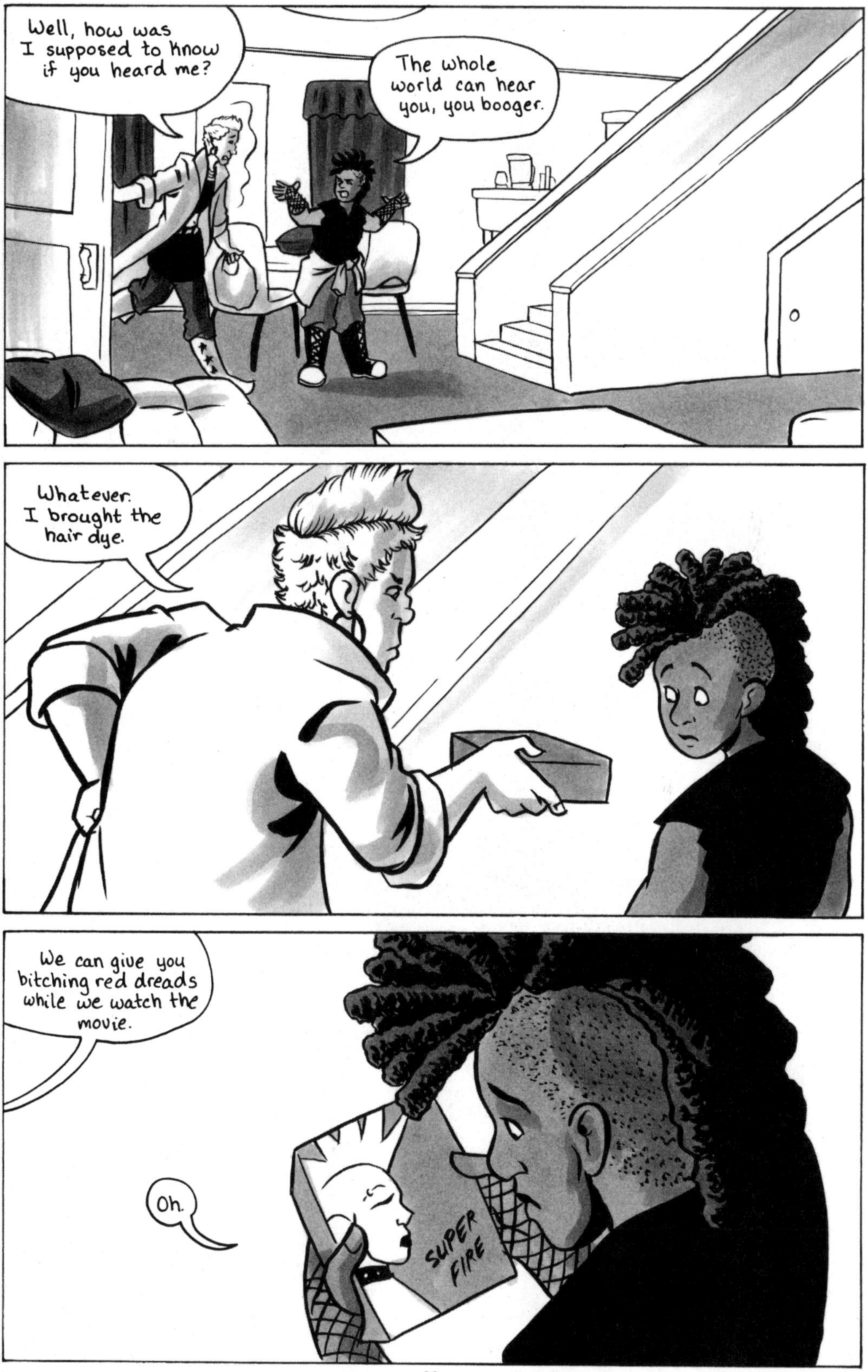
Well, how was I supposed to know if you heard me?
The whole world can hear you, you booger.
Whatever. I brought the hair dye.
We can give you bitching red dreads while we watch the movie.
Oh.
SUPER FIRE

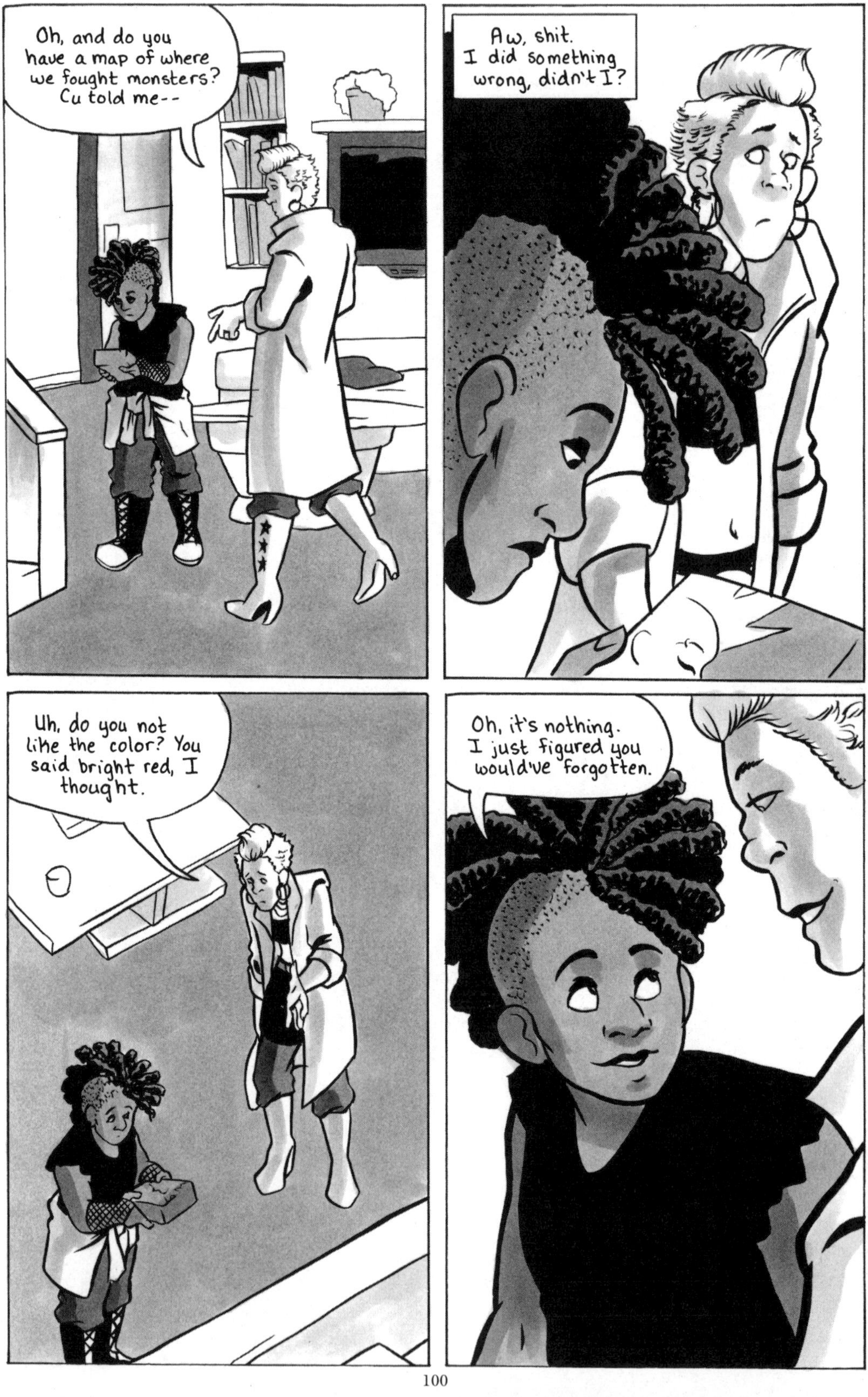
Oh, and do you have a map of where we fought monsters? Cu told me--
Aw, shit. I did something wrong, didn't I?
Uh, do you not like the color? You said bright red, I thought.
Oh, it's nothing. I just figured you would've forgotten.

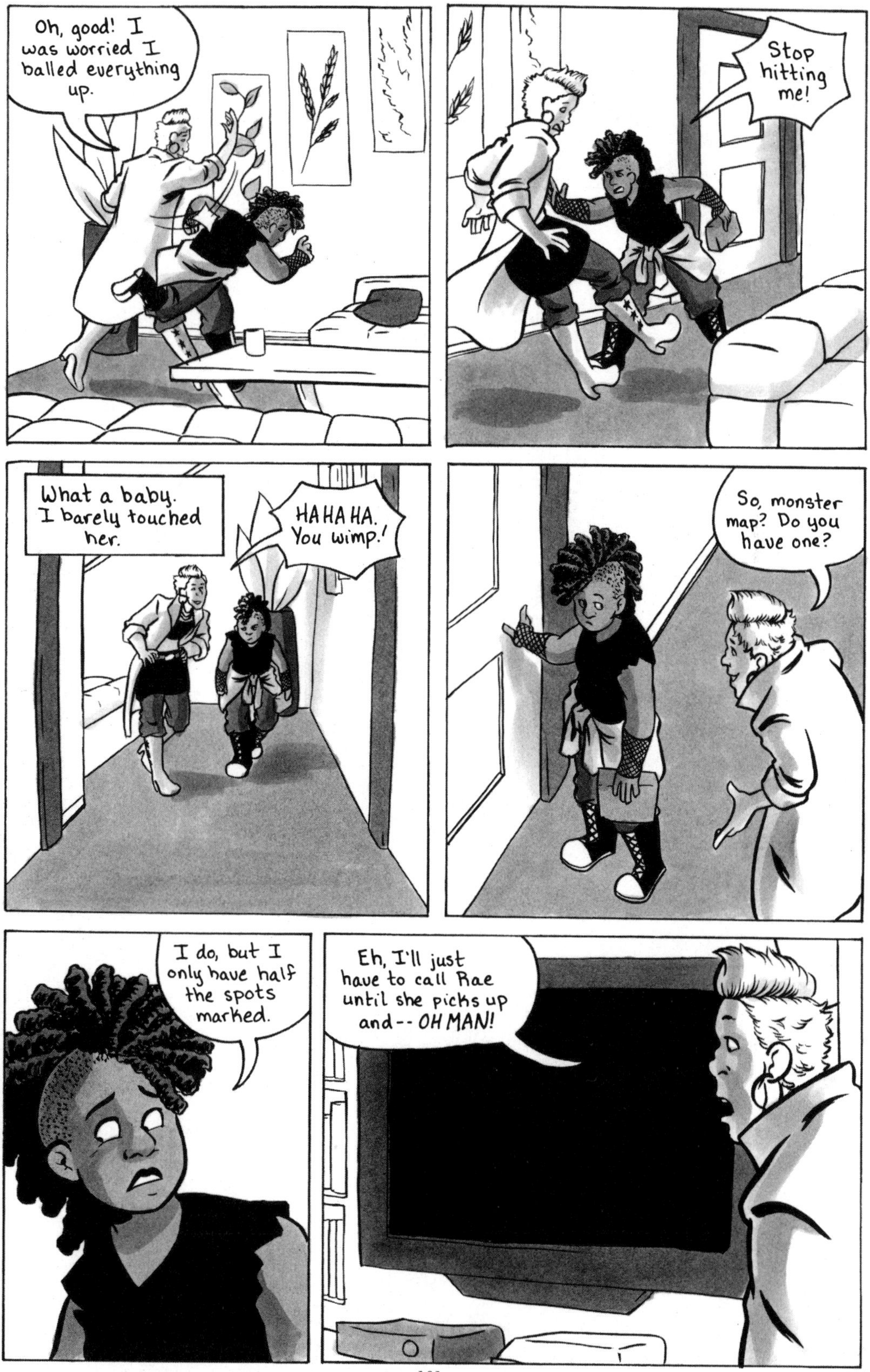
Oh, good! I was worried I balled everything up.
Stop hitting me!
What a baby. I barely touched her.
HAHAHA. You wimp!
So, monster map? Do you have one?
I do, but I only have half the spots marked.
Eh, I'll just have to call Rae until she picks up and-- OH MAN!

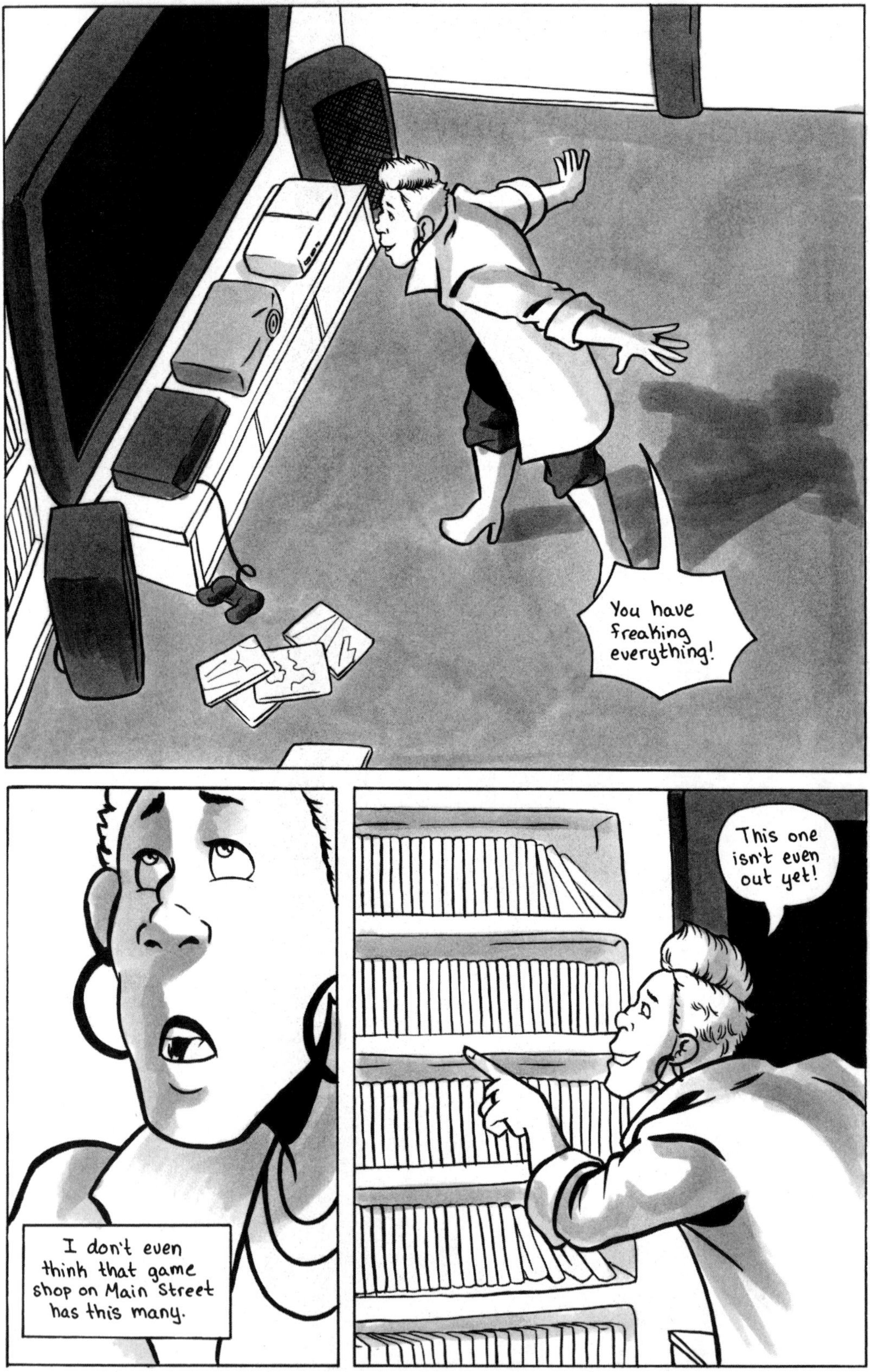

You have freaking everything!
I don't even think that game shop on Main Street has this many.
This one isn't even out yet!

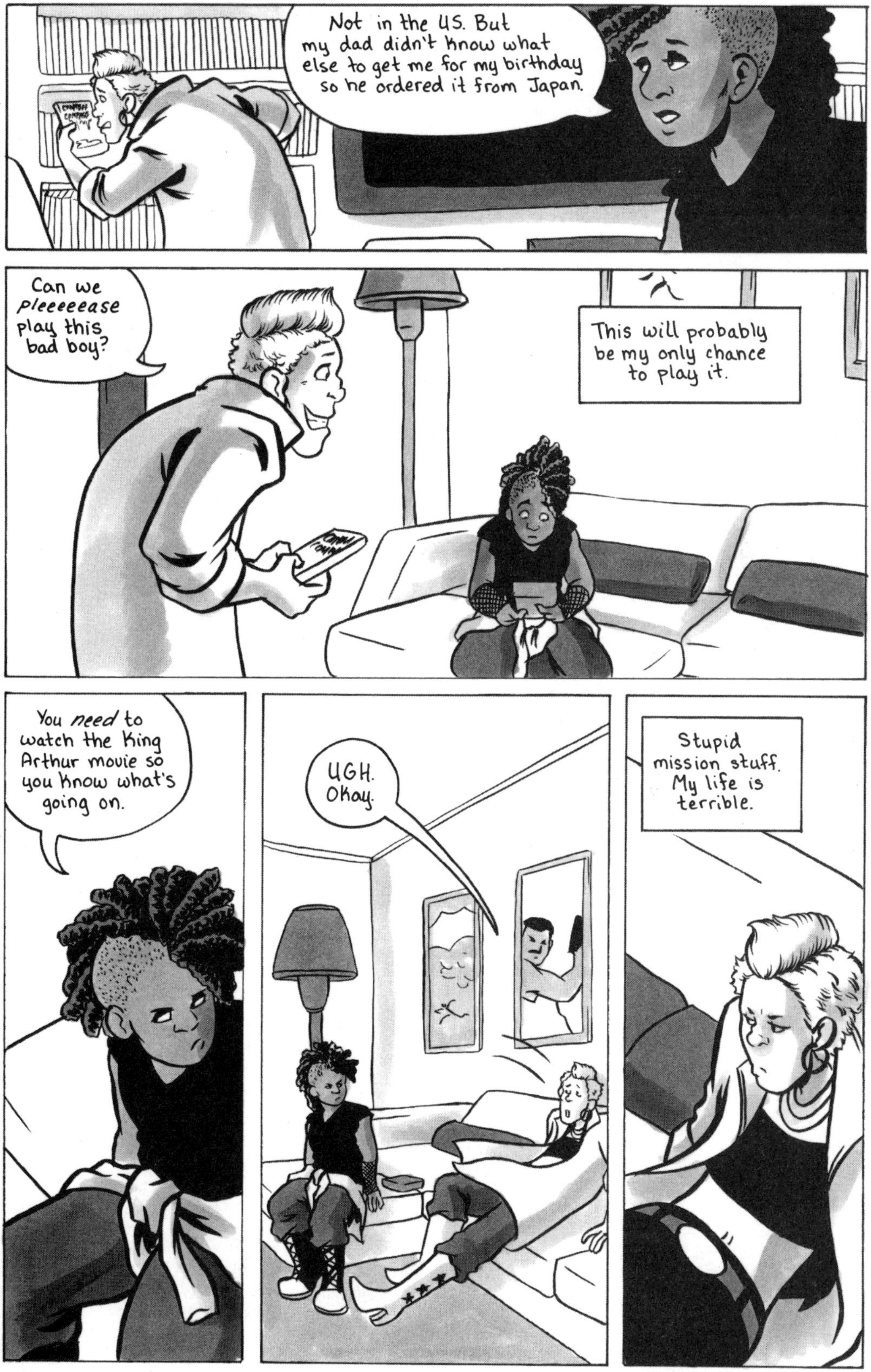
Not in the US. But my dad didn't know what else to get me for my birthday so he ordered it from Japan.
Can we *pleeeeease* play this bad boy?
This will probably be my only chance to play it.
You *need* to watch the King Arthur movie so you know what's going on.
UGH. Okay.
Stupid mission stuff. My life is terrible.

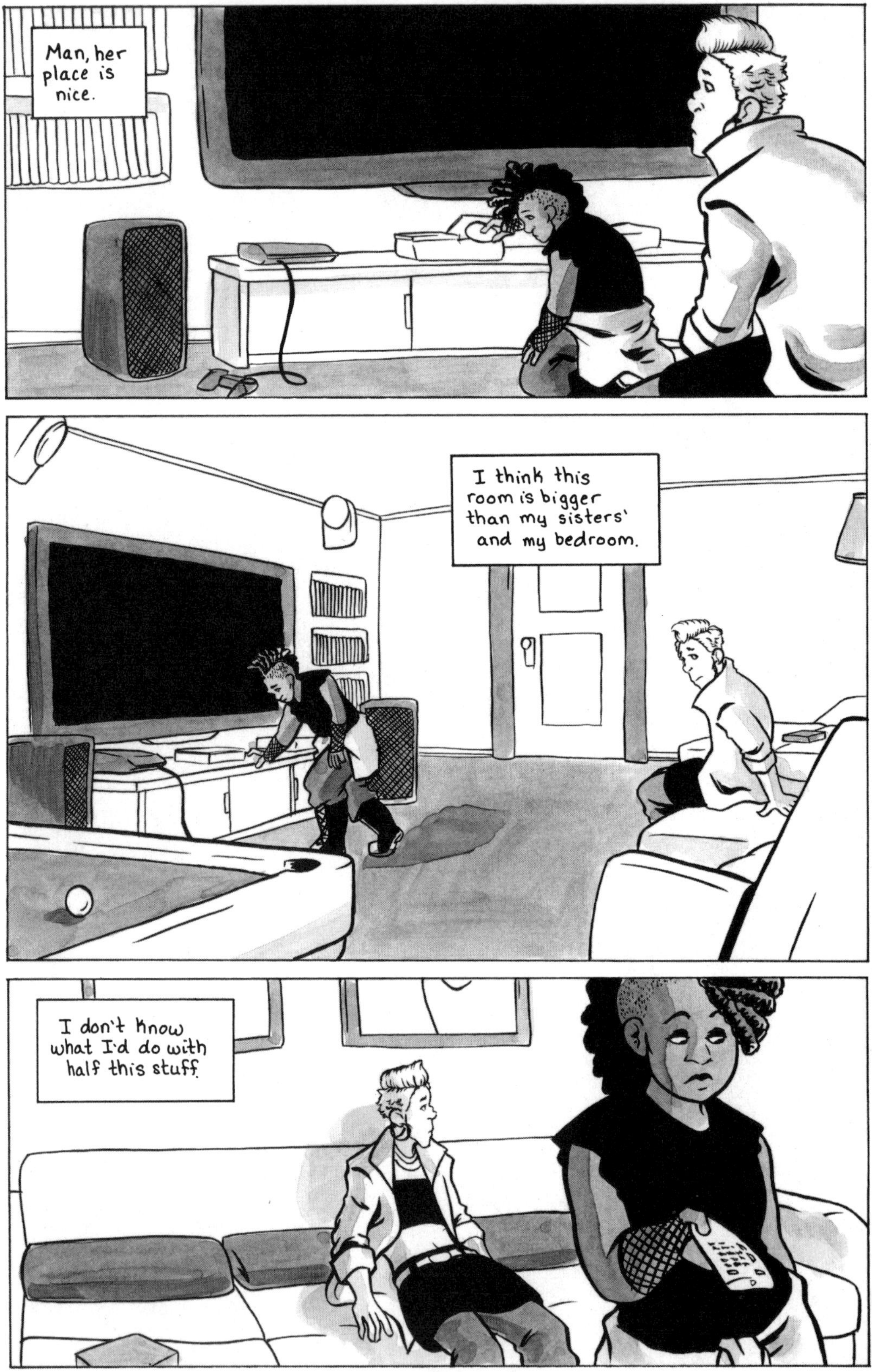
Man, her place is nice.
I think this room is bigger than my sisters' and my bedroom.
I don't know what I'd do with half this stuff.

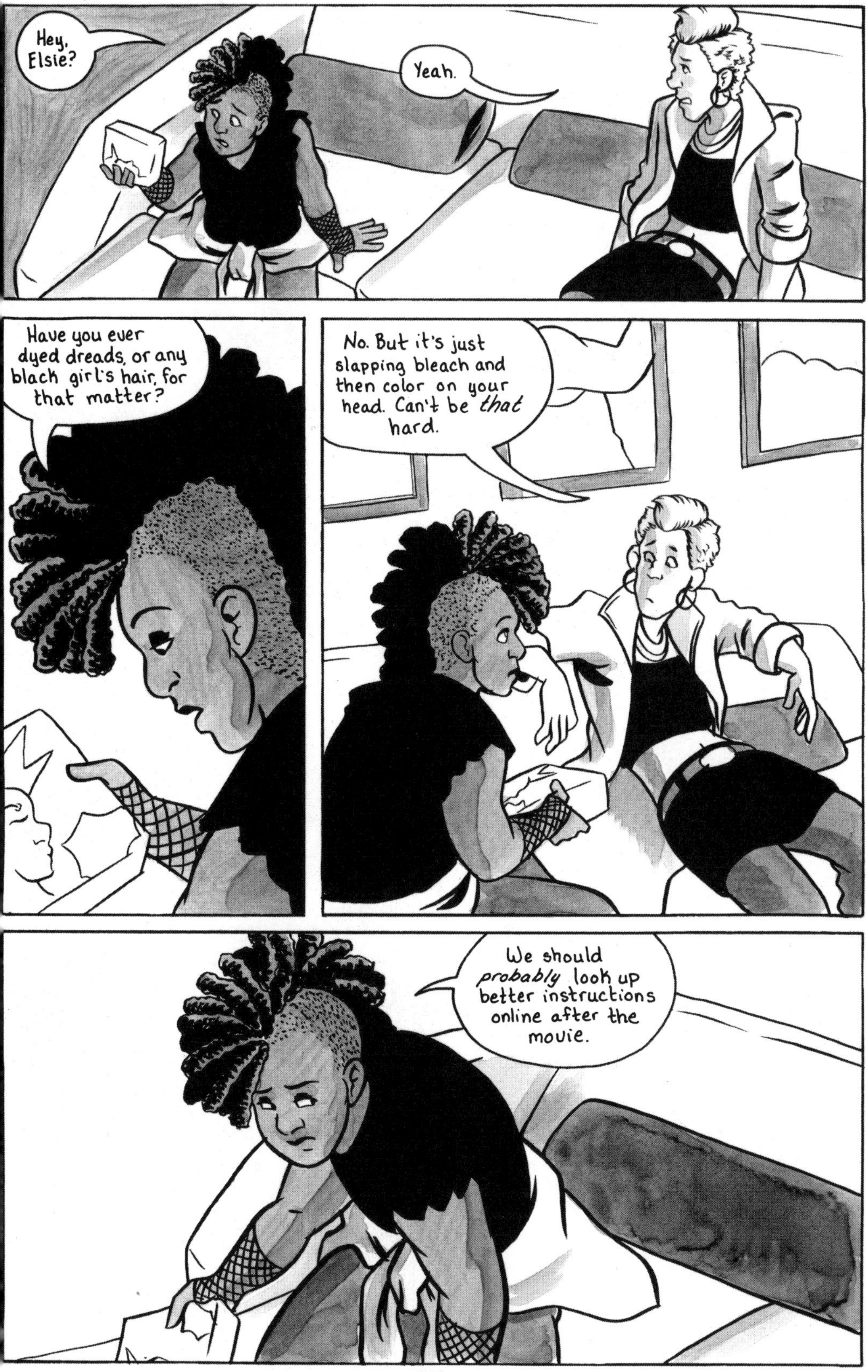

Hey, Elsie?
Yeah.
Have you ever dyed dreads, or any black girl's hair, for that matter?
No. But it's just slapping bleach and then color on your head. Can't be *that* hard.
We should *probably* look up better instructions online after the movie.

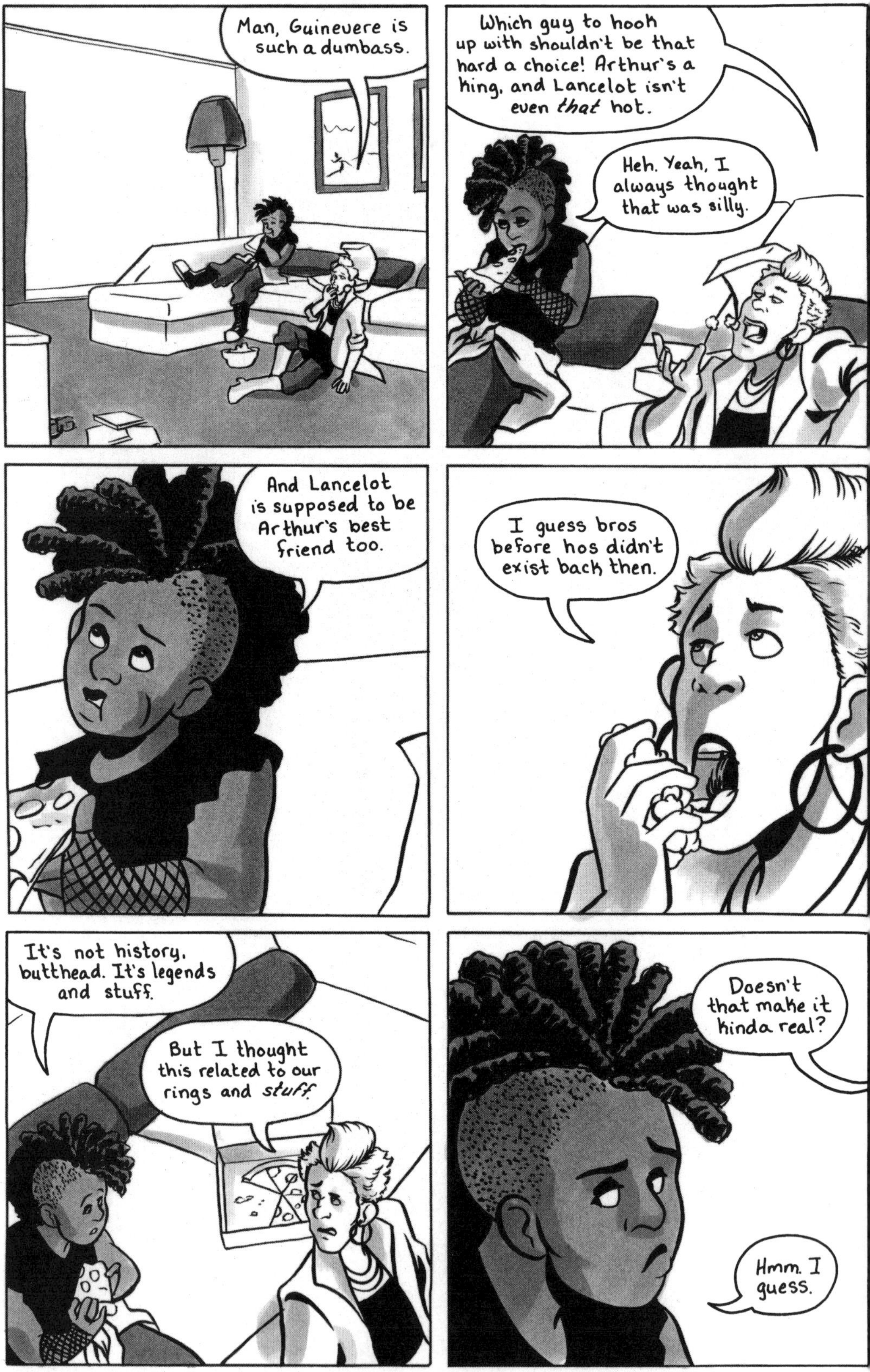
Man, Guinevere is such a dumbass.
Which guy to hook up with shouldn't be that hard a choice! Arthur's a king, and Lancelot isn't even *that* hot.
Heh. Yeah, I always thought that was silly.
And Lancelot is supposed to be Arthur's best friend too.
I guess bros before hos didn't exist back then.
It's not history, butthead. It's legends and stuff.
But I thought this related to our rings and *stuff*.
Doesn't that make it kinda real?
Hmm. I guess.

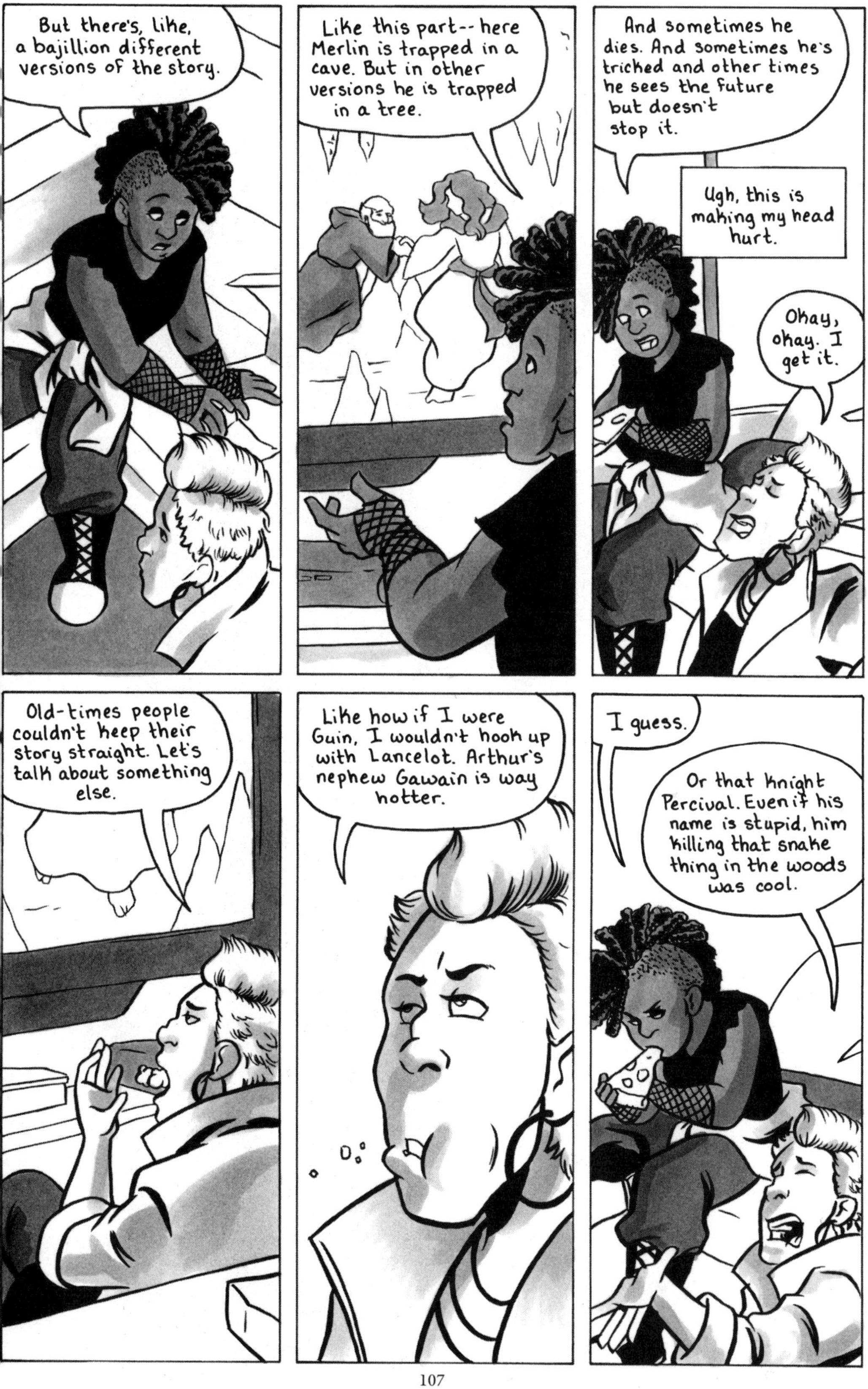

But there's, like, a bajillion different versions of the story.
Like this part-- here Merlin is trapped in a cave. But in other versions he is trapped in a tree.
And sometimes he dies. And sometimes he's tricked and other times he sees the future but doesn't stop it.
Ugh, this is making my head hurt.
Okay, okay. I get it.
Old-times people couldn't keep their story straight. Let's talk about something else.
Like how if I were Guin, I wouldn't hook up with Lancelot. Arthur's nephew Gawain is way hotter.
I guess.
Or that knight Percival. Even if his name is stupid, him killing that snake thing in the woods was cool.

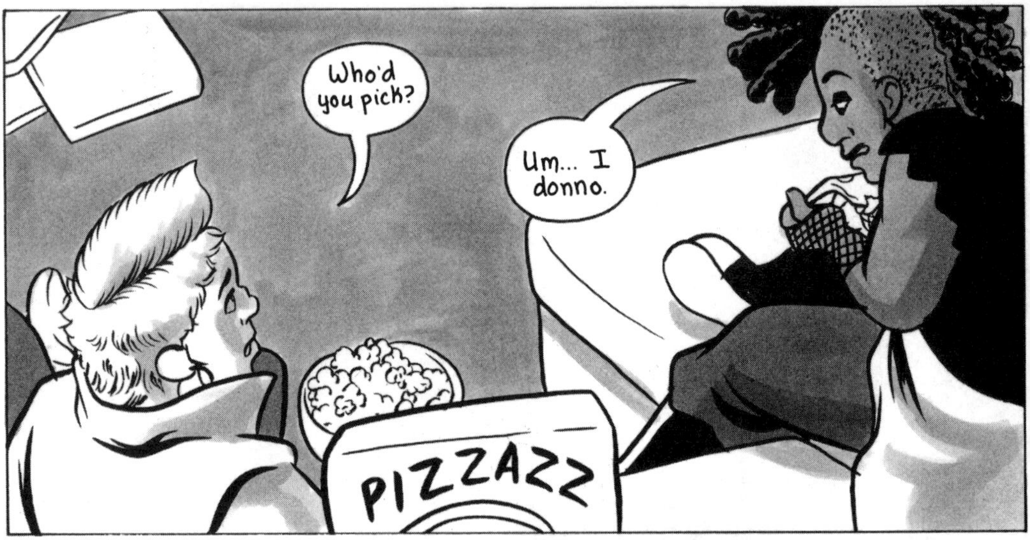
Who'd you pick?
Um... I donno.
PIZZAZZ

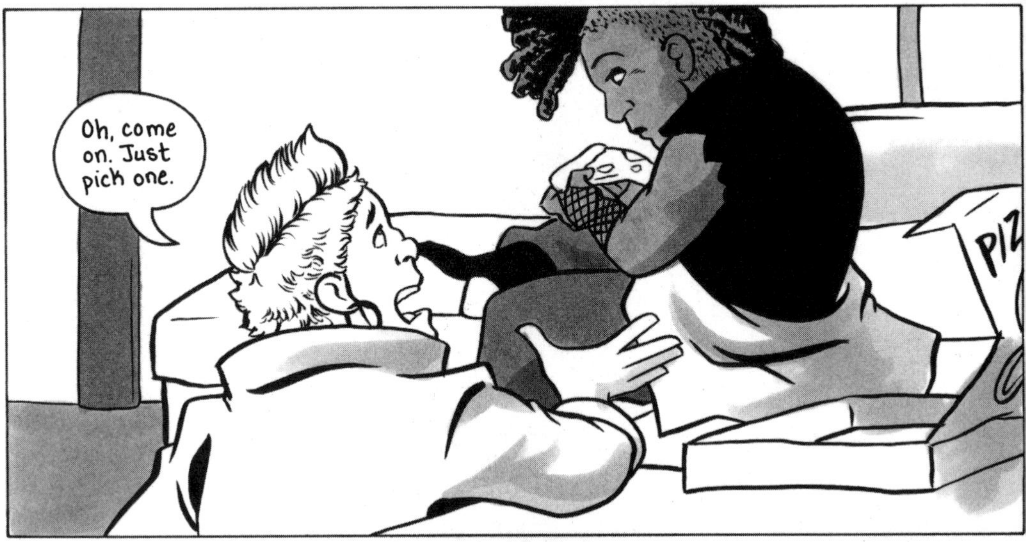
Oh, come on. Just pick one.

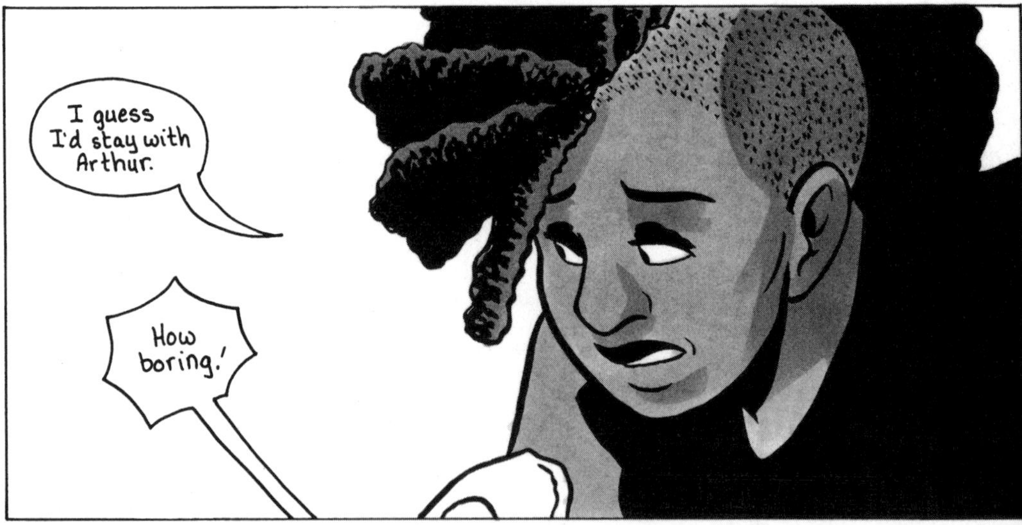
I guess I'd stay with Arthur.
How boring!

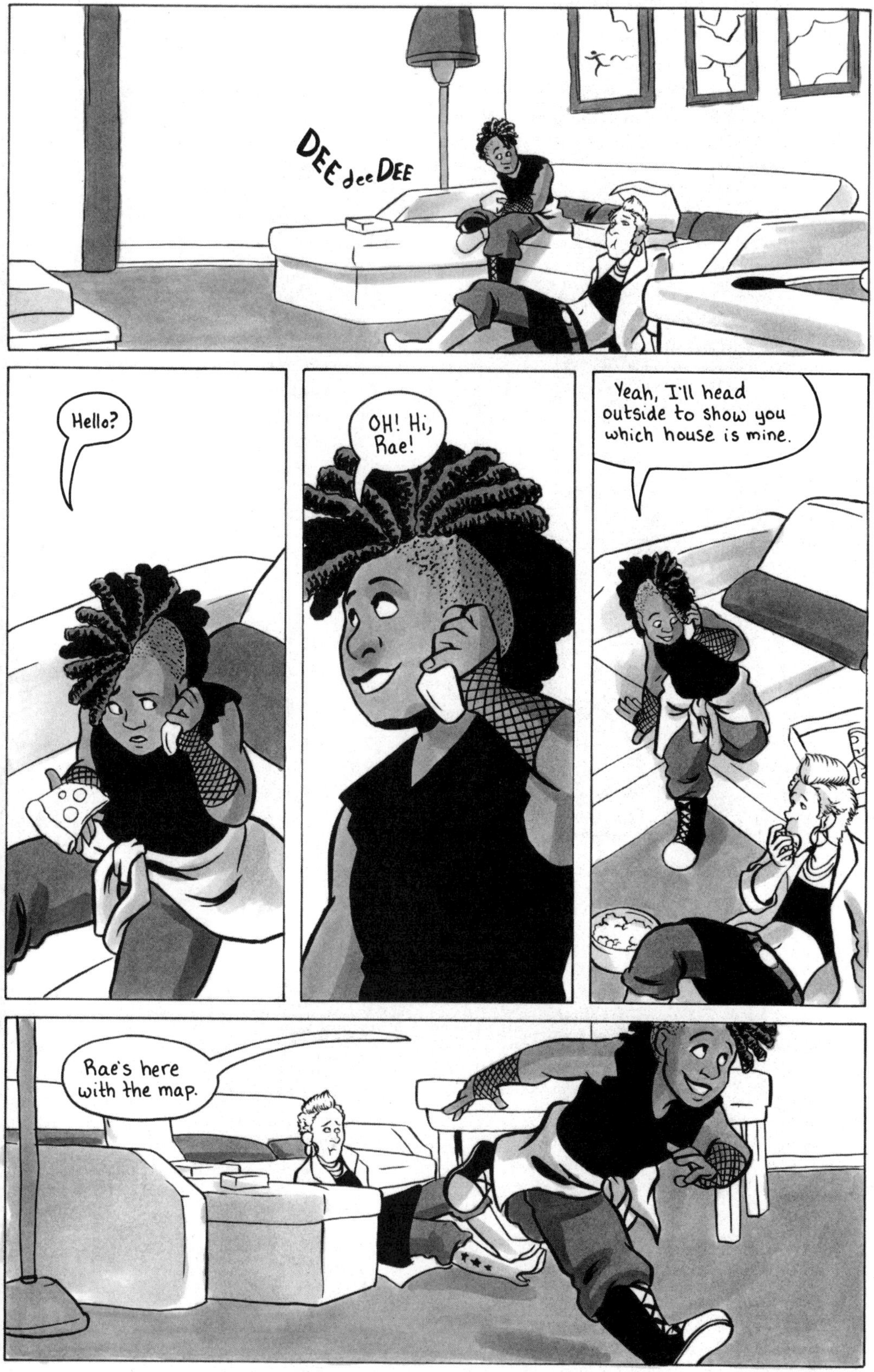
DEE dee DEE
Hello?
OH! Hi, Rae!
Yeah, I'll head outside to show you which house is mine.
Rae's here with the map.

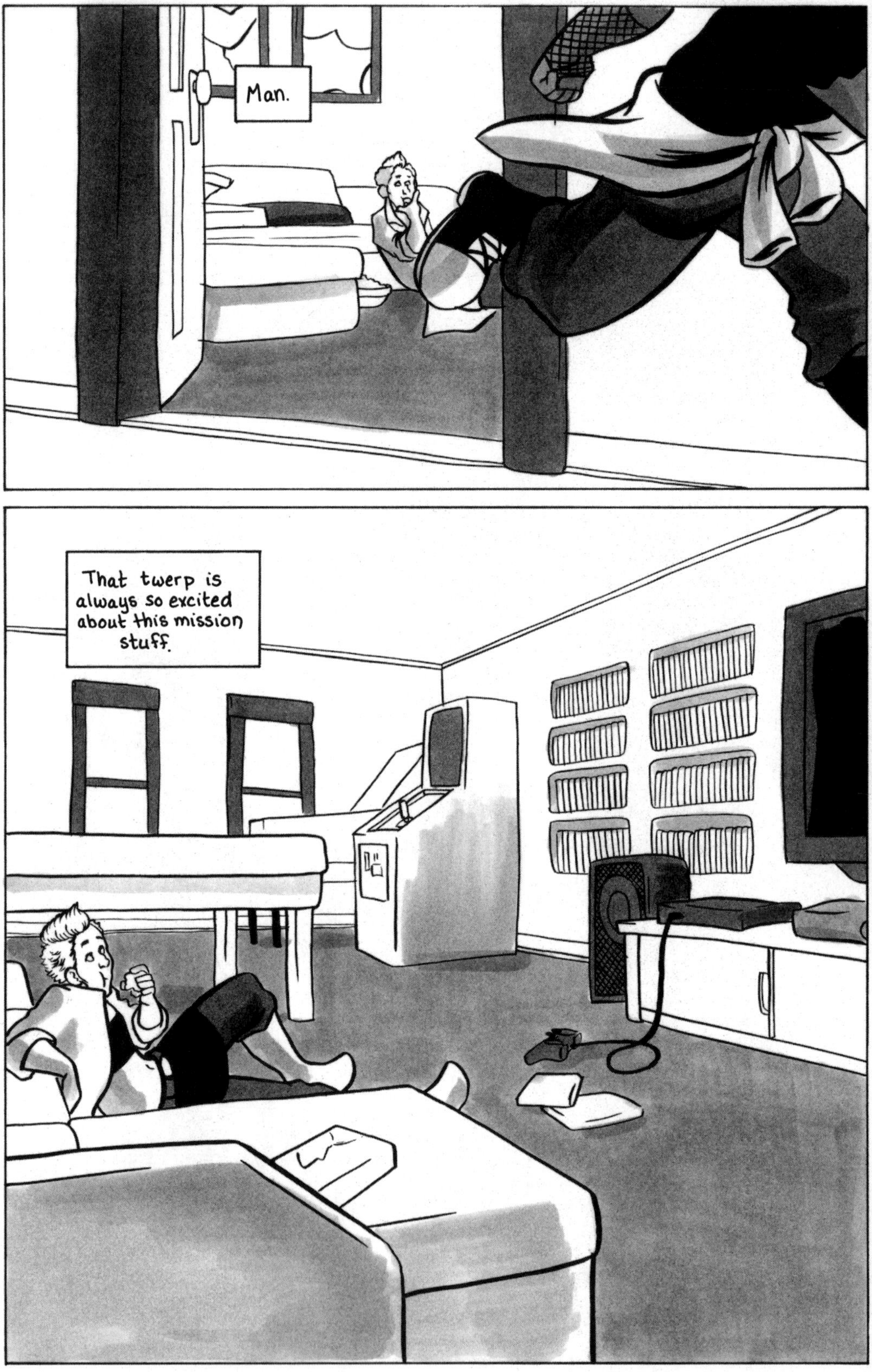
Man.
That twerp is always so excited about this mission stuff.

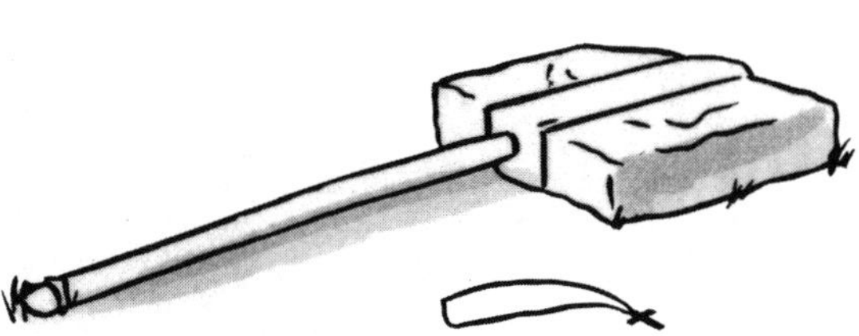

CHAPTER 6:

To Those Who Hardly Think about Us in Return

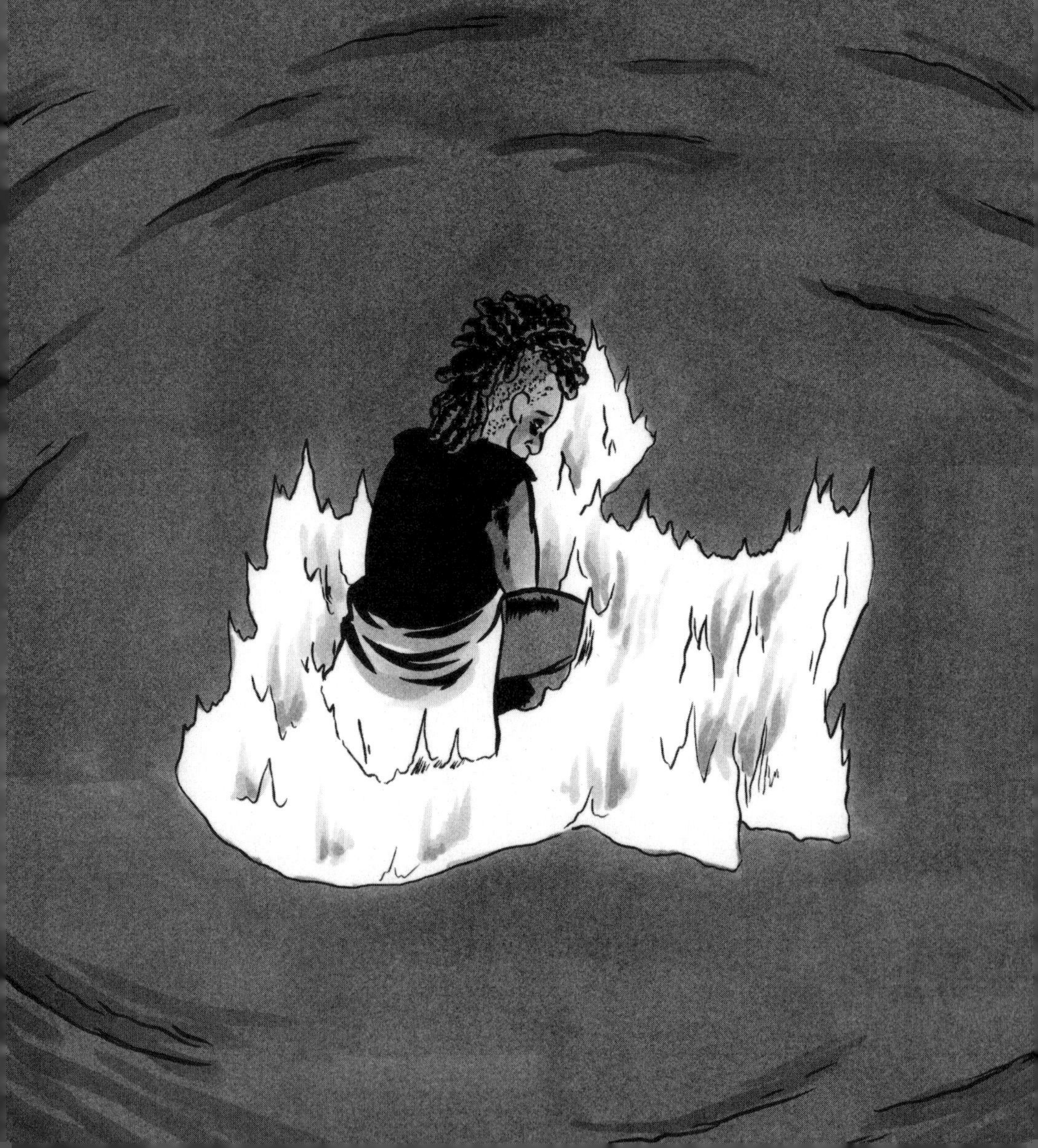

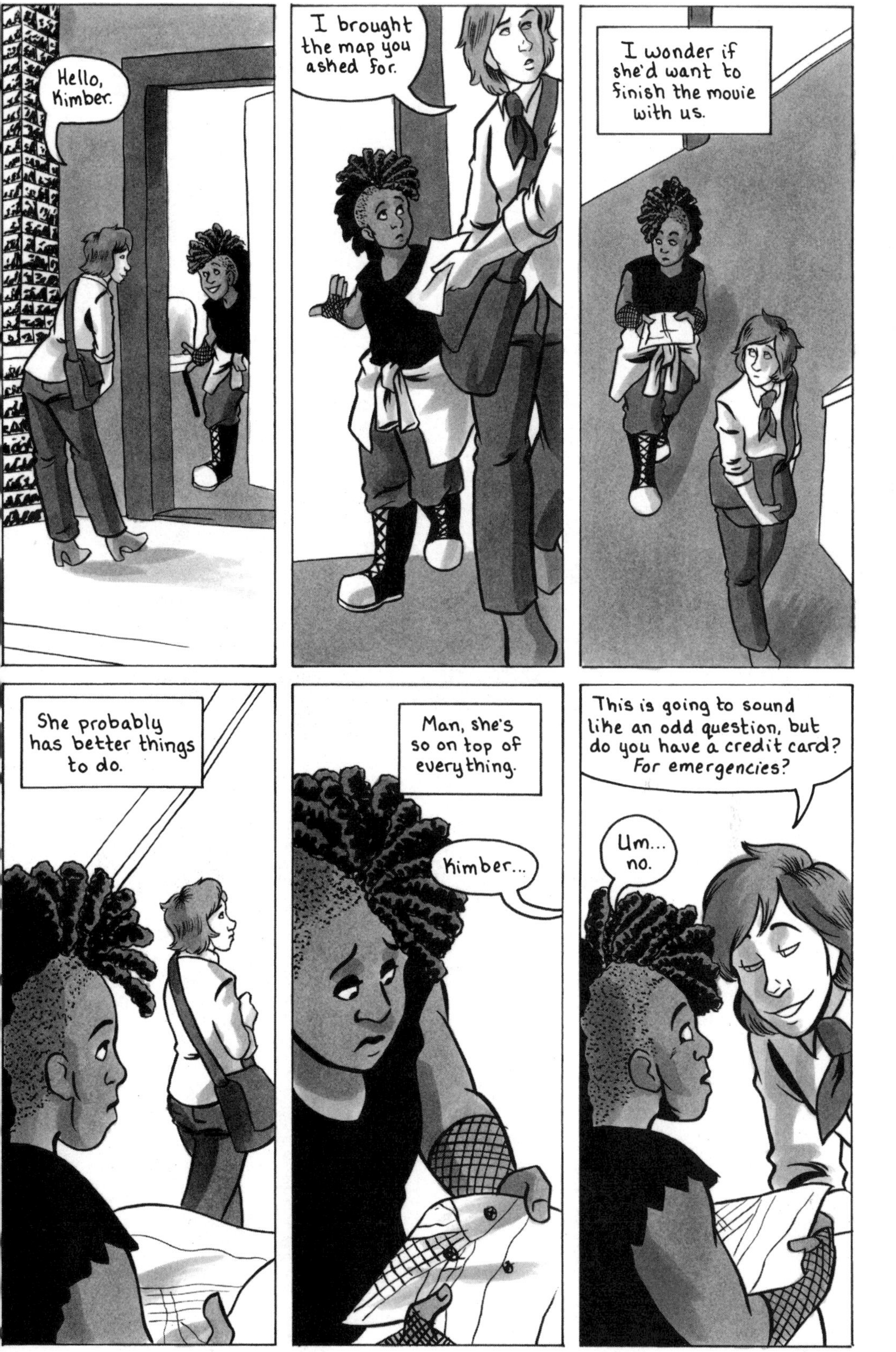
Hello, Kimber.
I brought the map you asked for.
I wonder if she'd want to finish the movie with us.
She probably has better things to do.
Man, she's so on top of everything.
Kimber...
This is going to sound like an odd question, but do you have a credit card? For emergencies?
Um... no.

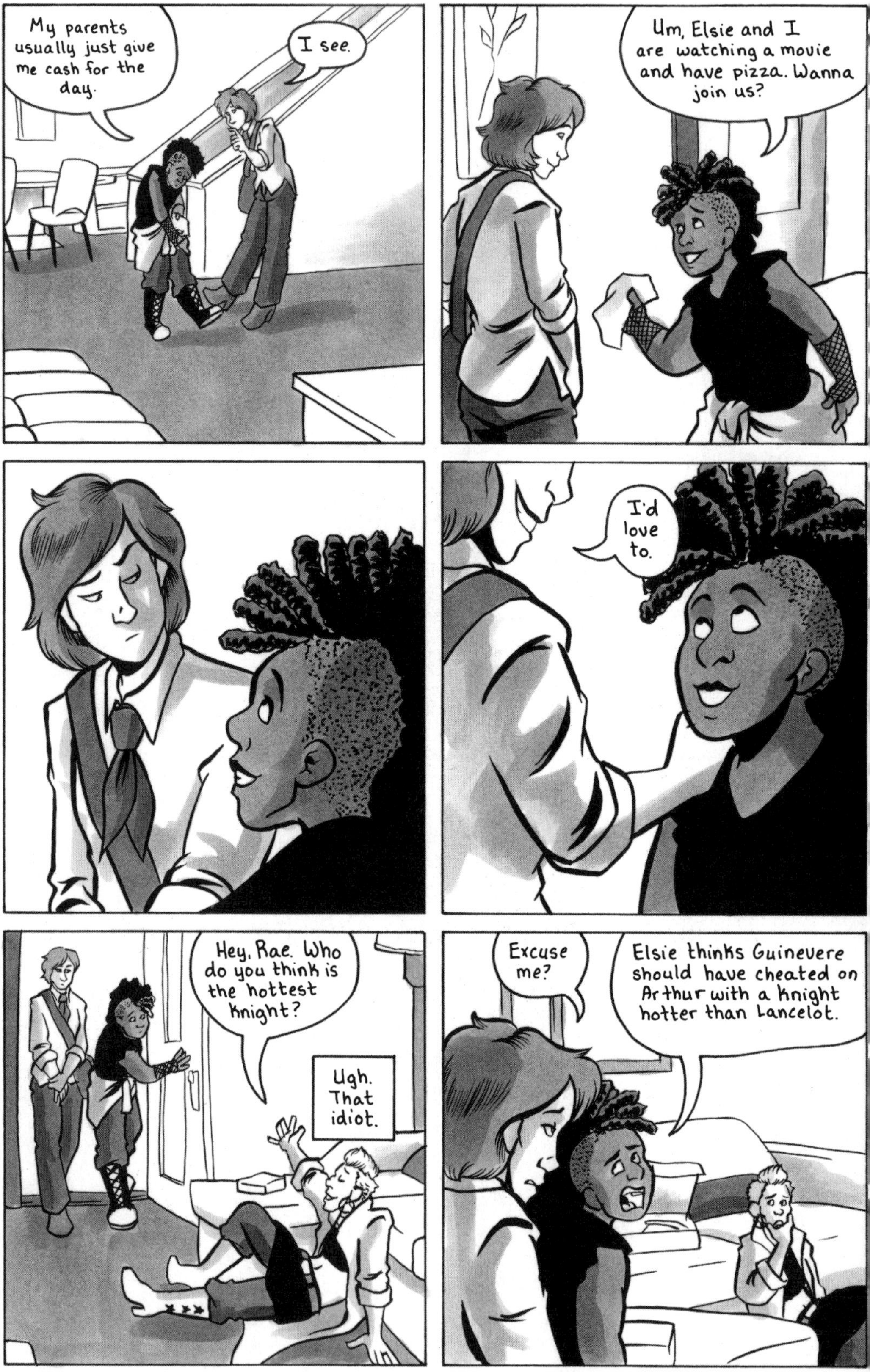

My parents usually just give me cash for the day.
I see.
Um, Elsie and I are watching a movie and have pizza. Wanna join us?
I'd love to.
Hey, Rae. Who do you think is the hottest knight?
Ugh. That idiot.
Excuse me?
Elsie thinks Guinevere should have cheated on Arthur with a knight hotter than Lancelot.

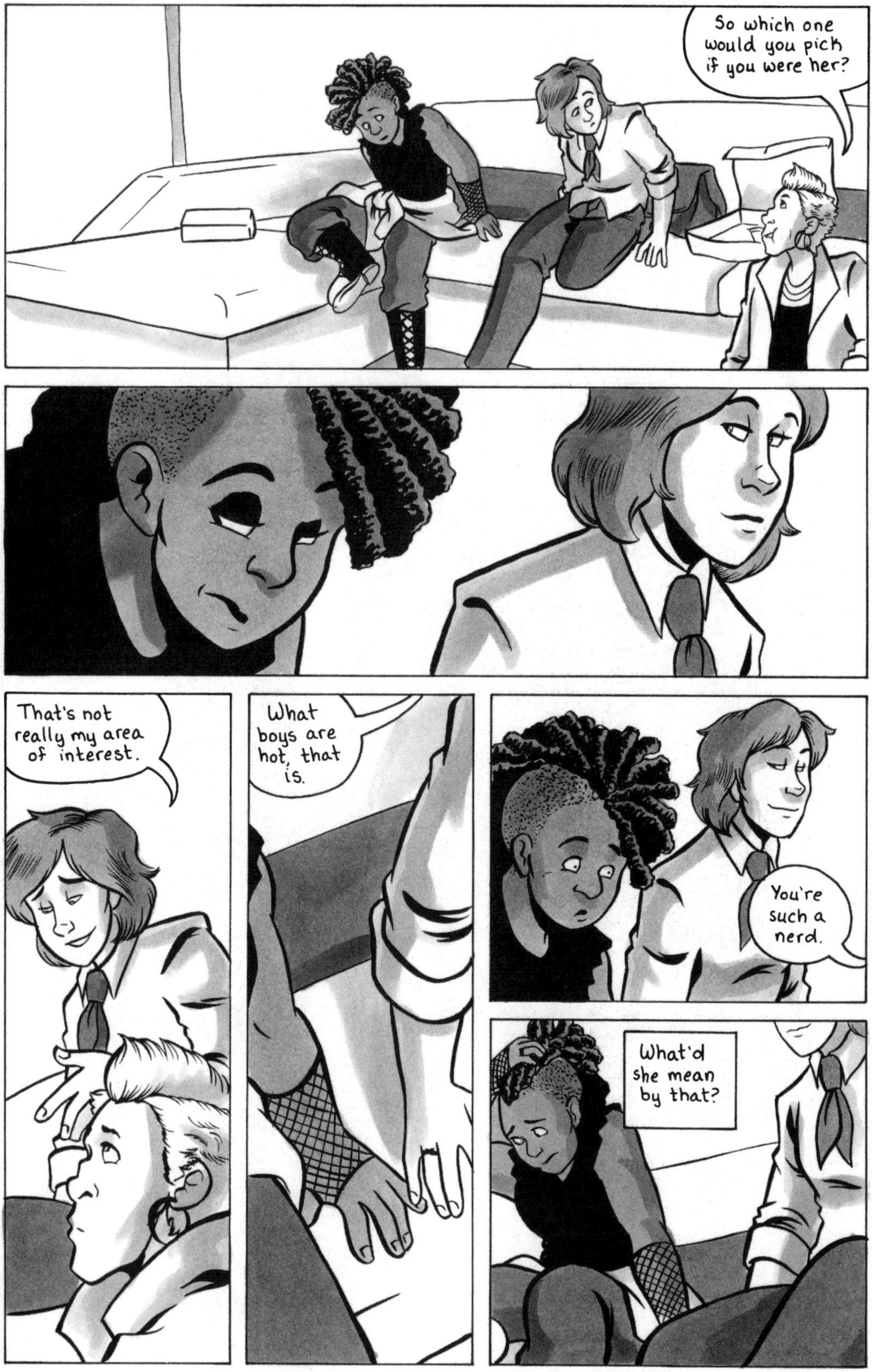
So which one would you pick if you were her?
That's not really my area of interest.
What boys are hot, that is.
You're such a nerd.
What'd she mean by that?

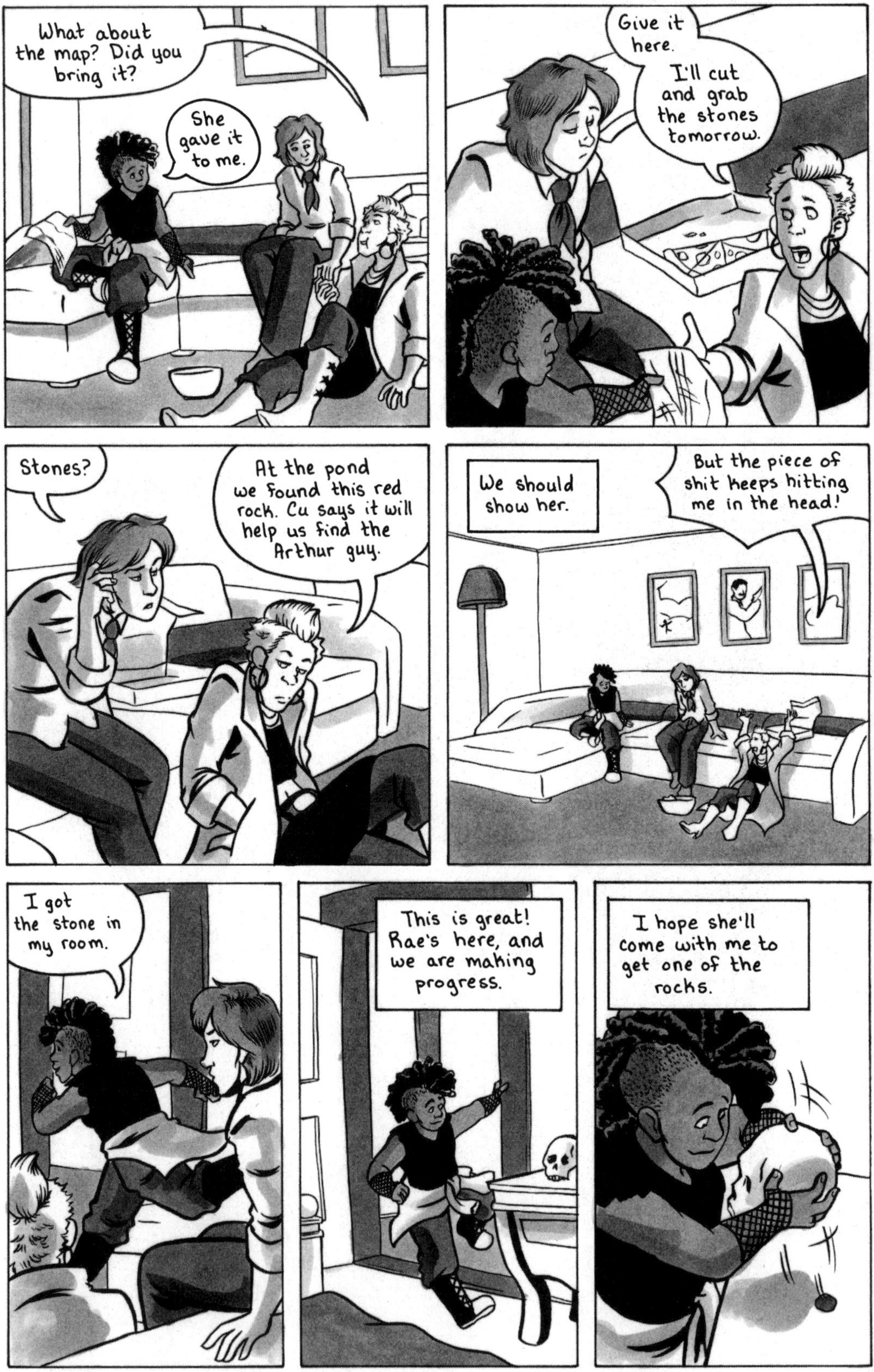
What about the map? Did you bring it?
She gave it to me.
Give it here.
I'll cut and grab the stones tomorrow.
Stones?
At the pond we found this red rock. Cu says it will help us find the Arthur guy.
We should show her.
But the piece of shit keeps hitting me in the head!
I got the stone in my room.
This is great! Rae's here, and we are making progress.
I hope she'll come with me to get one of the rocks.

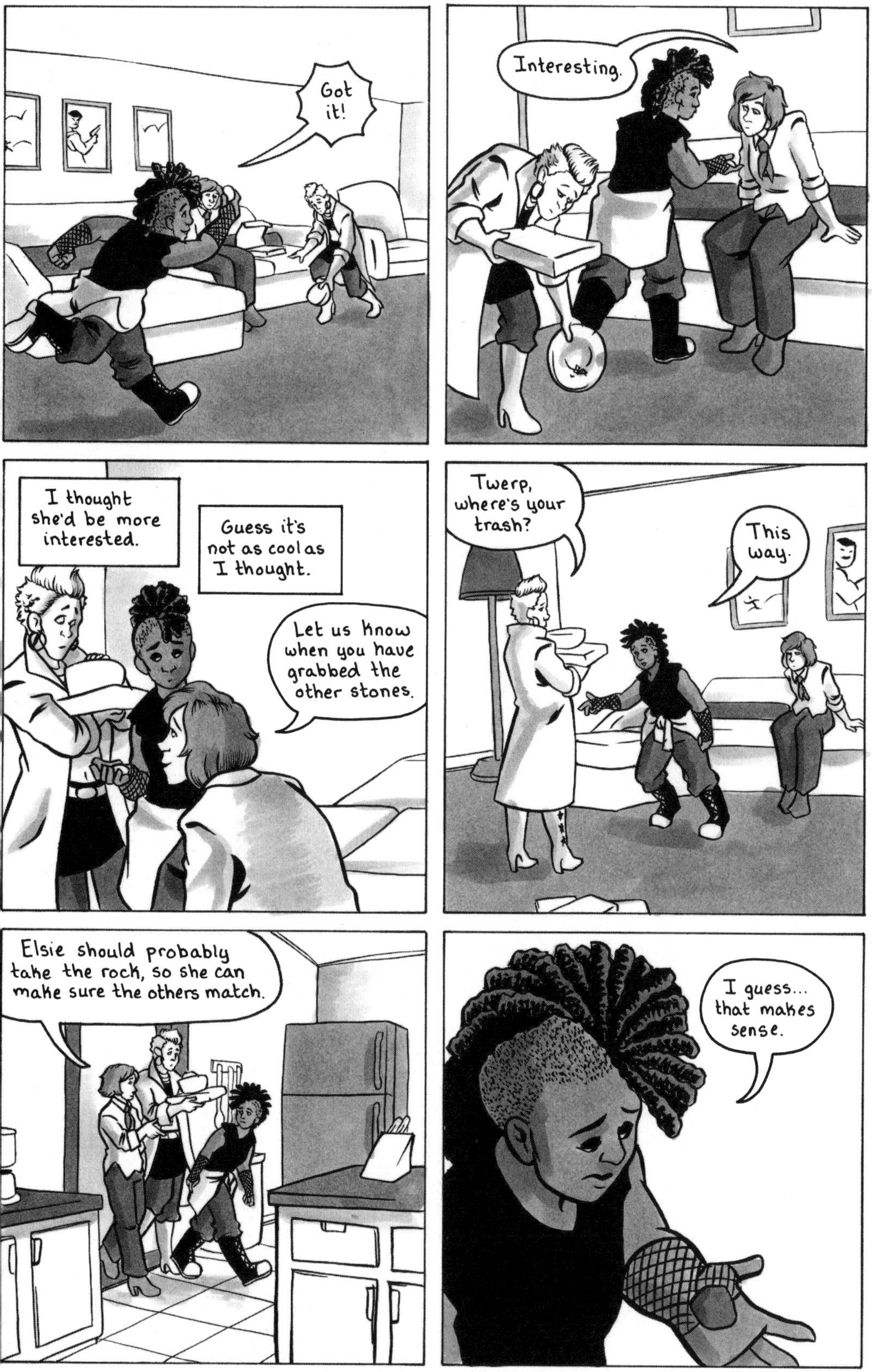
Got it!
Interesting.
I thought she'd be more interested.
Guess it's not as cool as I thought.
Let us know when you have grabbed the other stones.
Twerp, where's your trash?
This way.
Elsie should probably take the rock, so she can make sure the others match.
I guess... that makes sense.

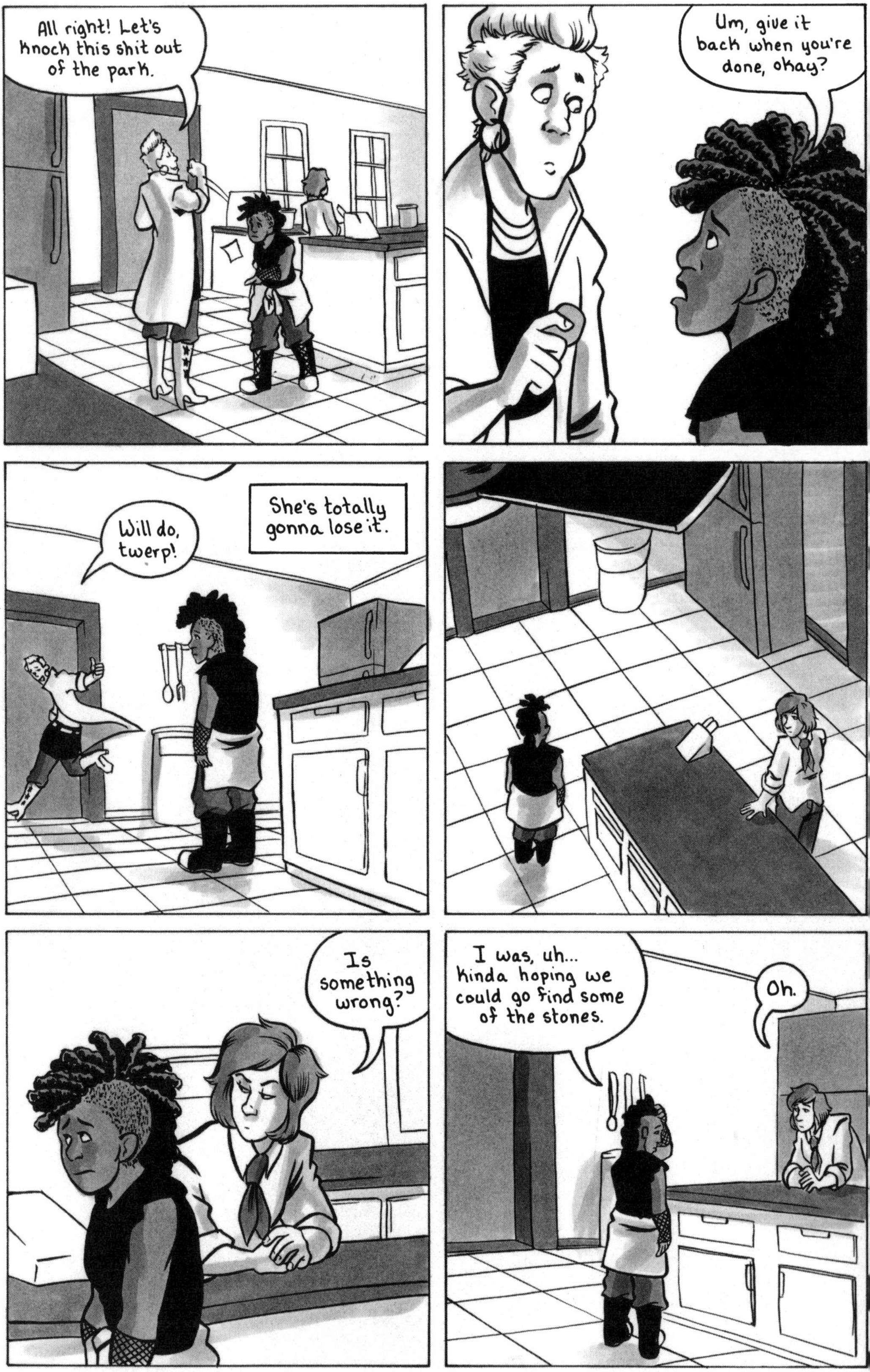
All right! Let's knock this shit out of the park.
Um, give it back when you're done, okay?
Will do, twerp!
She's totally gonna lose it.
Is something wrong?
I was, uh... kinda hoping we could go find some of the stones.
Oh.

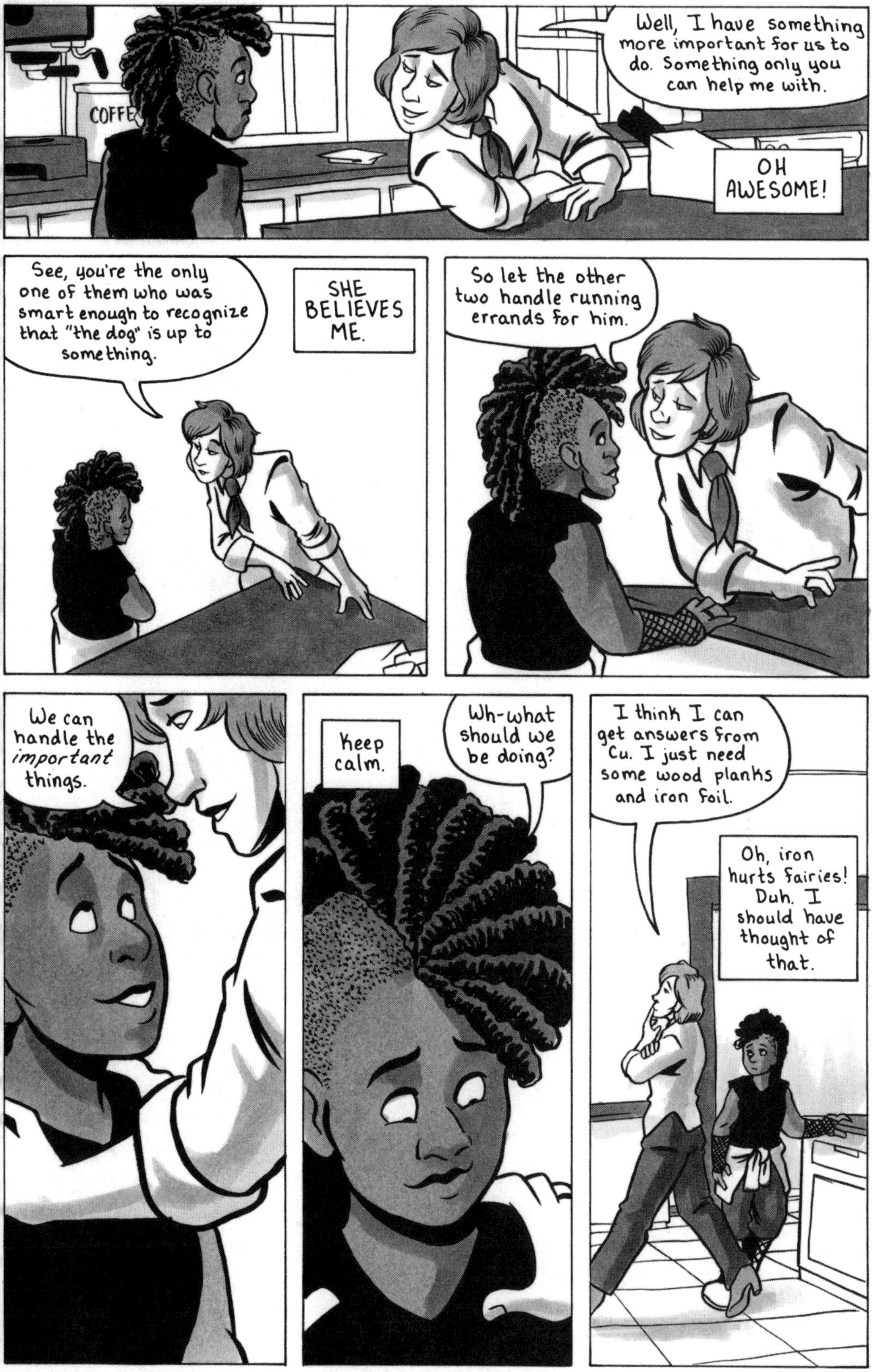
Well, I have something more important for us to do. Something only you can help me with.
OH AWESOME!
See, you're the only one of them who was smart enough to recognize that "the dog" is up to something.
SHE BELIEVES ME.
So let the other two handle running errands for him.
We can handle the *important* things.
Keep calm.
Wh-what should we be doing?
I think I can get answers from Cu. I just need some wood planks and iron foil.
Oh, iron hurts fairies! Duh. I should have thought of that.
COFFE

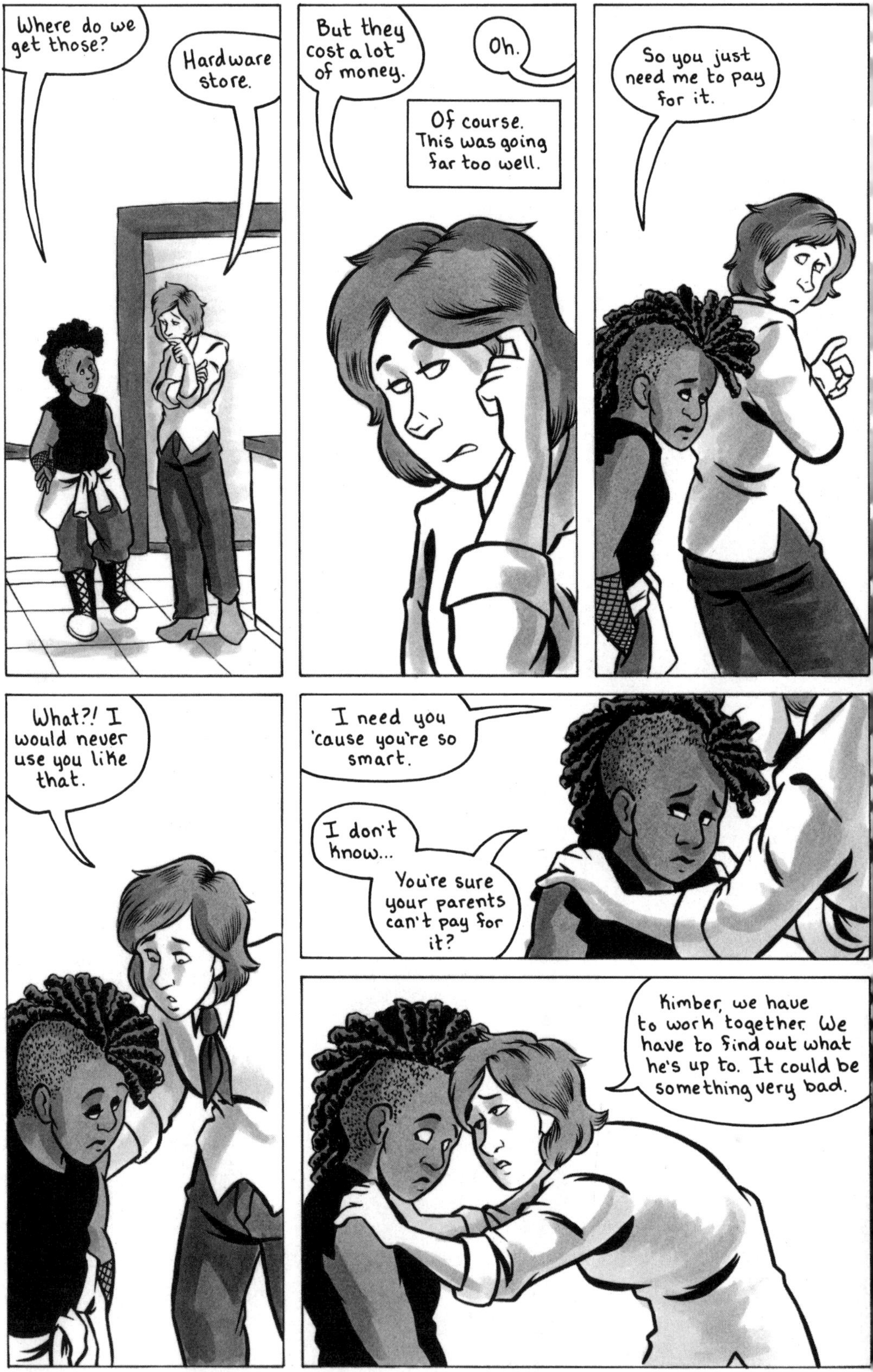
Where do we get those?
Hardware store.
But they cost a lot of money.
Oh.
Of course. This was going far too well.
So you just need me to pay for it.
What?! I would never use you like that.
I need you 'cause you're so smart.
I don't know...
You're sure your parents can't pay for it?
Kimber, we have to work together. We have to find out what he's up to. It could be something very bad.

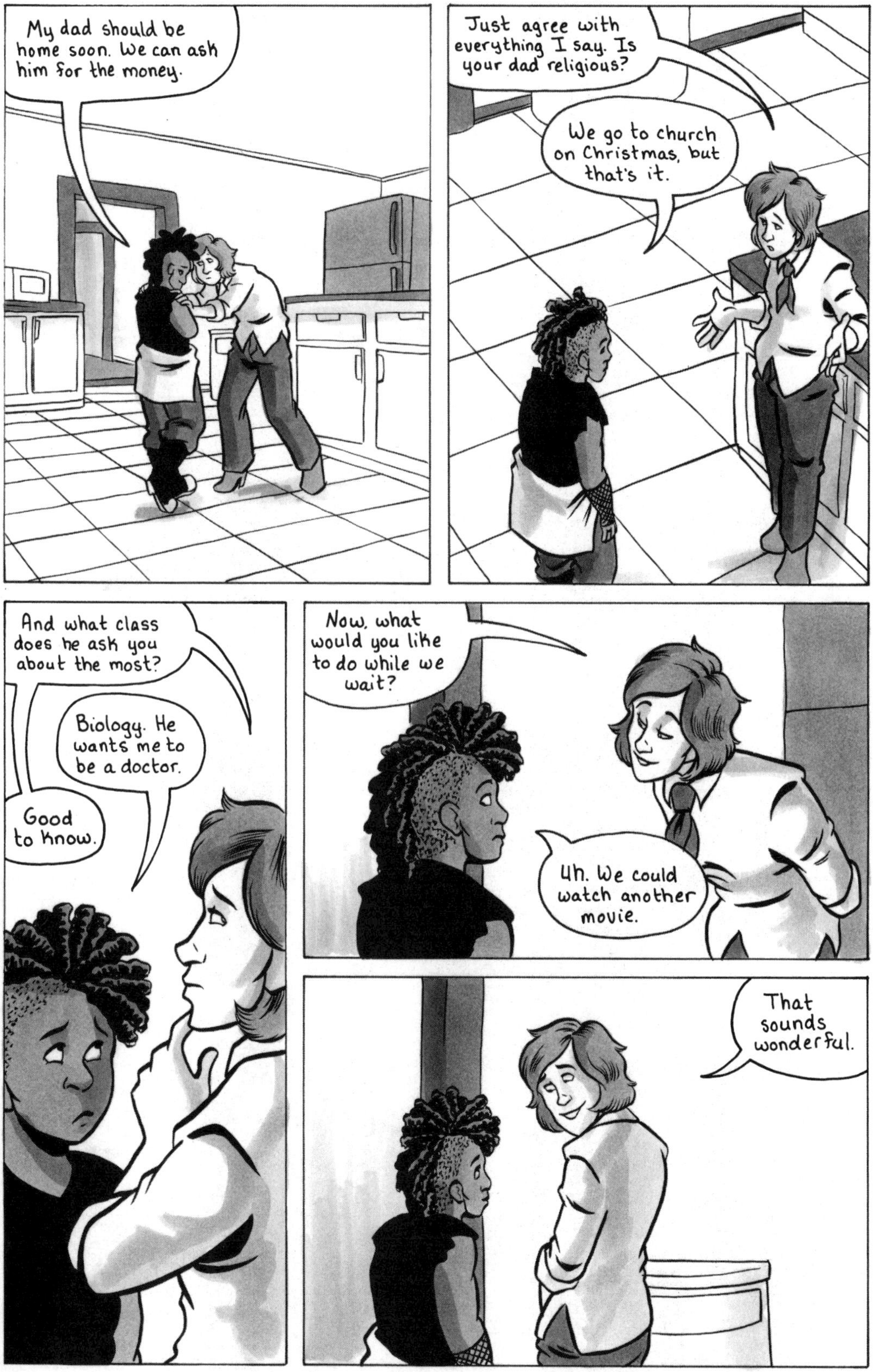
My dad should be home soon. We can ask him for the money.
Just agree with everything I say. Is your dad religious?
We go to church on Christmas, but that's it.
And what class does he ask you about the most?
Biology. He wants me to be a doctor.
Good to know.
Now, what would you like to do while we wait?
Uh. We could watch another movie.
That sounds wonderful.

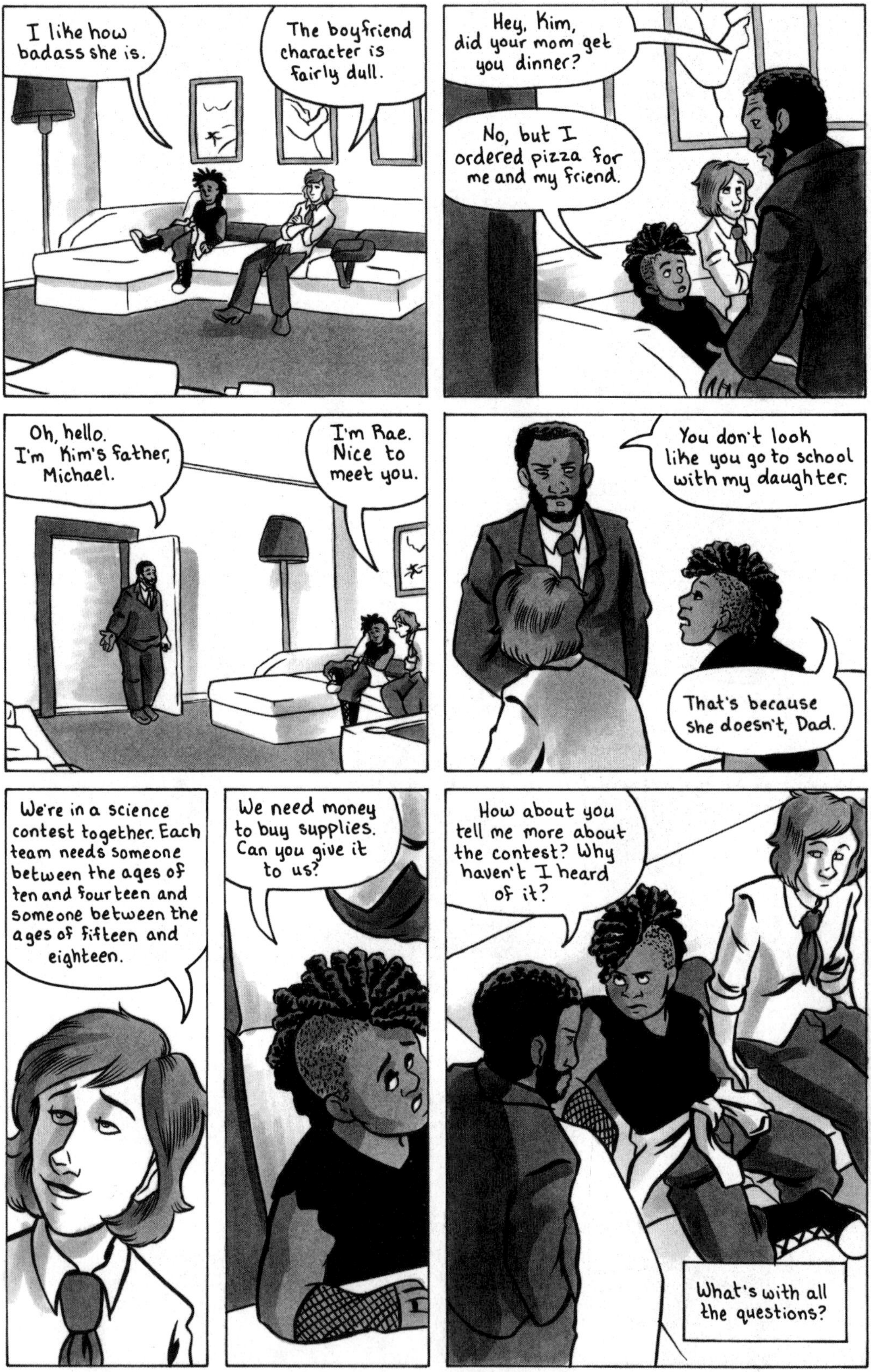
I like how badass she is.
The boyfriend character is fairly dull.
Hey, Kim, did your mom get you dinner?
No, but I ordered pizza for me and my friend.
Oh, hello. I'm Kim's father, Michael.
I'm Rae. Nice to meet you.
You don't look like you go to school with my daughter.
That's because she doesn't, Dad.
We're in a science contest together. Each team needs someone between the ages of ten and fourteen and someone between the ages of fifteen and eighteen.
We need money to buy supplies. Can you give it to us?
How about you tell me more about the contest? Why haven't I heard of it?
What's with all the questions?

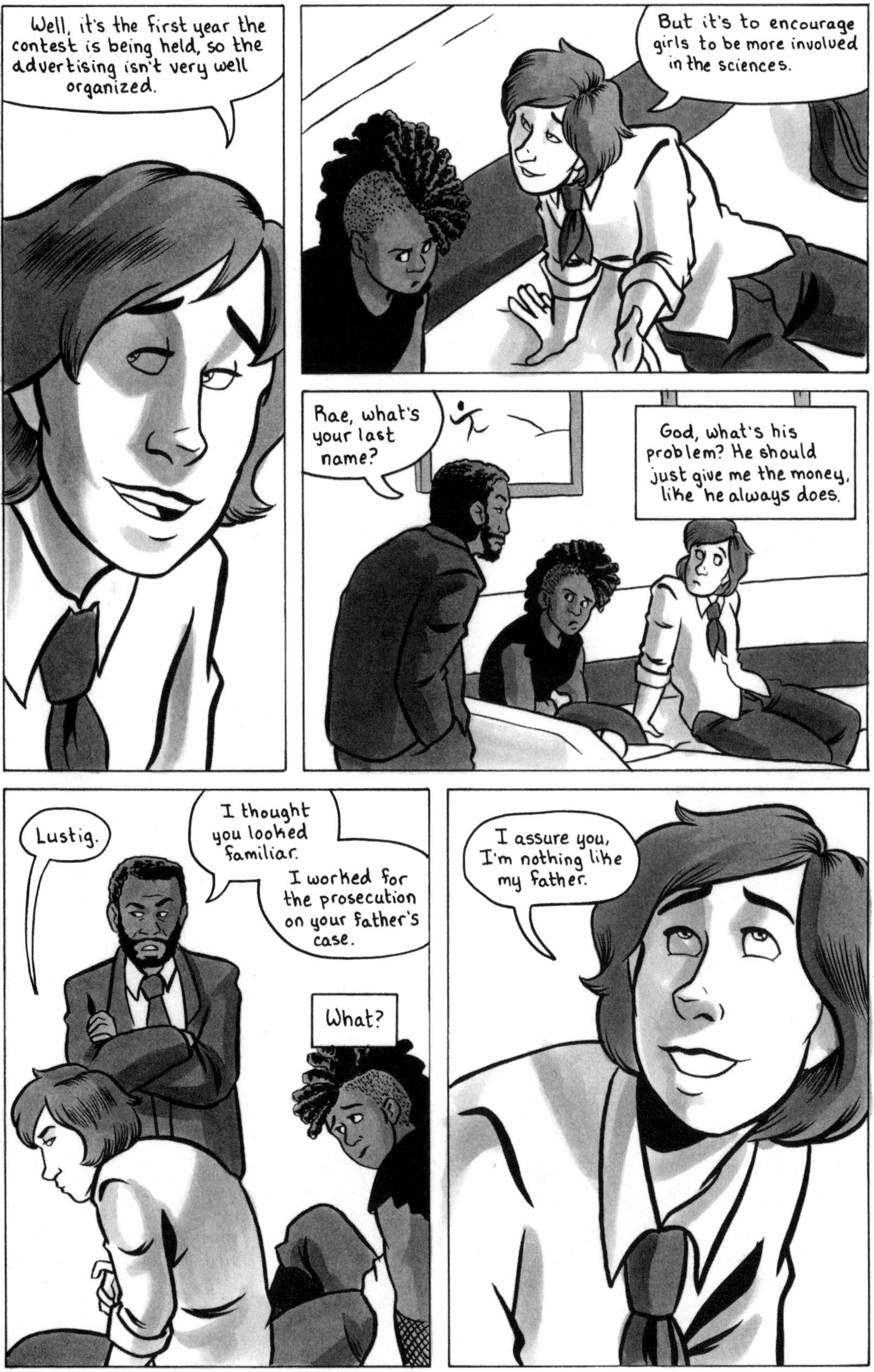
Well, it's the first year the contest is being held, so the advertising isn't very well organized.
But it's to encourage girls to be more involved in the sciences.
Rae, what's your last name?
God, what's his problem? He should just give me the money, like he always does.
Lustig.
I thought you looked familiar.
I worked for the prosecution on your father's case.
What?
I assure you, I'm nothing like my father.

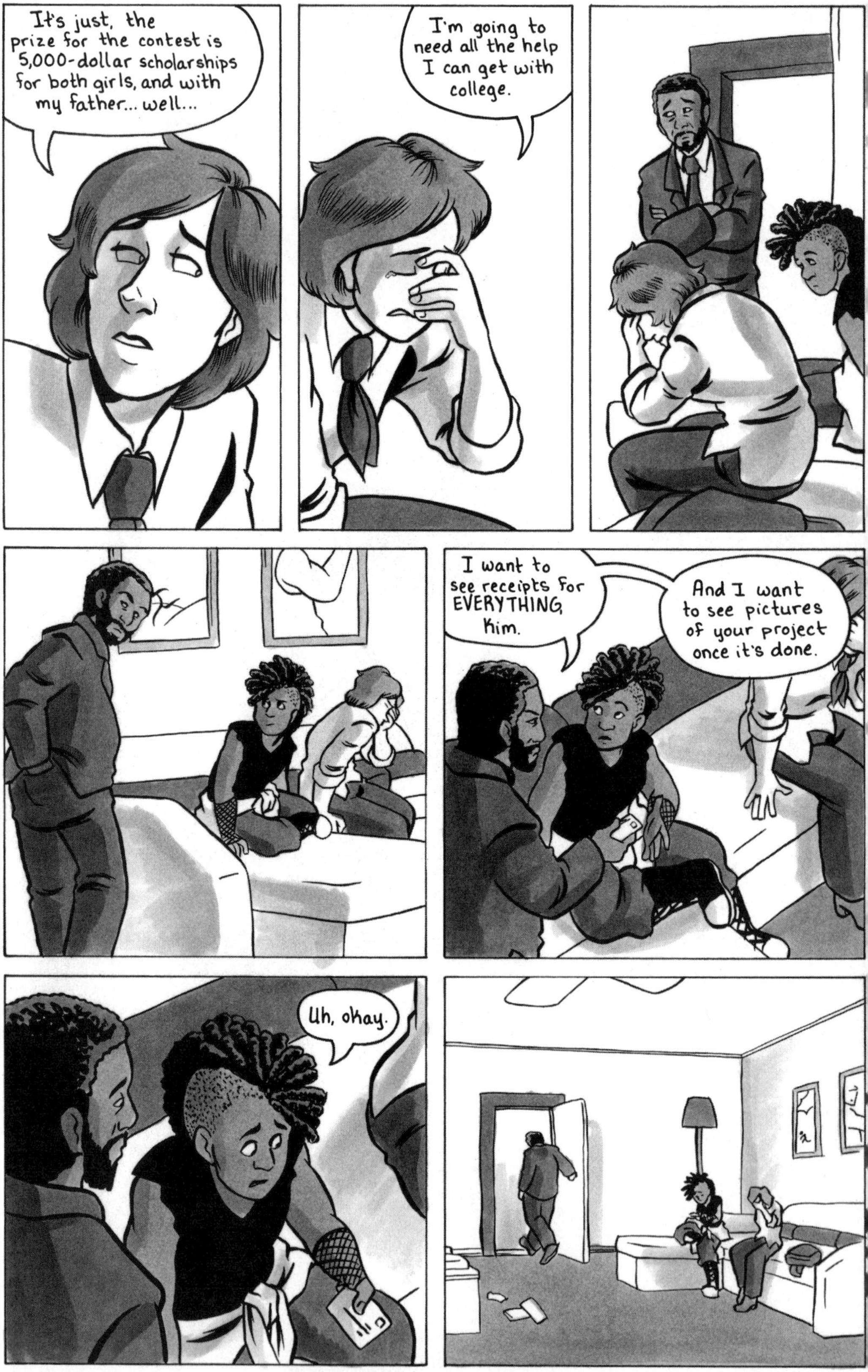
It's just, the prize for the contest is 5,000-dollar scholarships for both girls, and with my father... well...
I'm going to need all the help I can get with college.
I want to see receipts for EVERYTHING, Kim.
And I want to see pictures of your project once it's done.
Uh, okay.

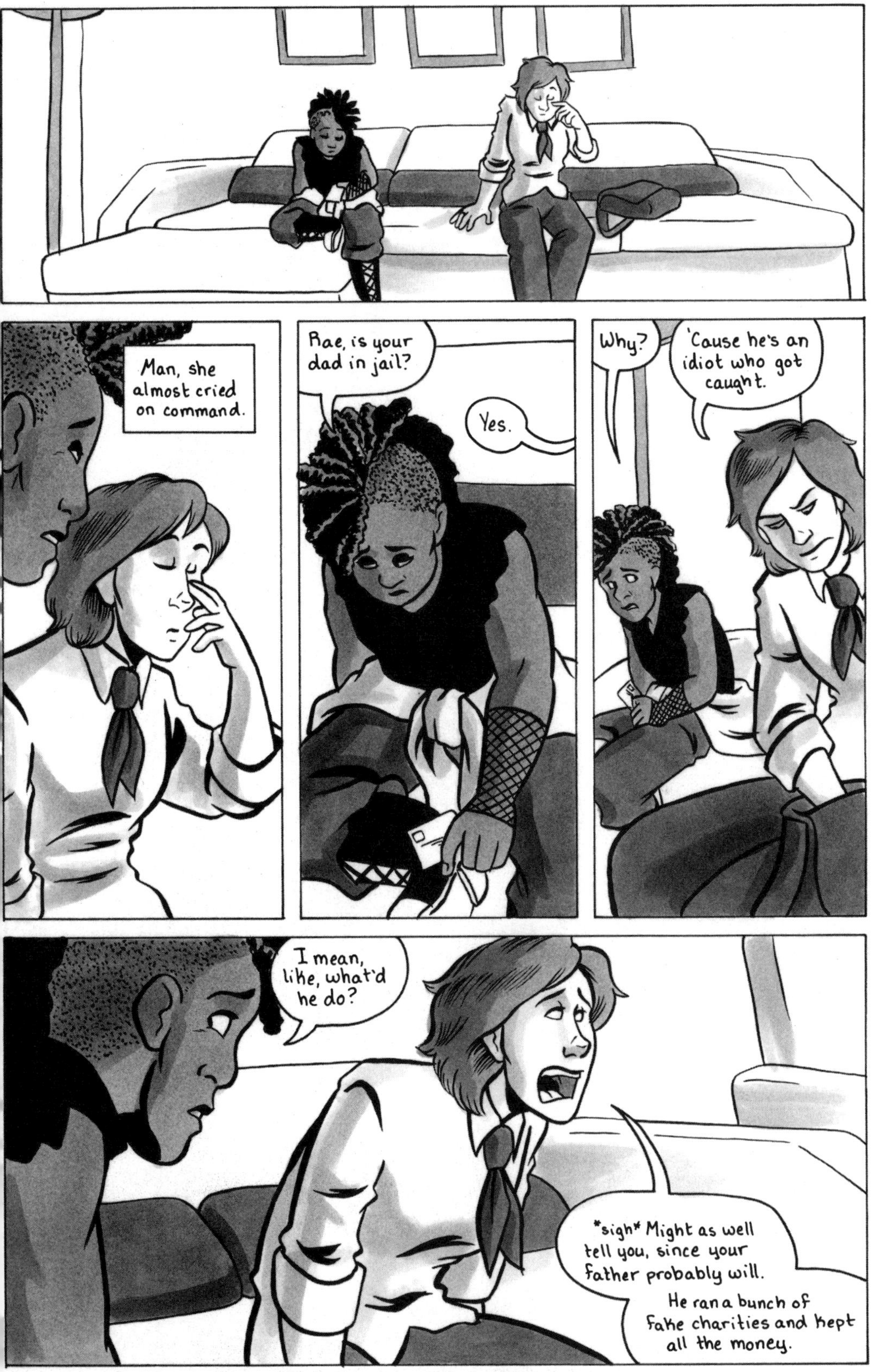

Man, she almost cried on command.
Rae, is your dad in jail?
Yes.
Why?
'Cause he's an idiot who got caught.
I mean, like, what'd he do?
sigh Might as well tell you, since your father probably will.
He ran a bunch of fake charities and kept all the money.

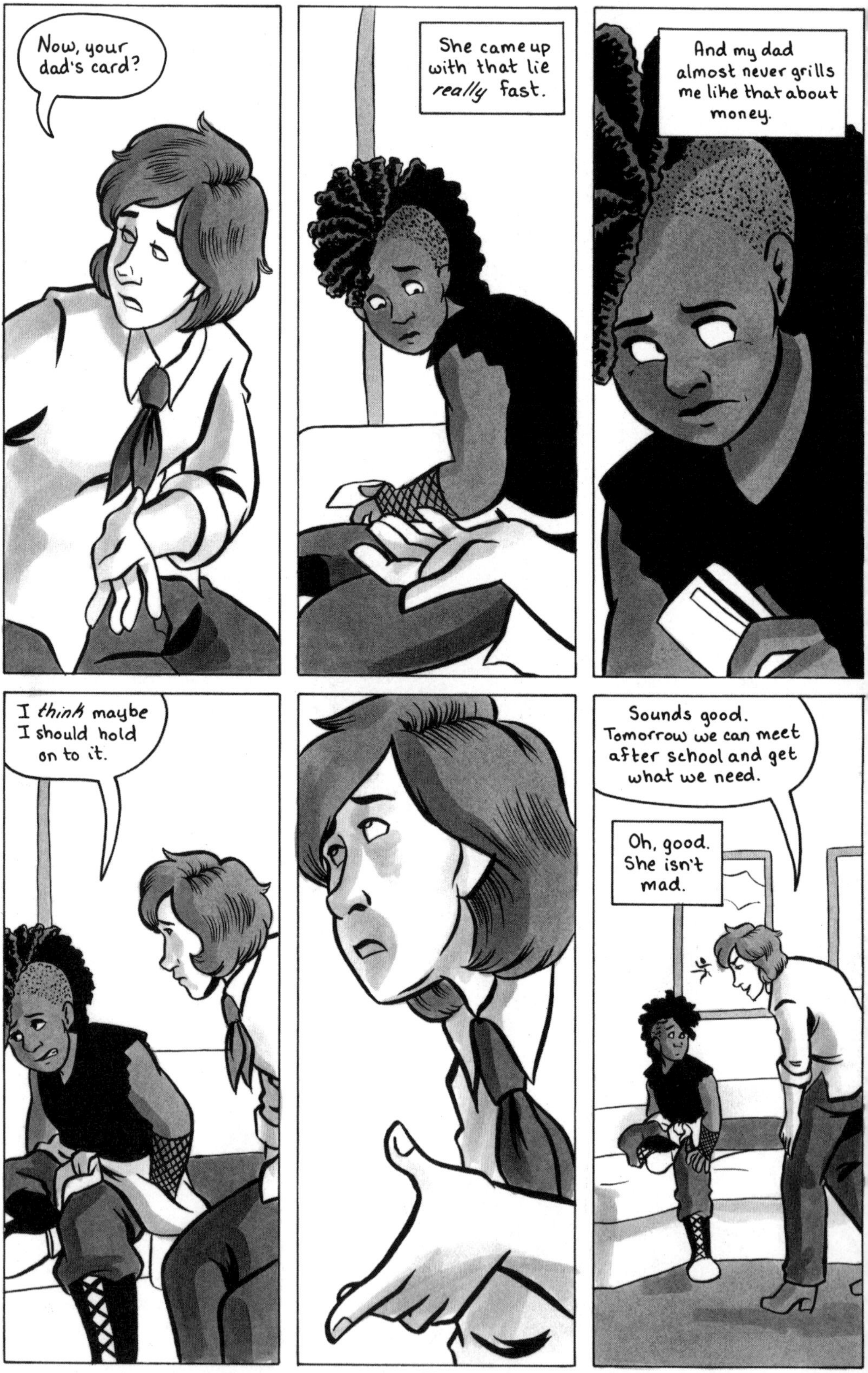
Now, your dad's card?
She came up with that lie *really* fast.
And my dad almost never grills me like that about money.
I *think* maybe I should hold on to it.
Sounds good. Tomorrow we can meet after school and get what we need.
Oh, good. She isn't mad.

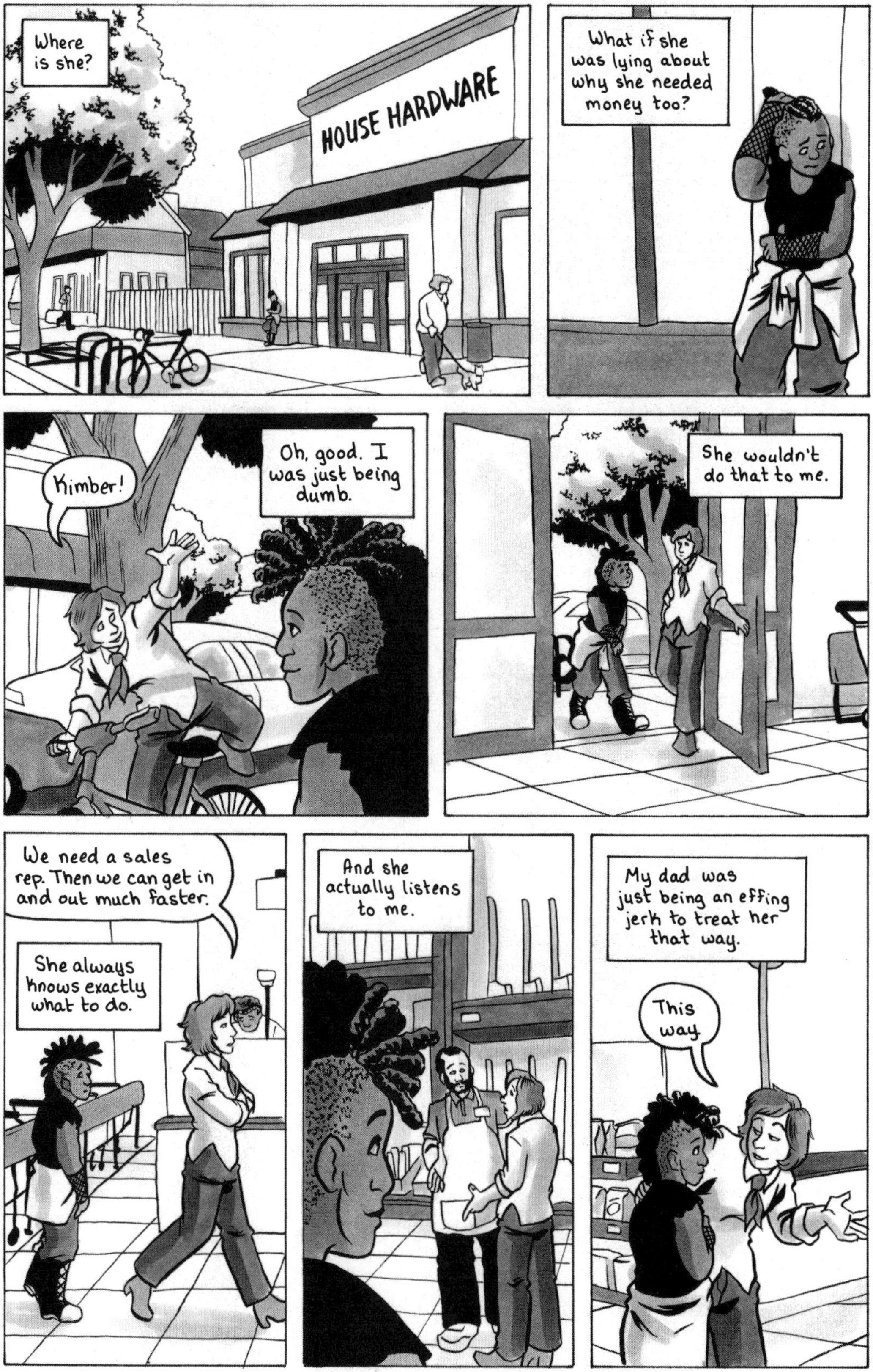
Where is she?
HOUSE HARDWARE
What if she was lying about why she needed money too?
Kimber!
Oh, good. I was just being dumb.
She wouldn't do that to me.
We need a sales rep. Then we can get in and out much faster.
She always knows exactly what to do.
And she actually listens to me.
My dad was just being an effing jerk to treat her that way.
This way.

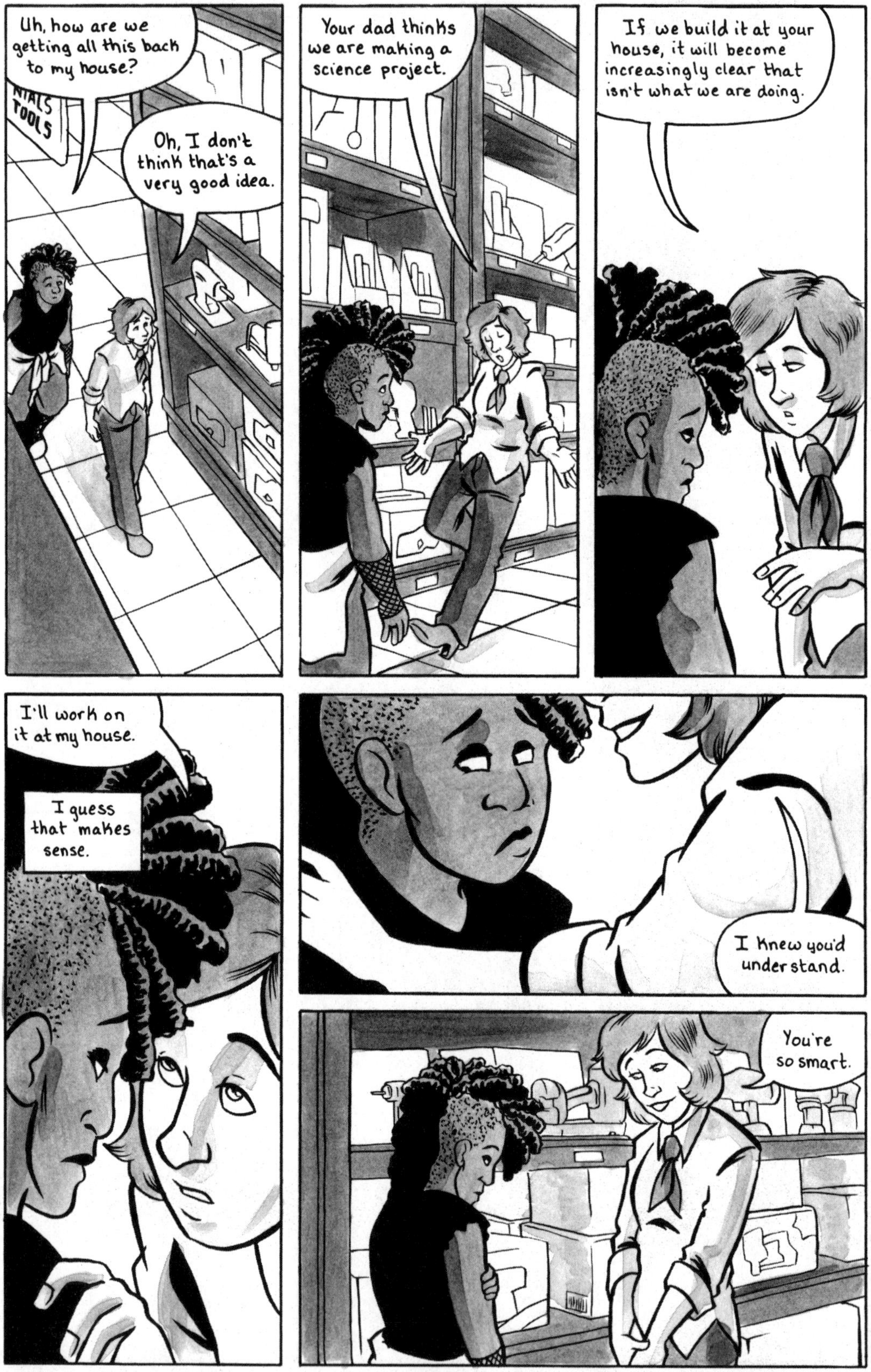
Uh, how are we getting all this back to my house?
Oh, I don't think that's a very good idea.
Your dad thinks we are making a science project.
If we build it at your house, it will become increasingly clear that isn't what we are doing.
I'll work on it at my house.
I guess that makes sense.
I knew you'd understand.
You're so smart.

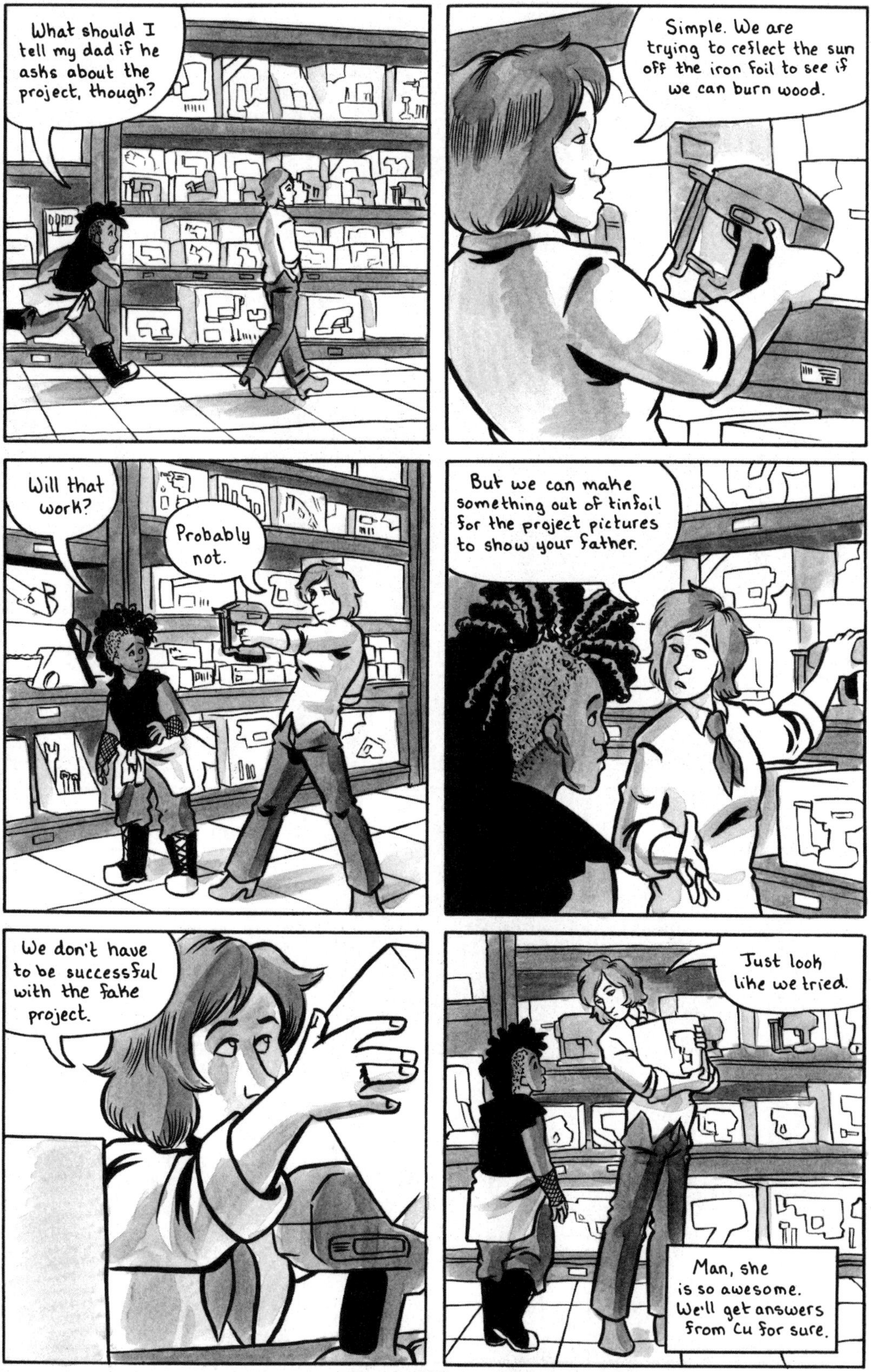
What should I tell my dad if he asks about the project, though?
Simple. We are trying to reflect the sun off the iron foil to see if we can burn wood.
Will that work?
Probably not.
But we can make something out of tinfoil for the project pictures to show your father.
We don't have to be successful with the fake project.
Just look like we tried.
Man, she is so awesome. We'll get answers from Cu for sure.

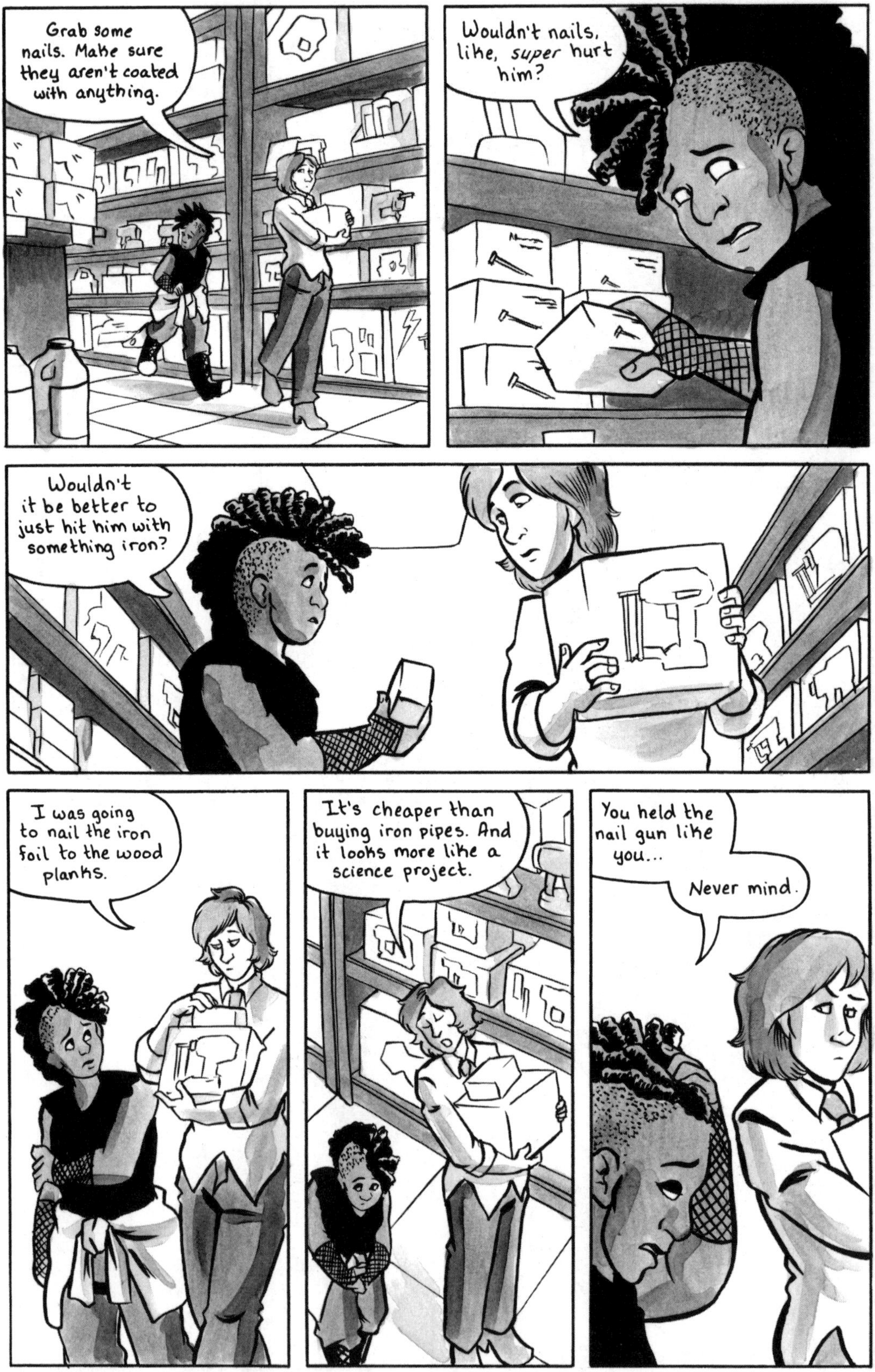
Grab some nails. Make sure they aren't coated with anything.
Wouldn't nails, like, *super* hurt him?
Wouldn't it be better to just hit him with something iron?
I was going to nail the iron foil to the wood planks.
It's cheaper than buying iron pipes. And it looks more like a science project.
You held the nail gun like you...
Never mind.

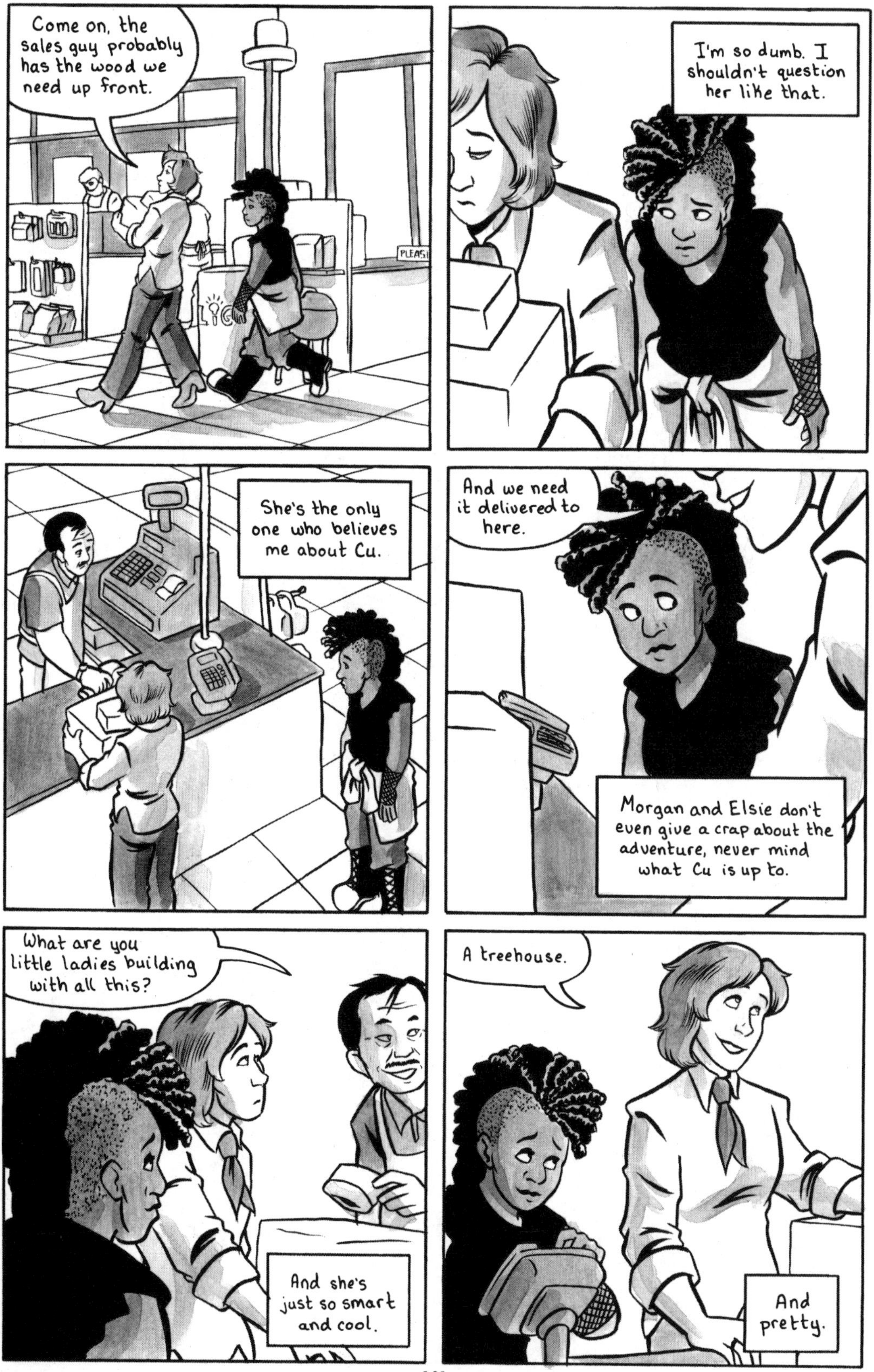
Come on, the sales guy probably has the wood we need up front.
PLEAS
I'm so dumb. I shouldn't question her like that.
She's the only one who believes me about Cu.
And we need it delivered to here.
Morgan and Elsie don't even give a crap about the adventure, never mind what Cu is up to.
What are you little ladies building with all this?
And she's just so smart and cool.
A treehouse.
And pretty.

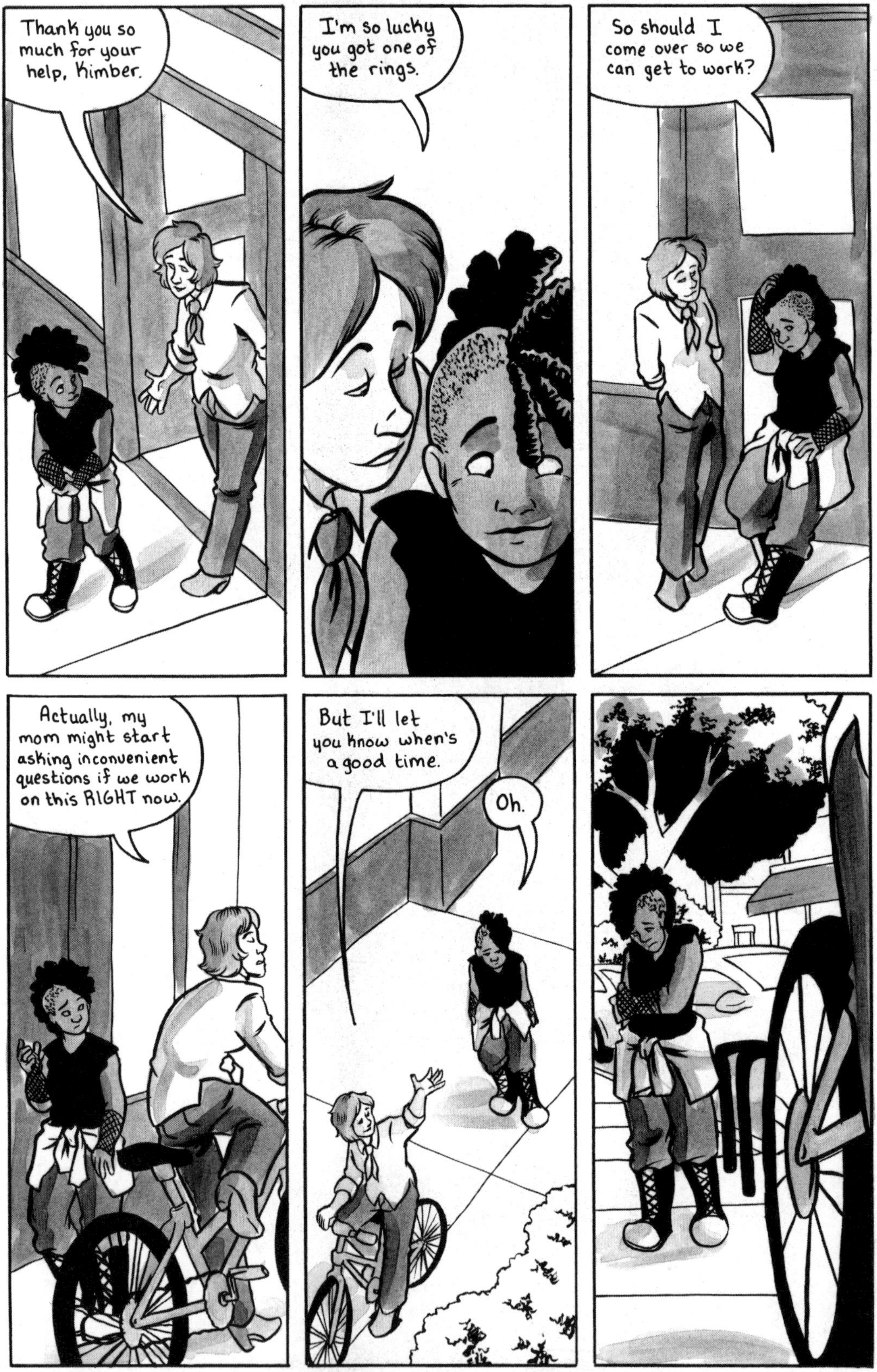

Thank you so much for your help, Kimber.
I'm so lucky you got one of the rings.
So should I come over so we can get to work?
Actually, my mom might start asking inconvenient questions if we work on this RIGHT now.
But I'll let you know when's a good time.
Oh.

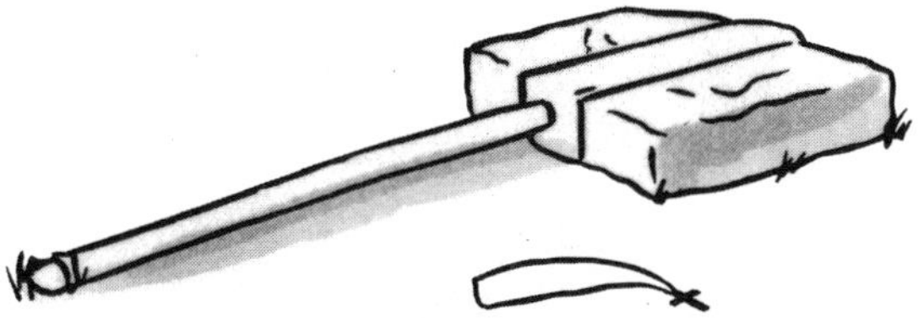

CHAPTER 7:

As All Decent Men Must Be, If You Assume That Decency Can't Exist

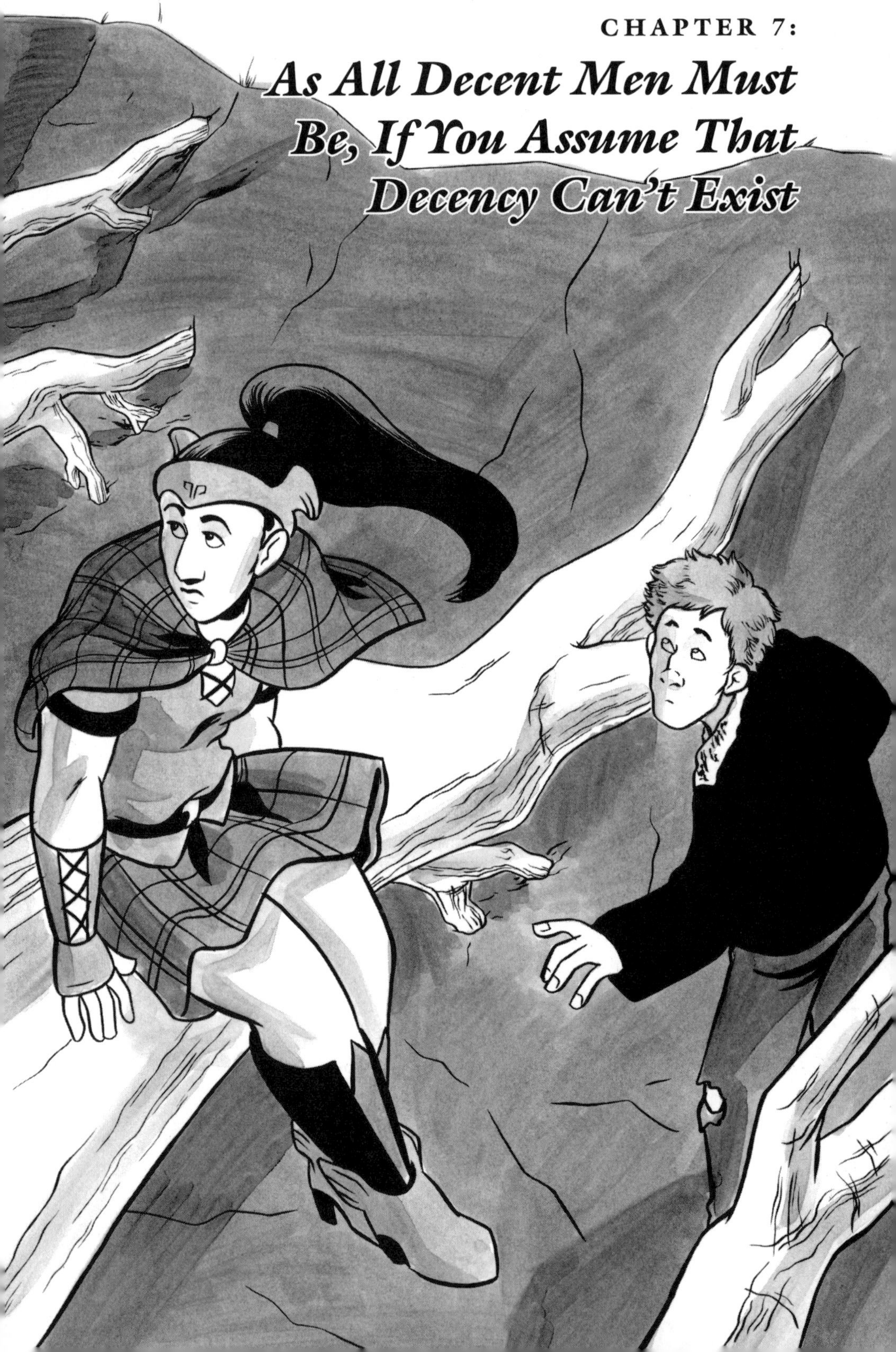

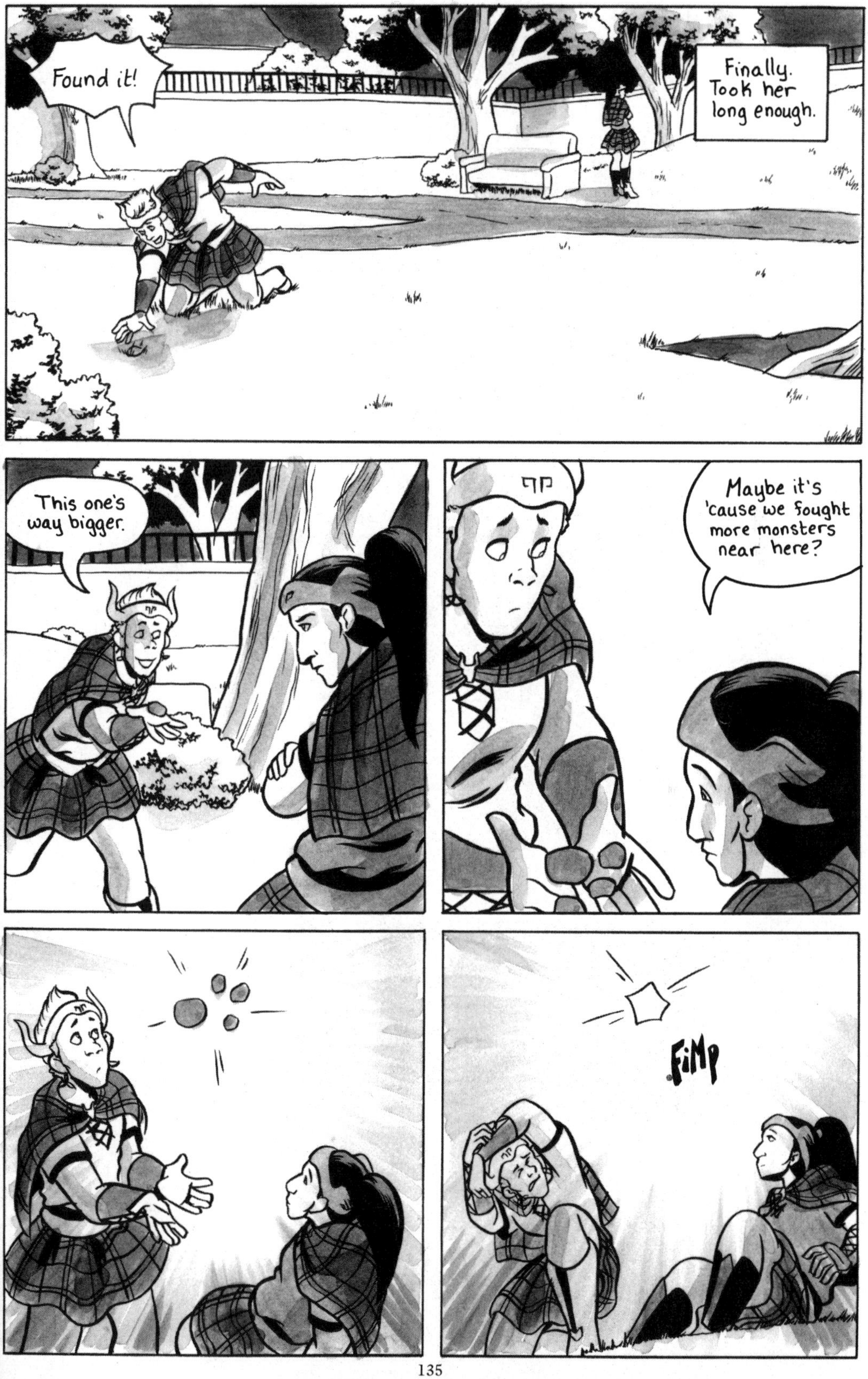
Found it!
Finally. Took her long enough.
This one's way bigger.
Maybe it's 'cause we fought more monsters near here?
FiMp

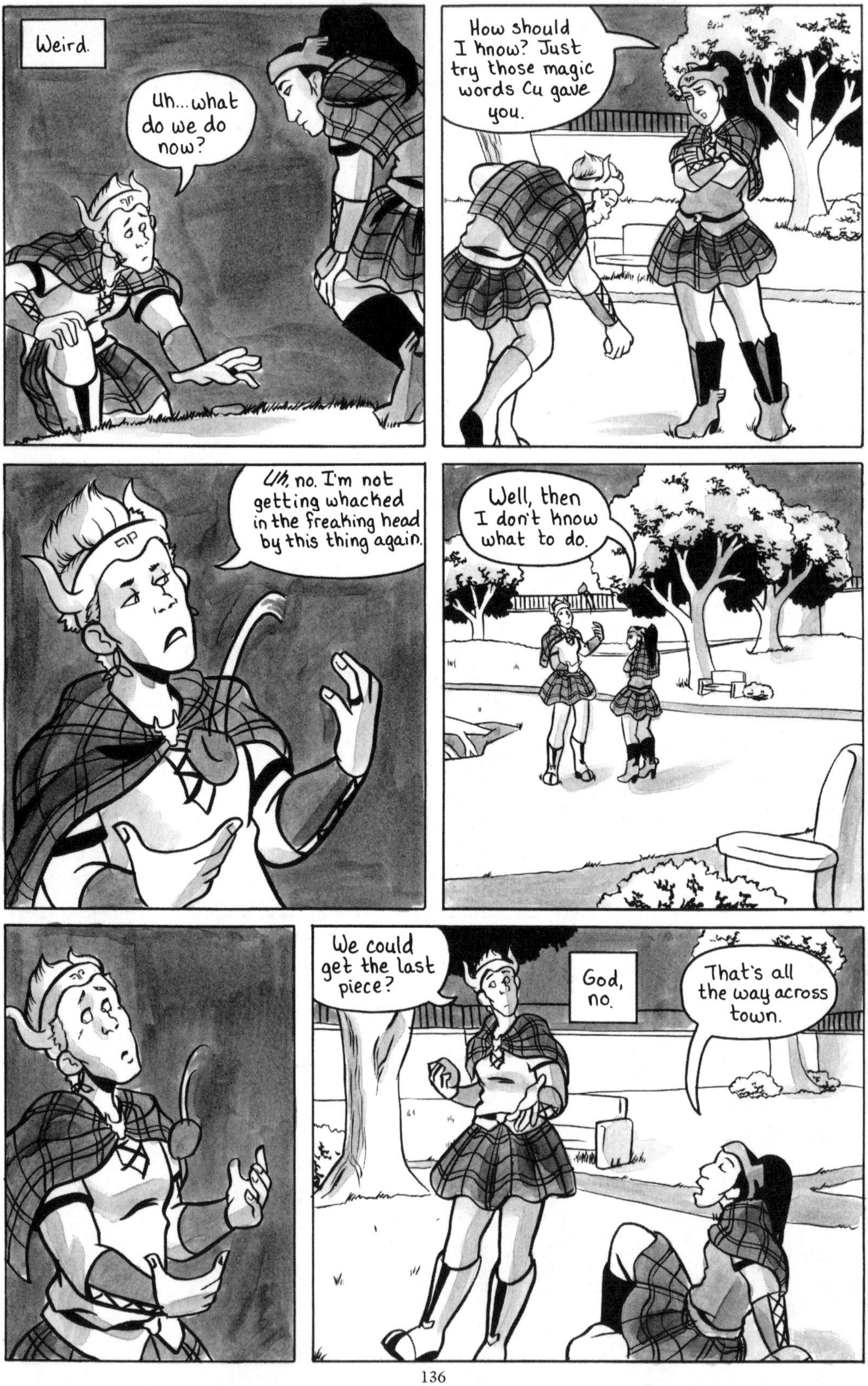
Weird.
Uh... what do we do now?
How should I know? Just try those magic words Cu gave you.
Uh, no. I'm not getting whacked in the freaking head by this thing again.
Well, then I don't know what to do.
We could get the last piece?
God, no.
That's all the way across town.

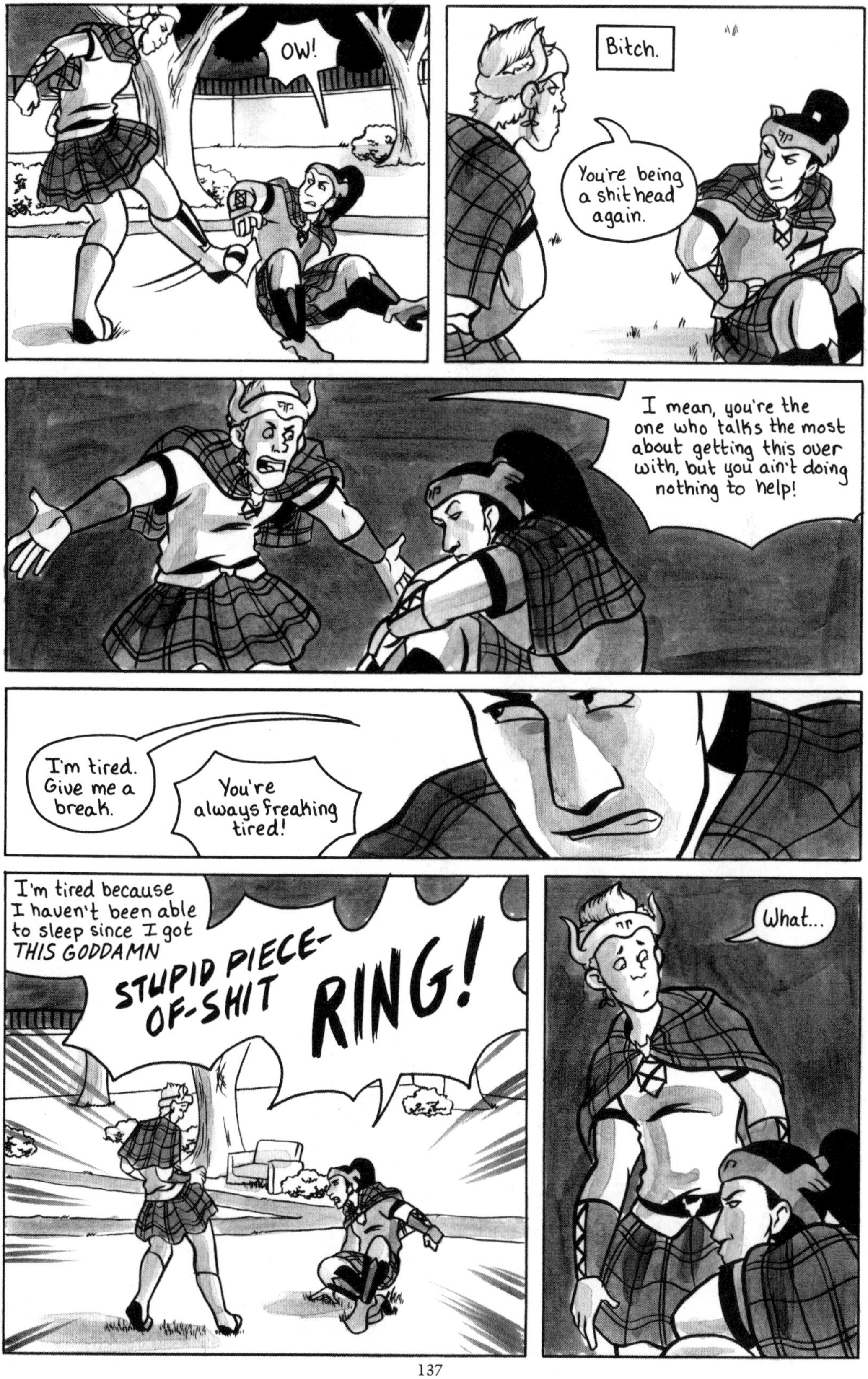
OW!
Bitch.
You're being a shithead again.
I mean, you're the one who talks the most about getting this over with, but you ain't doing nothing to help!
I'm tired. Give me a break.
You're always freaking tired!
I'm tired because I haven't been able to sleep since I got THIS GODDAMN
STUPID PIECE-OF-SHIT RING!
What...

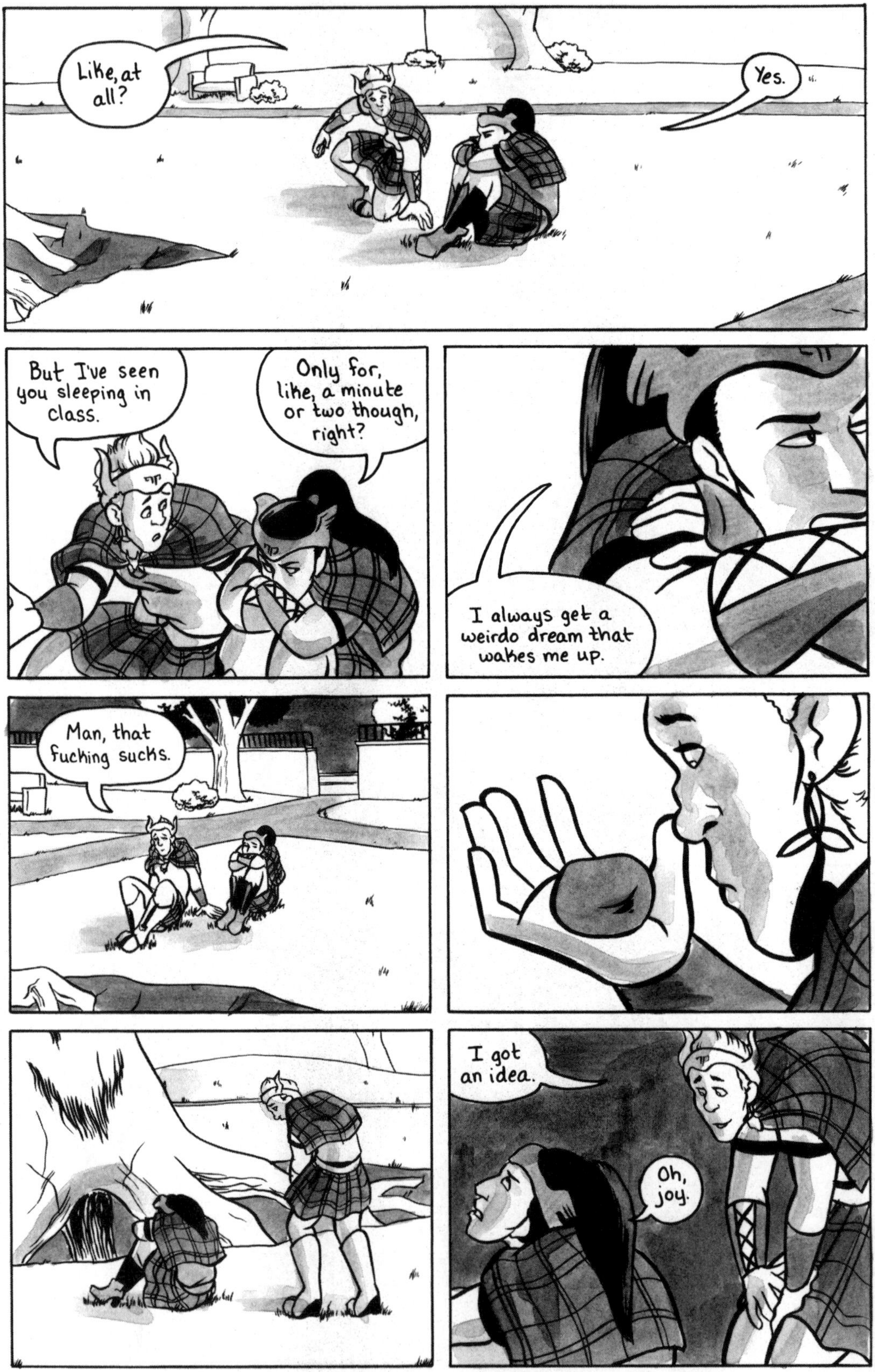
Like, at all?
Yes.
But I've seen you sleeping in class.
Only for, like, a minute or two though, right?
I always get a weirdo dream that wakes me up.
Man, that fucking sucks.
I got an idea.
Oh, joy.

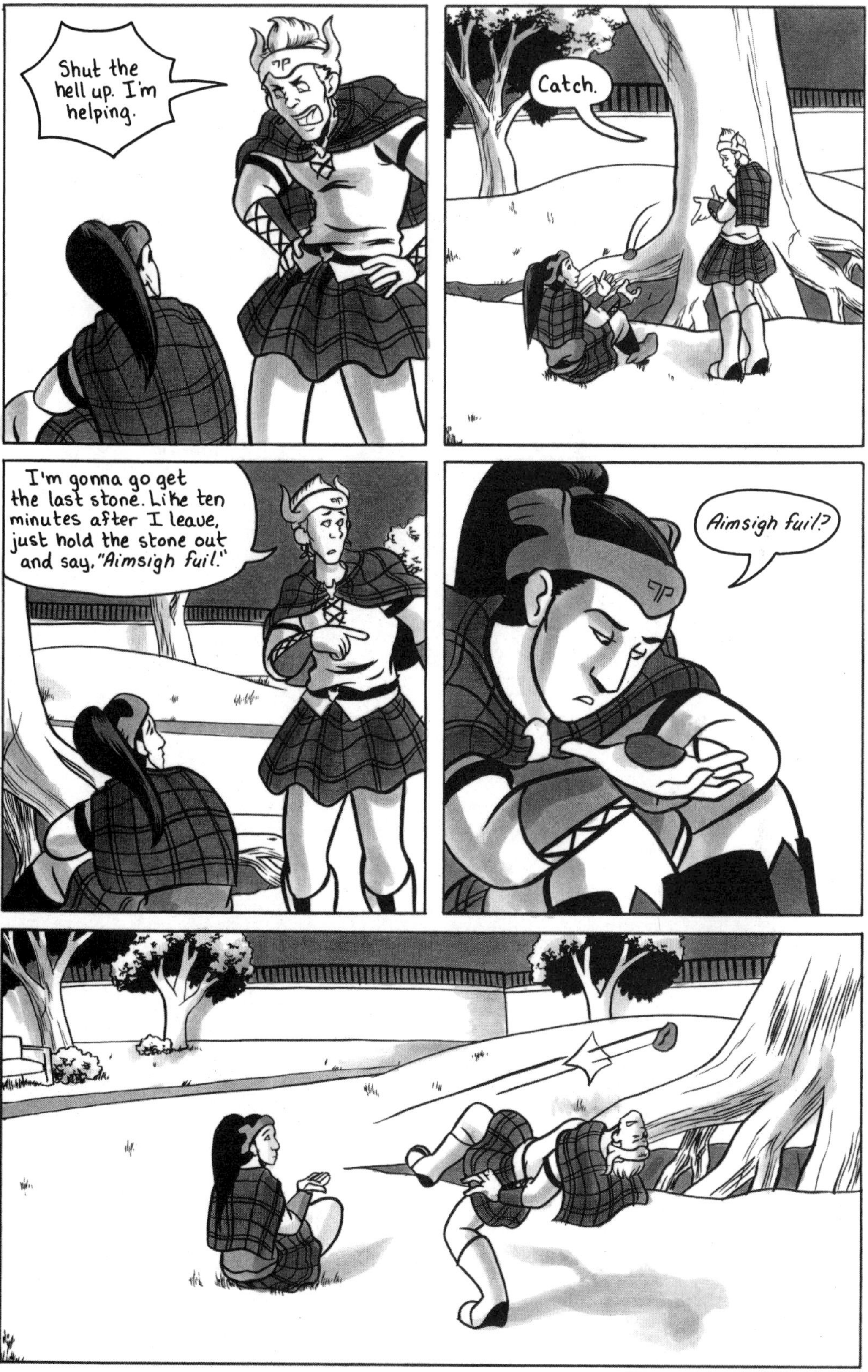
Shut the hell up. I'm helping.
Catch.
I'm gonna go get the last stone. Like ten minutes after I leave, just hold the stone out and say, "Aimsigh fuil."
Aimsigh fuil?

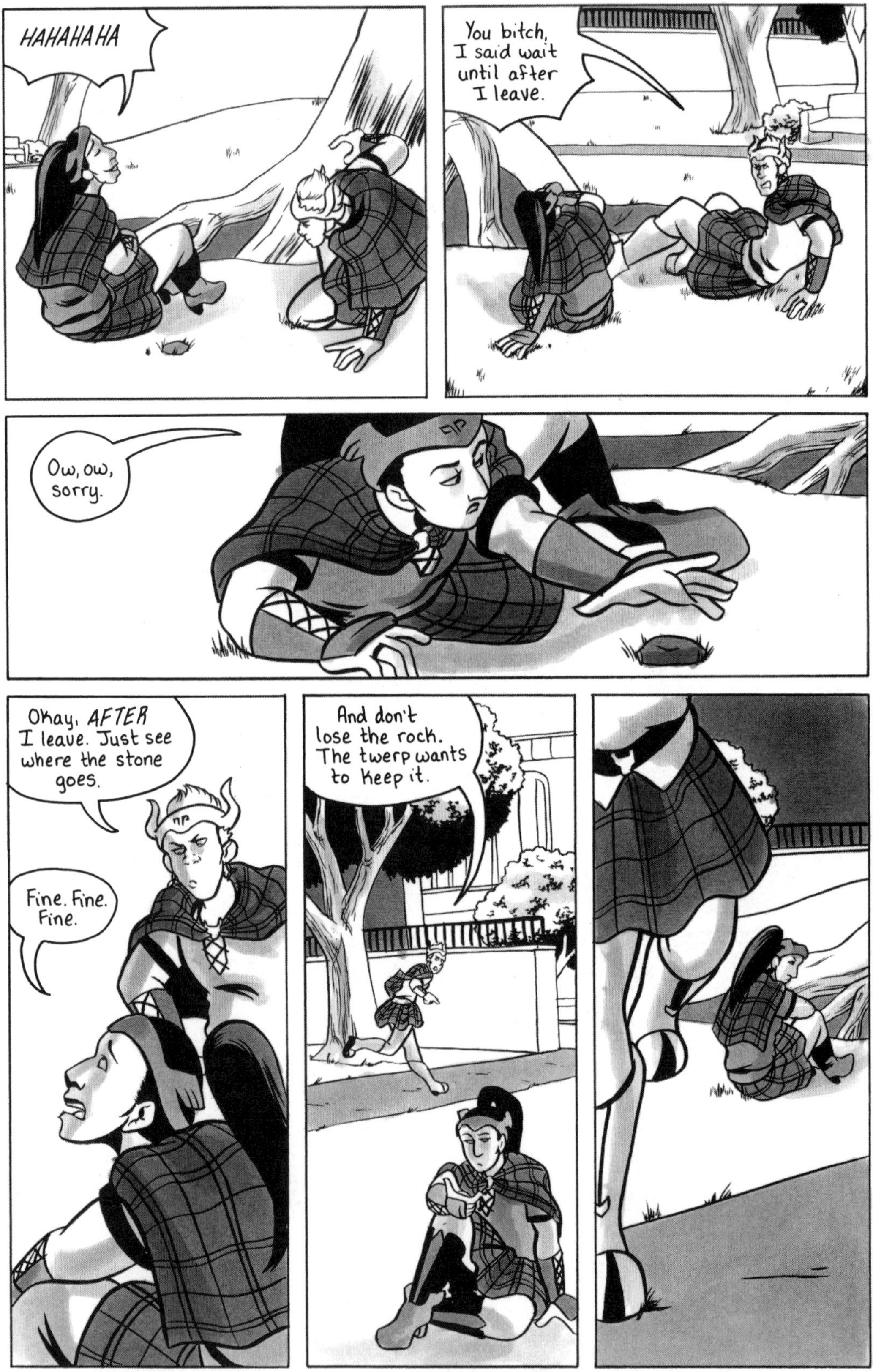
HAHAHAHA
You bitch, I said wait until after I leave.
Ow, ow, sorry.
Okay, AFTER I leave. Just see where the stone goes.
Fine. Fine. Fine.
And don't lose the rock. The twerp wants to keep it.

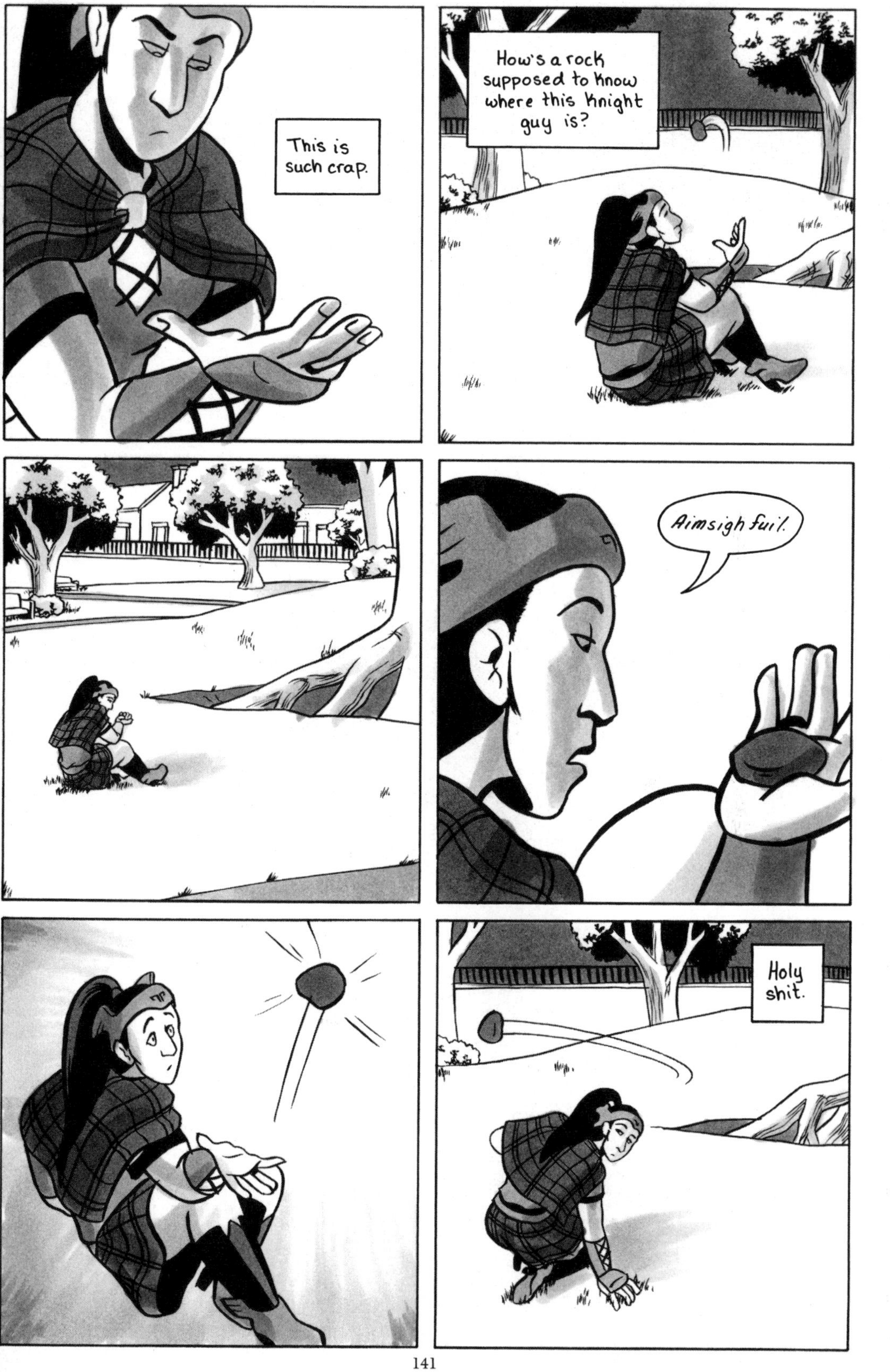
This is such crap.
How's a rock supposed to know where this knight guy is?
Aimsigh fuil.
Holy shit.

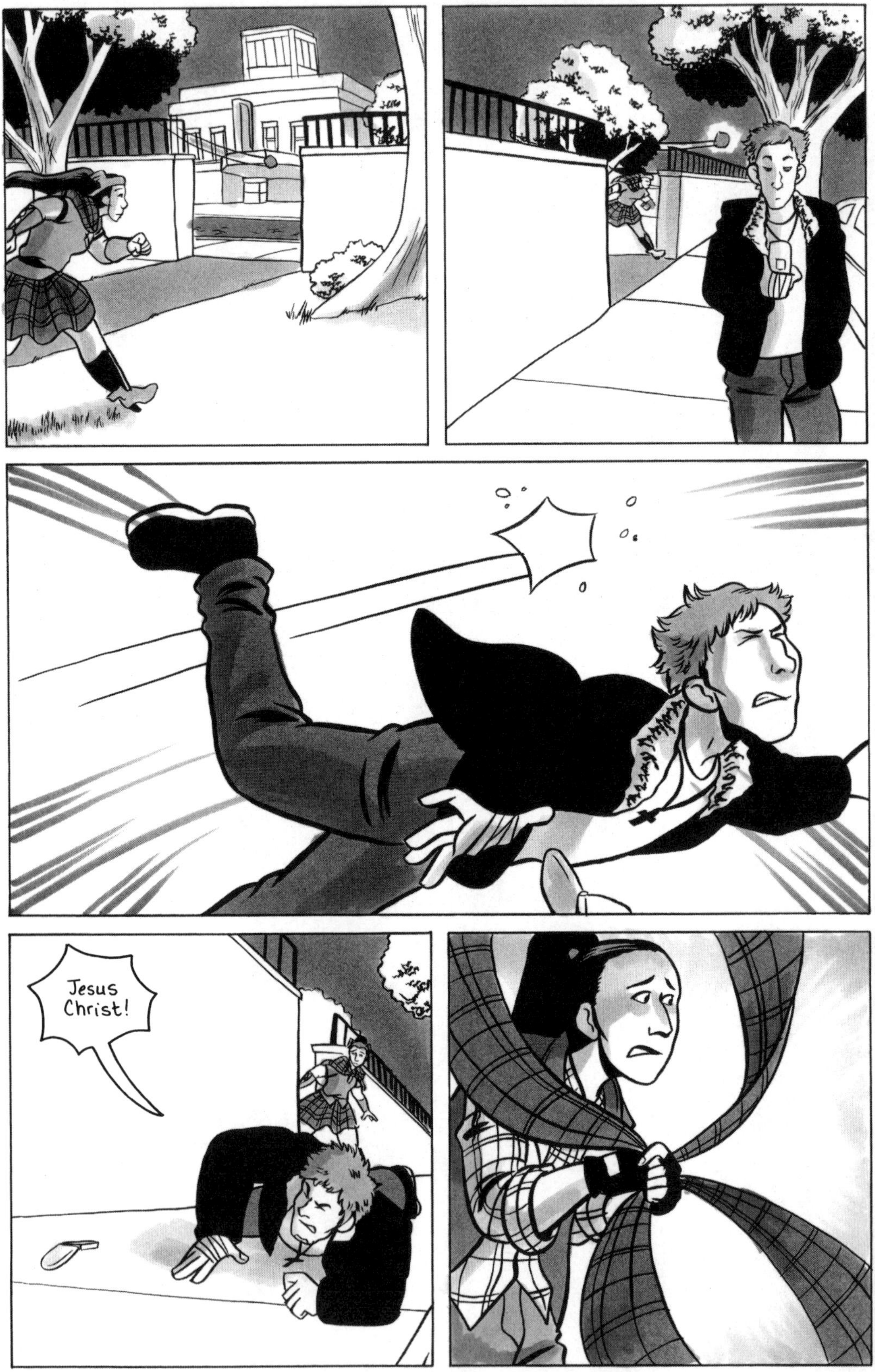
Jesus Christ!

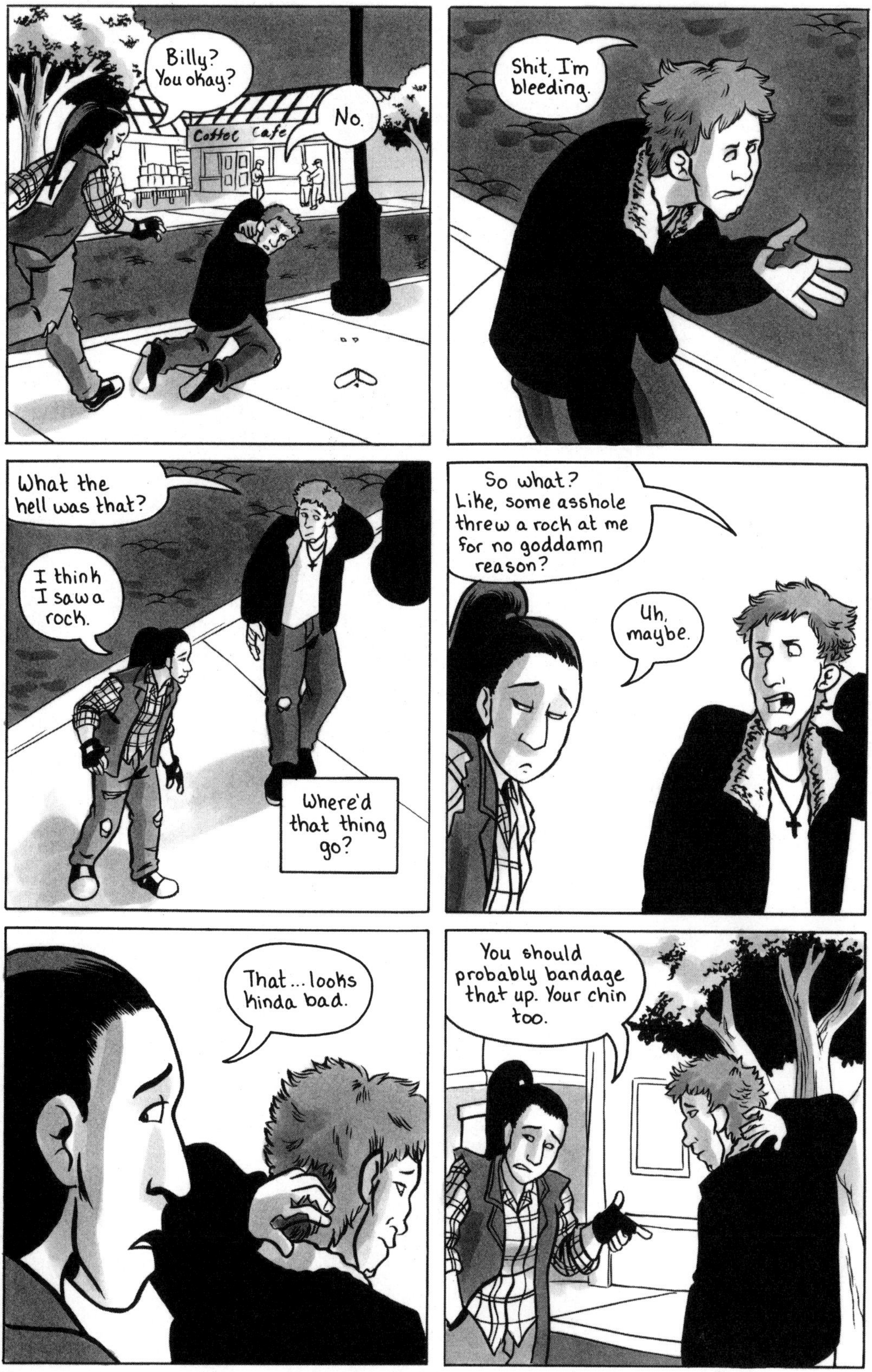
Billy? You okay?
Coffee Cafe
No.
Shit, I'm bleeding.
What the hell was that?
I think I saw a rock.
Where'd that thing go?
So what? Like, some asshole threw a rock at me for no goddamn reason?
Uh, maybe.
That... looks kinda bad.
You should probably bandage that up. Your chin too.

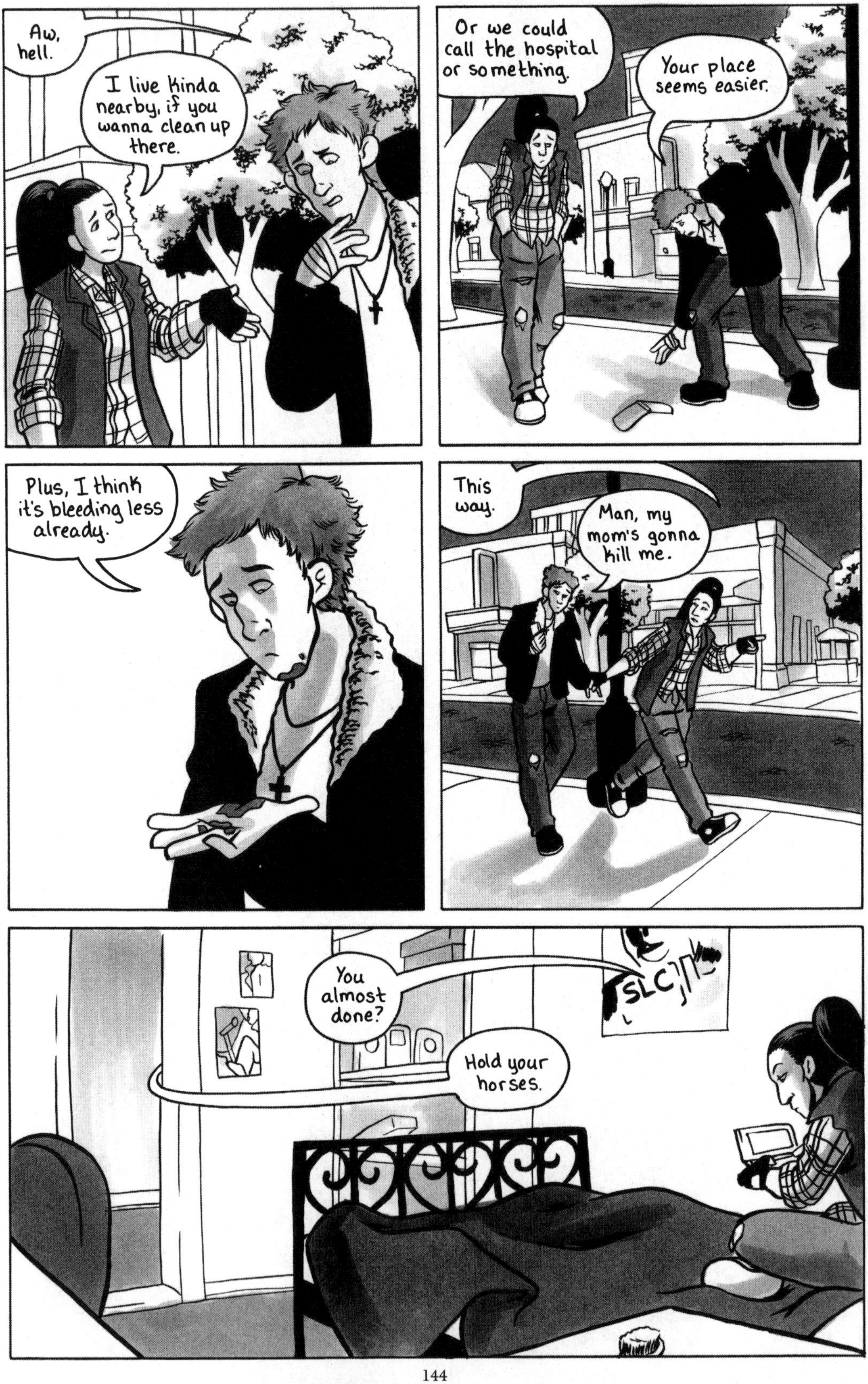
Aw, hell.
I live kinda nearby, if you wanna clean up there.
Or we could call the hospital or something.
Your place seems easier.
Plus, I think it's bleeding less already.
This way.
Man, my mom's gonna kill me.
SLC
You almost done?
Hold your horses.

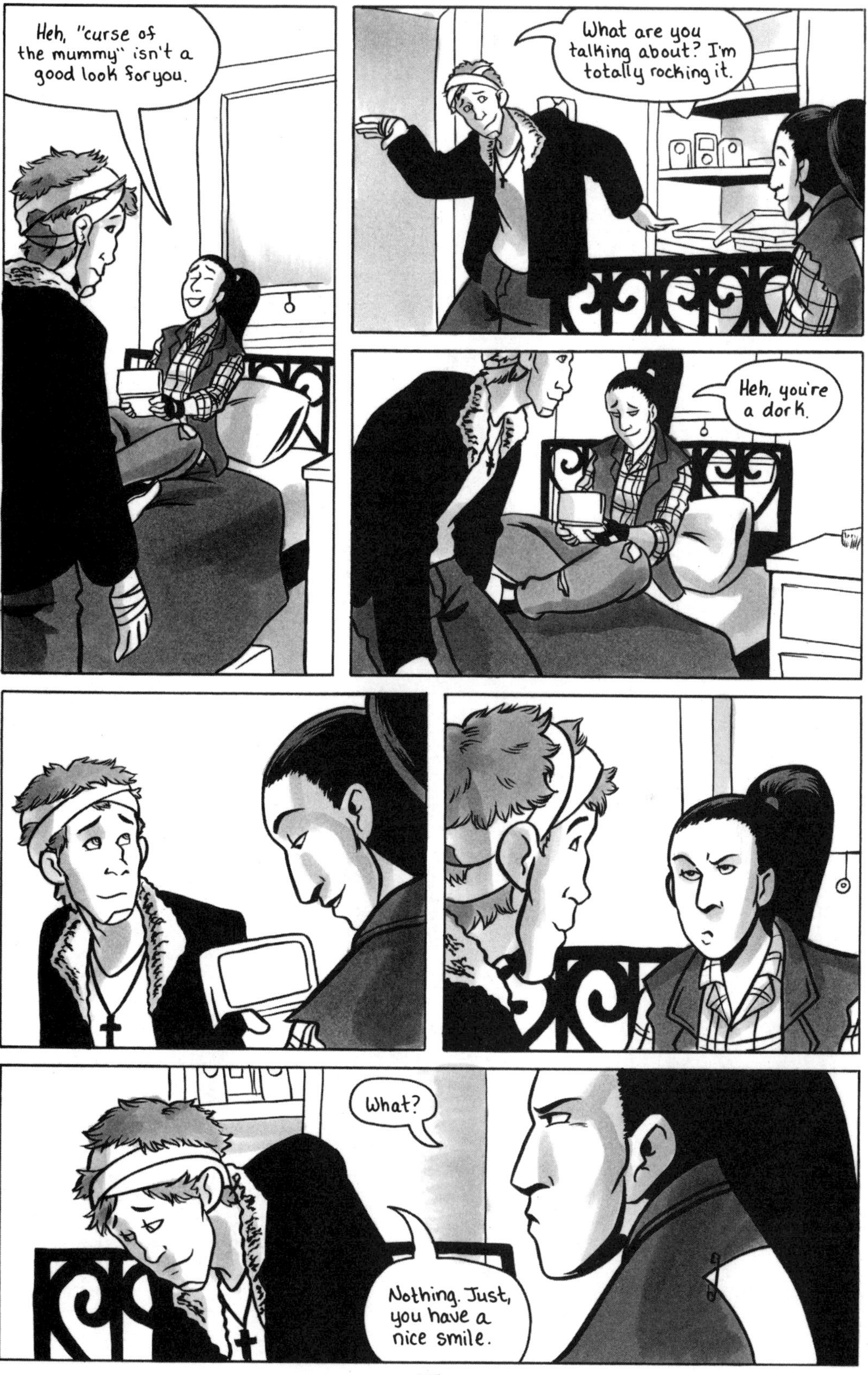

Heh, "curse of the mummy" isn't a good look for you.
What are you talking about? I'm totally rocking it.
Heh, you're a dork.
What?
Nothing. Just, you have a nice smile.

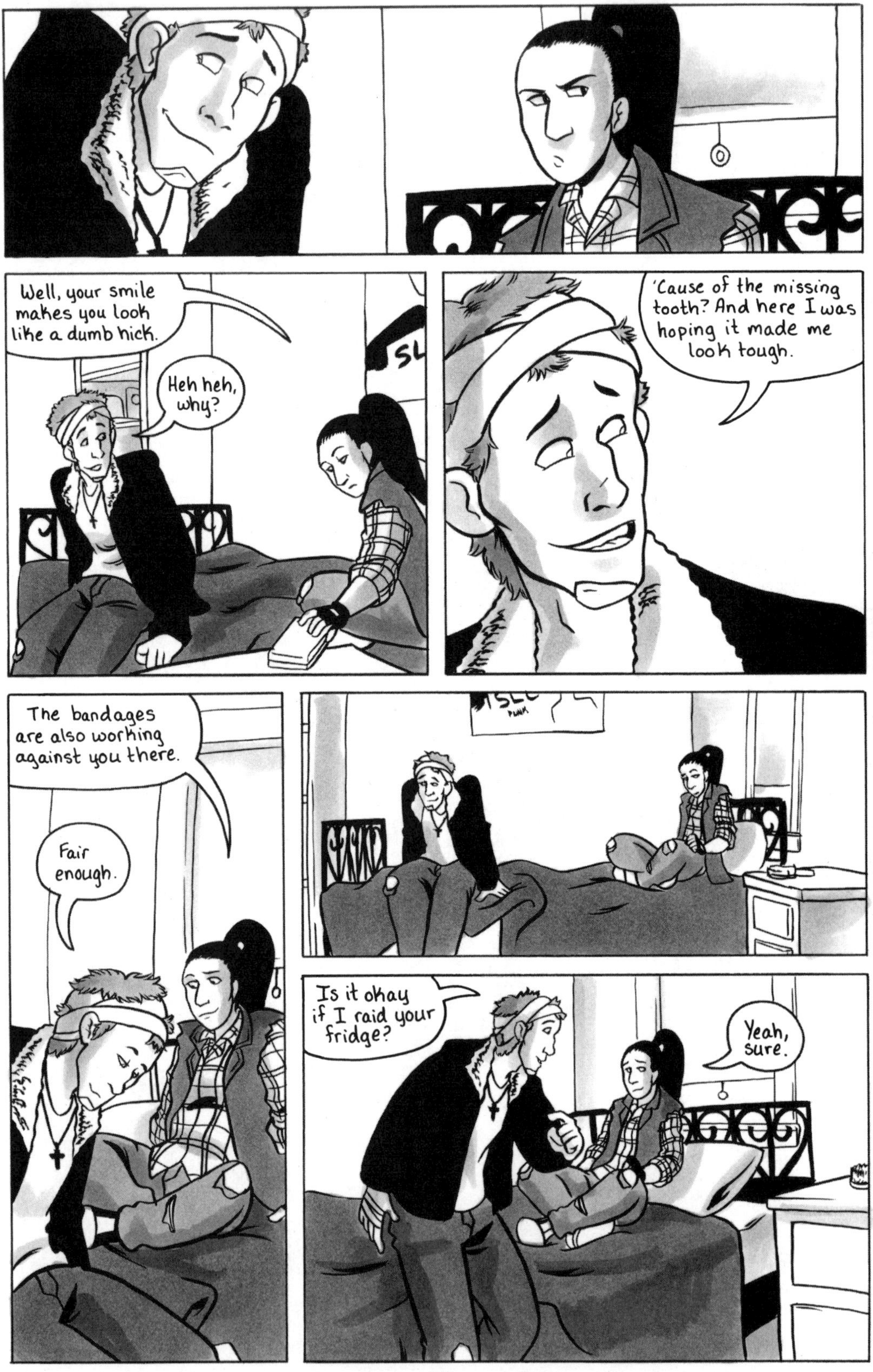
Well, your smile makes you look like a dumb hick.
Heh heh, why?
'Cause of the missing tooth? And here I was hoping it made me look tough.
The bandages are also working against you there.
Fair enough.
Is it okay if I raid your fridge?
Yeah, sure.

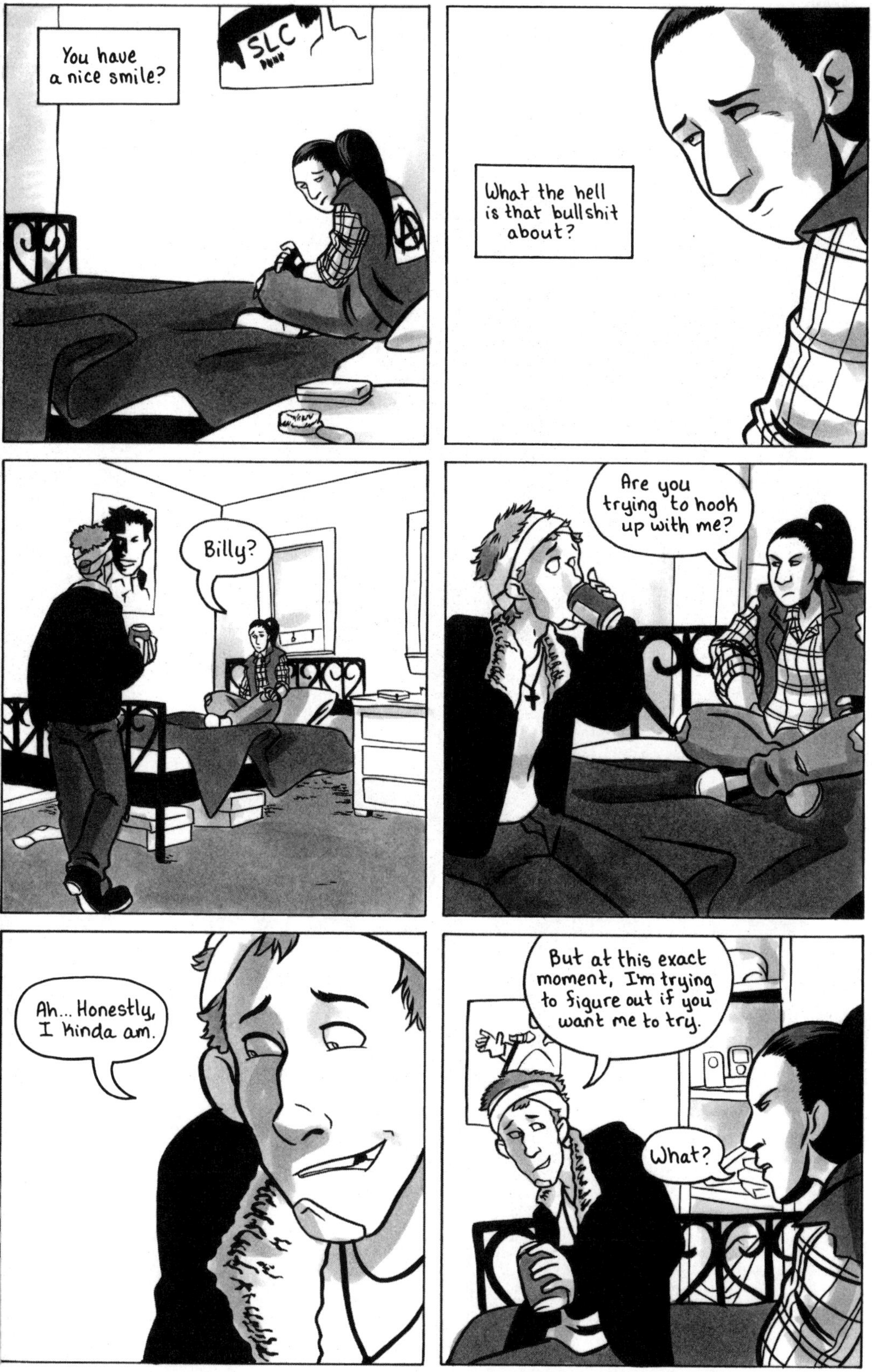
You have a nice smile?
SLC
What the hell is that bullshit about?
Billy?
Are you trying to hook up with me?
Ah... Honestly, I kinda am.
But at this exact moment, I'm trying to figure out if you want me to try.
What?

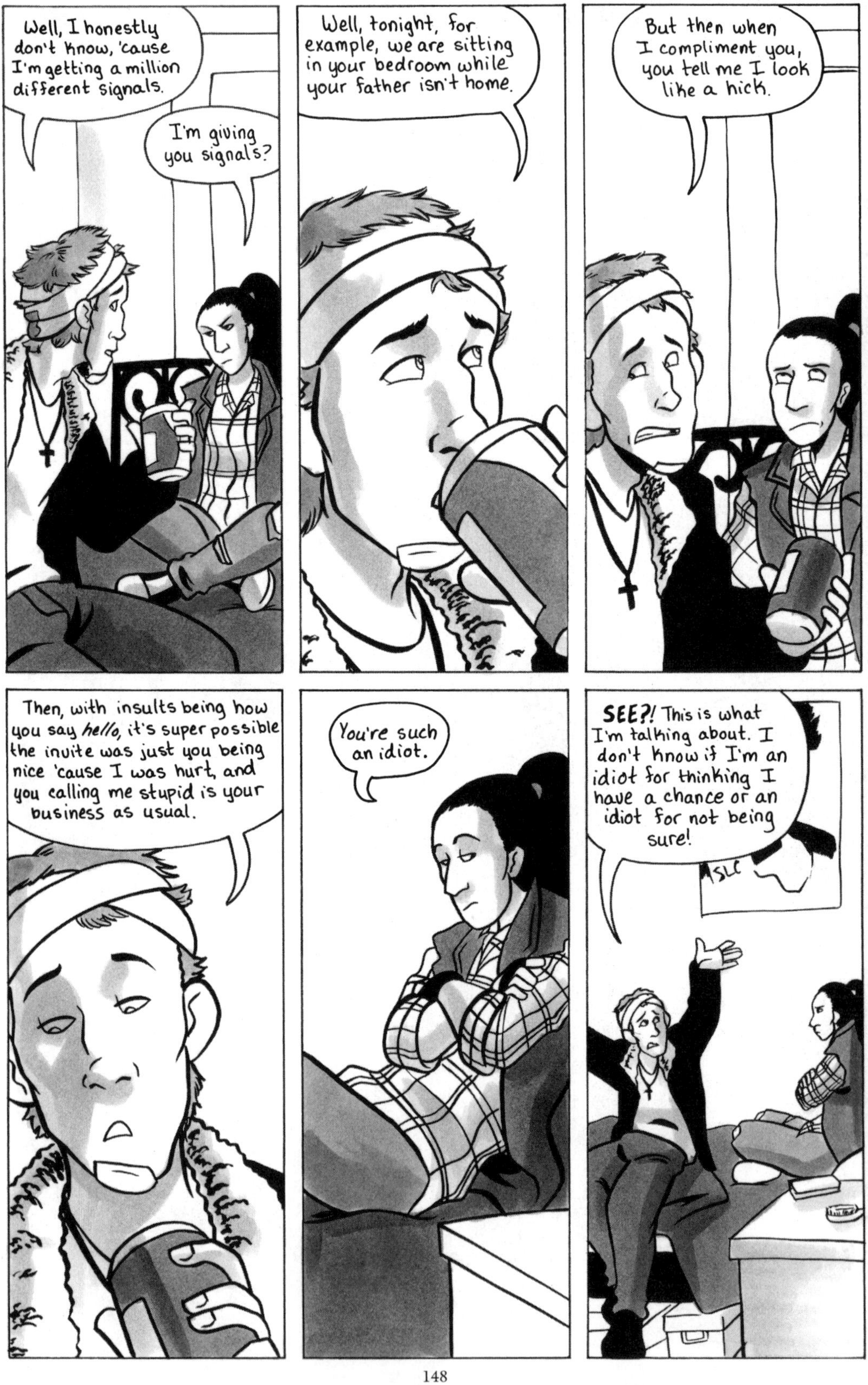
Well, I honestly don't know, 'cause I'm getting a million different signals.
I'm giving you signals?
Well, tonight, for example, we are sitting in your bedroom while your father isn't home.
But then when I compliment you, you tell me I look like a hick.
Then, with insults being how you say *hello*, it's super possible the invite was just you being nice 'cause I was hurt, and you calling me stupid is your business as usual.
You're such an idiot.
SEE?! This is what I'm talking about. I don't know if I'm an idiot for thinking I have a chance or an idiot for not being sure!
SLC

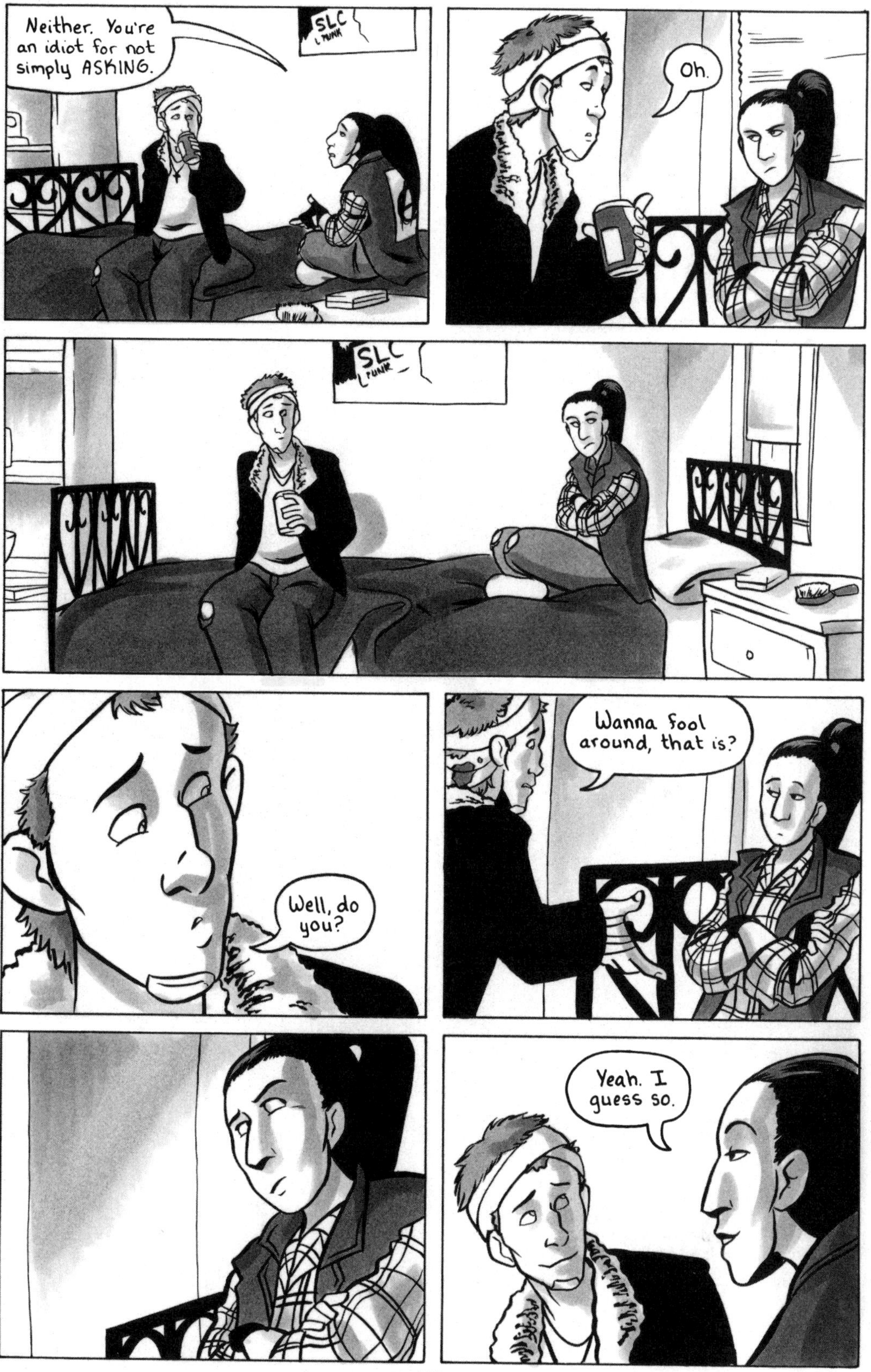
SLC PUNK
Neither. You're an idiot for not simply ASKING.
Oh.
SLC PUNK
Well, do you?
Wanna fool around, that is?
Yeah. I guess so.

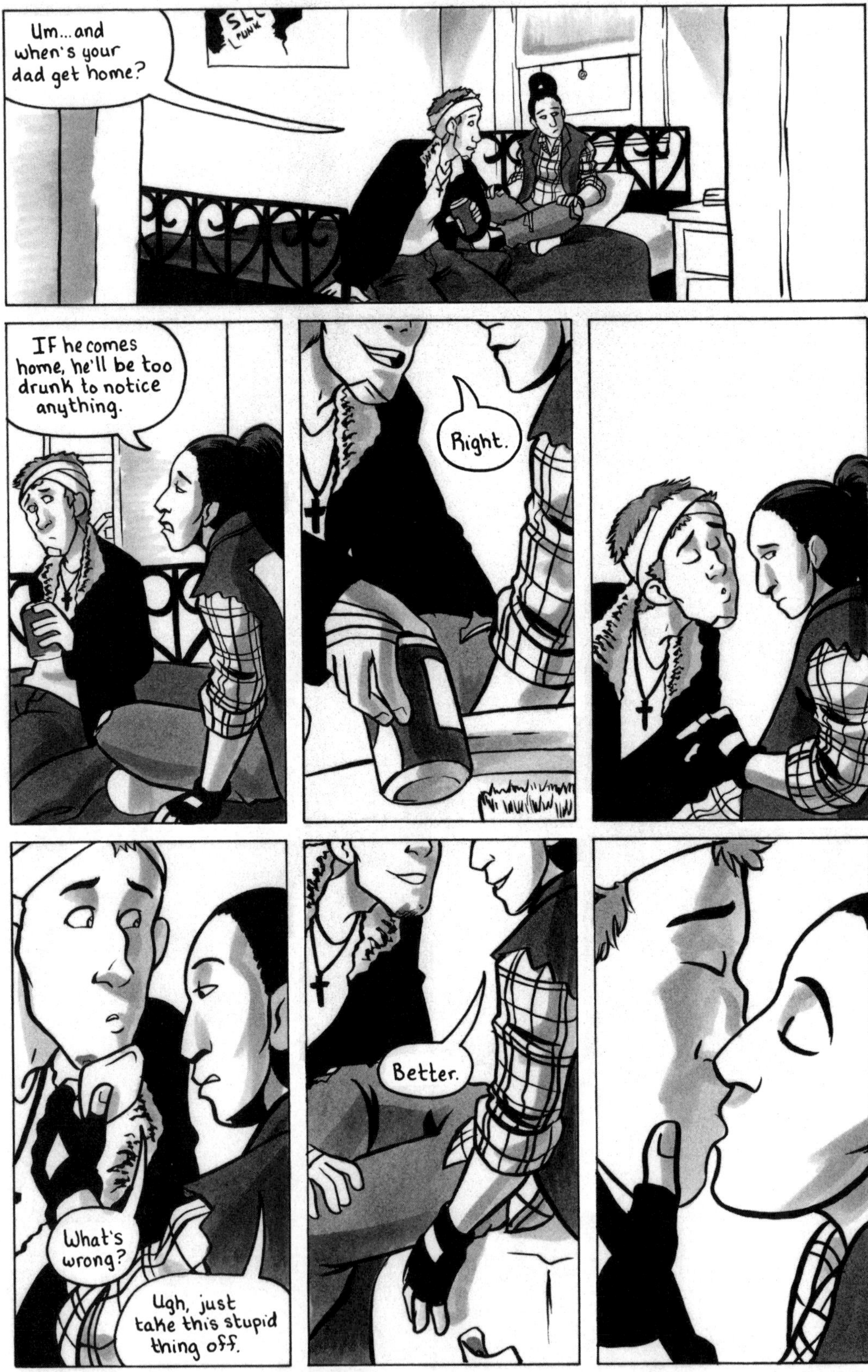
SLC PUNK
Um... and when's your dad get home?
If he comes home, he'll be too drunk to notice anything.
Right.
What's wrong?
Ugh, just take this stupid thing off.
Better.

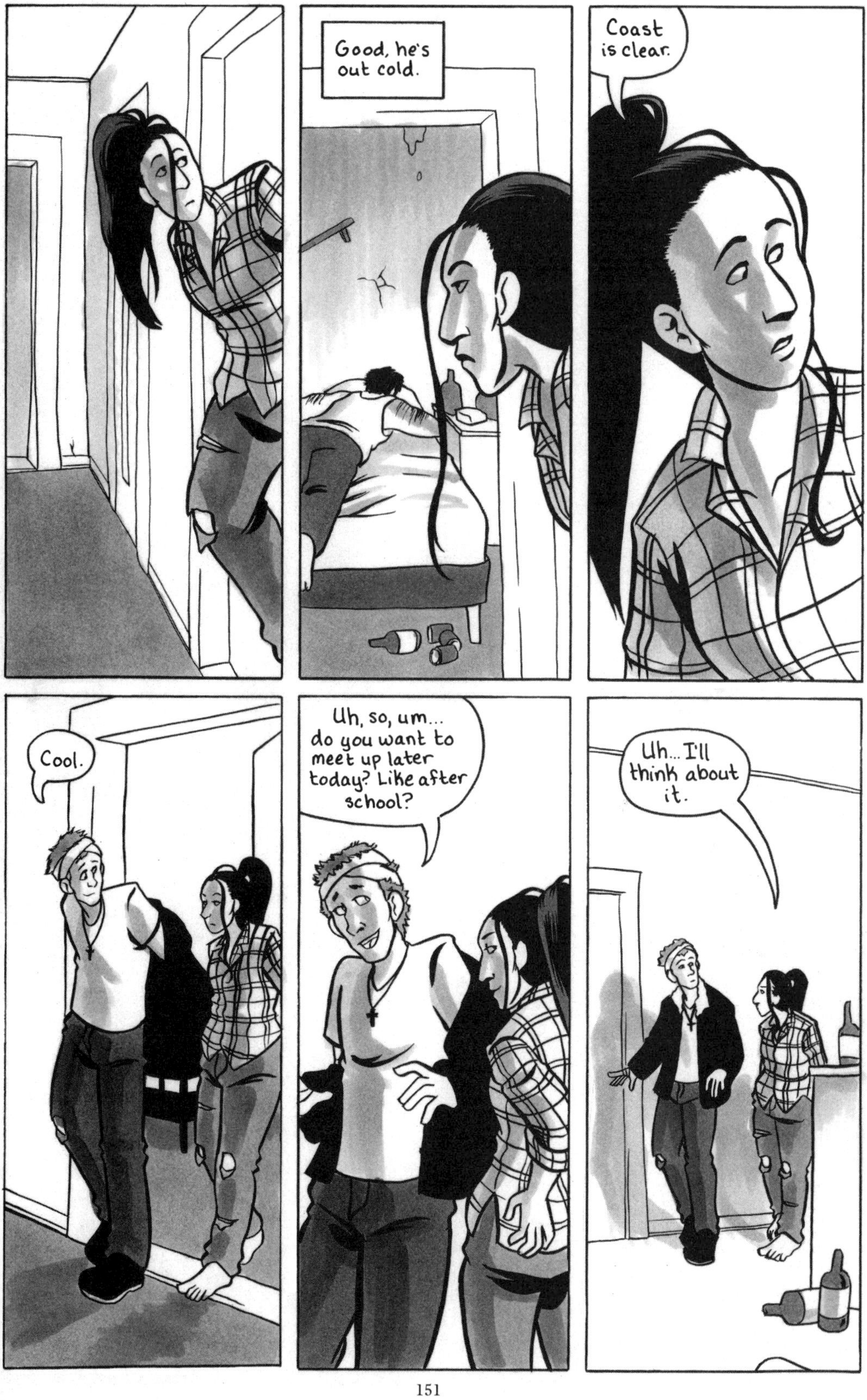
Good, he's out cold.
Coast is clear.
Cool.
Uh, so, um... do you want to meet up later today? Like after school?
Uh... I'll think about it.

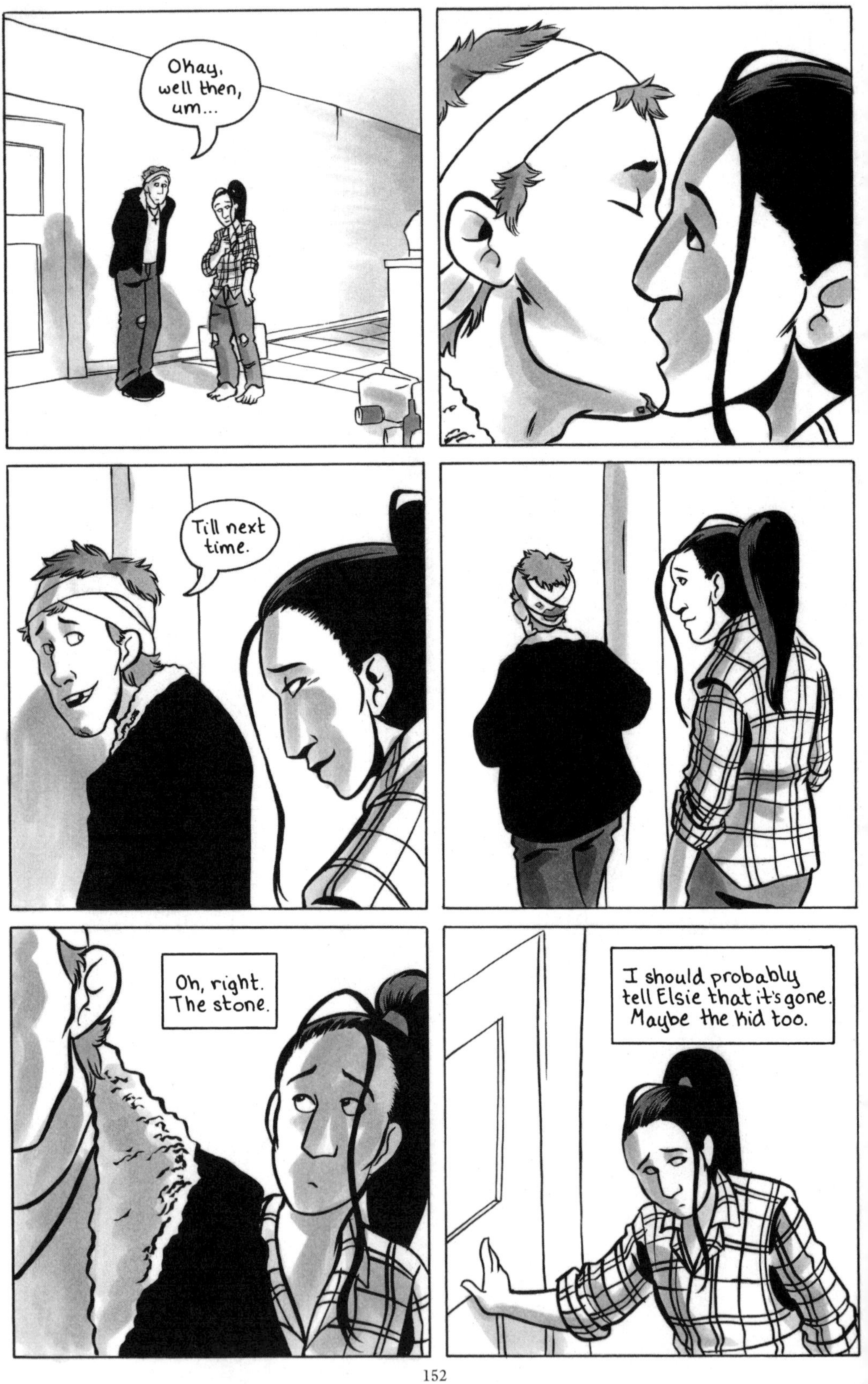
Okay, well then, um...
Till next time.
Oh, right. The stone.
I should probably tell Elsie that it's gone. Maybe the kid too.

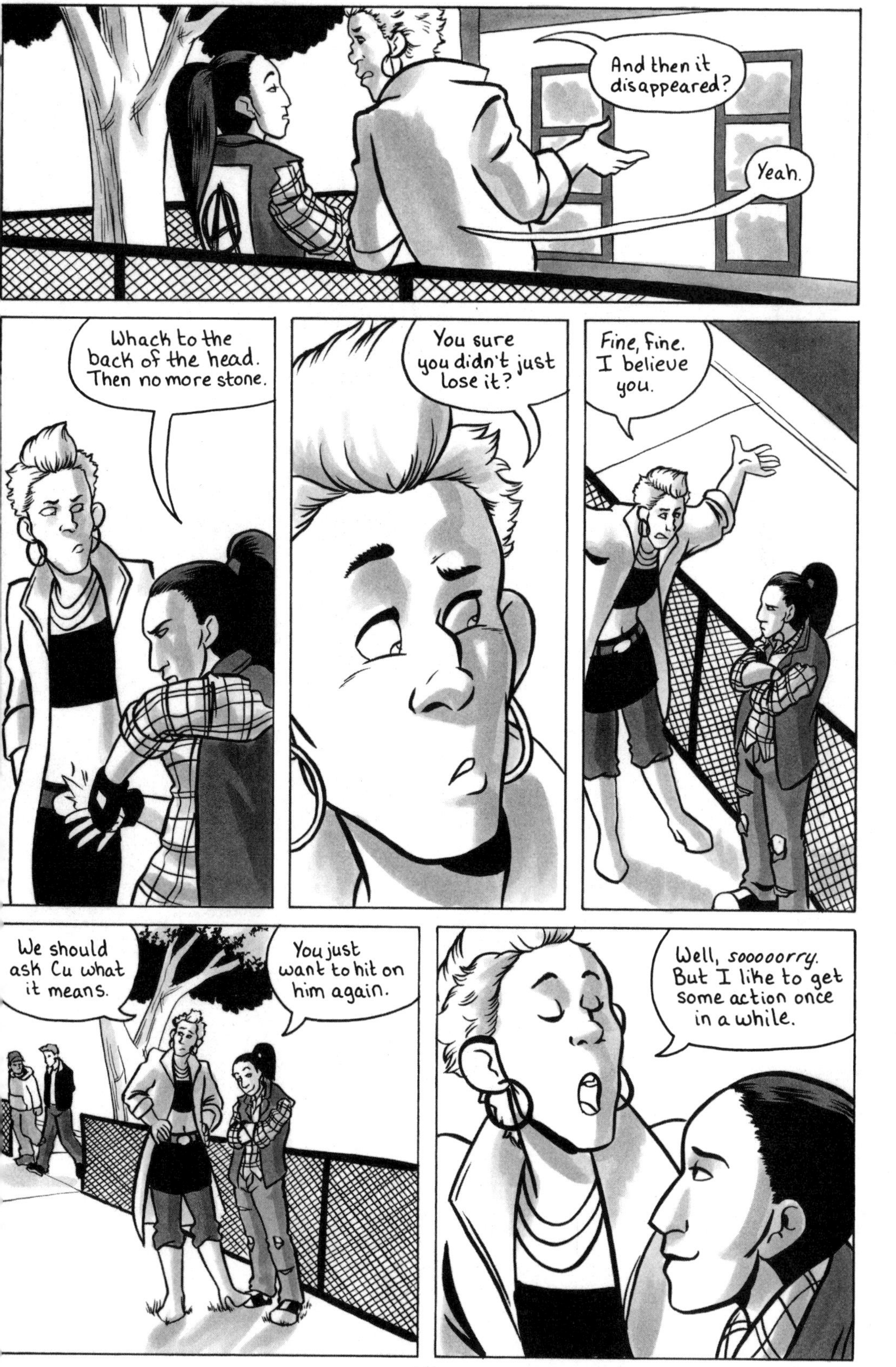
And then it disappeared?
Yeah.
Whack to the back of the head. Then no more stone.
You sure you didn't just lose it?
Fine, fine. I believe you.
We should ask Cu what it means.
You just want to hit on him again.
Well, *sooooorry.* But I like to get some action once in a while.

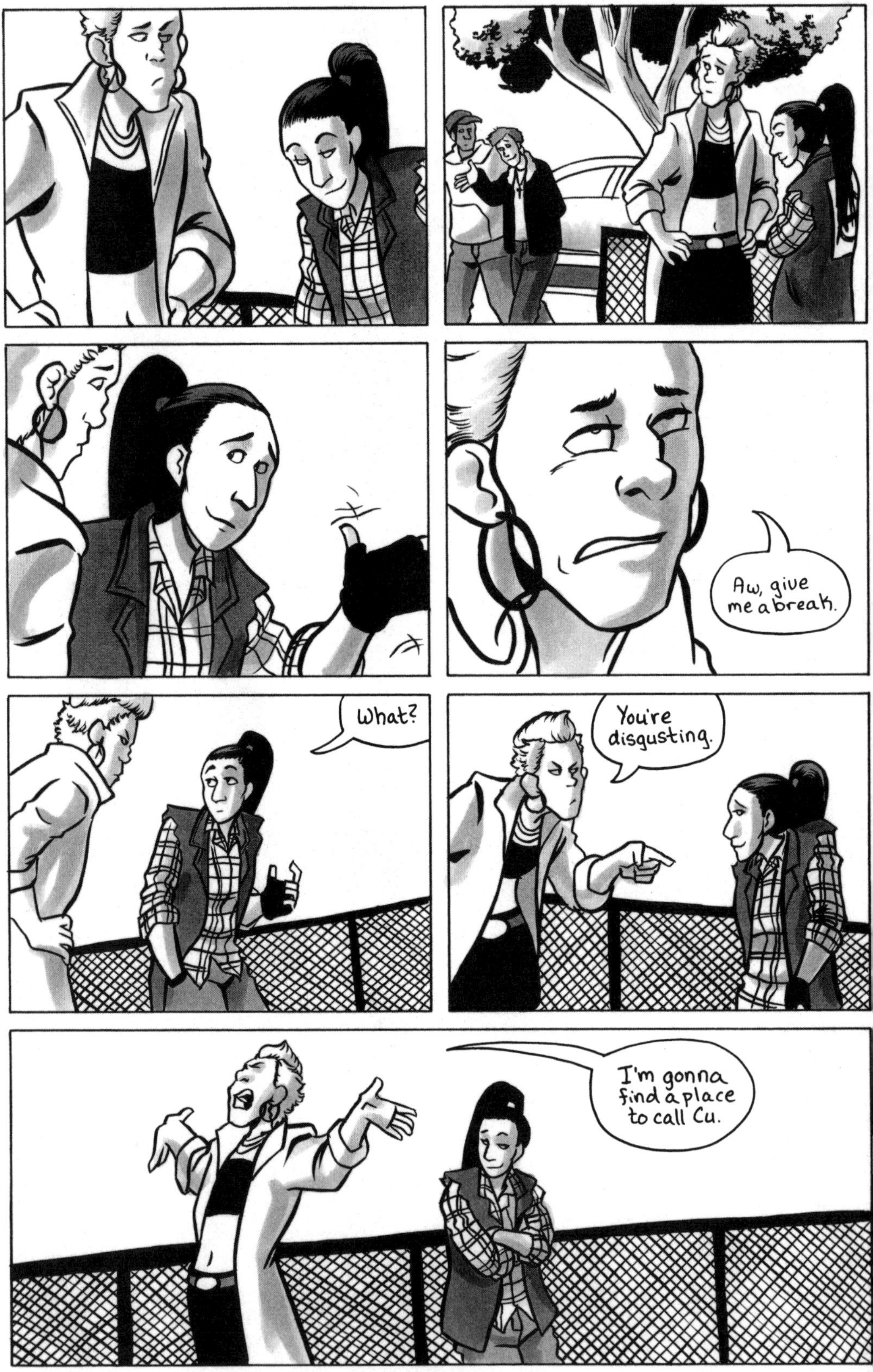
Aw, give me a break.
What?
You're disgusting.
I'm gonna find a place to call Cu.

CHAPTER 8:

It Is Only the People Who Are Lacking, or Bad, or Inferior, Who Have to Be Good at Things

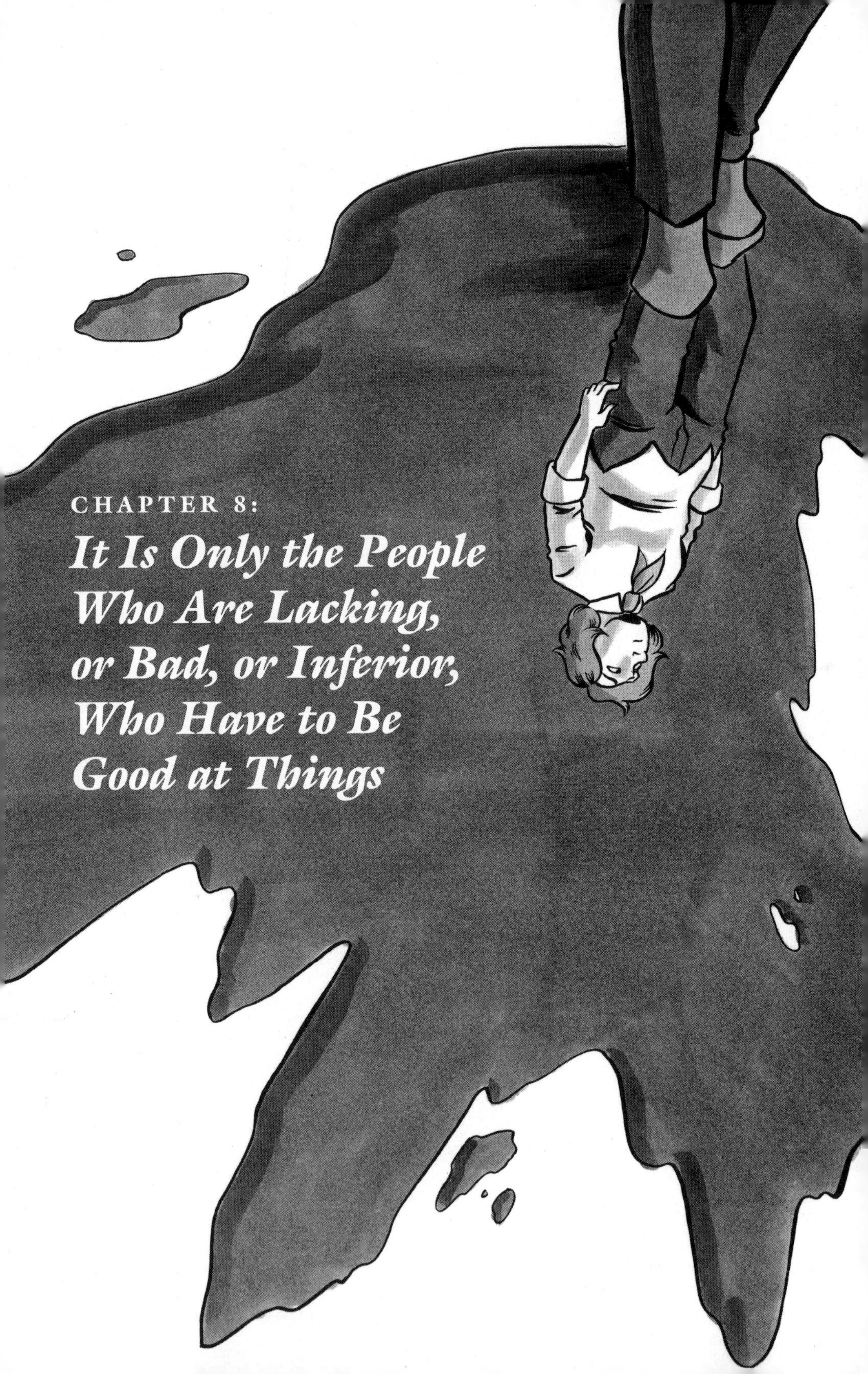

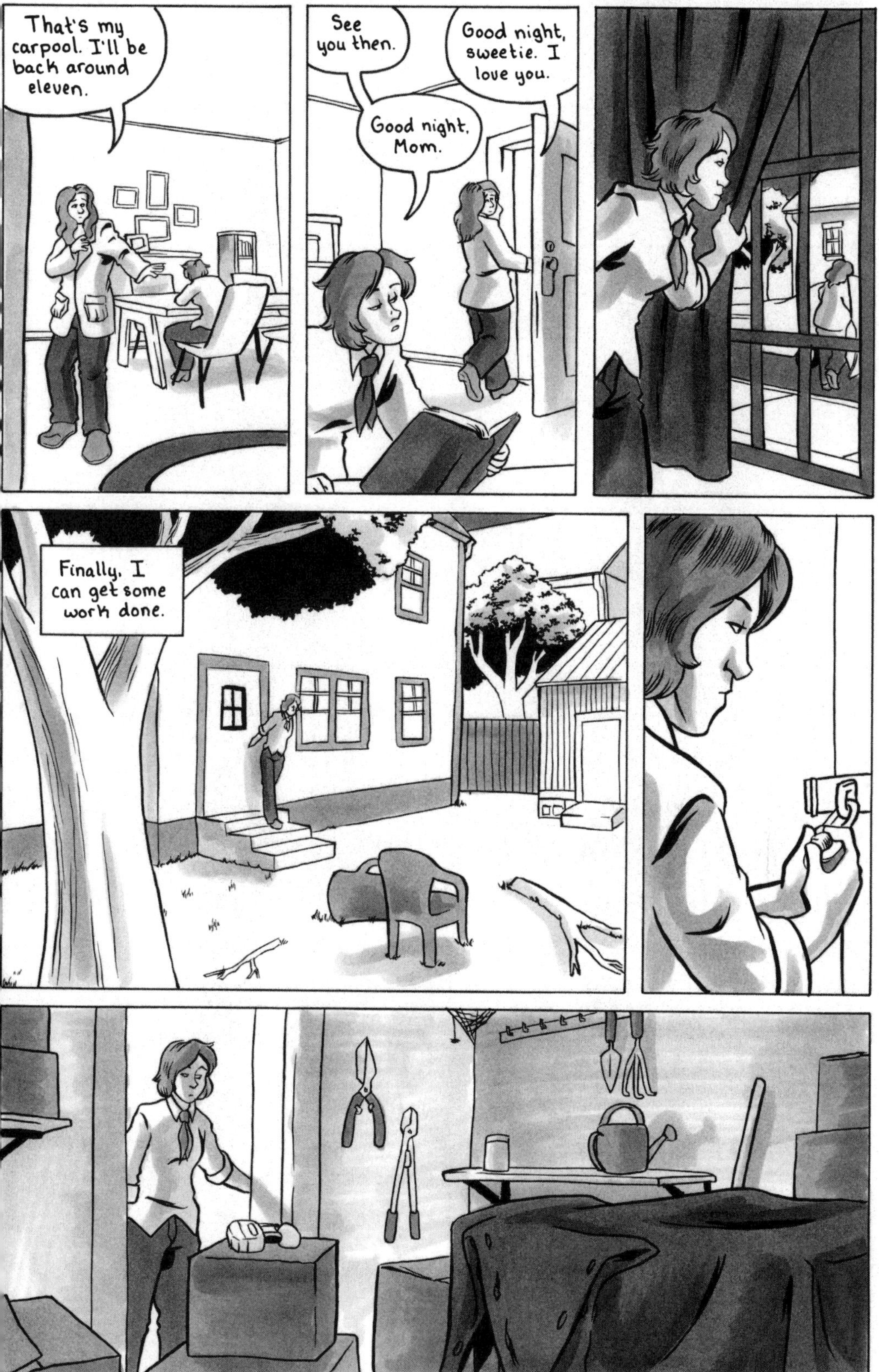
That's my carpool. I'll be back around eleven.
See you then.
Good night, sweetie. I love you.
Good night, Mom.
Finally, I can get some work done.

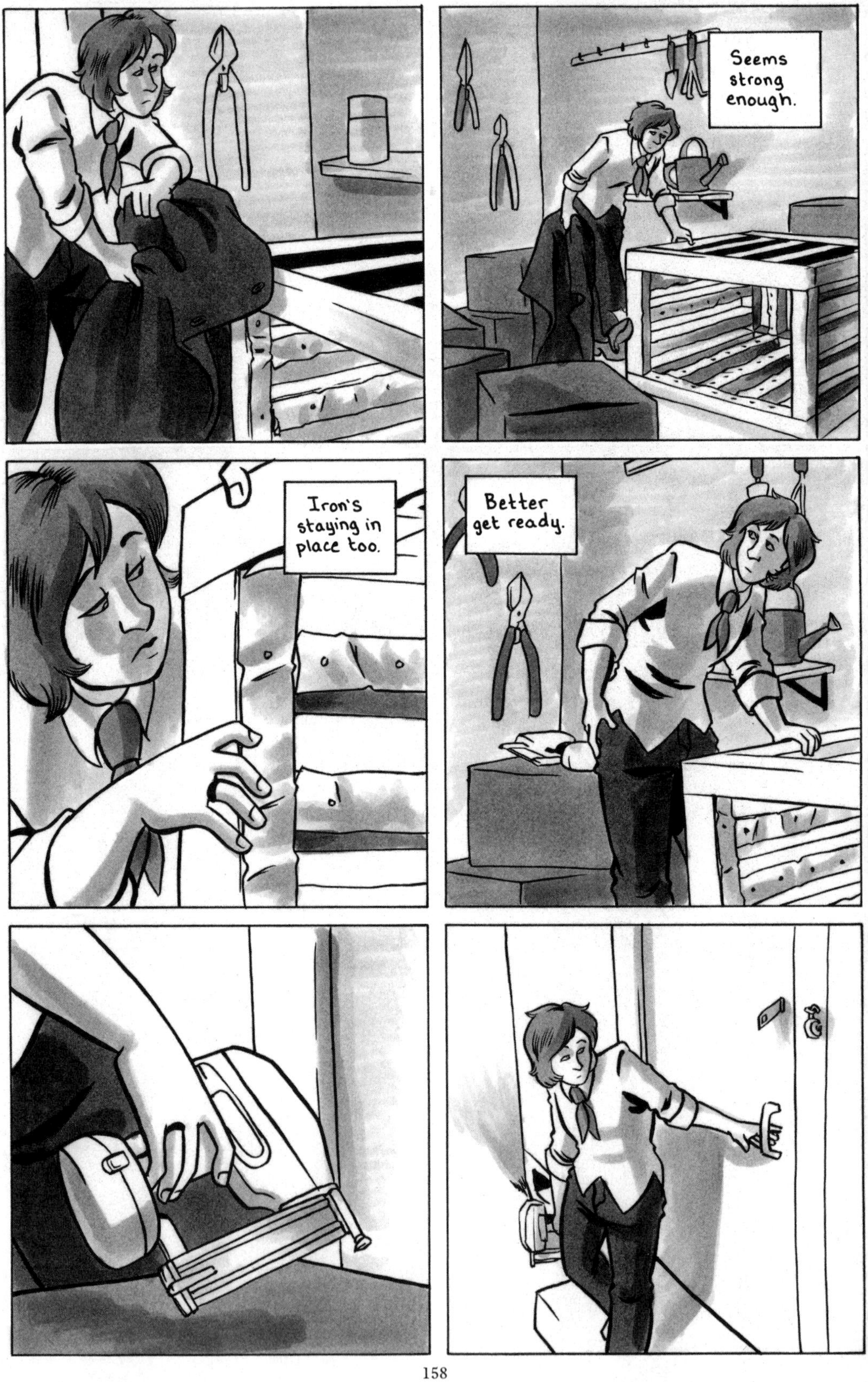
Seems strong enough.
Iron's staying in place too.
Better get ready.

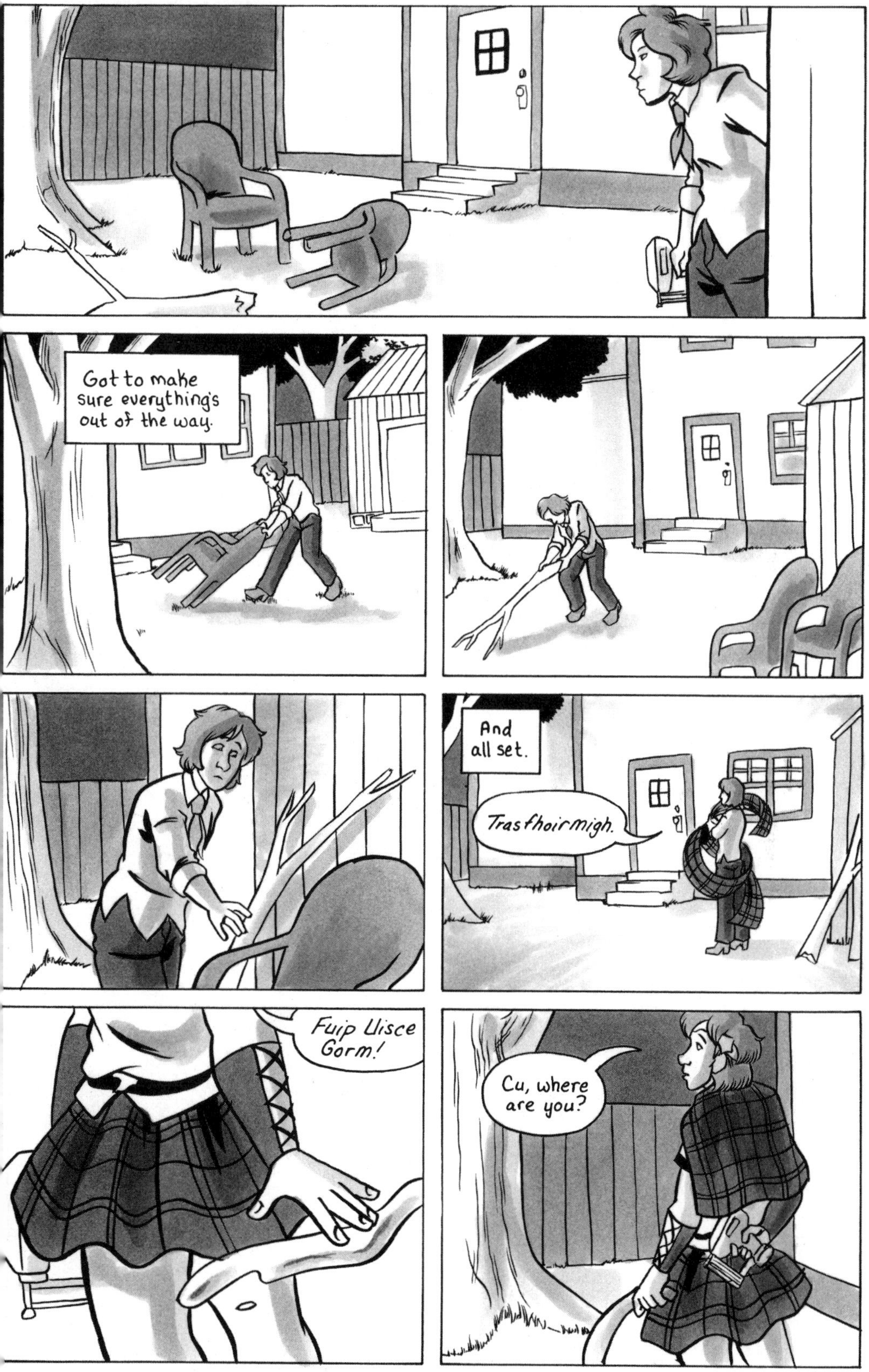
Got to make sure everything's out of the way.
And all set.
Trasfhoirmigh.
Fuip Uisce Gorm!
Cu, where are you?

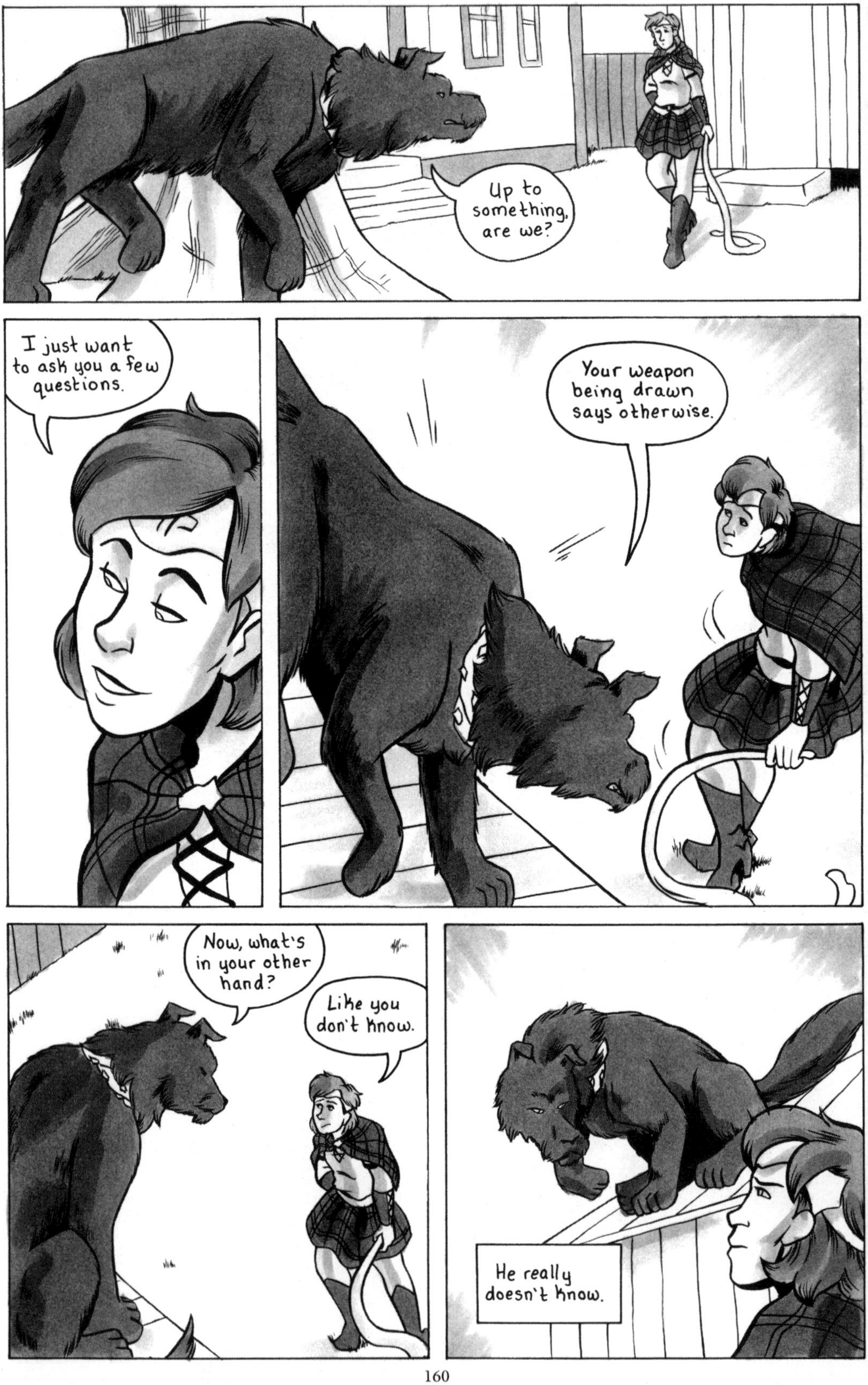
Up to something, are we?
I just want to ask you a few questions.
Your weapon being drawn says otherwise.
Now, what's in your other hand?
Like you don't know.
He really doesn't know.

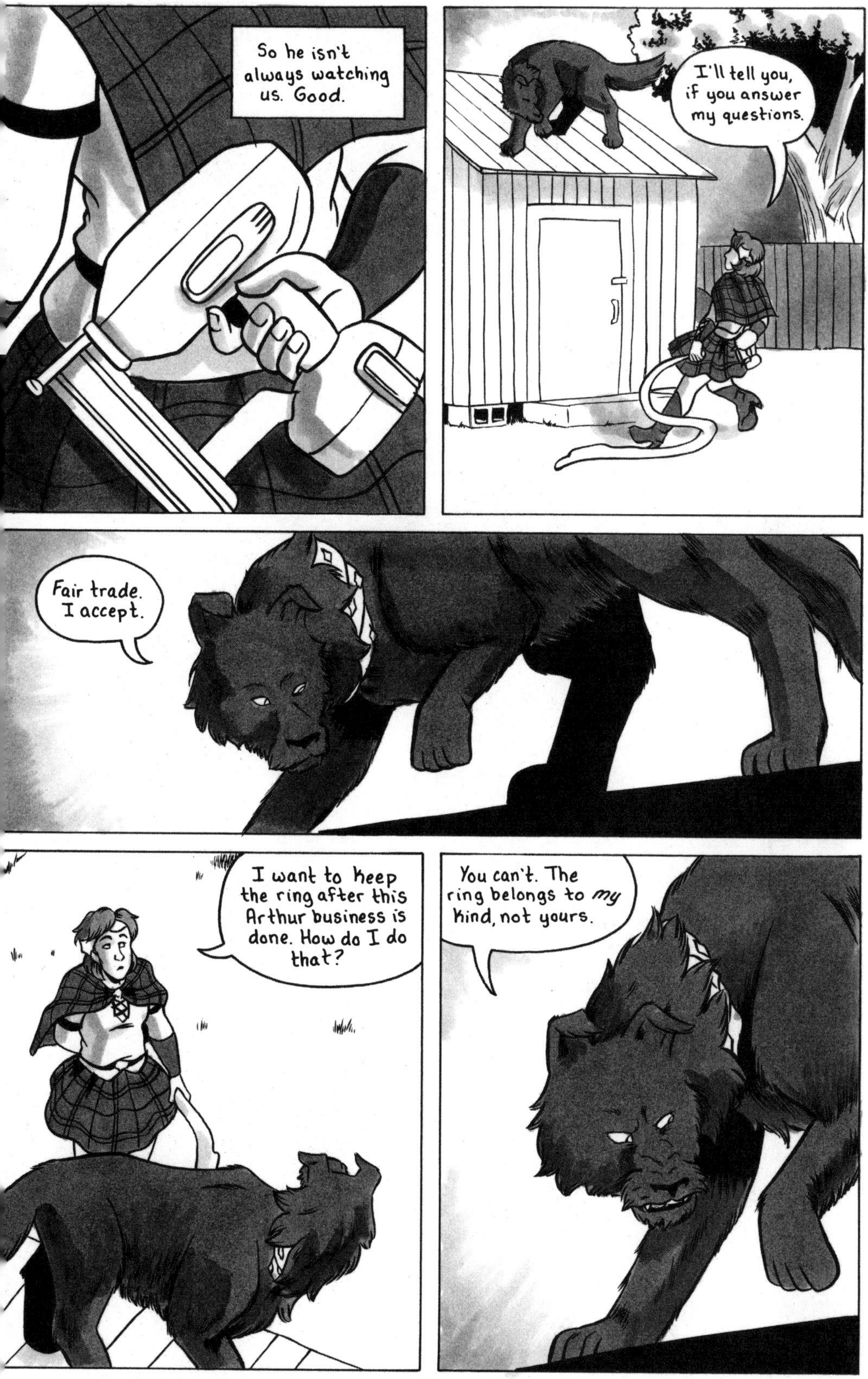
So he isn't always watching us. Good.
I'll tell you, if you answer my questions.
Fair trade. I accept.
I want to keep the ring after this Arthur business is done. How do I do that?
You can't. The ring belongs to *my* kind, not yours.

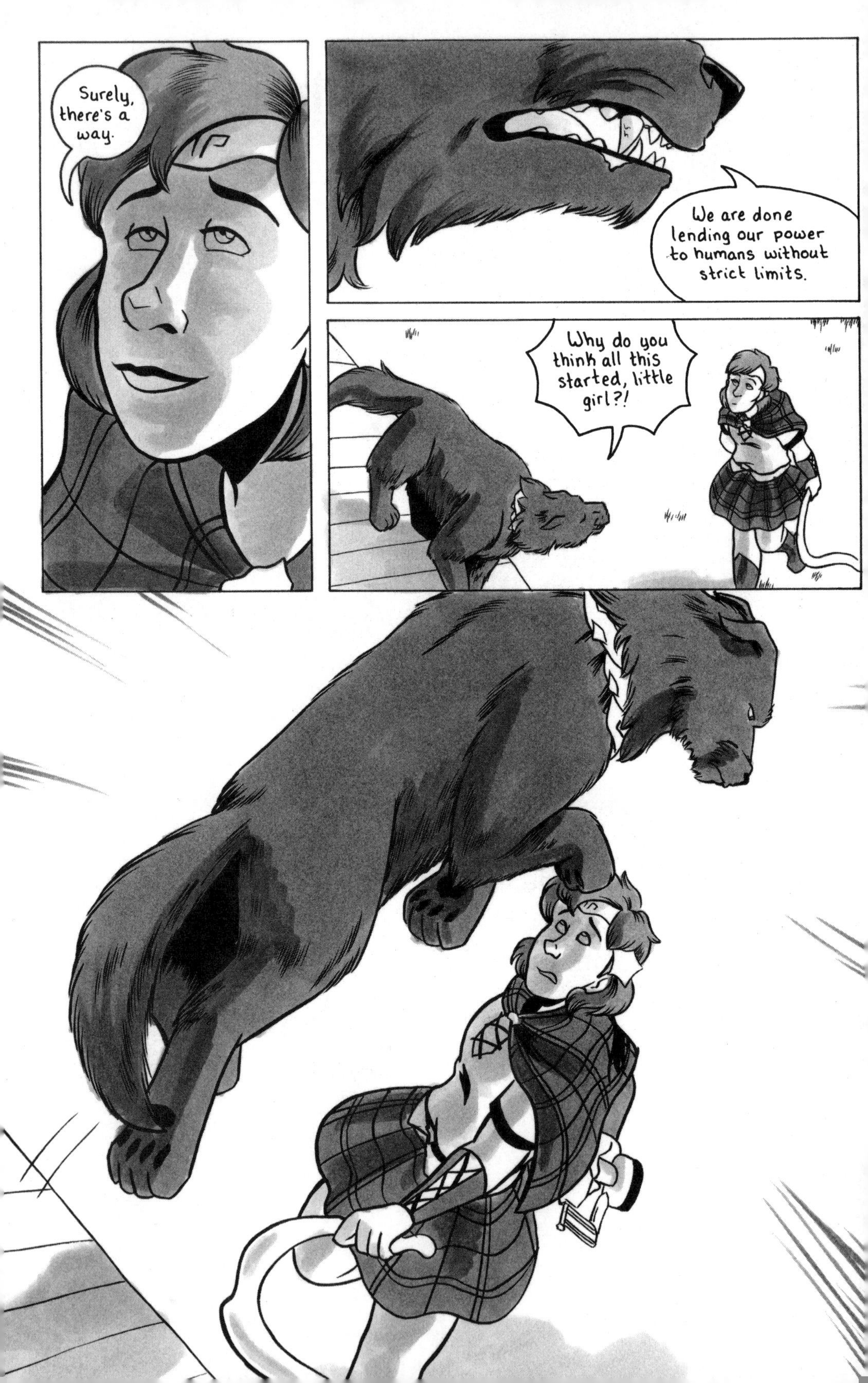

Surely, there's a way.
We are done lending our power to humans without strict limits.
Why do you think all this started, little girl?!

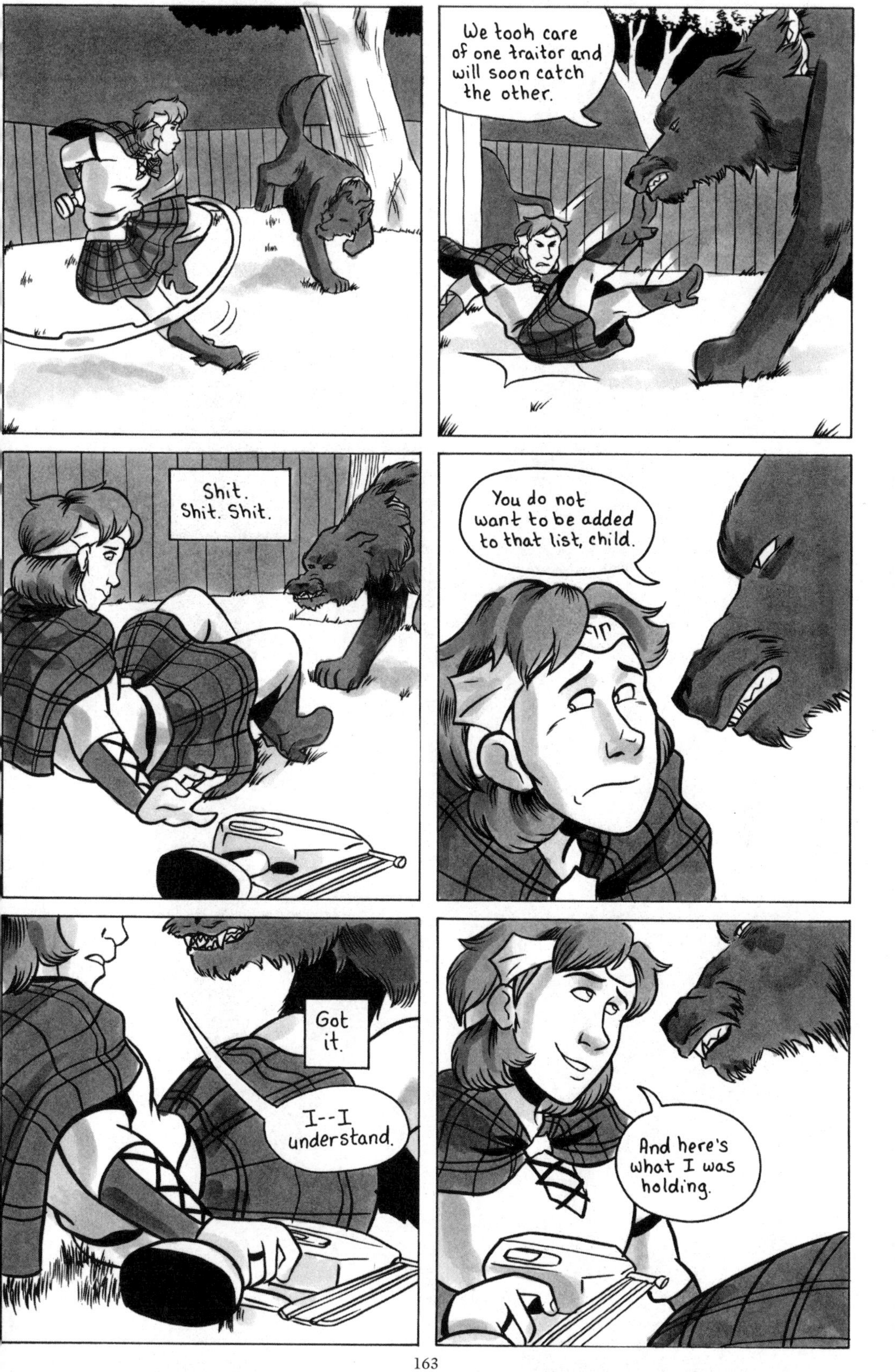
We took care of one traitor and will soon catch the other.
Shit. Shit. Shit.
You do not want to be added to that list, child.
Got it.
I--I understand.
And here's what I was holding.

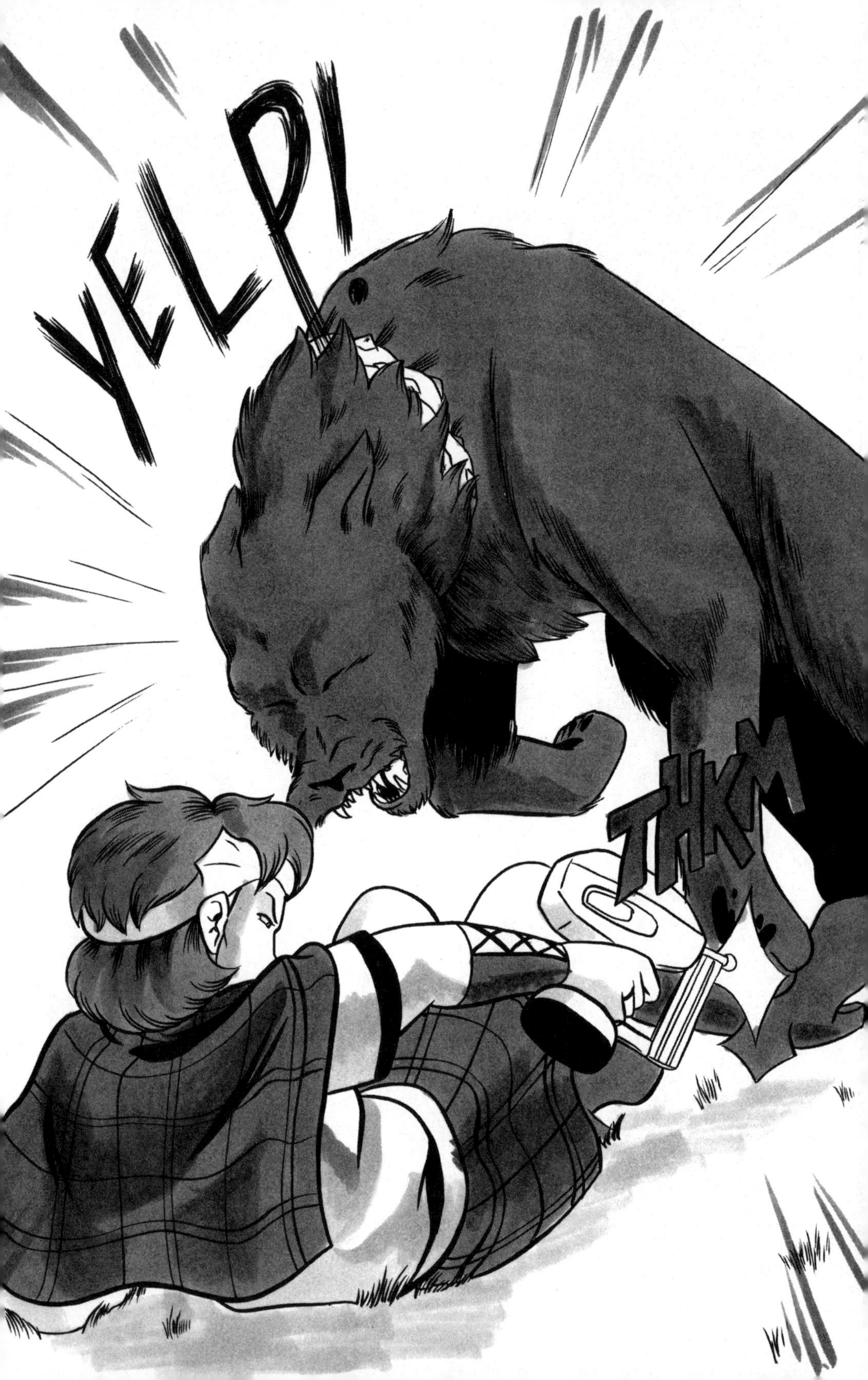
YELP!
THKM

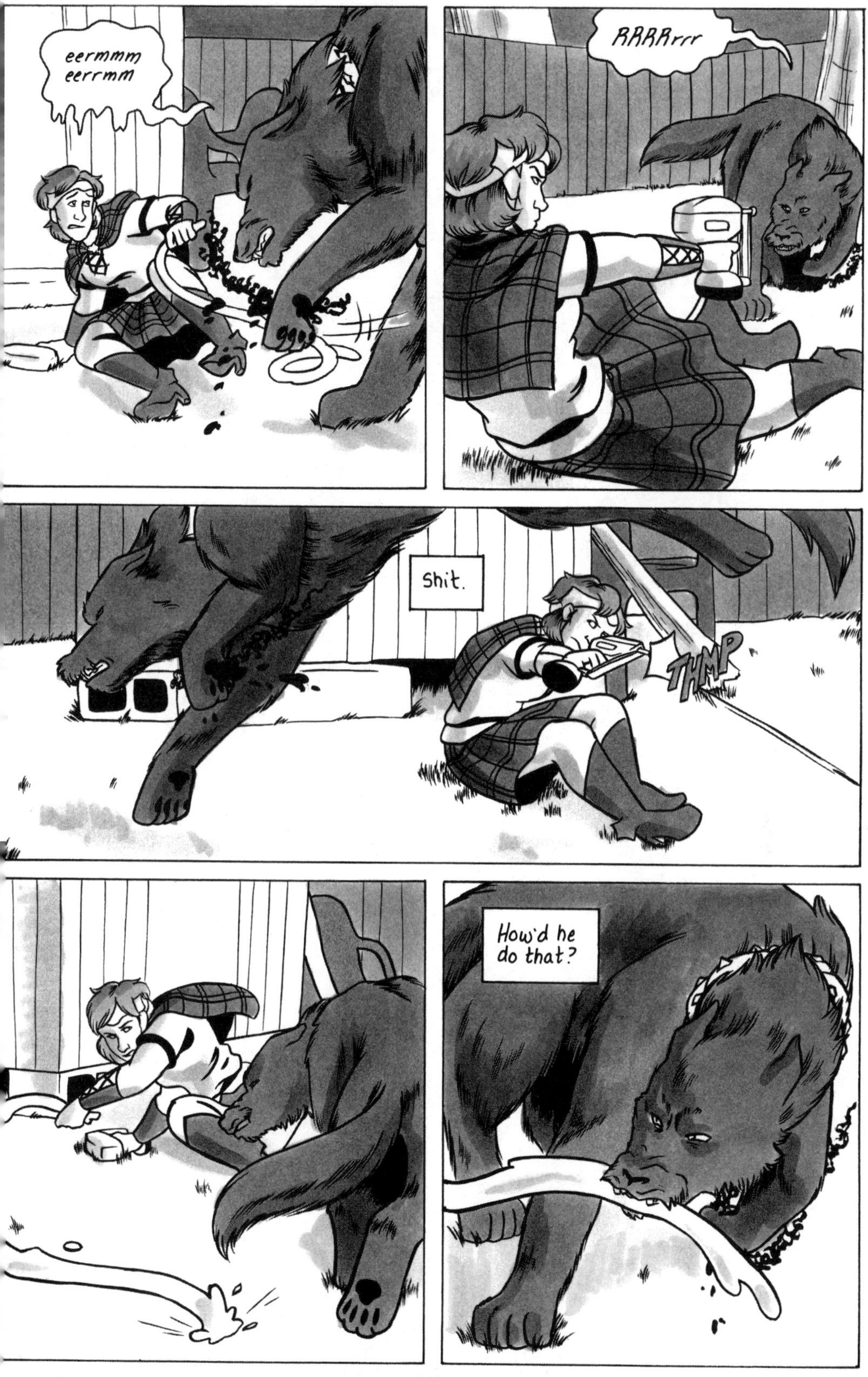
eermmm
eerrmm
RRRRrrr
shit.
THMP
How'd he do that?

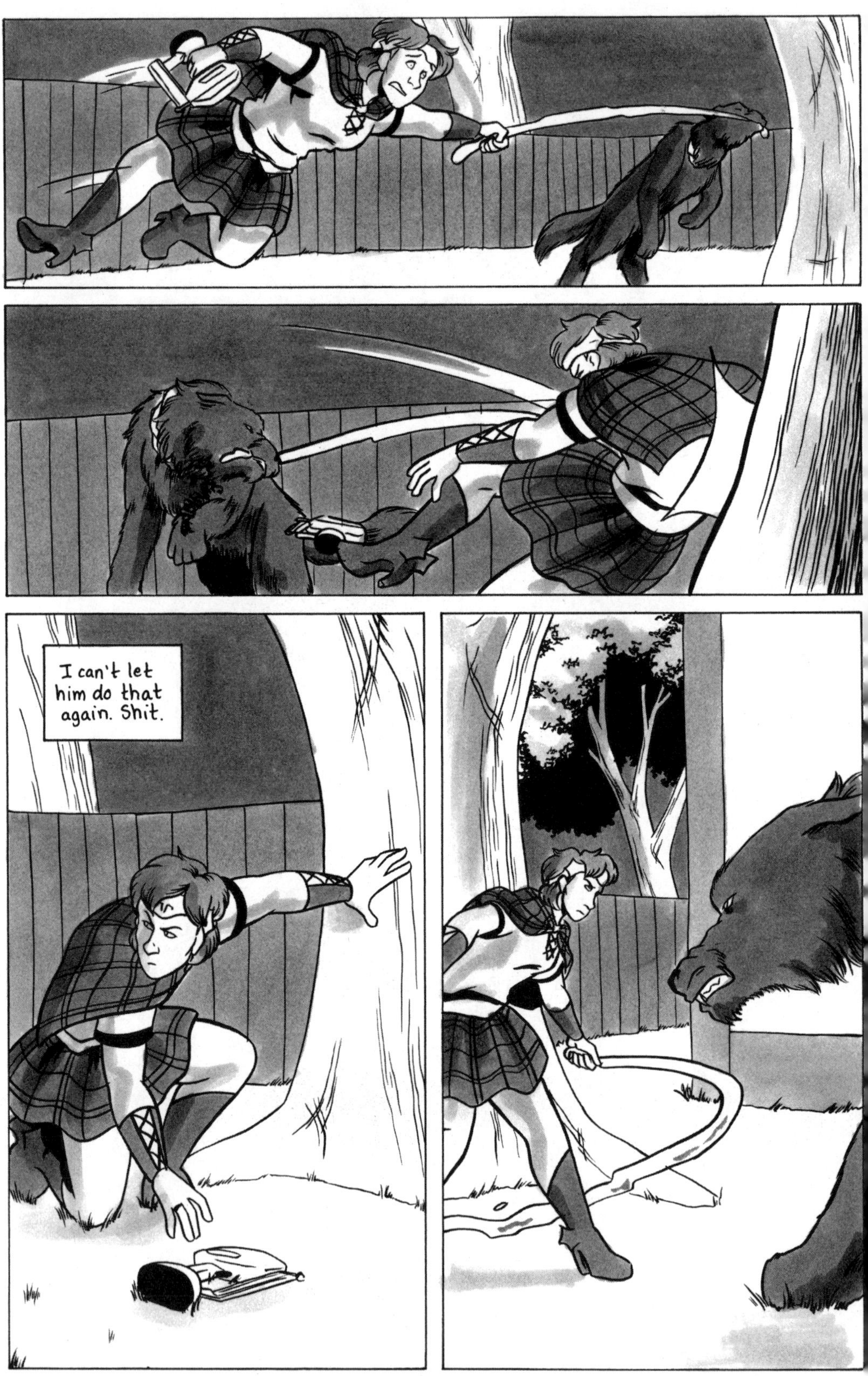
I can't let him do that again. Shit.

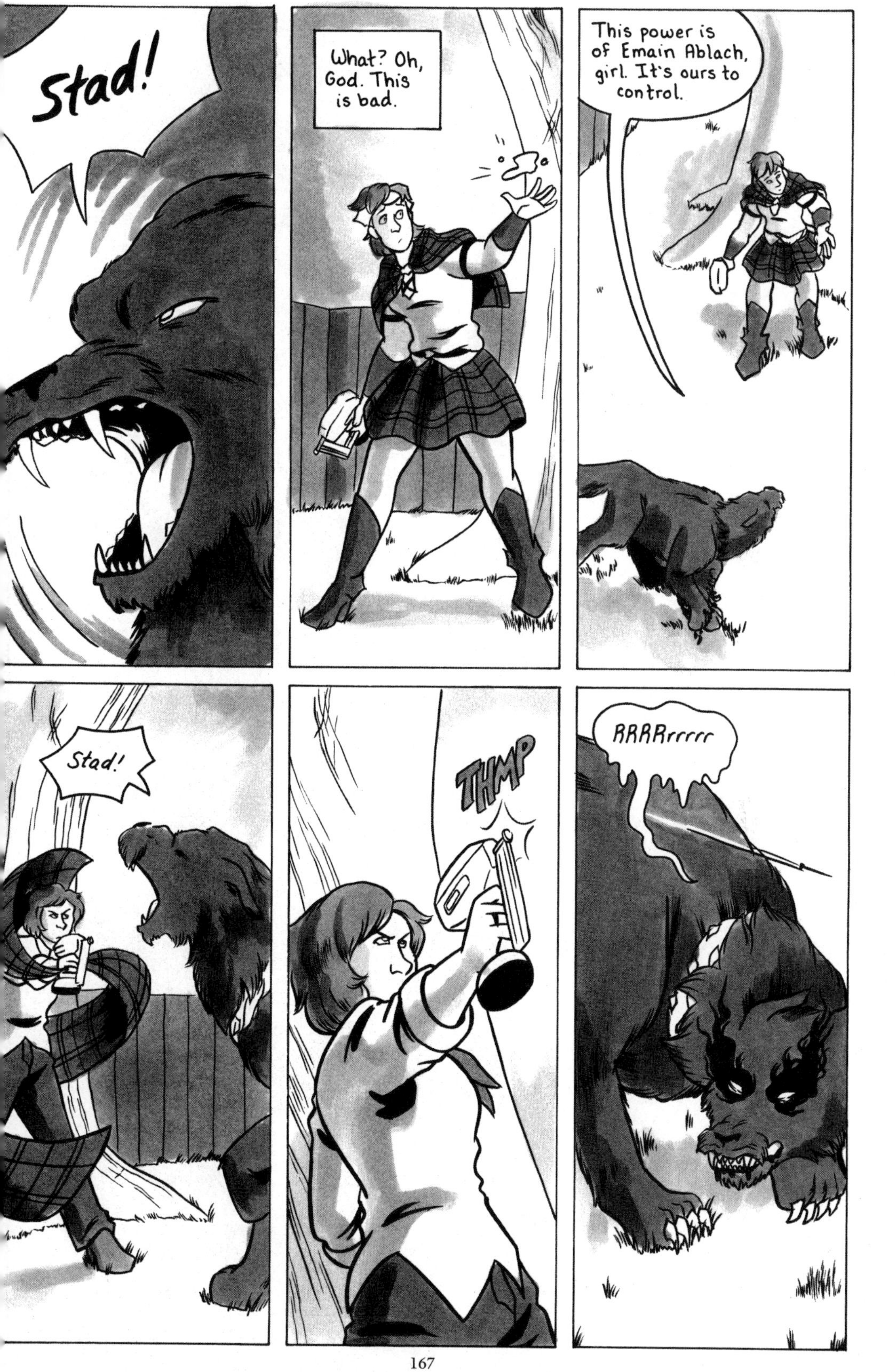
Stad!
What? Oh, God. This is bad.
This power is of Emain Ablach, girl. It's ours to control.
Stad!
THMP
RRRRrrrrr

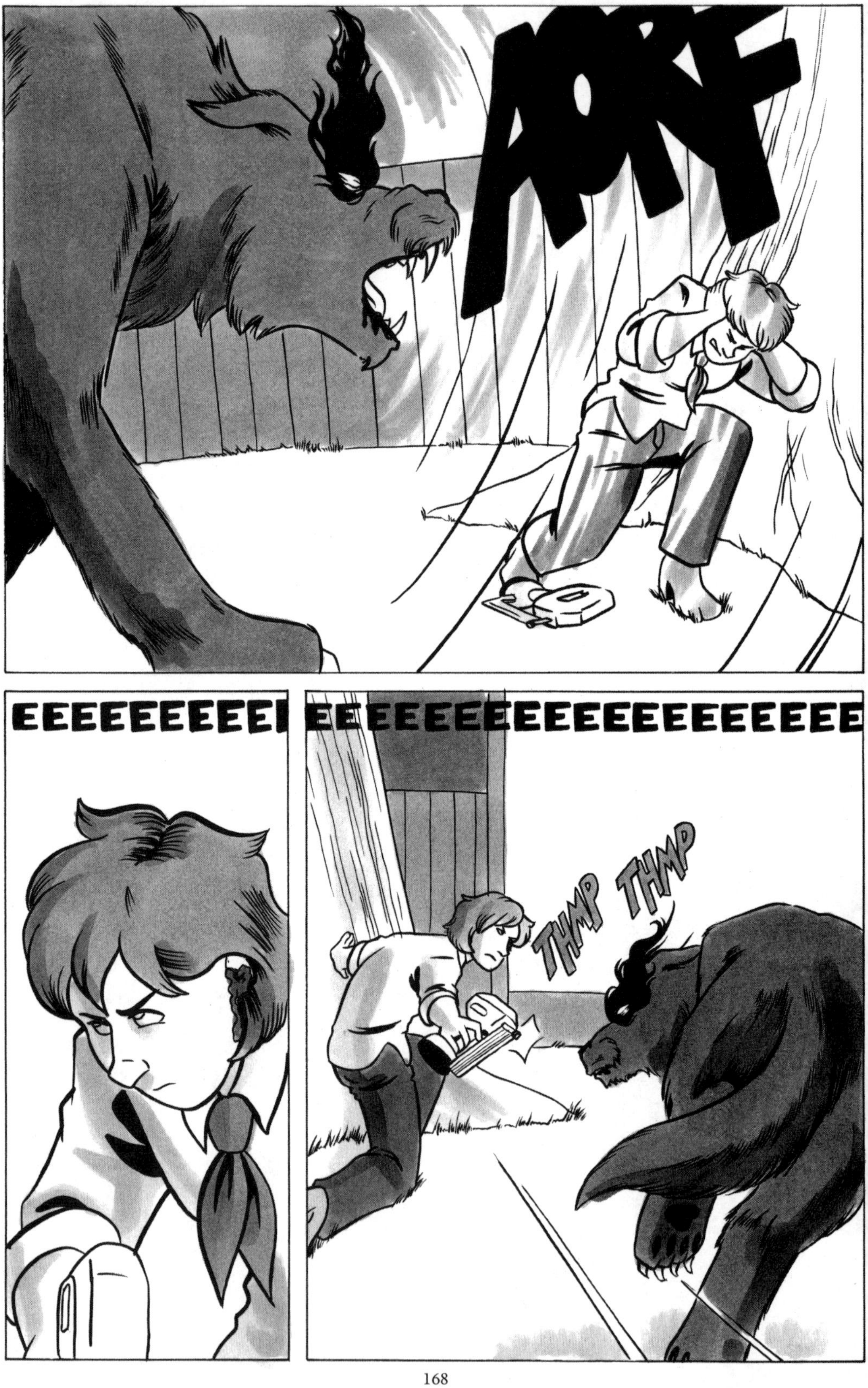
AORF
EEEEEEEEEEE
EEEEEEEEEEEEEEEEEEEEEE
THMP THMP

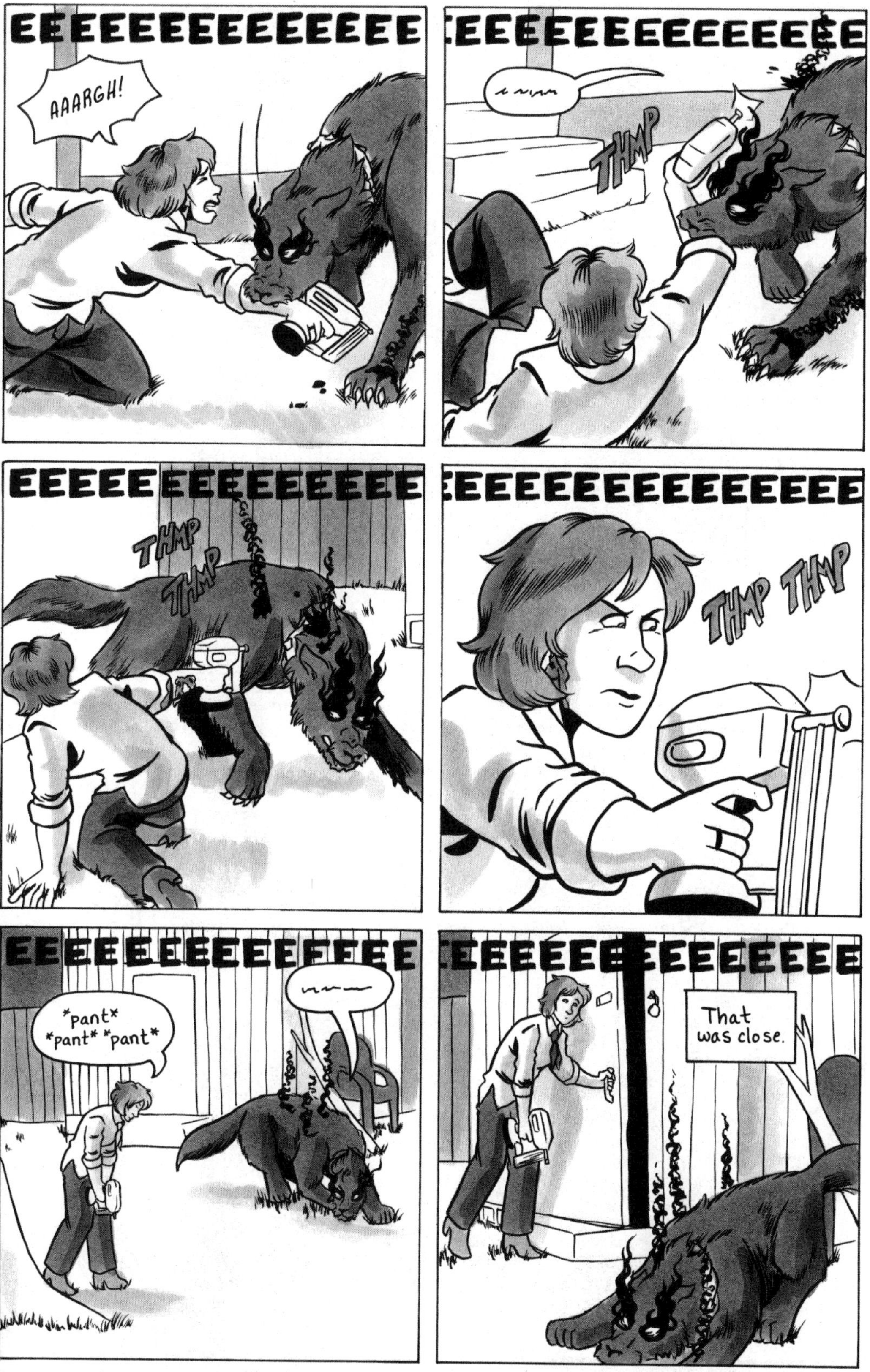
EEEEEEEEEEEEEE
AAARGH!
EEEEEEEEEEEEEE
THMP
EEEEEEEEEEEEEE
THMP
THMP
EEEEEEEEEEEEEE
THMP THMP
EEEEEEEEEEEEEE
pant
pant *pant*
EEEEEEEEEEEEEE
That was close.

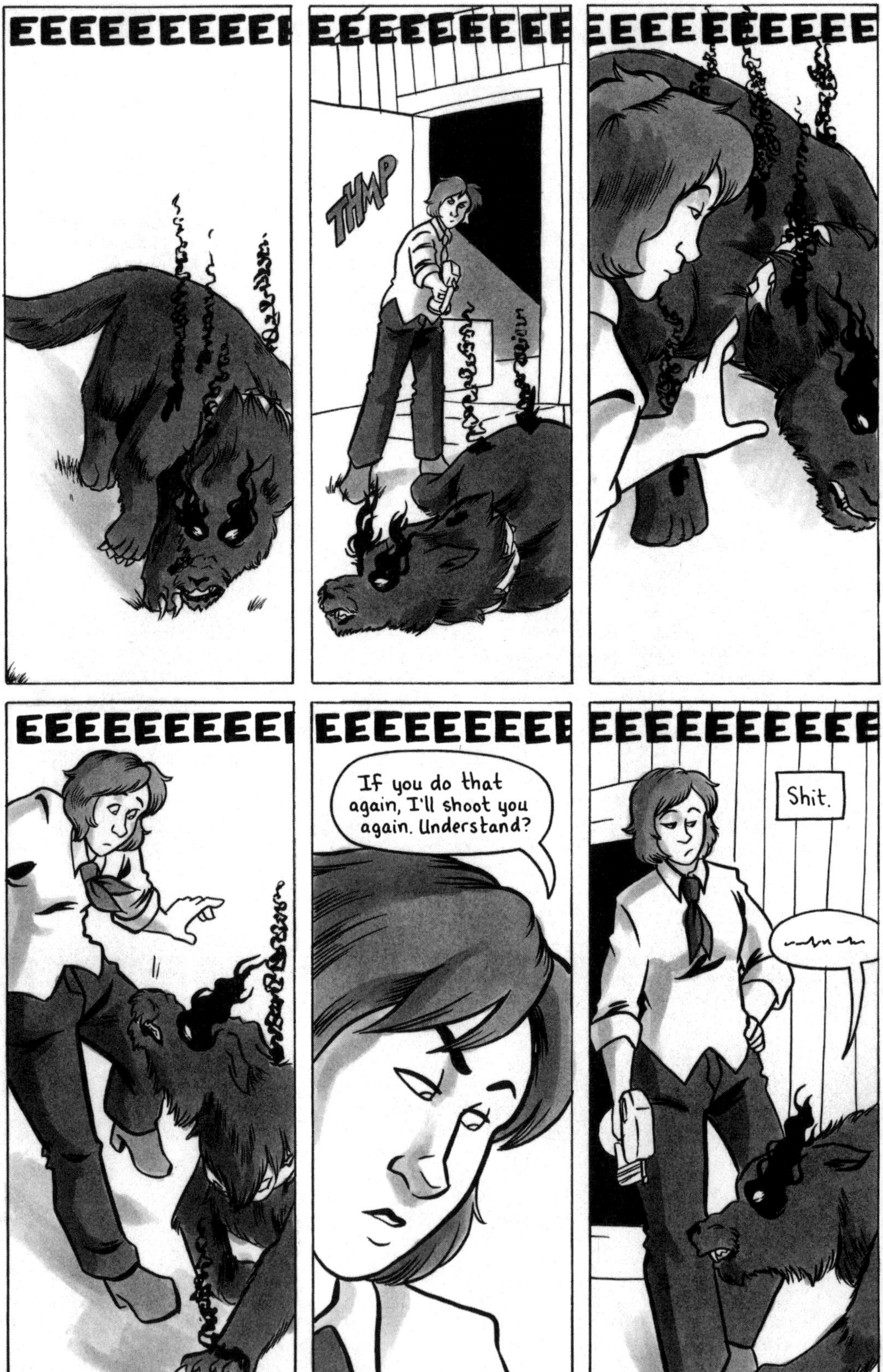
EEEEEEEEEEE
EEEEEEEEEEE
EEEEEEEEEEE
THMP
EEEEEEEEEEE
EEEEEEEEEEE
If you do that again, I'll shoot you again. Understand?
EEEEEEEEEEE
Shit.

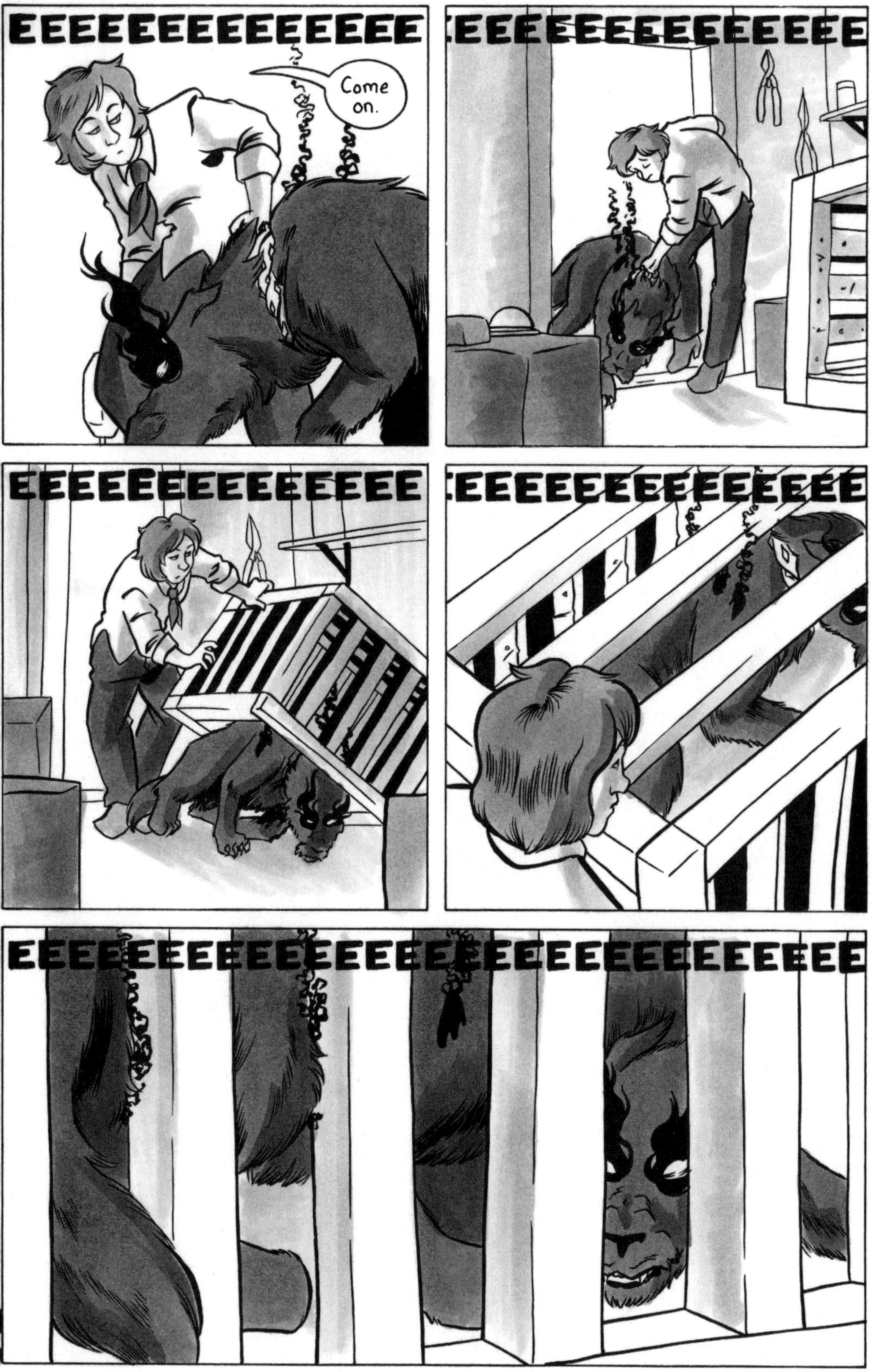
EEEEEEEEEEEEE
Come on.
EEEEEEEEEEEEEE
EEEEEEEEEEEEE
EEEEEEEEEEEEEE
EEEEEEEEEEEEEEEEEEEEEEEEEE

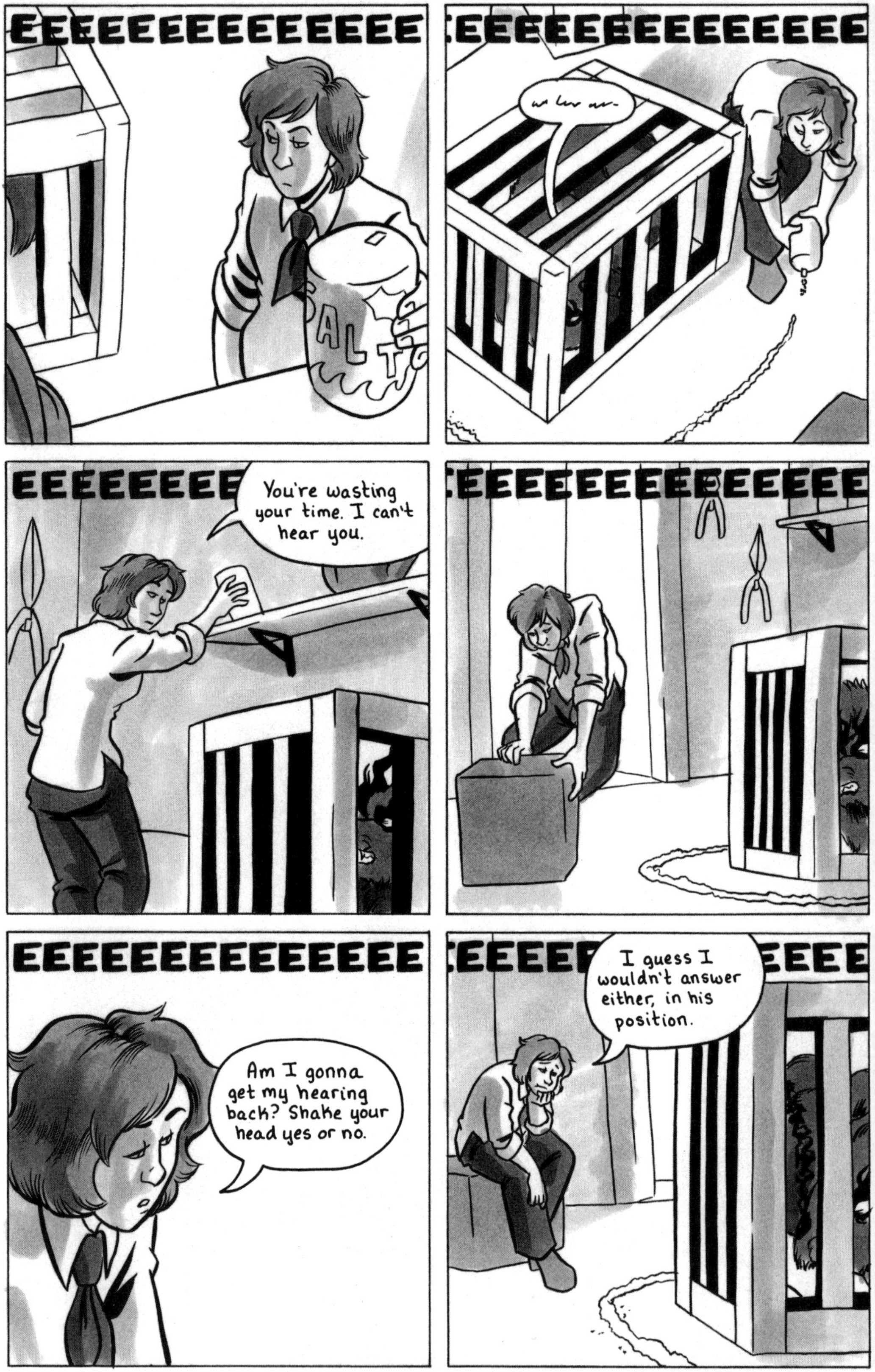
EEEEEEEEEEEEEEE
EEEEEEEEEEEEEEE
EEEEEEEE
You're wasting your time. I can't hear you.
EEEEEEEEEEEEEE
EEEEEEEEEEEEEEE
Am I gonna get my hearing back? Shake your head yes or no.
EEEEE
I guess I wouldn't answer either, in his position.
EEEE

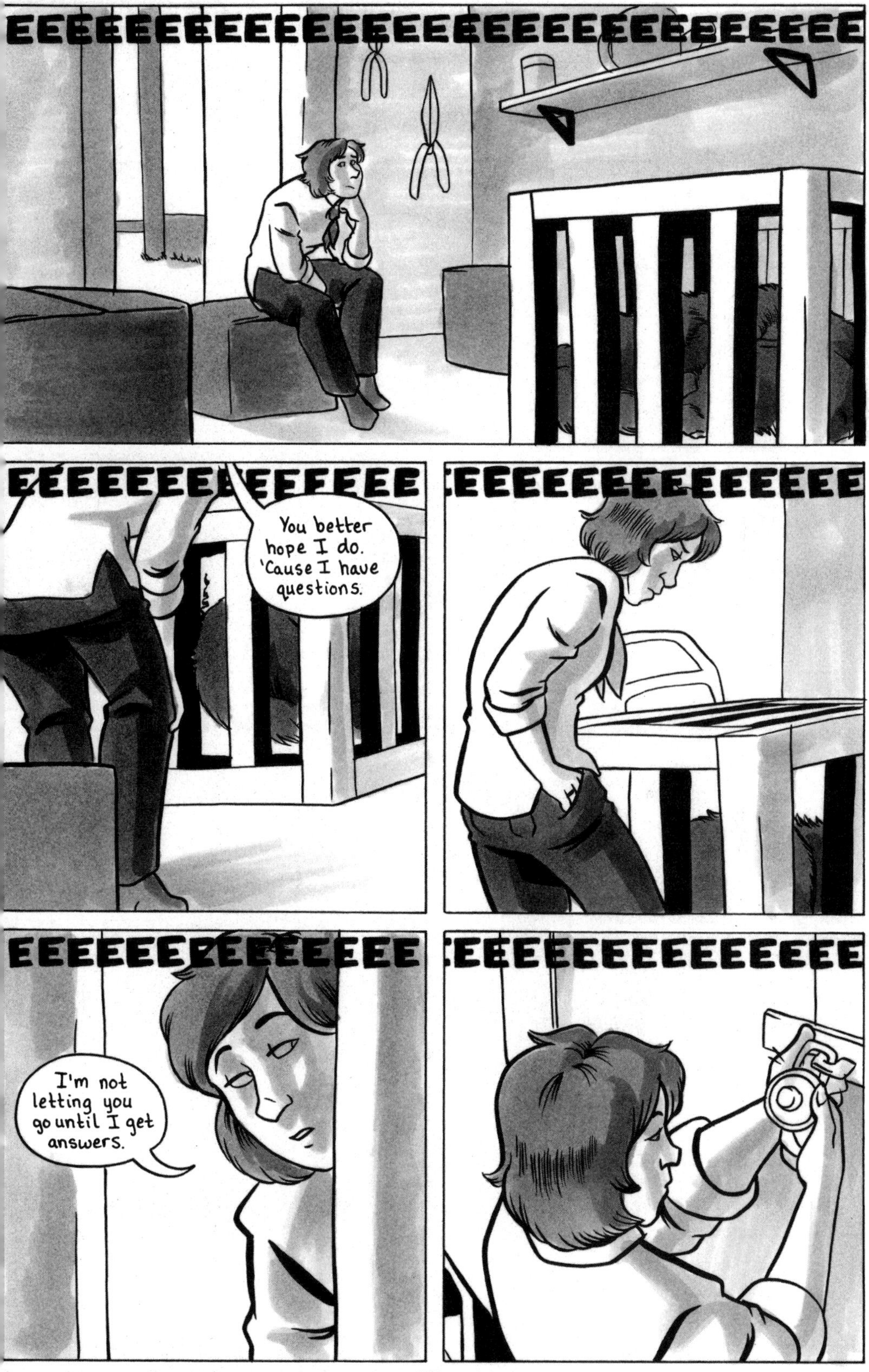
EEEEEEEEEEEEEEEEEEEEEEEEEEEEEEE
EEEEEEEEEEEEEEEE
You better hope I do. 'Cause I have questions.
EEEEEEEEEEEEEEEEE
EEEEEEEEEEEEEEEE
I'm not letting you go until I get answers.
EEEEEEEEEEEEEEEEE

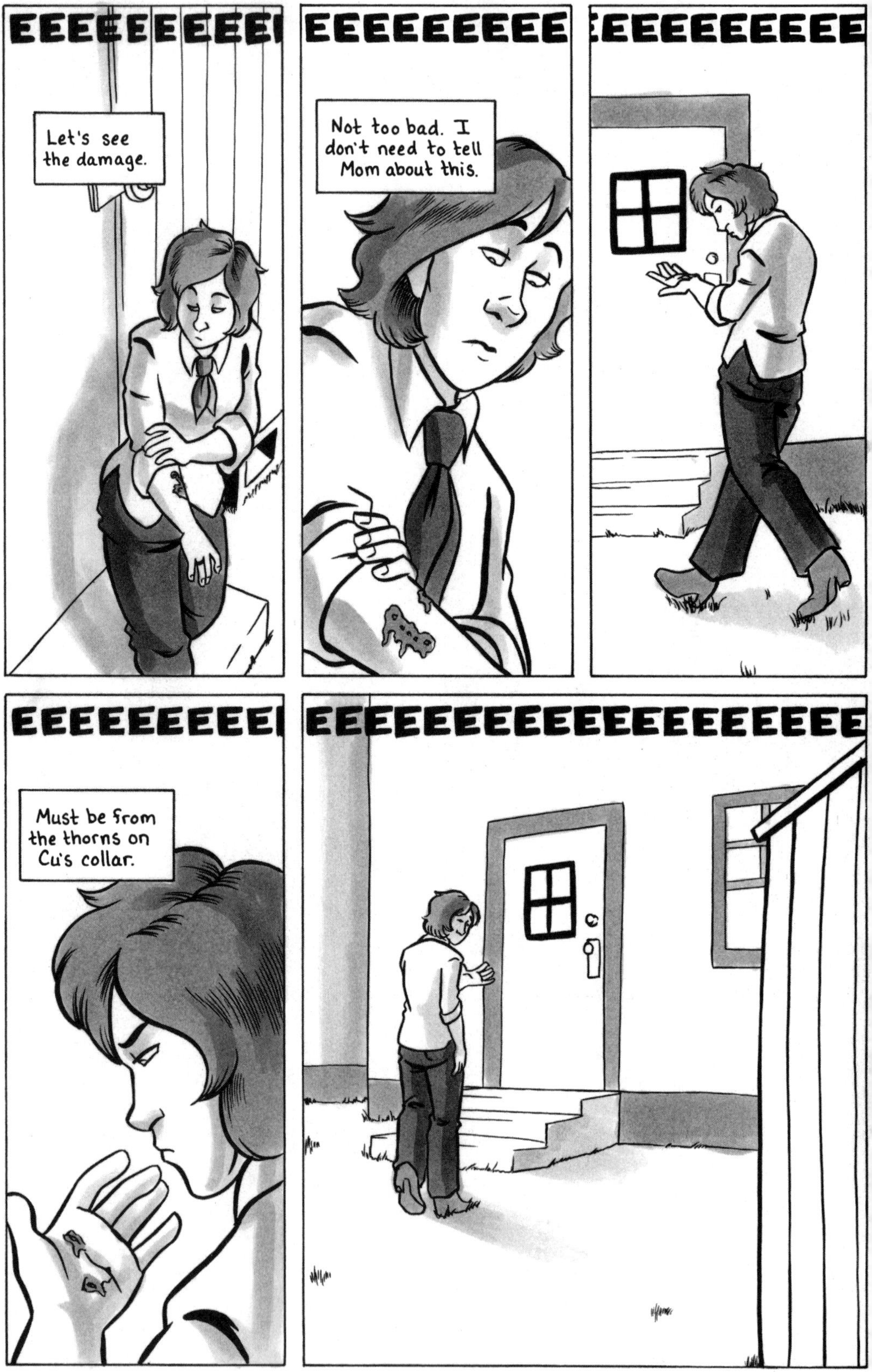
EEEEEEEEEEEE
Let's see the damage.
EEEEEEEEEE
Not too bad. I don't need to tell Mom about this.
EEEEEEEEEEE
EEEEEEEEEEE
Must be from the thorns on Cu's collar.
EEEEEEEEEEEEEEEEEEEEE

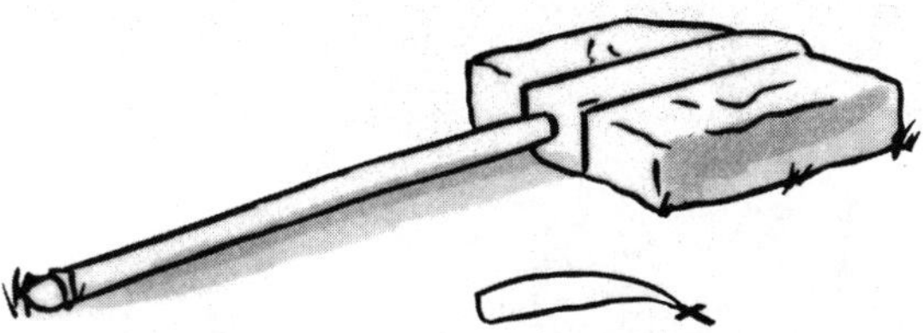

CHAPTER 9: *Neither Clever nor Sensitive, but He Was Loyal*

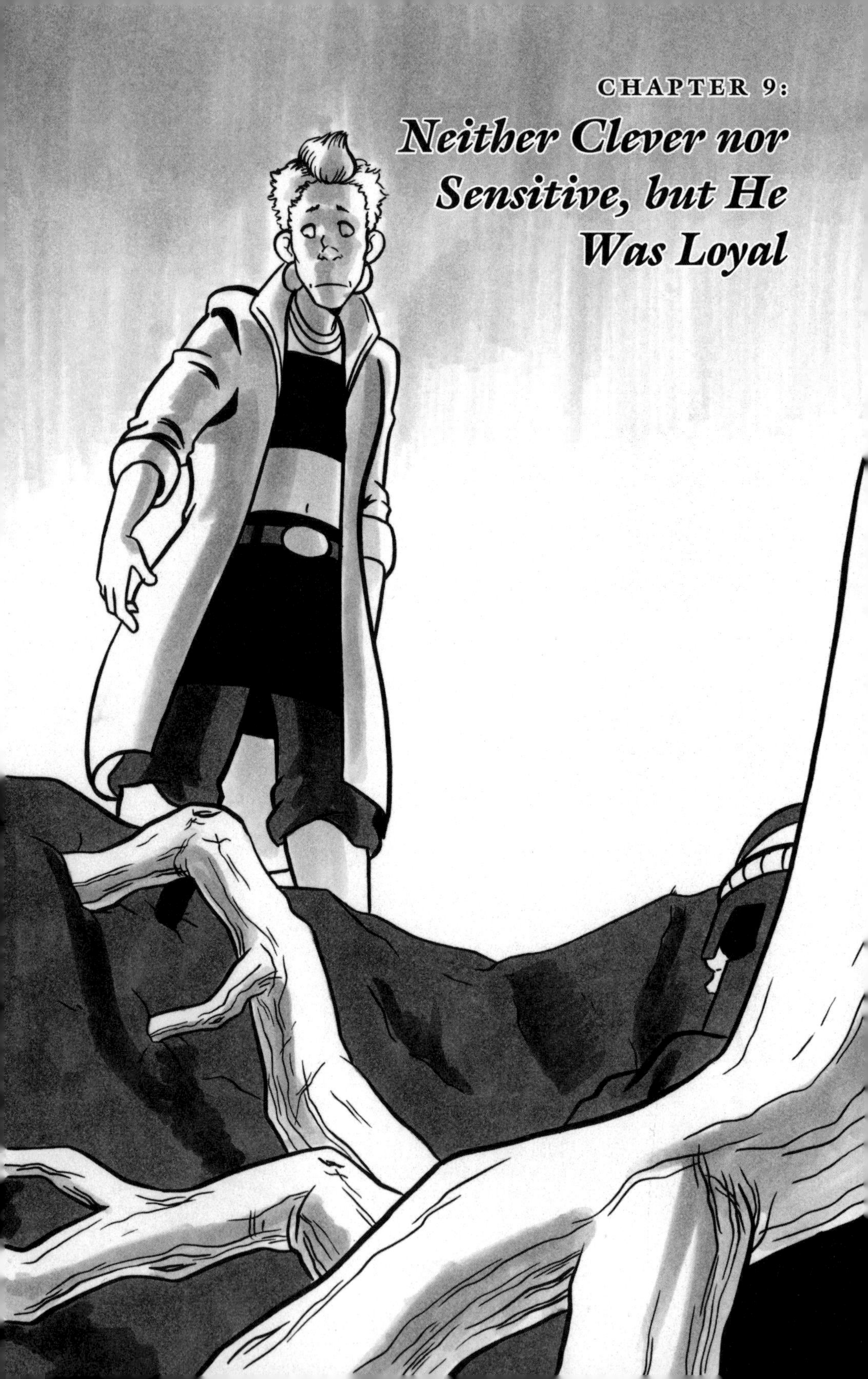

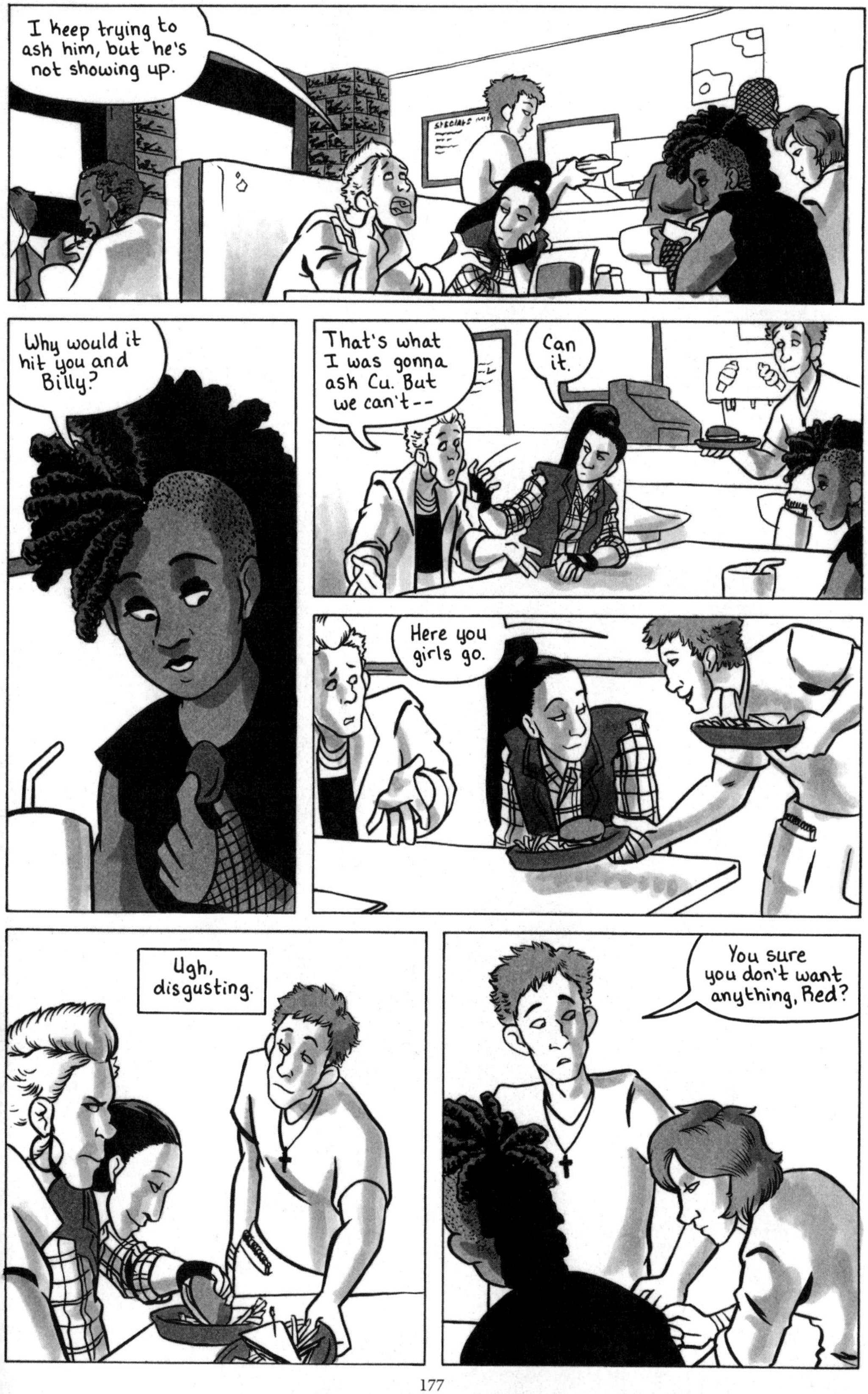
I keep trying to ask him, but he's not showing up.
Why would it hit you and Billy?
That's what I was gonna ask Cu. But we can't--
Can it.
Here you girls go.
Ugh, disgusting.
You sure you don't want anything, Red?

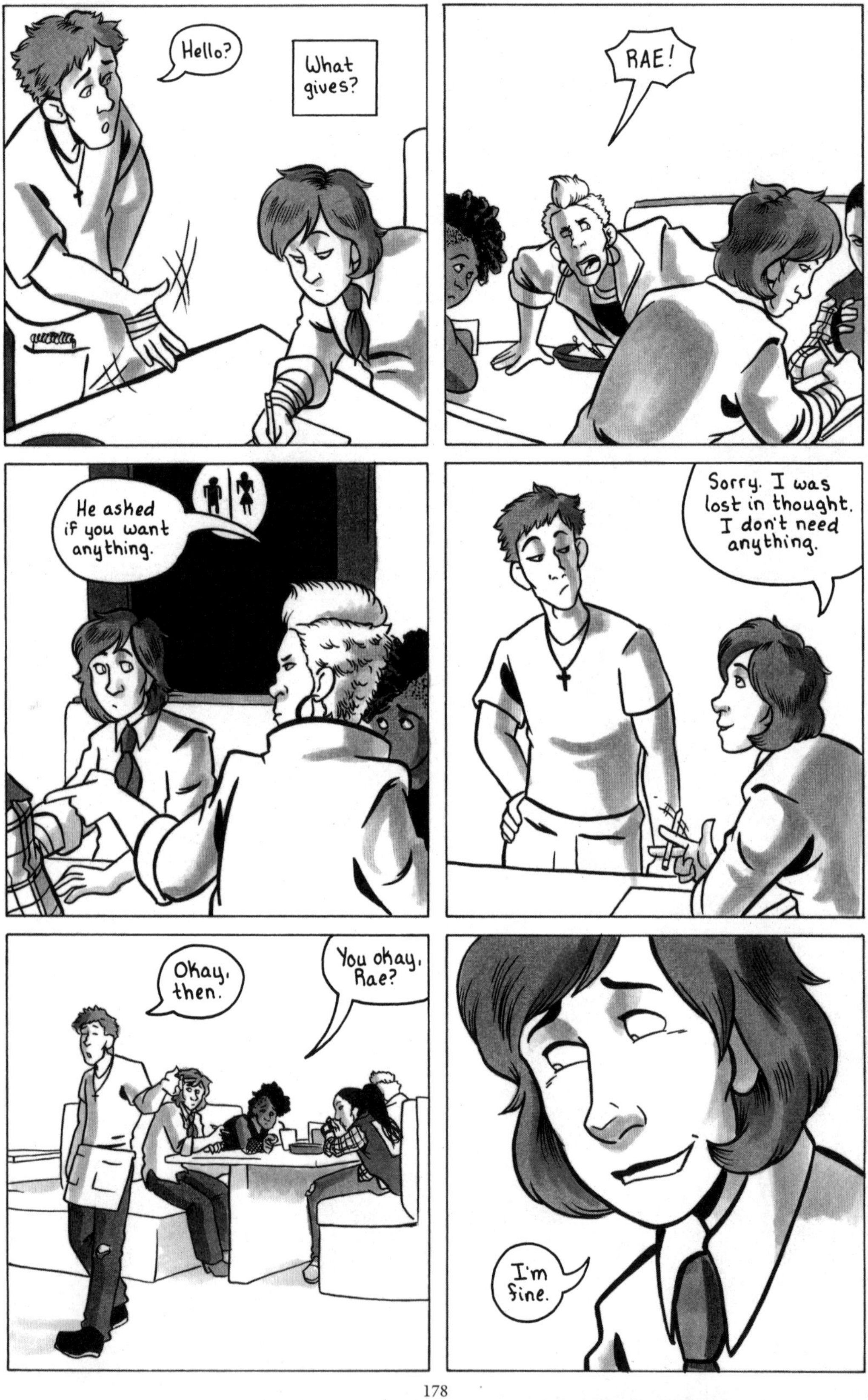

Hello?
What gives?
RAE!
He asked if you want anything.
Sorry. I was lost in thought. I don't need anything.
Okay, then.
You okay, Rae?
I'm fine.

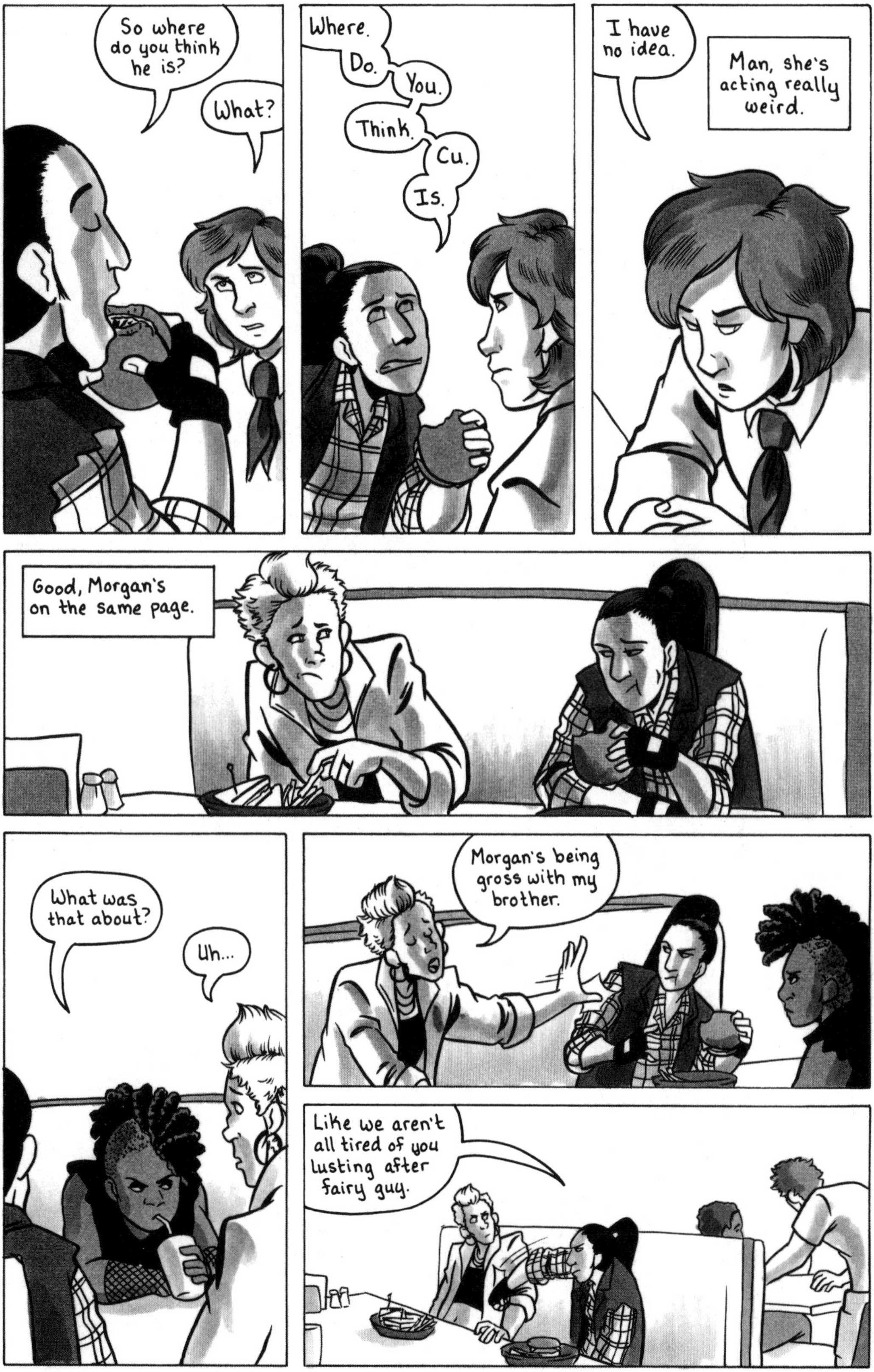
So where do you think he is?
What?
Where. Do. You. Think. Cu. Is.
I have no idea.
Man, she's acting really weird.
Good, Morgan's on the same page.
What was that about?
Uh...
Morgan's being gross with my brother.
Like we aren't all tired of you lusting after fairy guy.

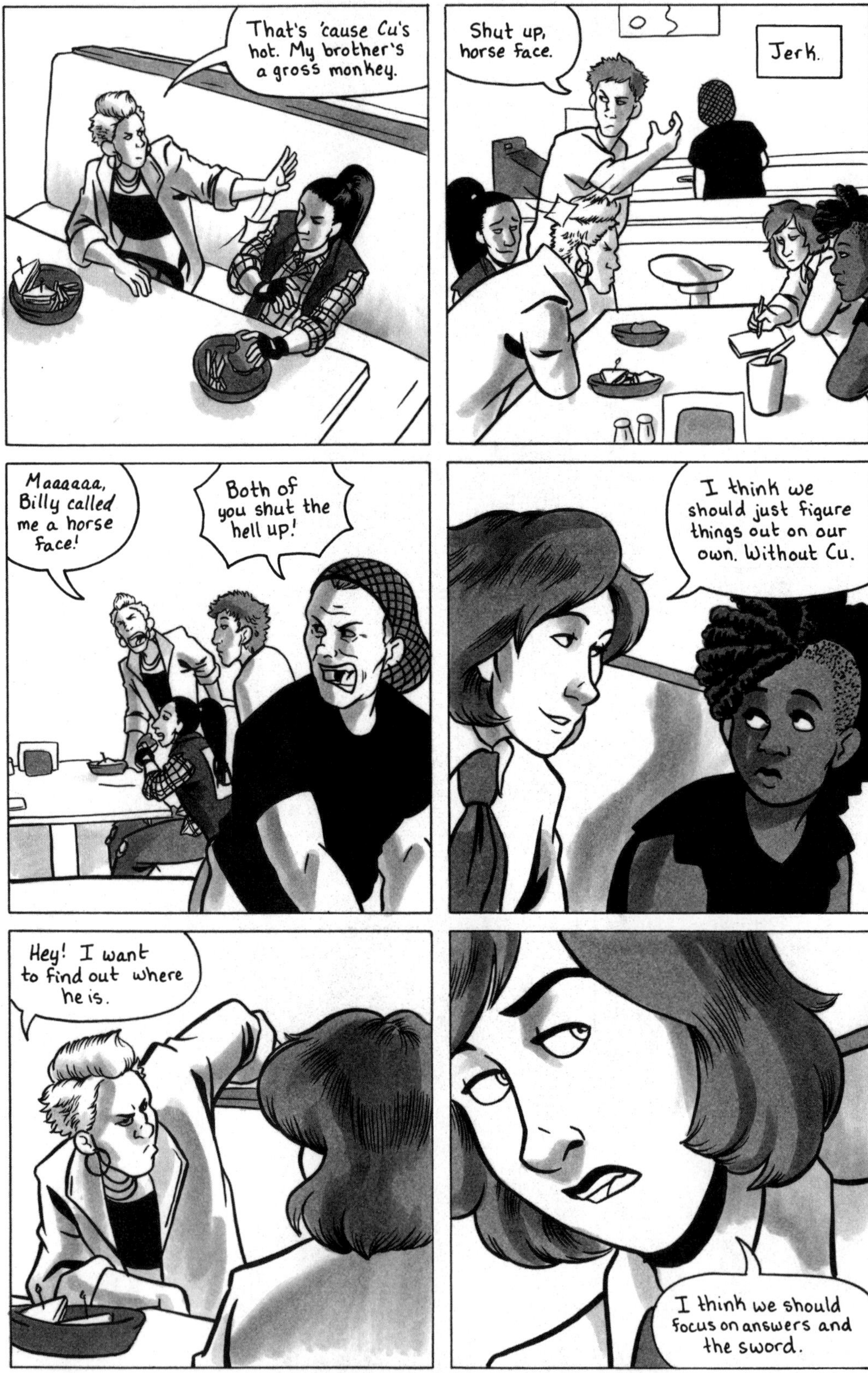
That's 'cause Cu's hot. My brother's a gross monkey.
Shut up, horse face.
Jerk.
Maaaaaa, Billy called me a horse face!
Both of you shut the hell up!
I think we should just figure things out on our own. Without Cu.
Hey! I want to find out where he is.
I think we should focus on answers and the sword.

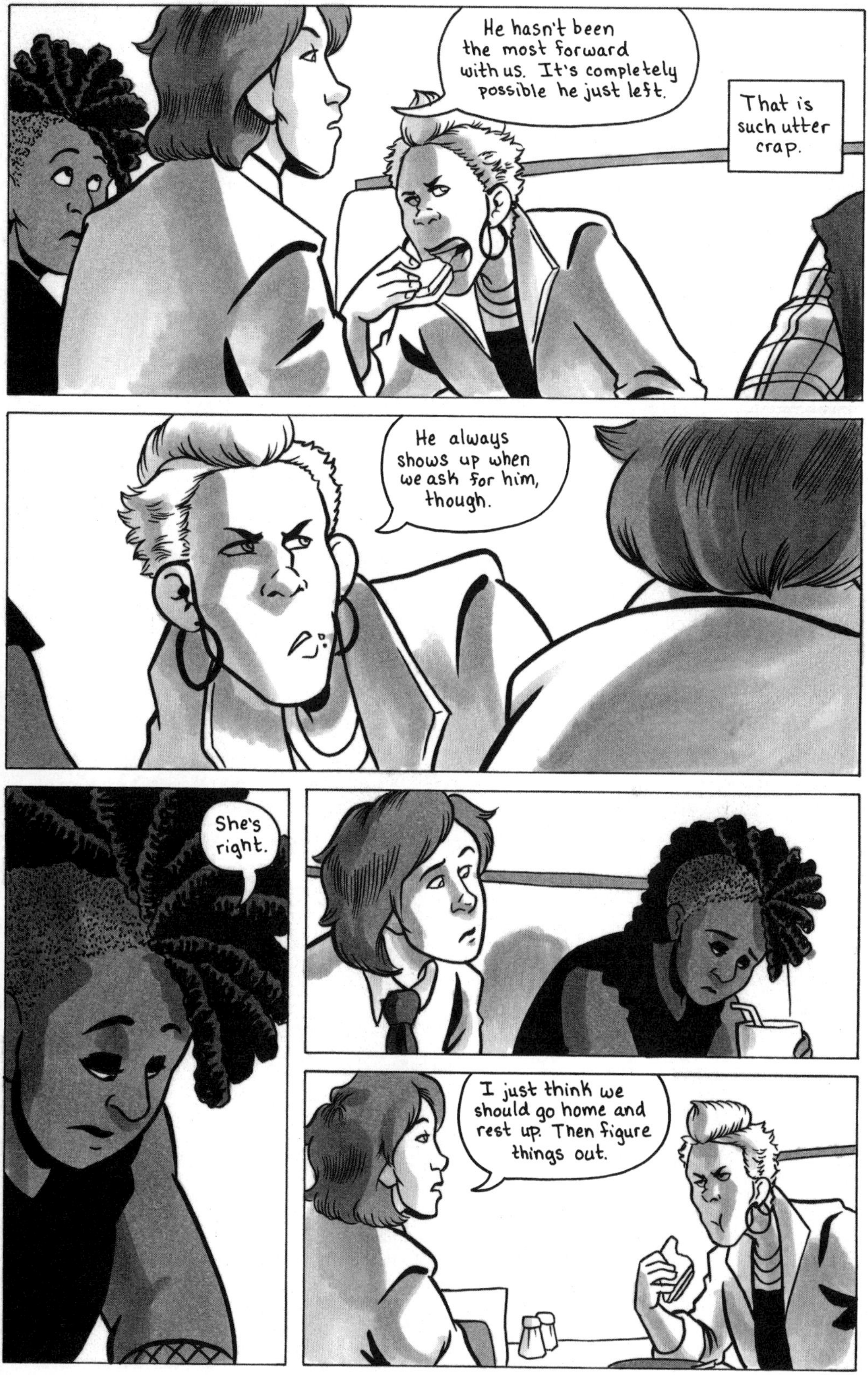
He hasn't been the most forward with us. It's completely possible he just left.
That is such utter crap.
He always shows up when we ask for him, though.
She's right.
I just think we should go home and rest up. Then figure things out.

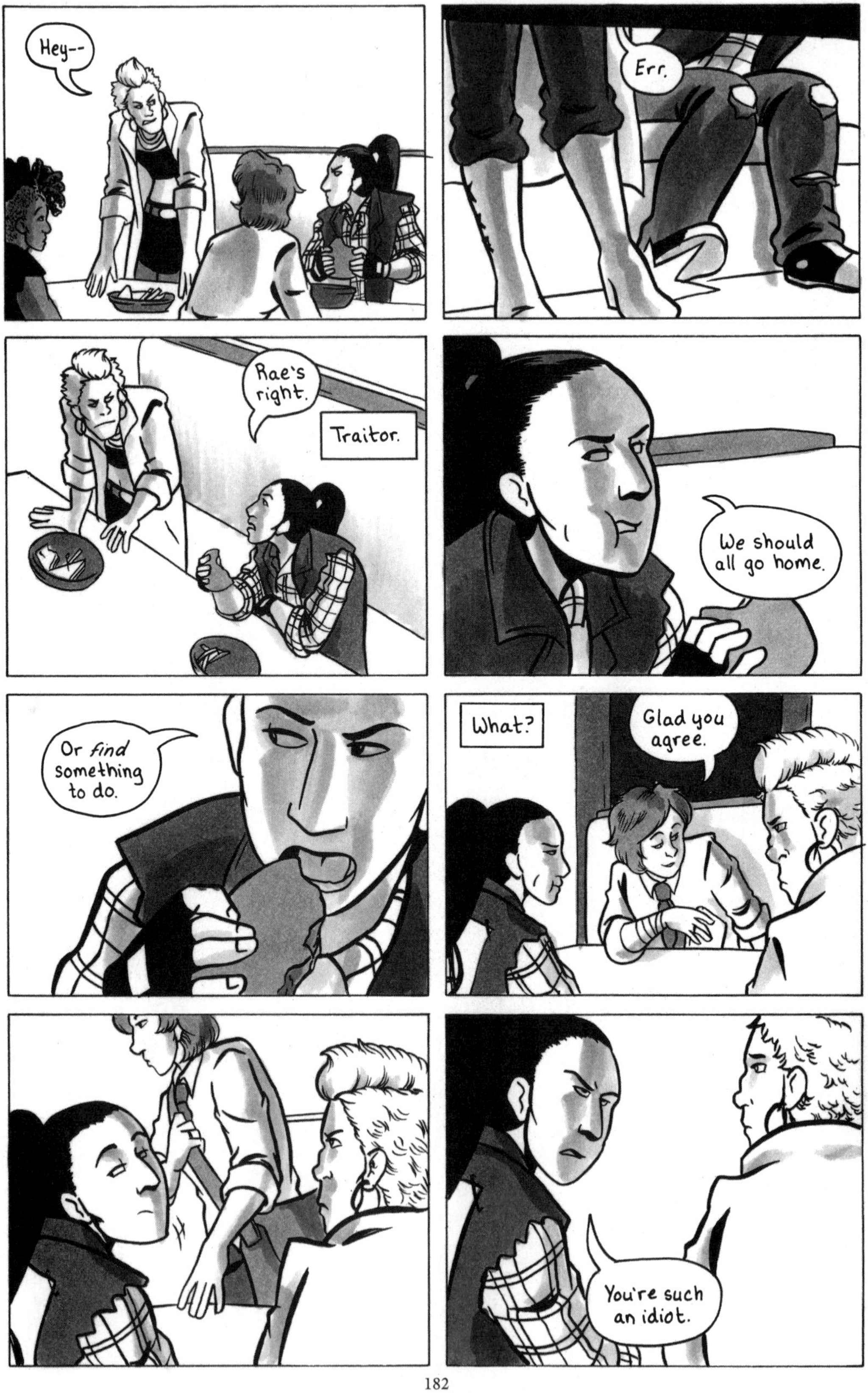
Hey--
Err.
Rae's right.
Traitor.
We should all go home.
Or *find* something to do.
What?
Glad you agree.
You're such an idiot.

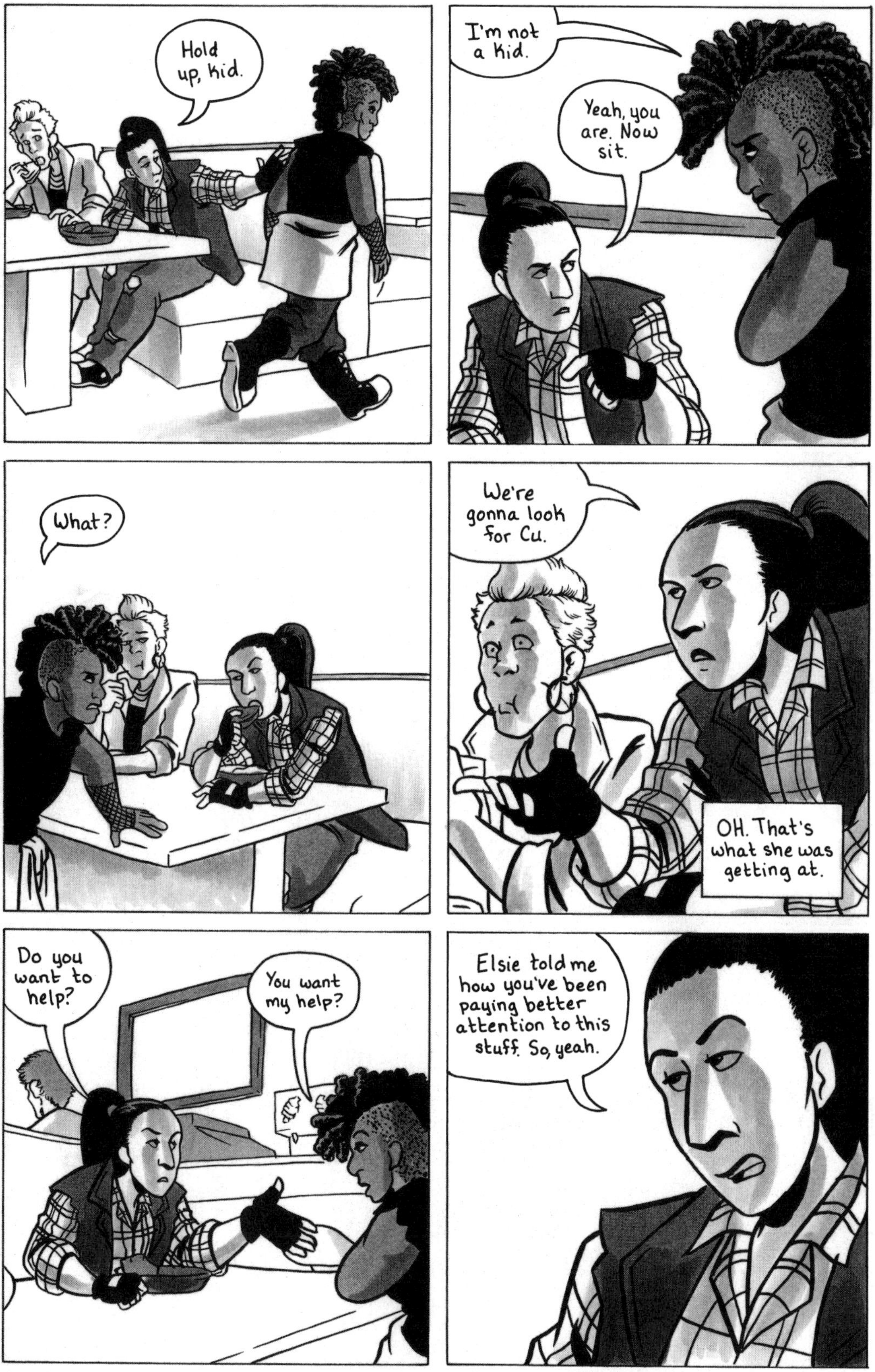
Hold up, kid.
I'm not a kid.
Yeah, you are. Now sit.
What?
We're gonna look for Cu.
OH. That's what she was getting at.
Do you want to help?
You want my help?
Elsie told me how you've been paying better attention to this stuff. So, yeah.

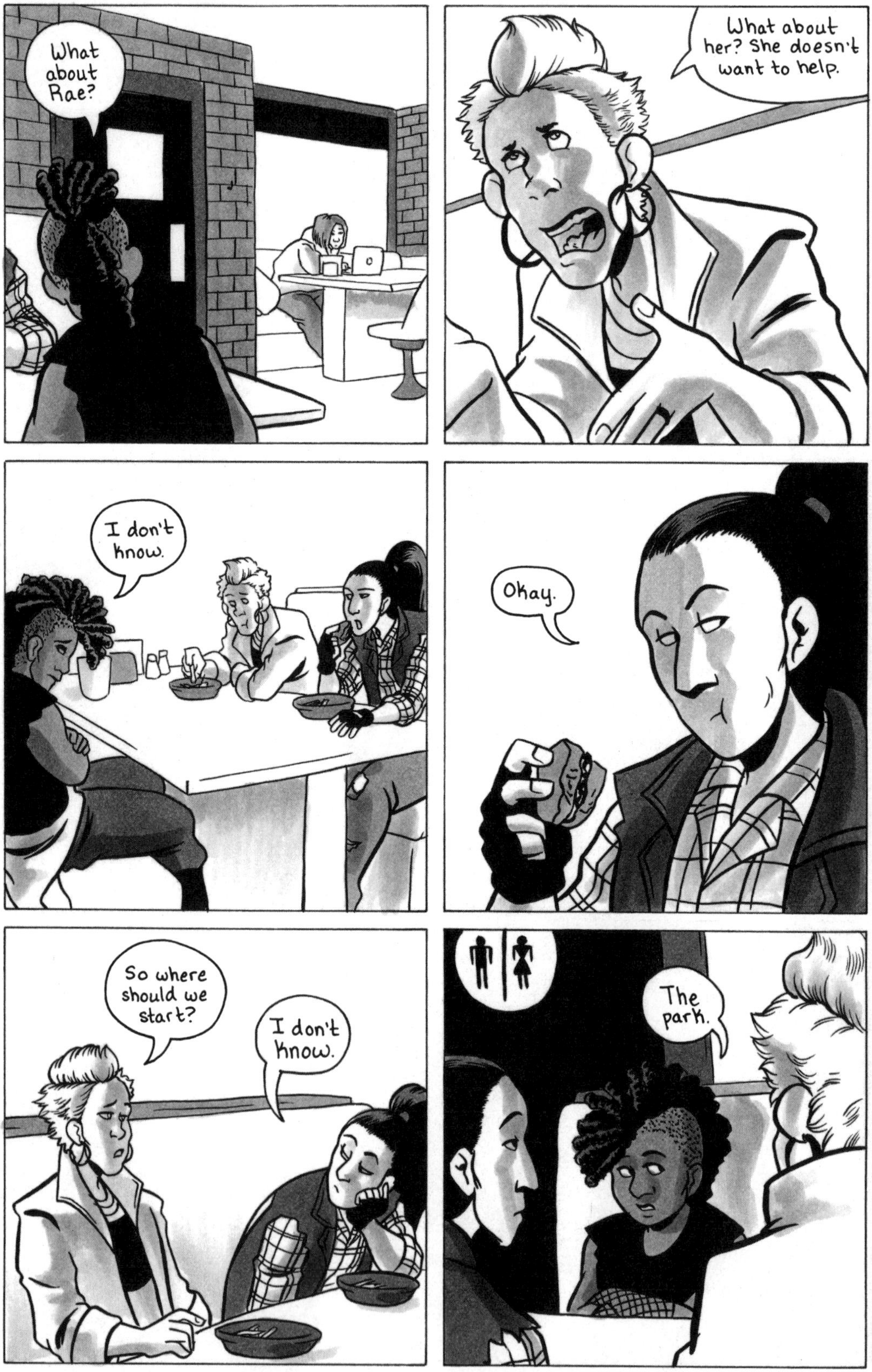
What about Rae?
What about her? She doesn't want to help.
I don't know.
Okay.
So where should we start?
I don't know.
The park.

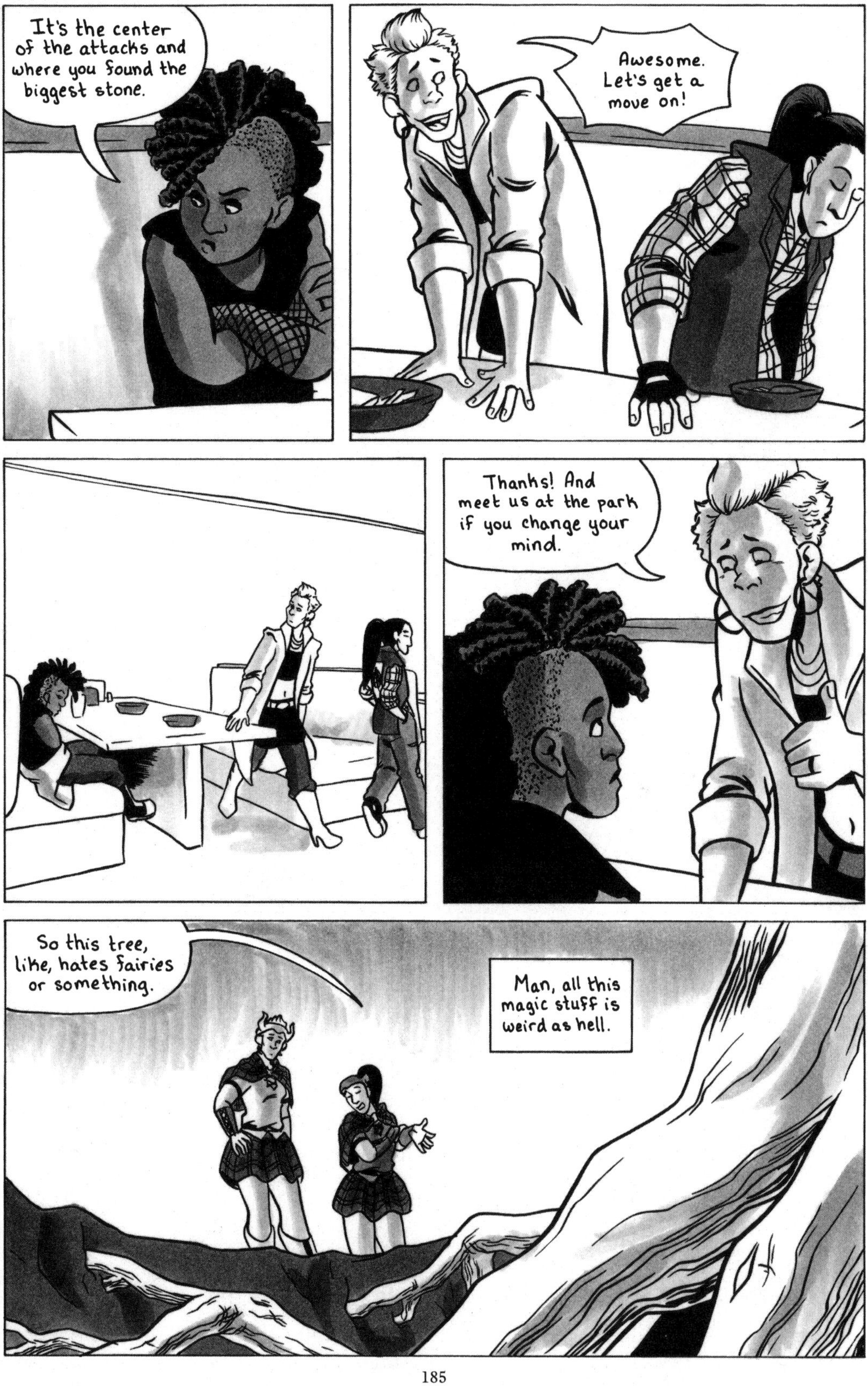

It's the center of the attacks and where you found the biggest stone.
Awesome. Let's get a move on!
Thanks! And meet us at the park if you change your mind.
So this tree, like, hates fairies or something.
Man, all this magic stuff is weird as hell.

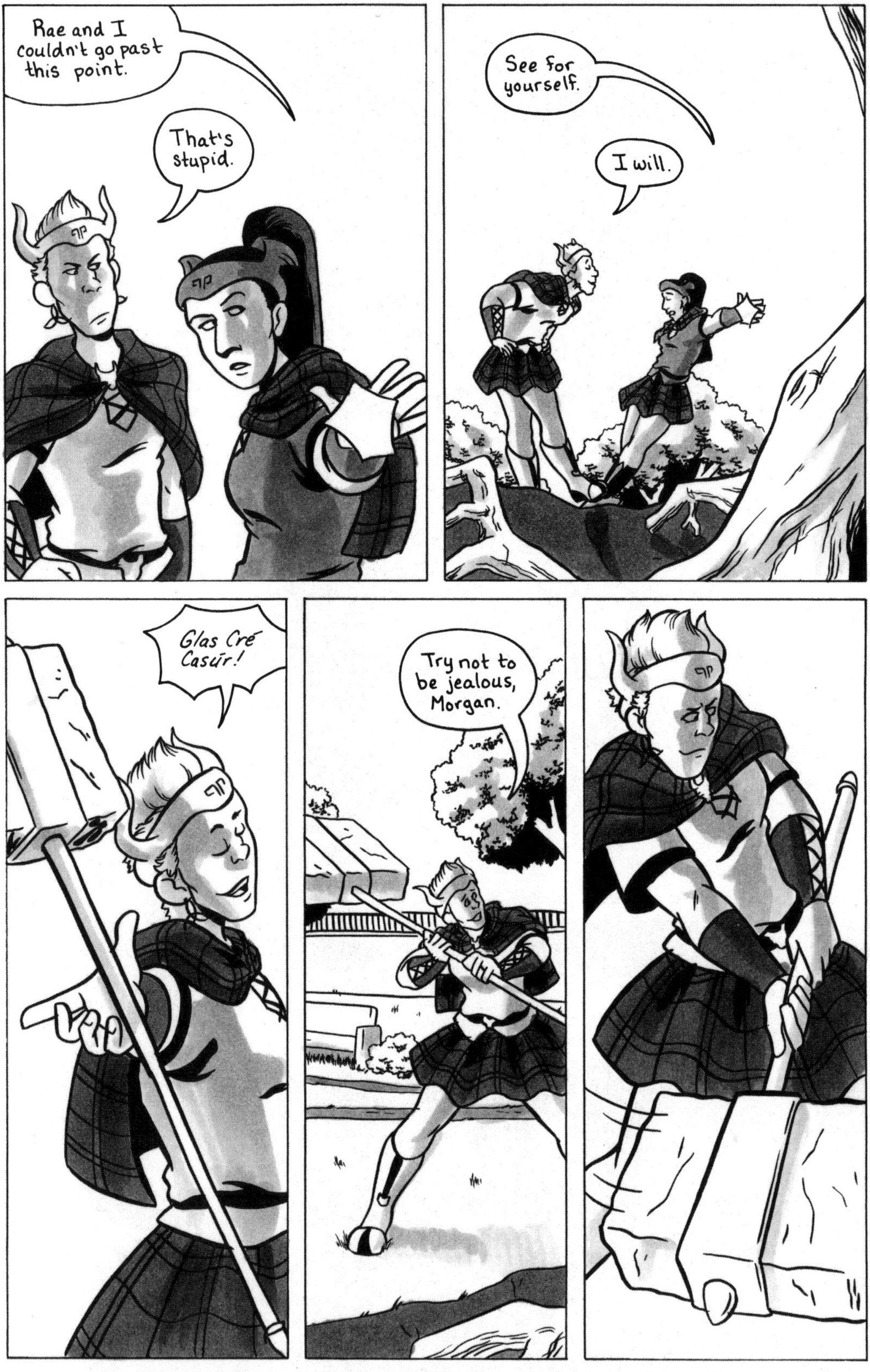
Rae and I couldn't go past this point.
That's stupid.
See for yourself.
I will.
Glas Cré Casúr!
Try not to be jealous, Morgan.

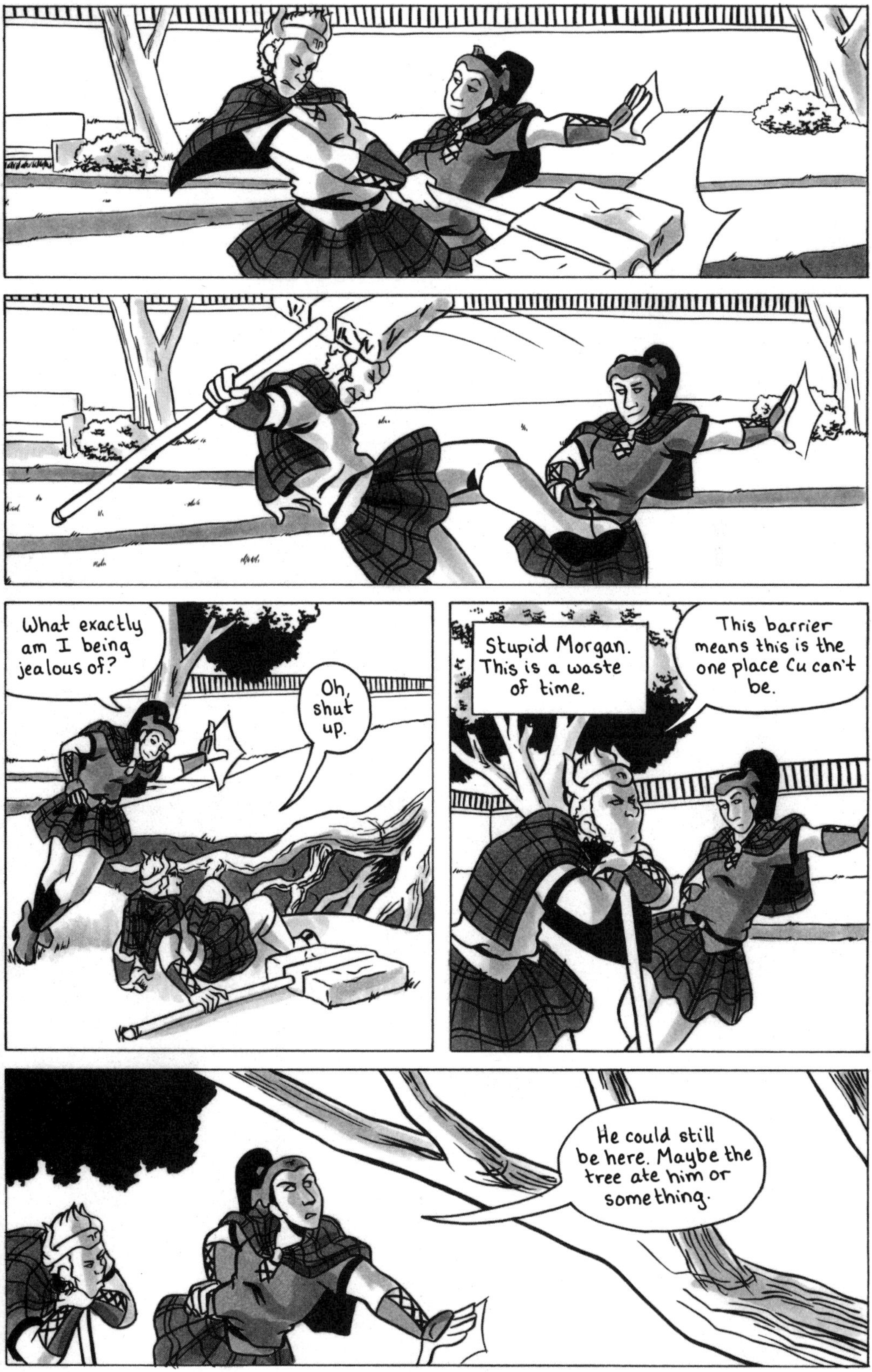
What exactly am I being jealous of?
Oh, shut up.
Stupid Morgan. This is a waste of time.
This barrier means this is the one place Cu can't be.
He could still be here. Maybe the tree ate him or something.

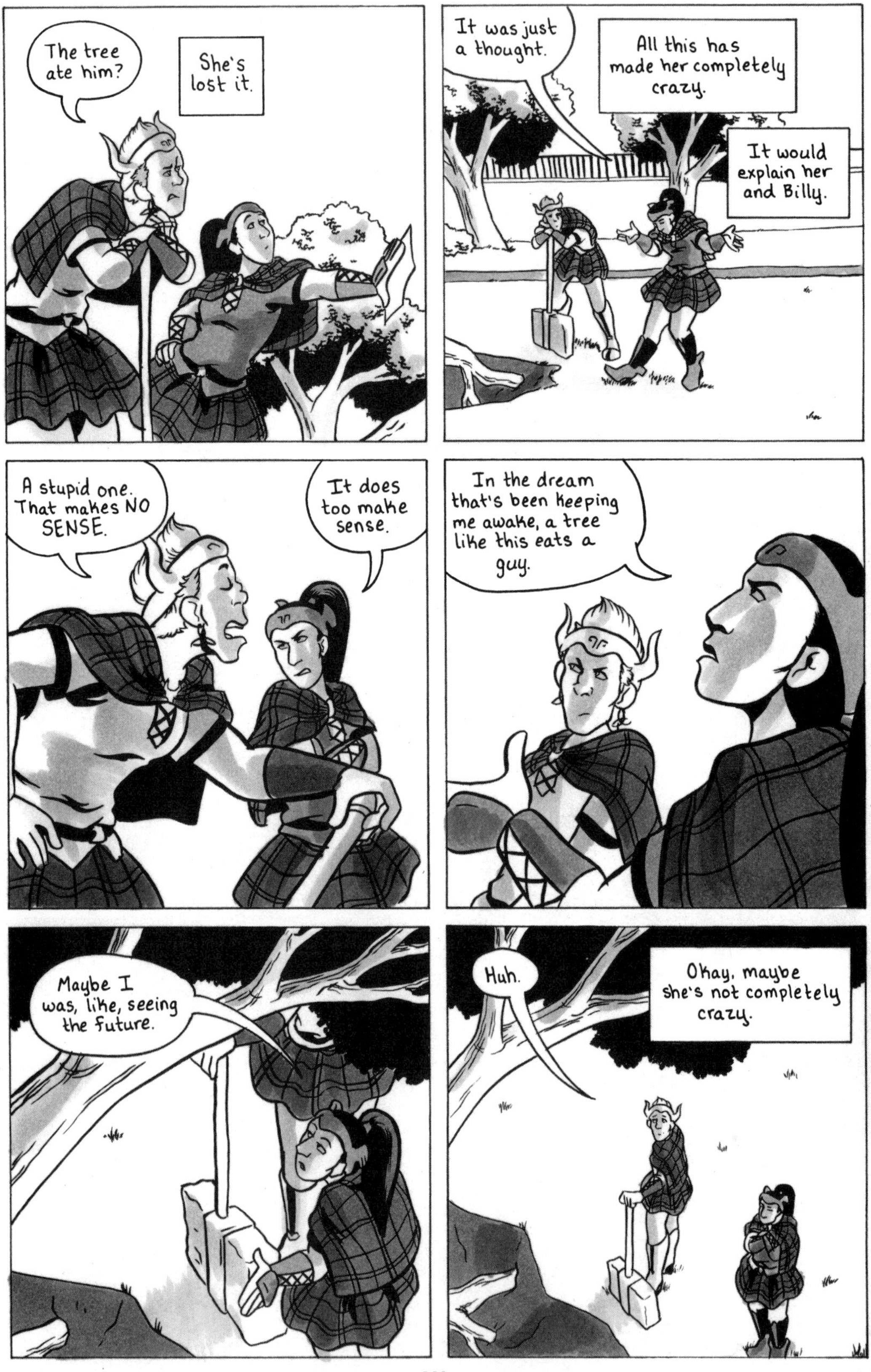
The tree ate him?
She's lost it.
It was just a thought.
All this has made her completely crazy.
It would explain her and Billy.
A stupid one. That makes NO SENSE.
It does too make sense.
In the dream that's been keeping me awake, a tree like this eats a guy.
Maybe I was, like, seeing the future.
Huh.
Okay, maybe she's not completely crazy.

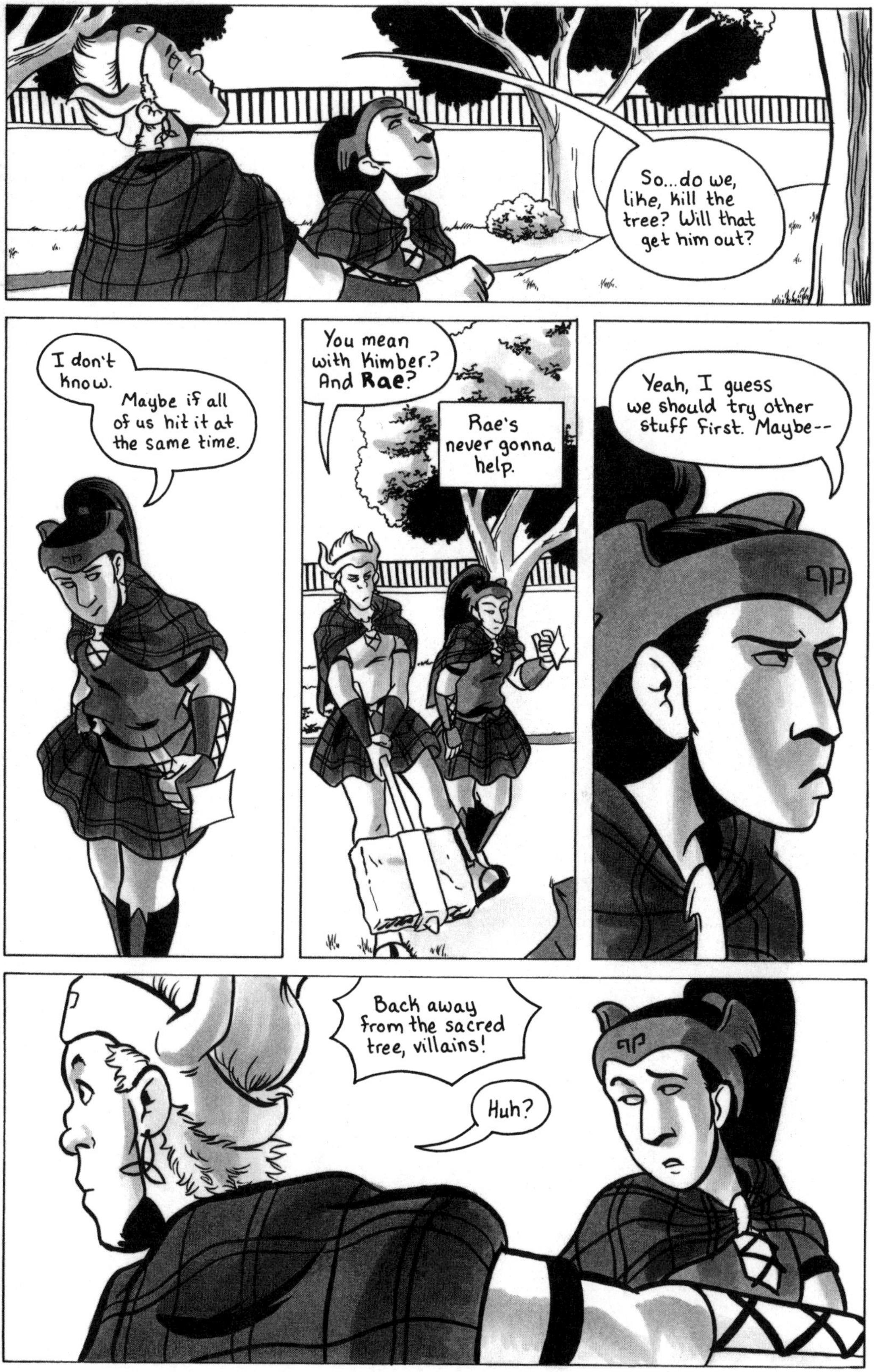
So...do we, like, kill the tree? Will that get him out?
I don't know.
Maybe if all of us hit it at the same time.
You mean with Kimber? And **Rae**?
Rae's never gonna help.
Yeah, I guess we should try other stuff first. Maybe--
Back away from the sacred tree, villains!
Huh?

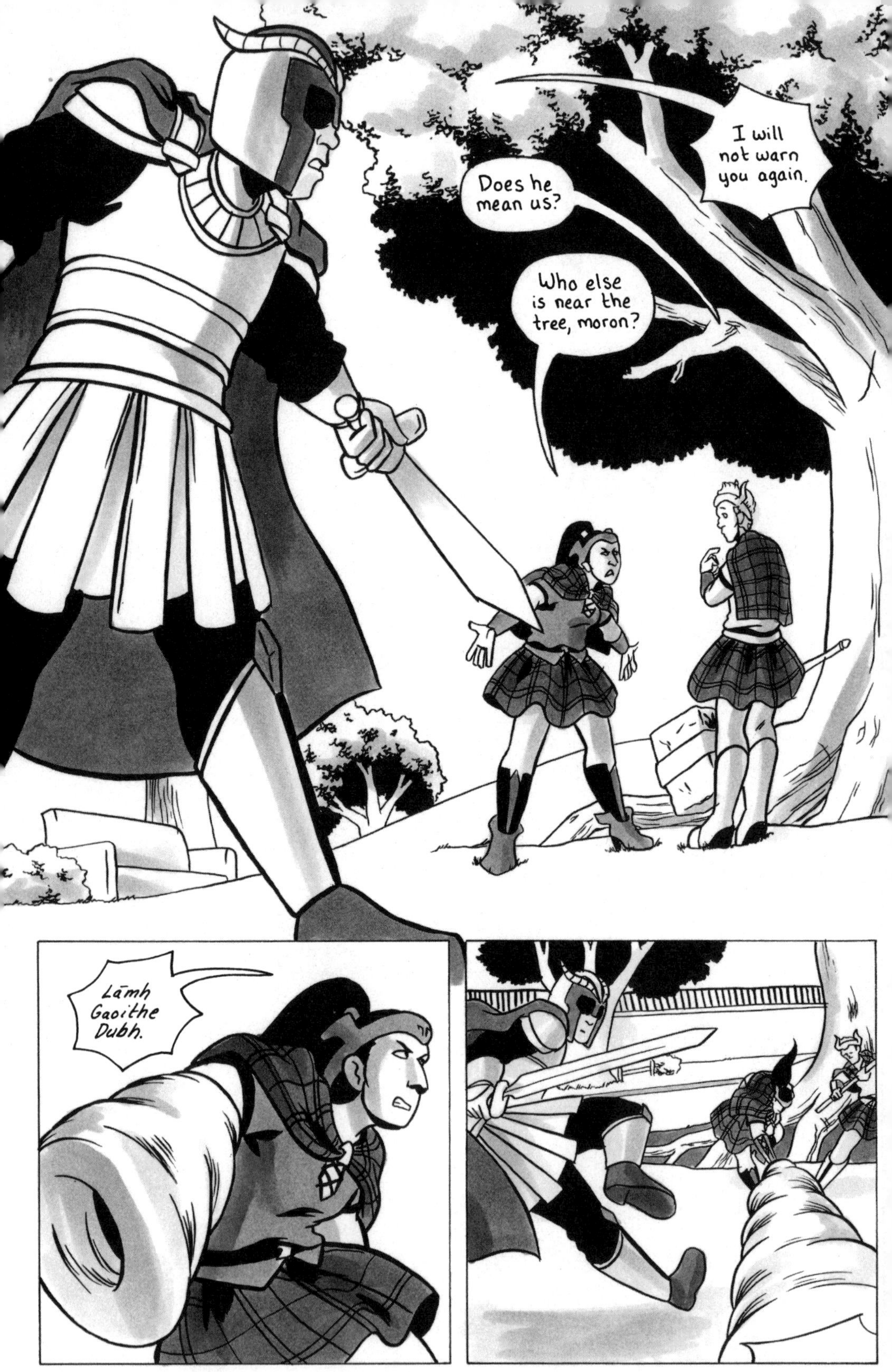
I will not warn you again.
Does he mean us?
Who else is near the tree, moron?
Lāmh Gaoithe Dubh.

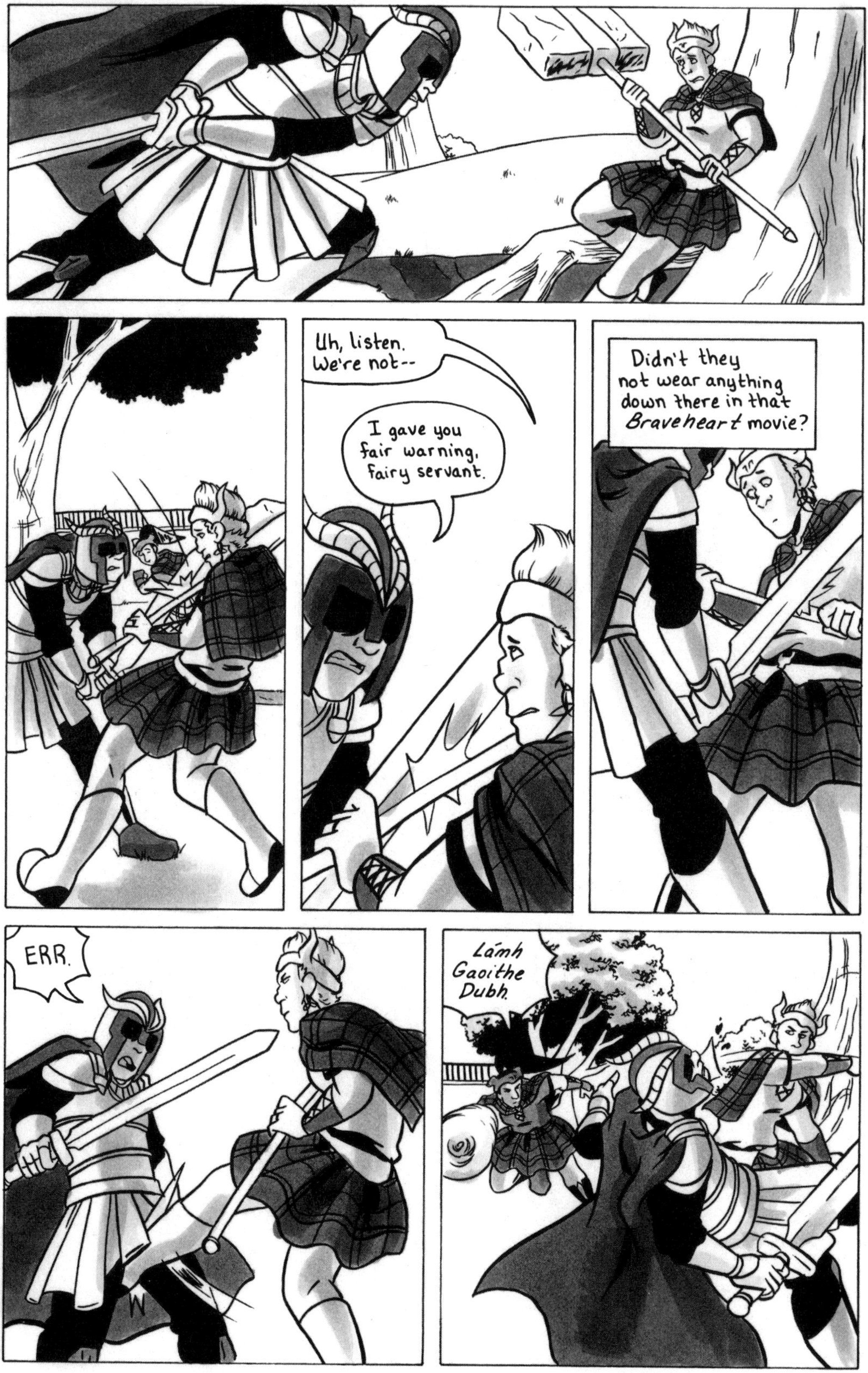

Uh, listen. We're not--
I gave you fair warning, fairy servant.
Didn't they not wear anything down there in that *Braveheart* movie?
ERR.
Lámh Gaoithe Dubh.

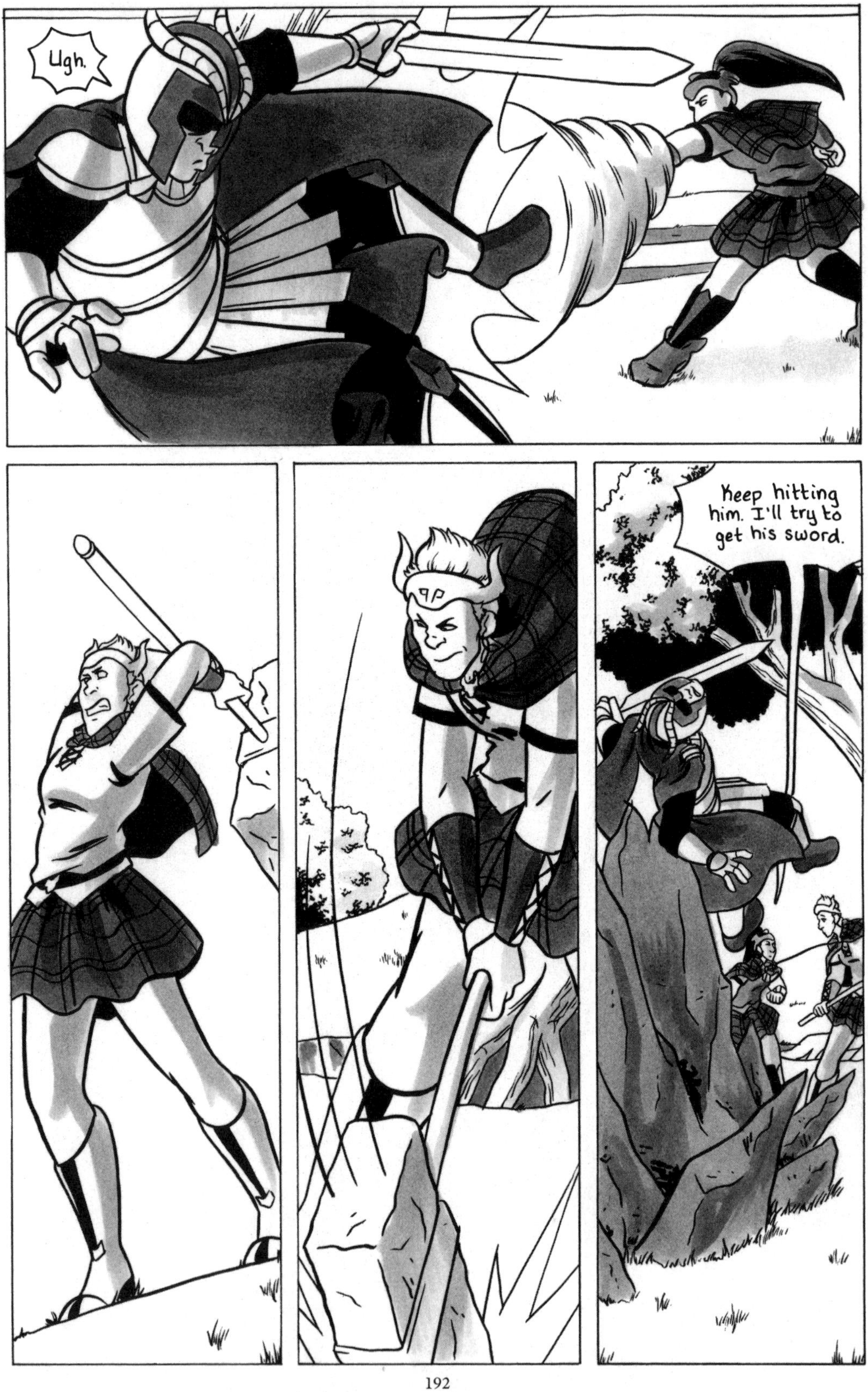
Ugh.
Keep hitting him. I'll try to get his sword.

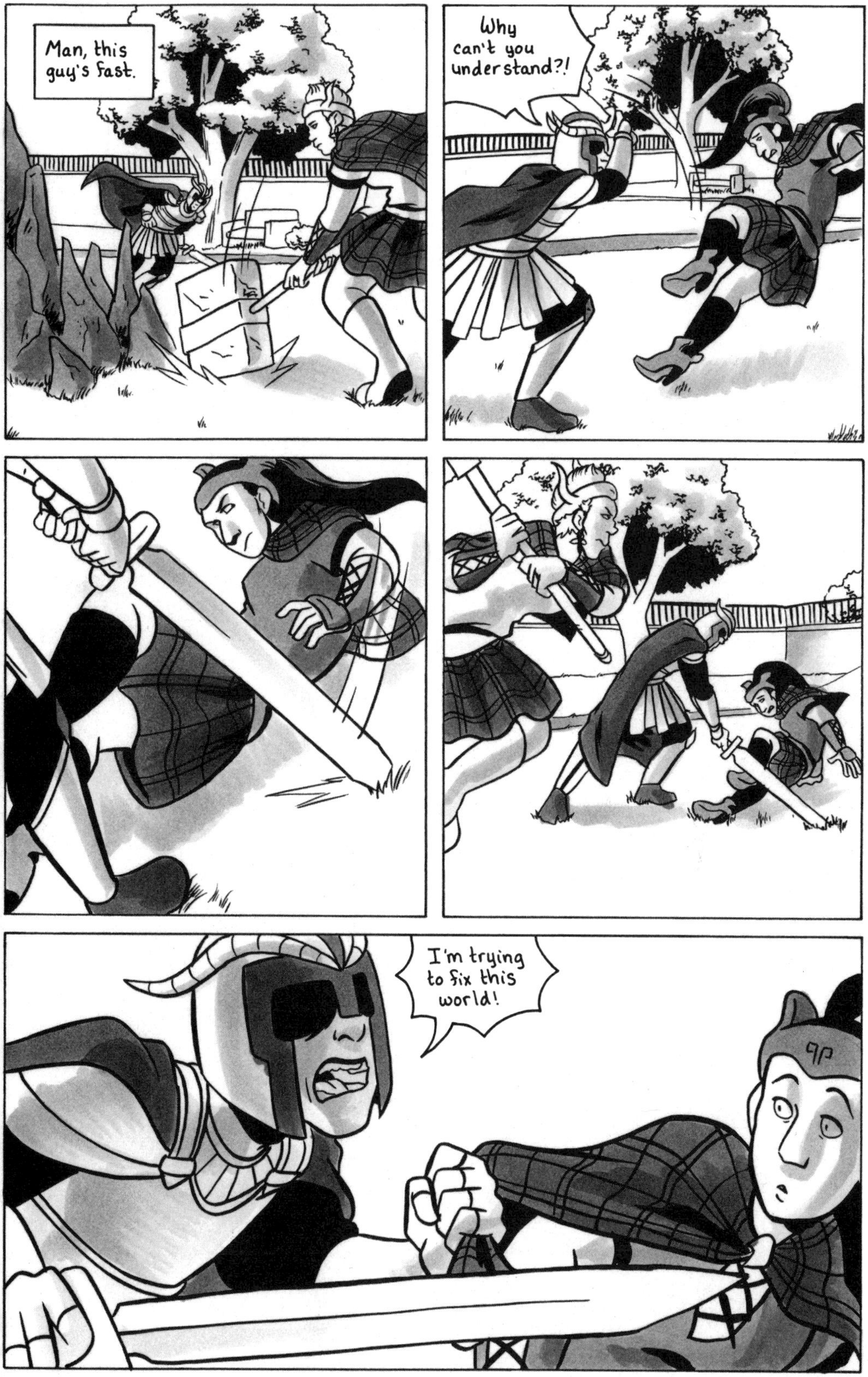
Man, this guy's fast.
Why can't you understand?!
I'm trying to fix this world!

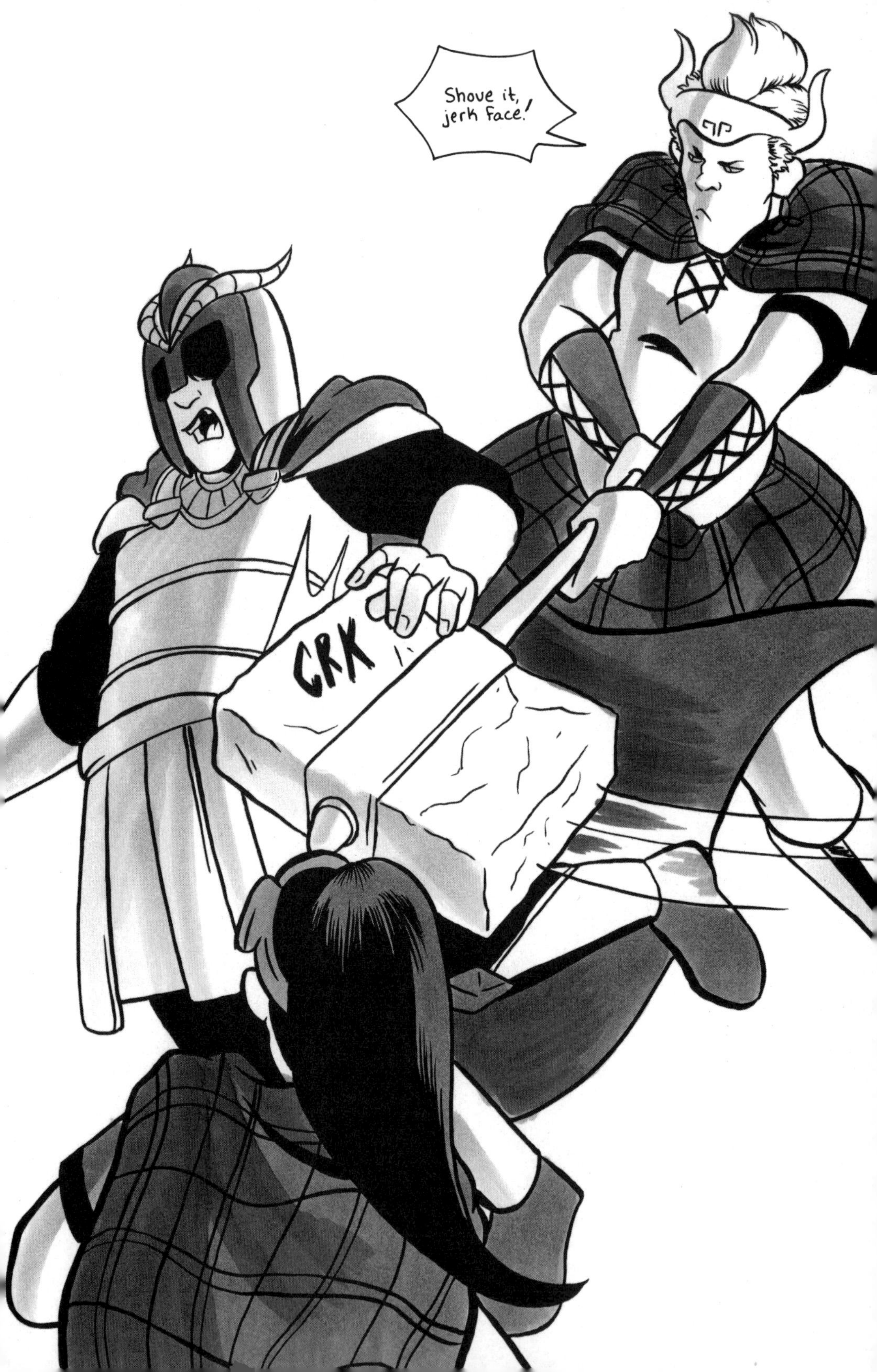
Shove it, jerk face!
GRK

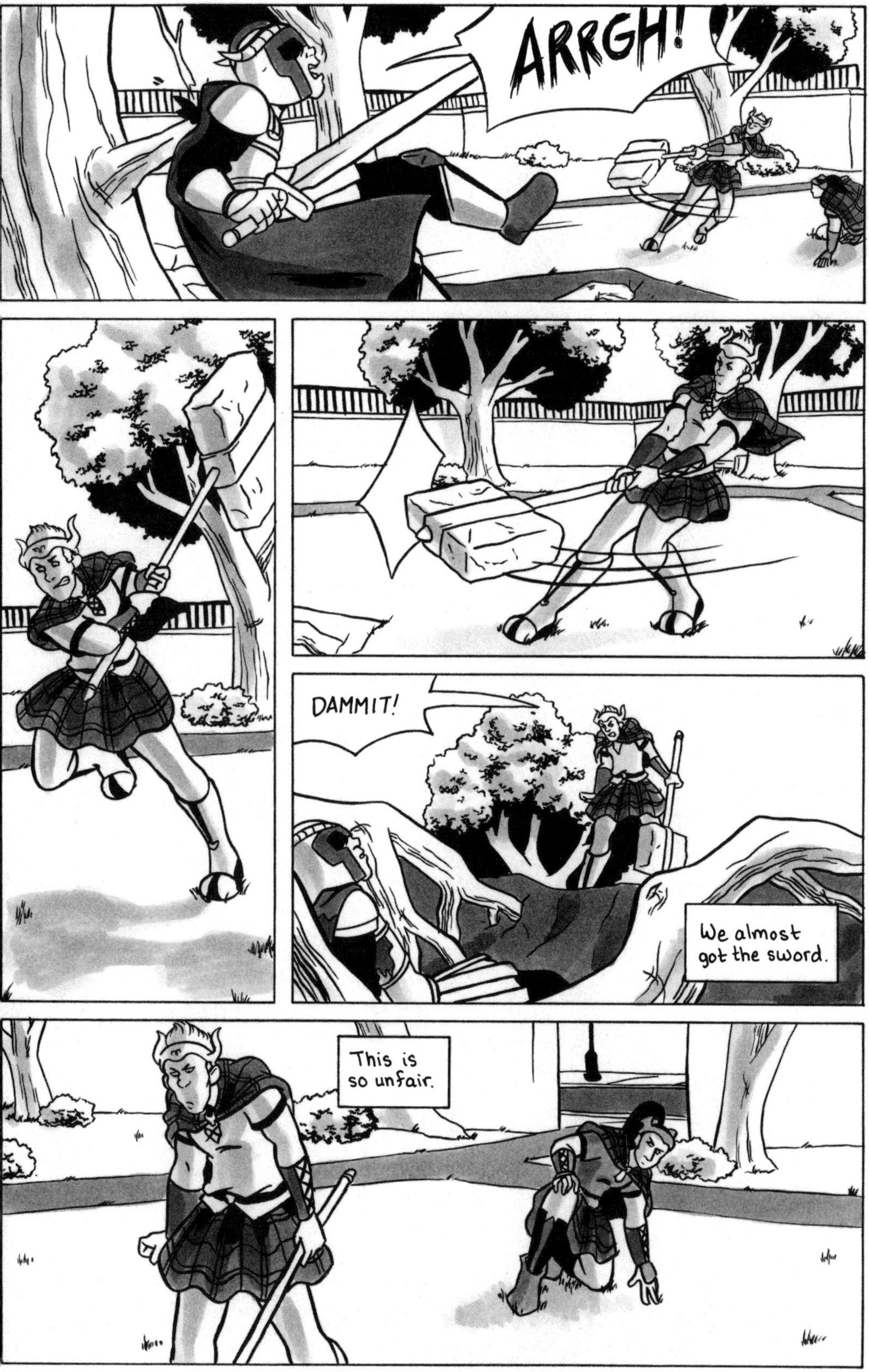
ARRGH!
DAMMIT!
We almost got the sword.
This is so unfair.

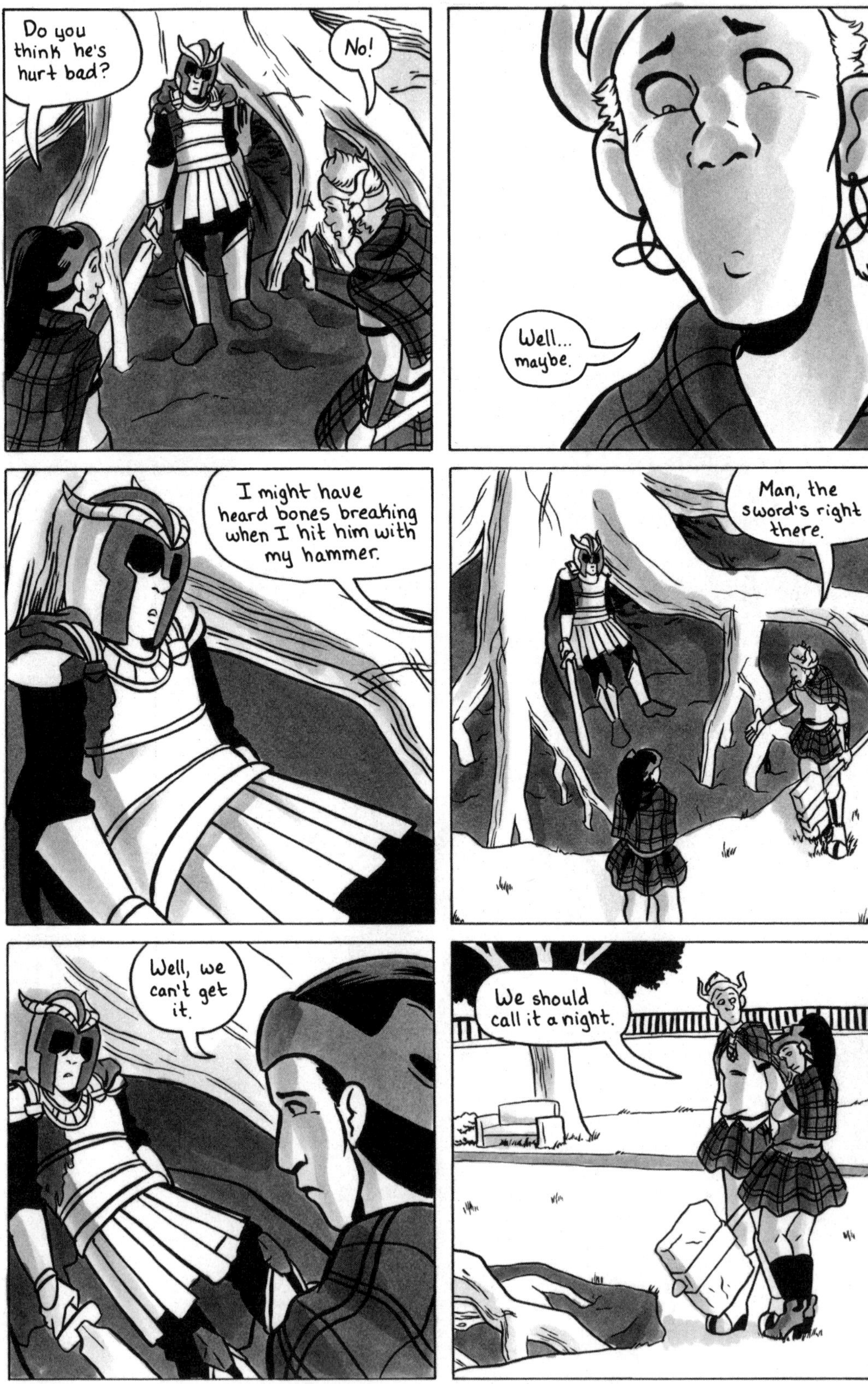
Do you think he's hurt bad?
No!
Well... maybe.
I might have heard bones breaking when I hit him with my hammer.
Man, the sword's right there.
Well, we can't get it.
We should call it a night.

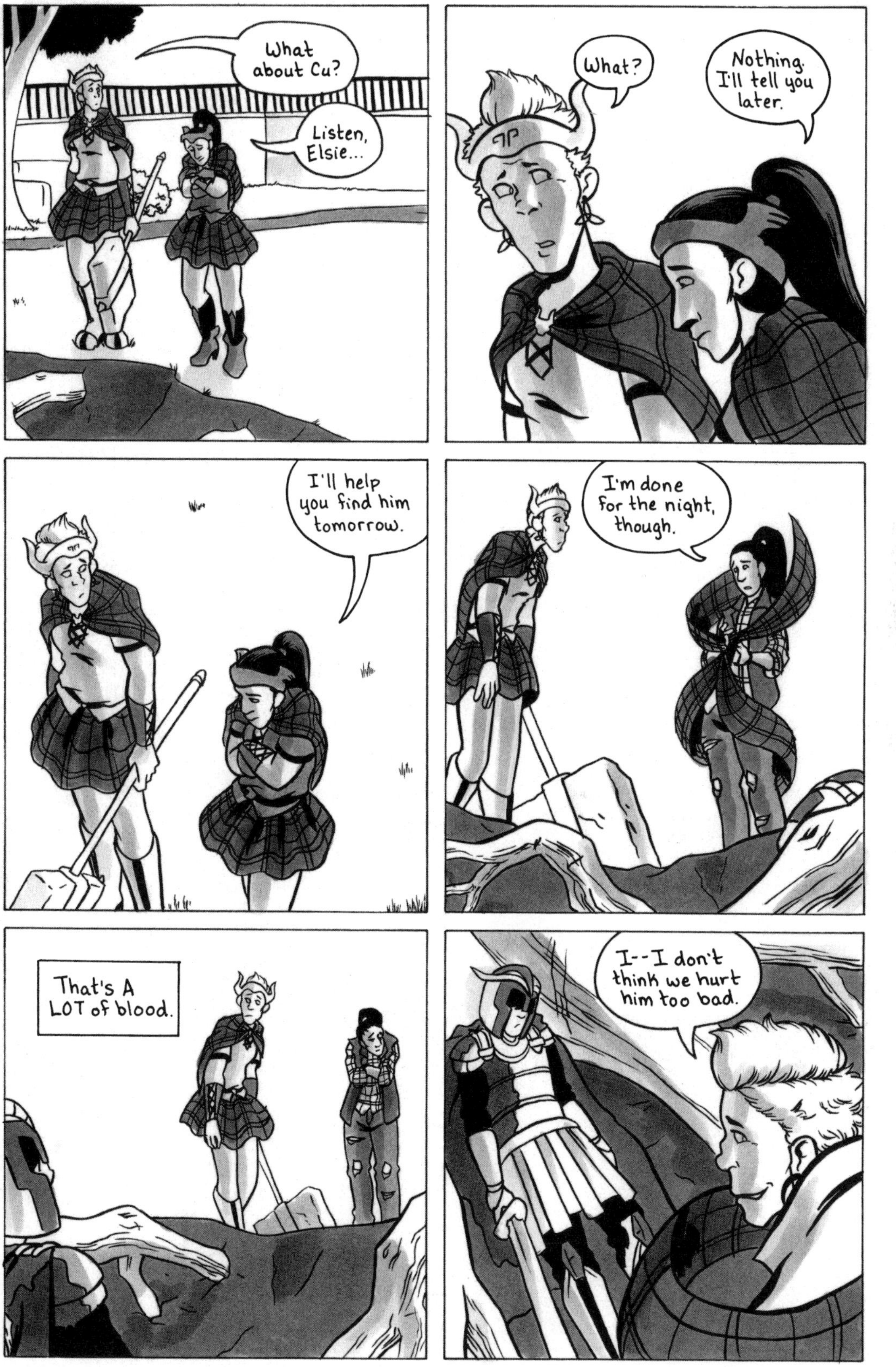
What about Cu?
Listen, Elsie...
What?
Nothing. I'll tell you later.
I'll help you find him tomorrow.
I'm done for the night, though.
That's A LOT of blood.
I--I don't think we hurt him too bad.

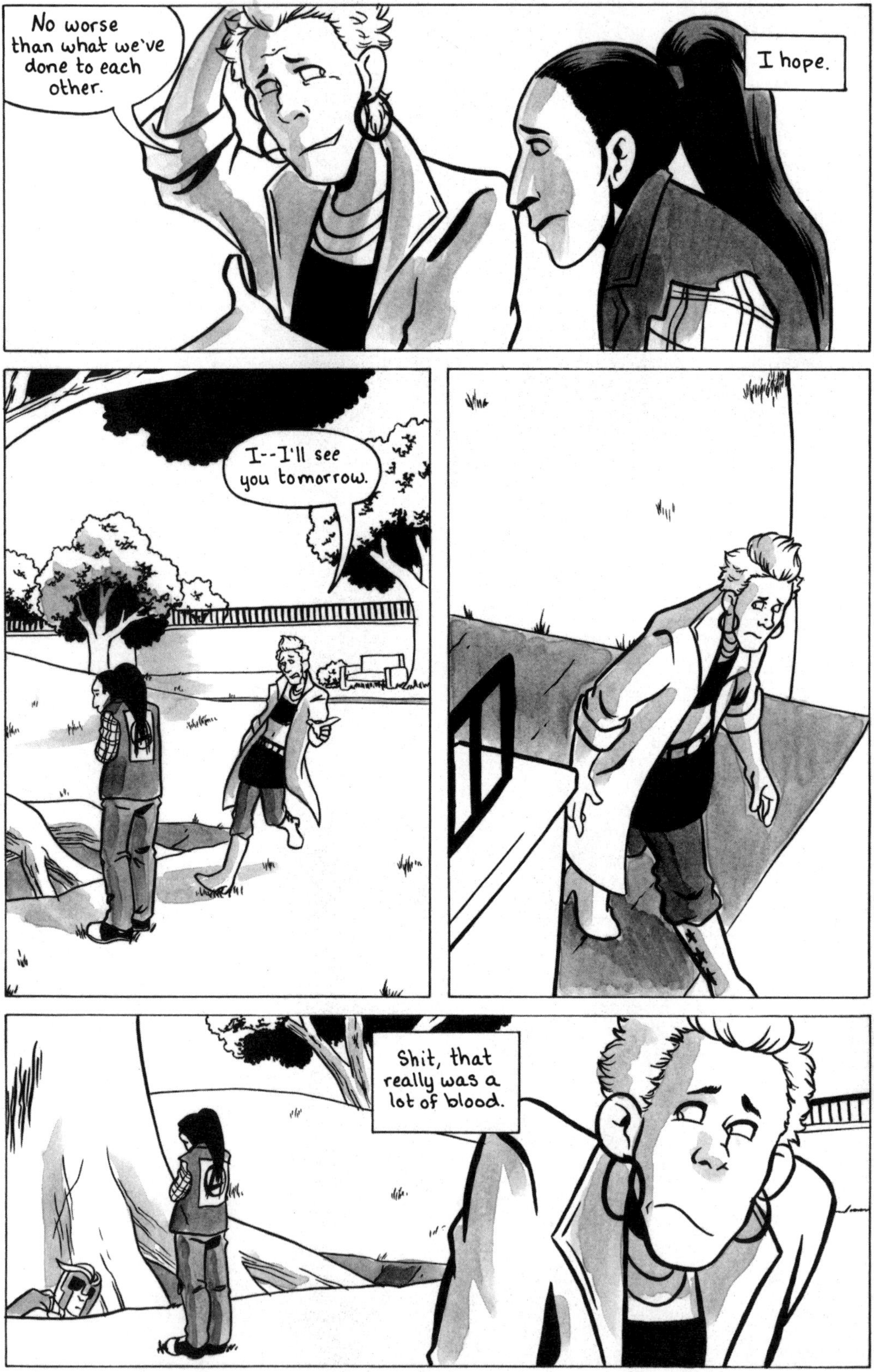

No worse than what we've done to each other.
I hope.
I--I'll see you tomorrow.
Shit, that really was a lot of blood.

CHAPTER 10:

The Poor Fellow Had Never Been Cut Out to Be a Villain

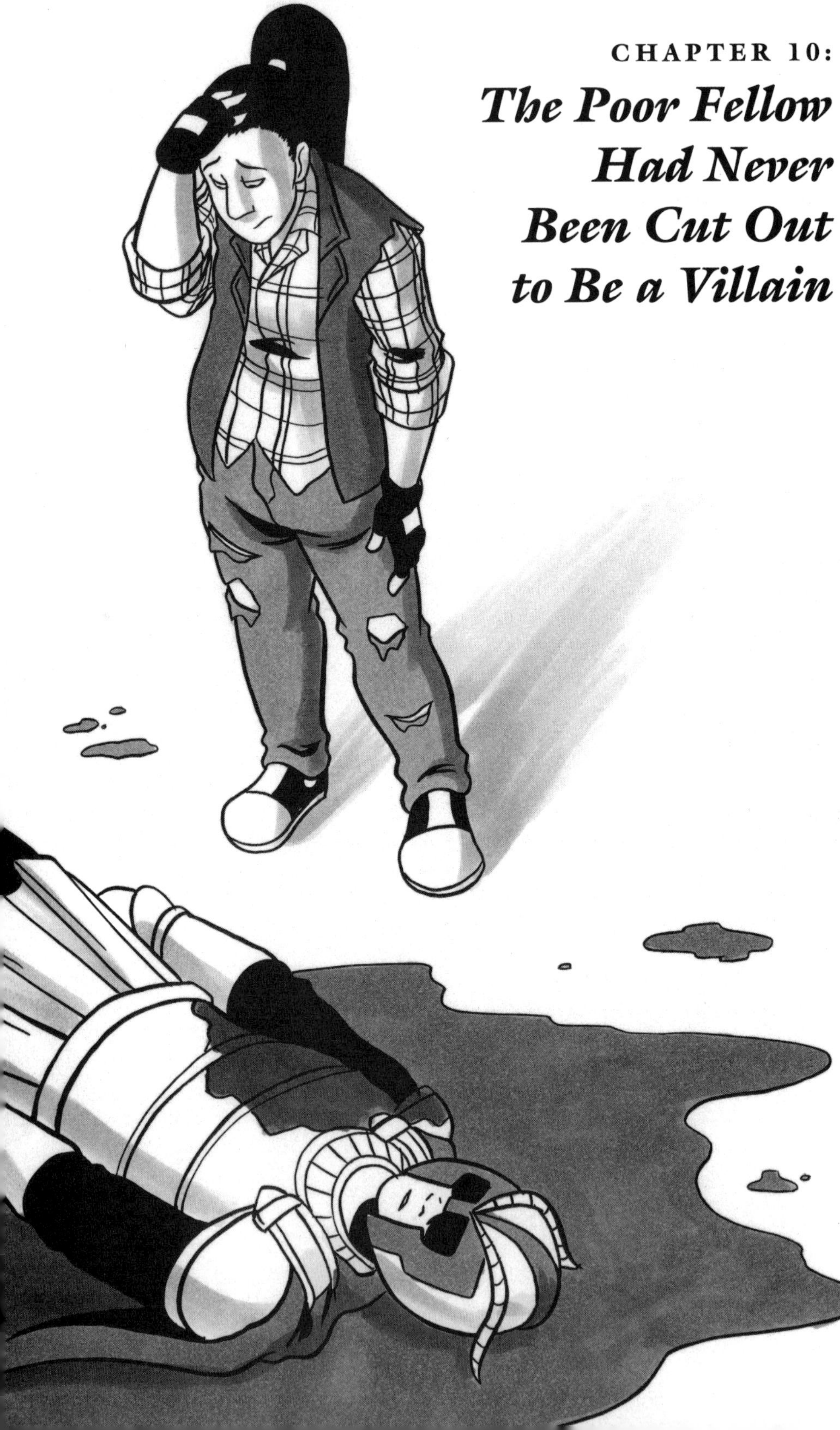

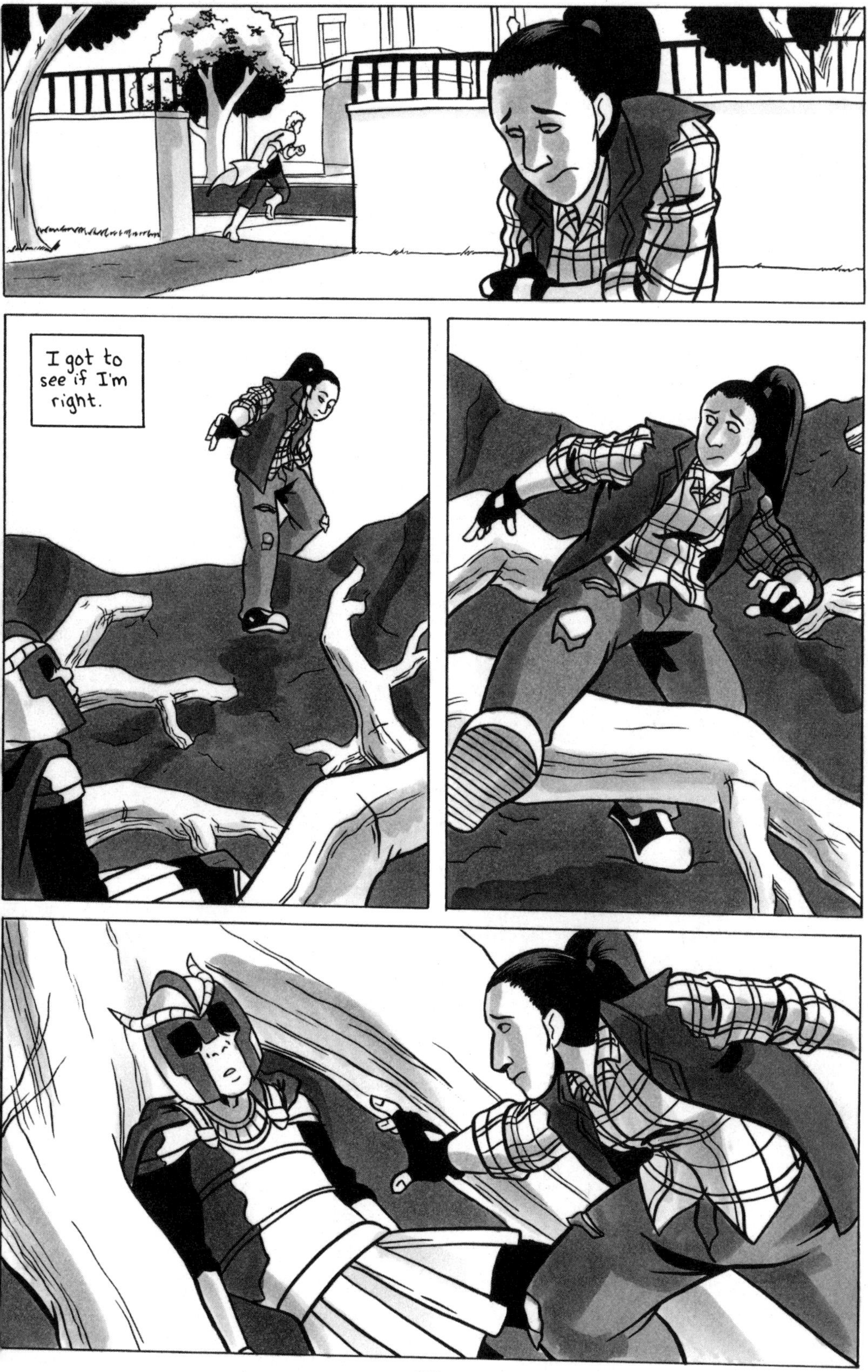
I got to see if I'm right.

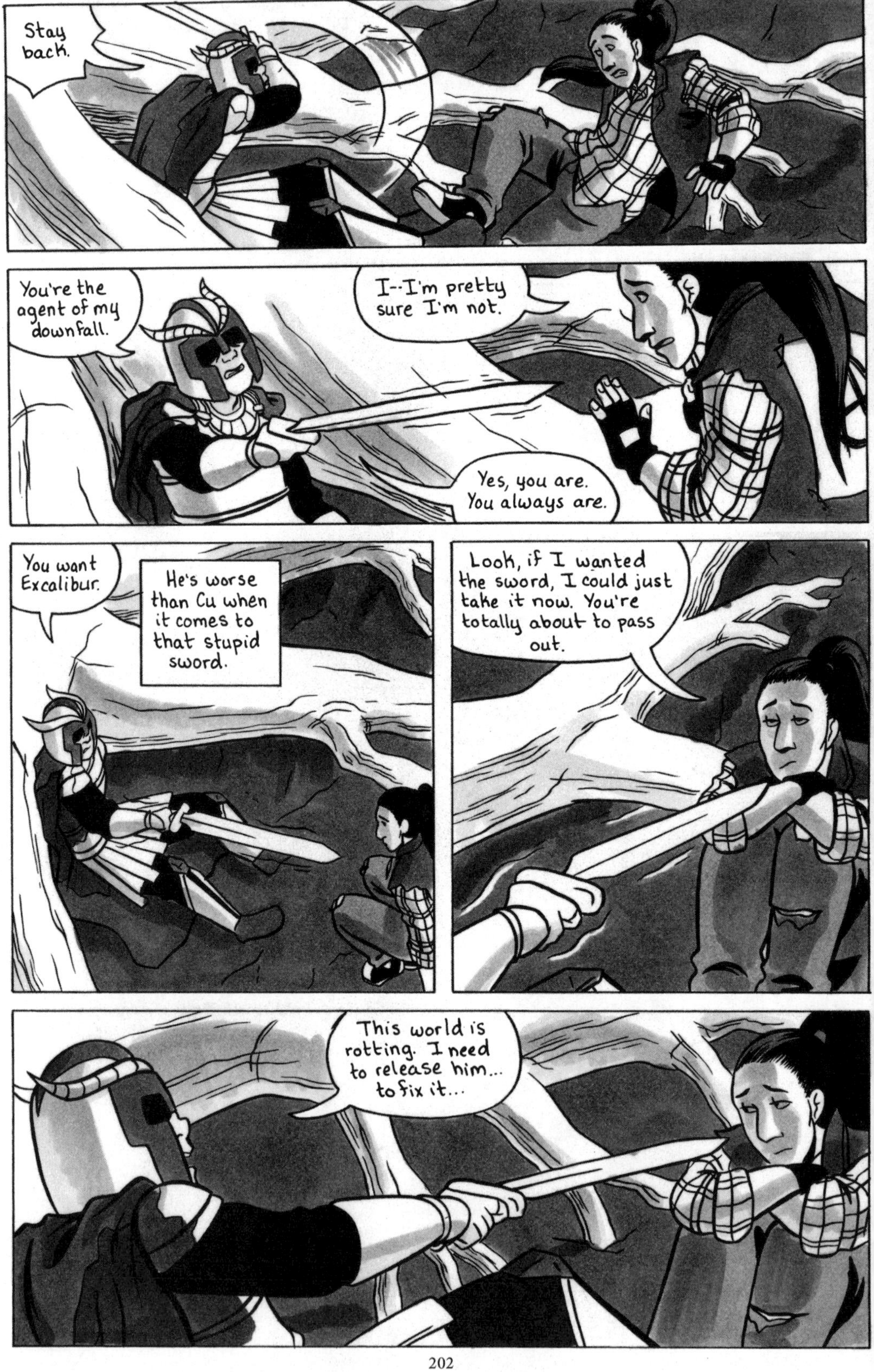
Stay back.
You're the agent of my downfall.
I--I'm pretty sure I'm not.
Yes, you are. You always are.
You want Excalibur.
He's worse than Cu when it comes to that stupid sword.
Look, if I wanted the sword, I could just take it now. You're totally about to pass out.
This world is rotting. I need to release him... to fix it...

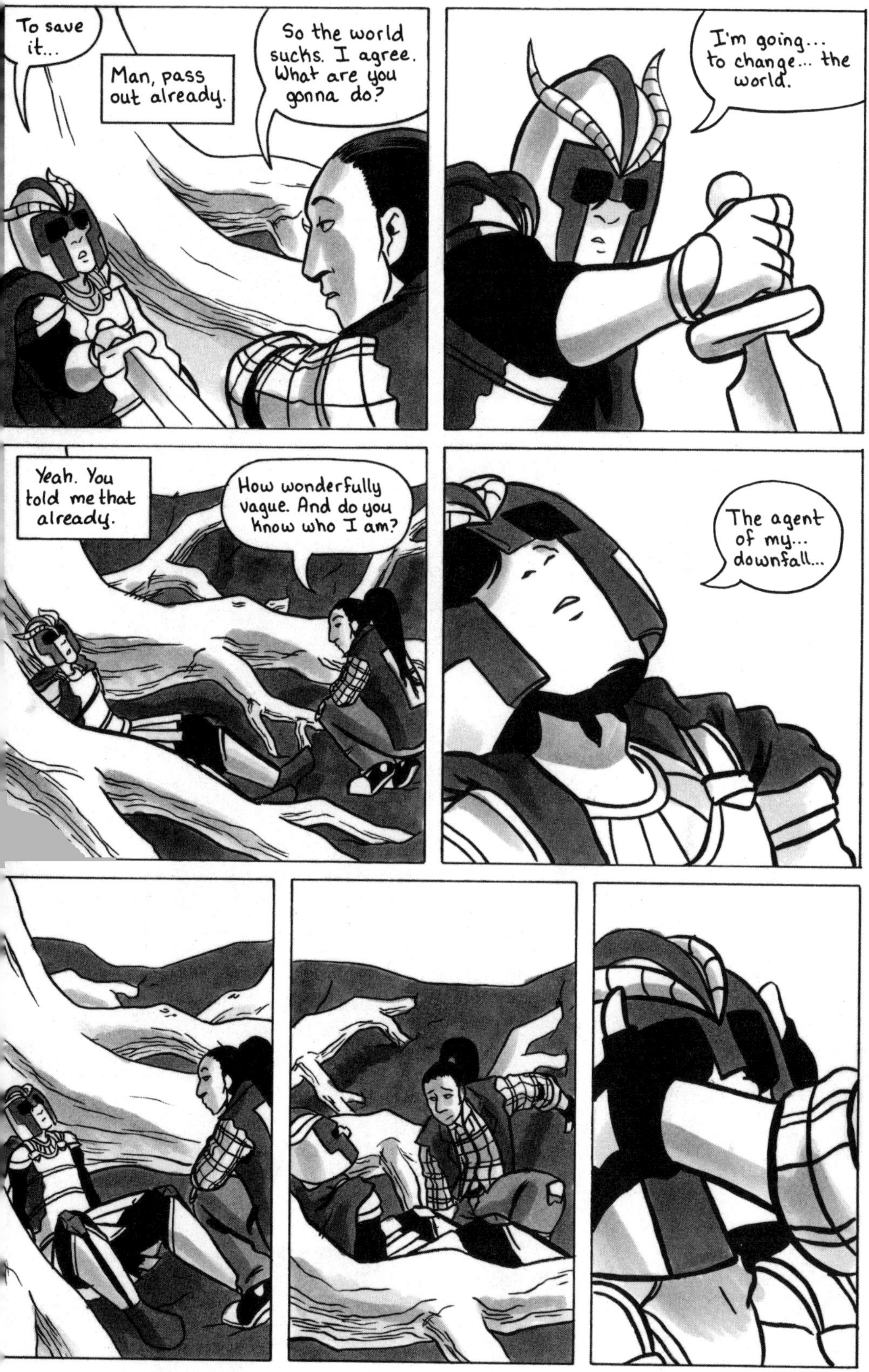
To save it...
Man, pass out already.
So the world sucks. I agree. What are you gonna do?
I'm going... to change... the world.
Yeah. You told me that already.
How wonderfully vague. And do you know who I am?
The agent of my... downfall...

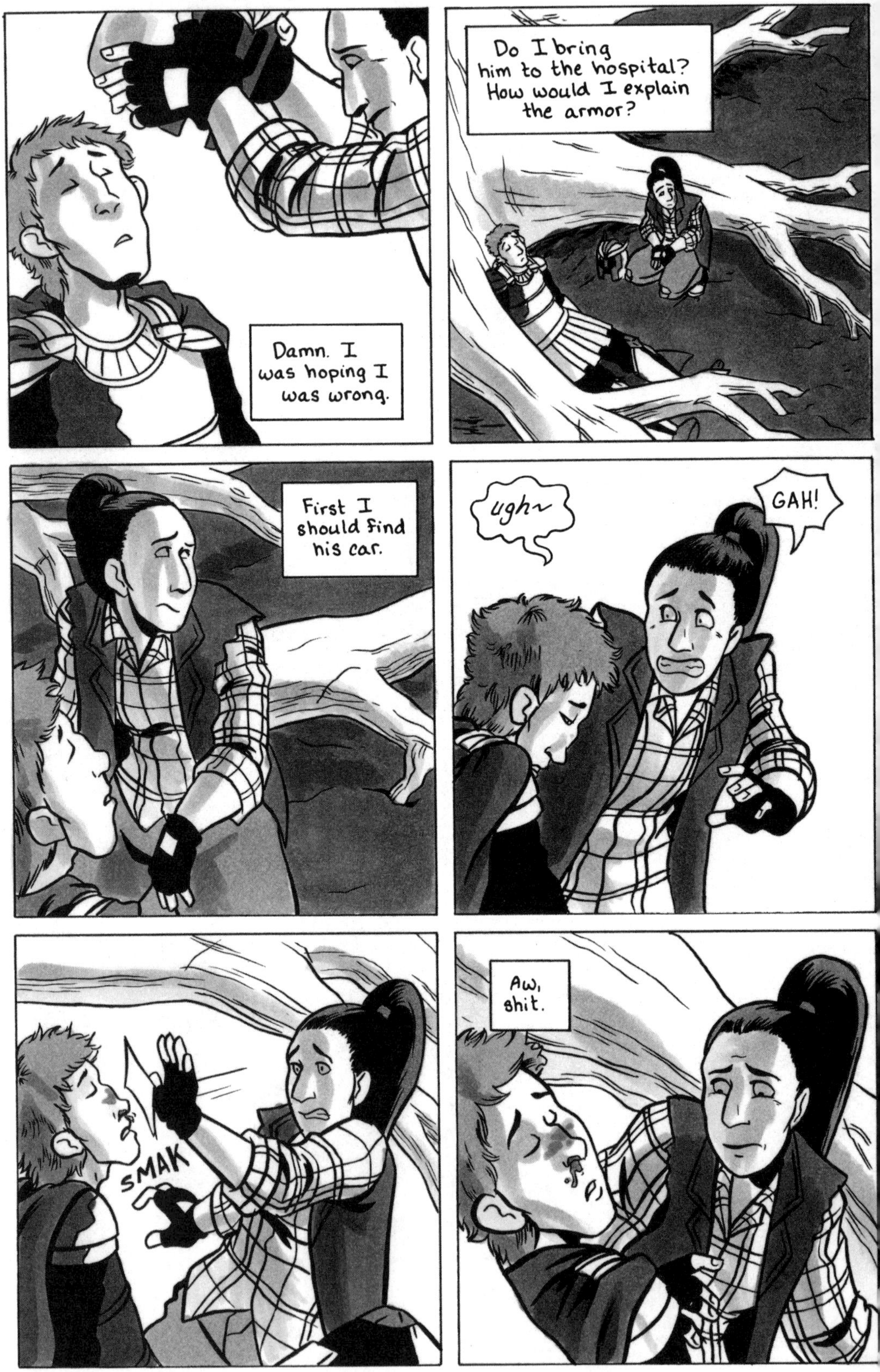
Damn. I was hoping I was wrong.
Do I bring him to the hospital? How would I explain the armor?
First I should find his car.
ugh~
GAH!
SMAK
Aw, shit.

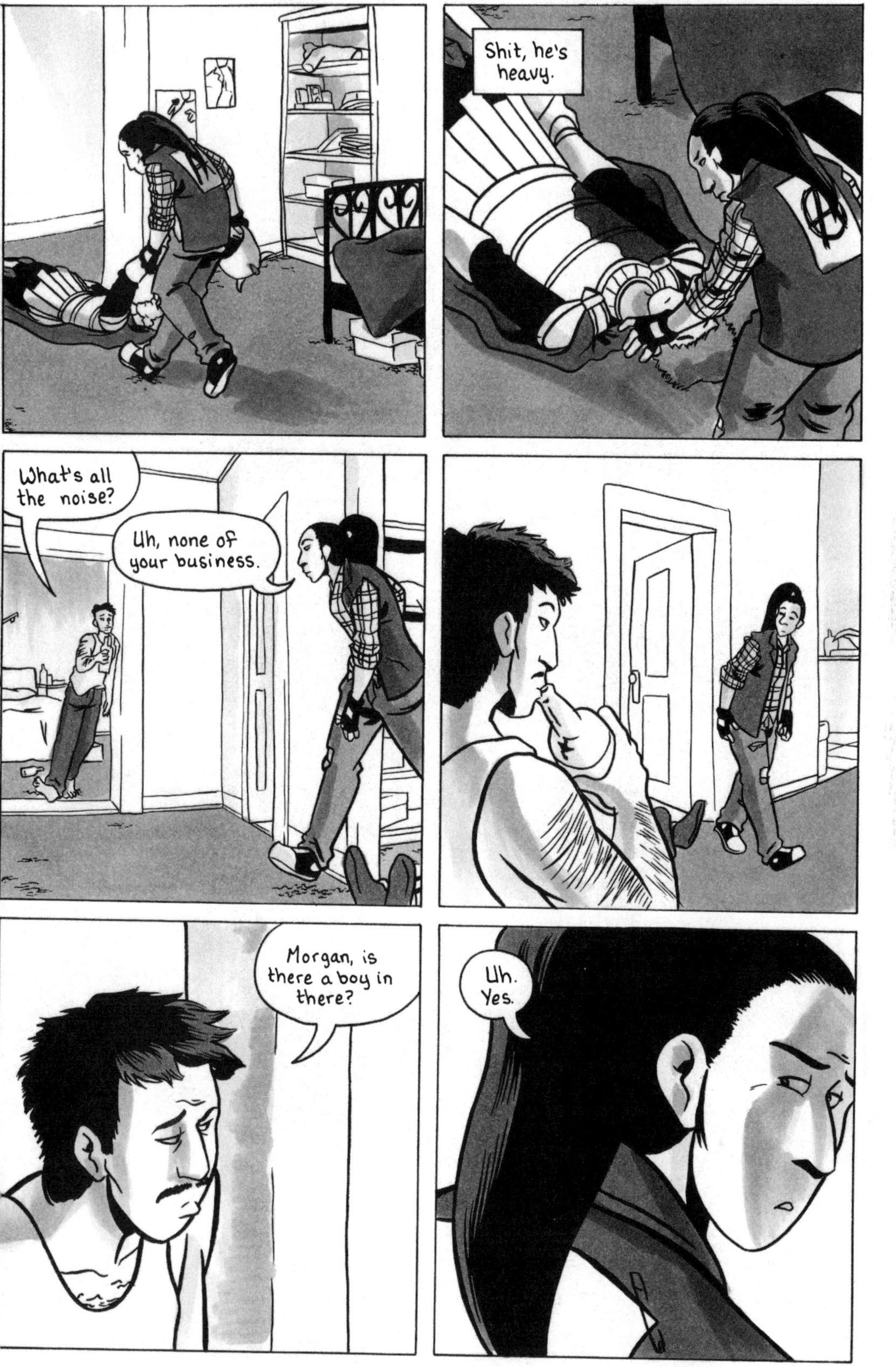
Shit, he's heavy.
What's all the noise?
Uh, none of your business.
Morgan, is there a boy in there?
Uh. Yes.

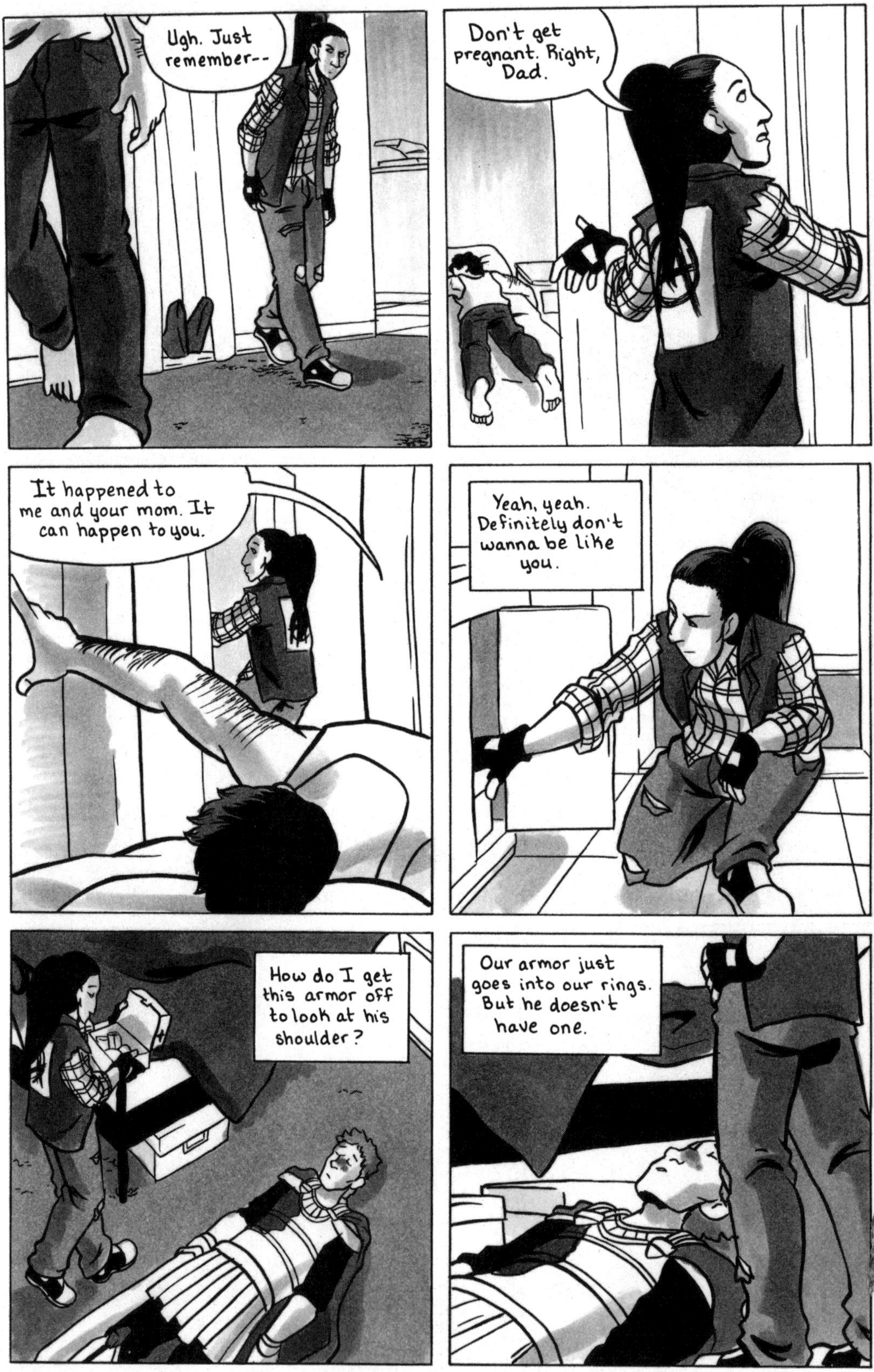
Ugh. Just remember--
Don't get pregnant. Right, Dad.
It happened to me and your mom. It can happen to you.
Yeah, yeah. Definitely don't wanna be like you.
How do I get this armor off to look at his shoulder?
Our armor just goes into our rings. But he doesn't have one.

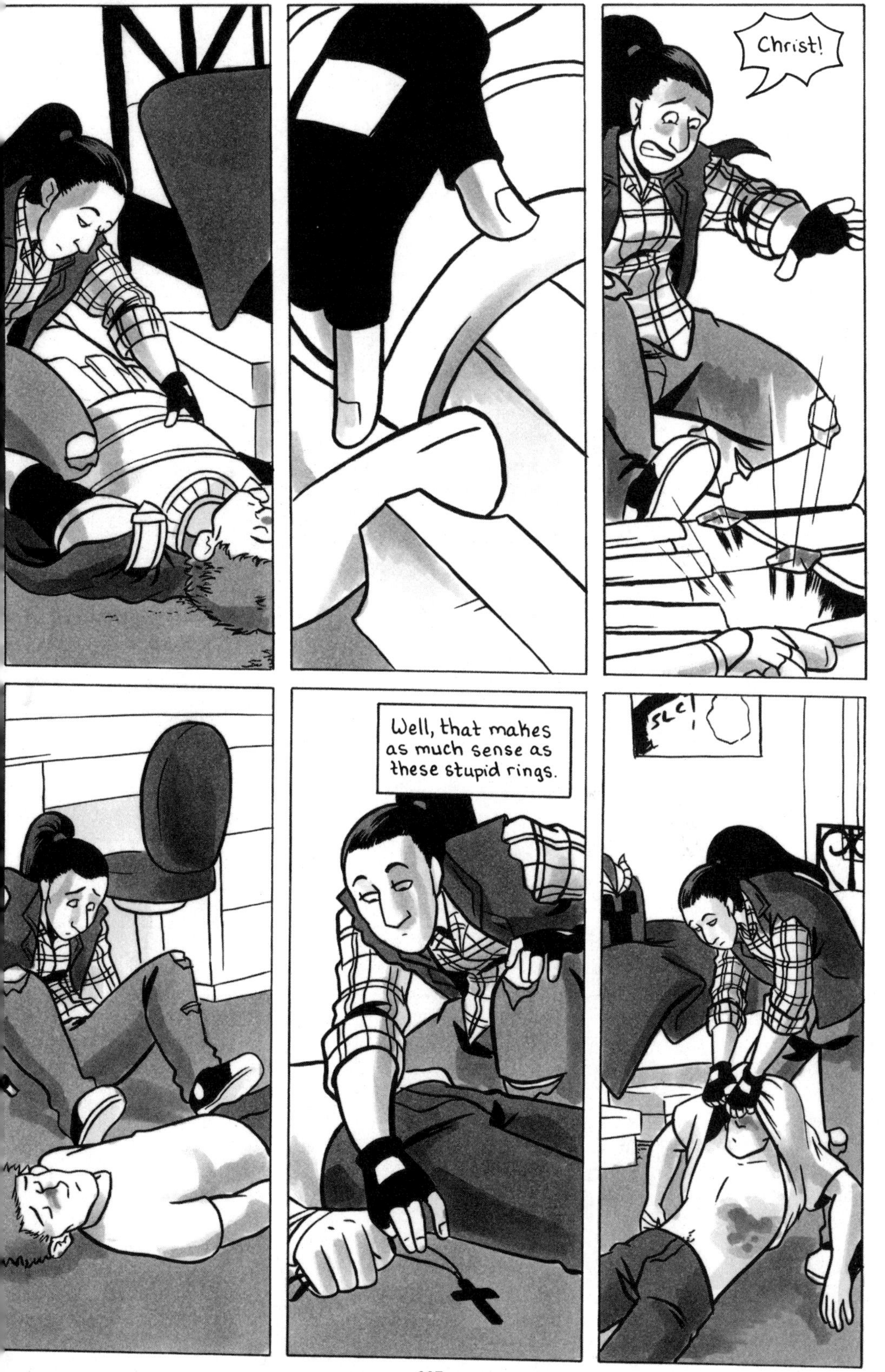
Christ!
Well, that makes as much sense as these stupid rings.

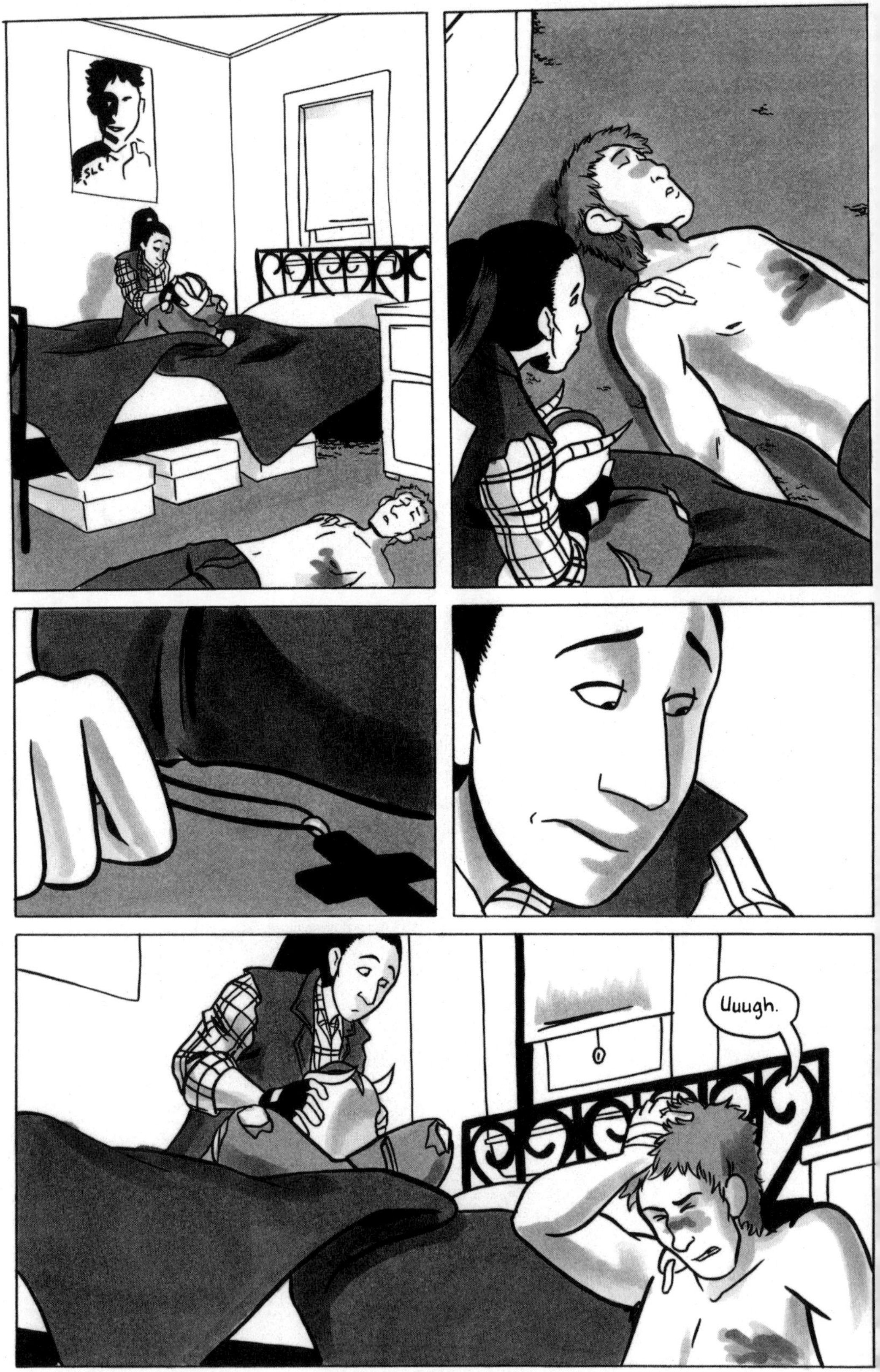
Uuugh.

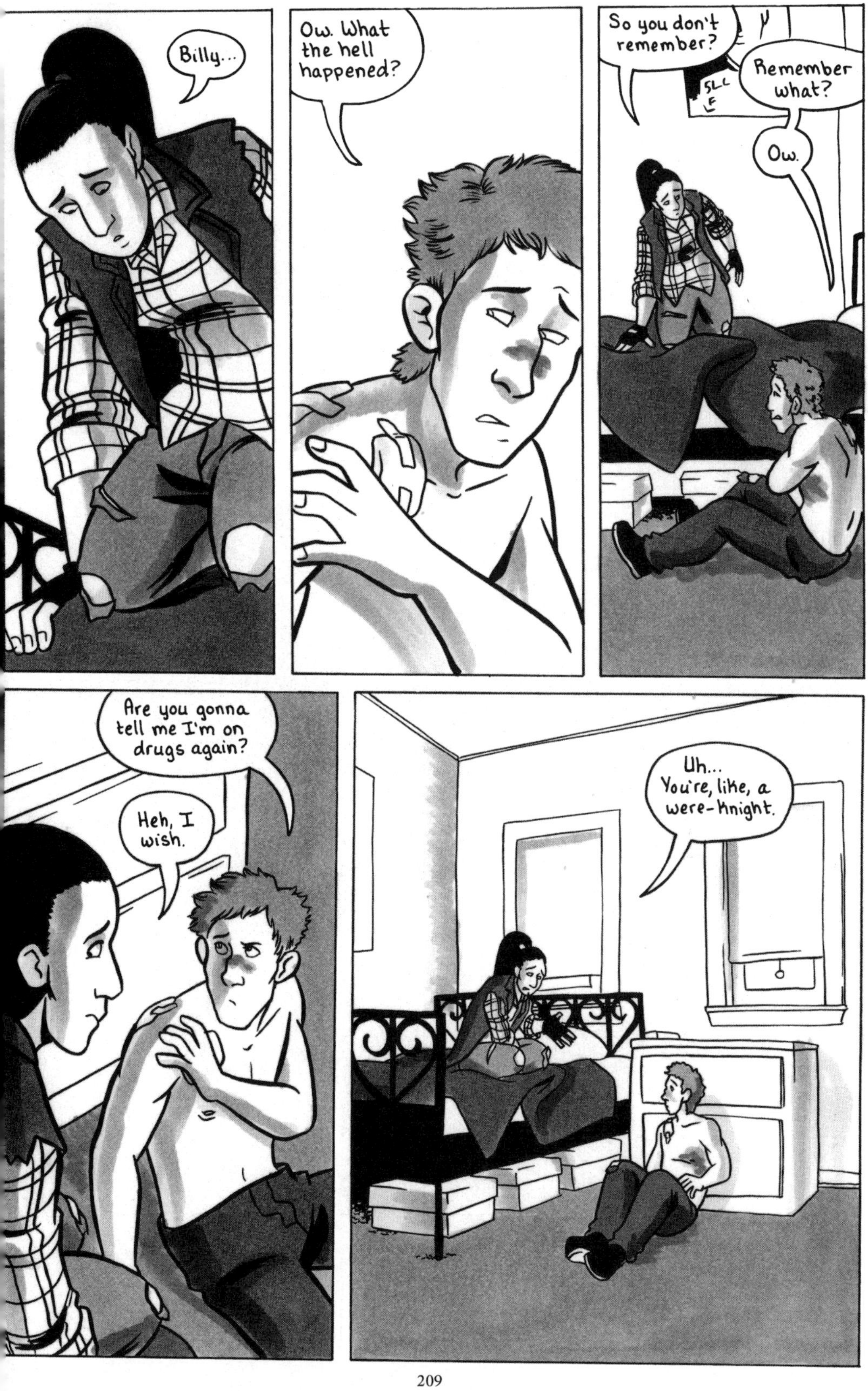
Billy...
Ow. What the hell happened?
So you don't remember?
Remember what?
Ow.
Are you gonna tell me I'm on drugs again?
Heh, I wish.
Uh... You're, like, a were-knight.

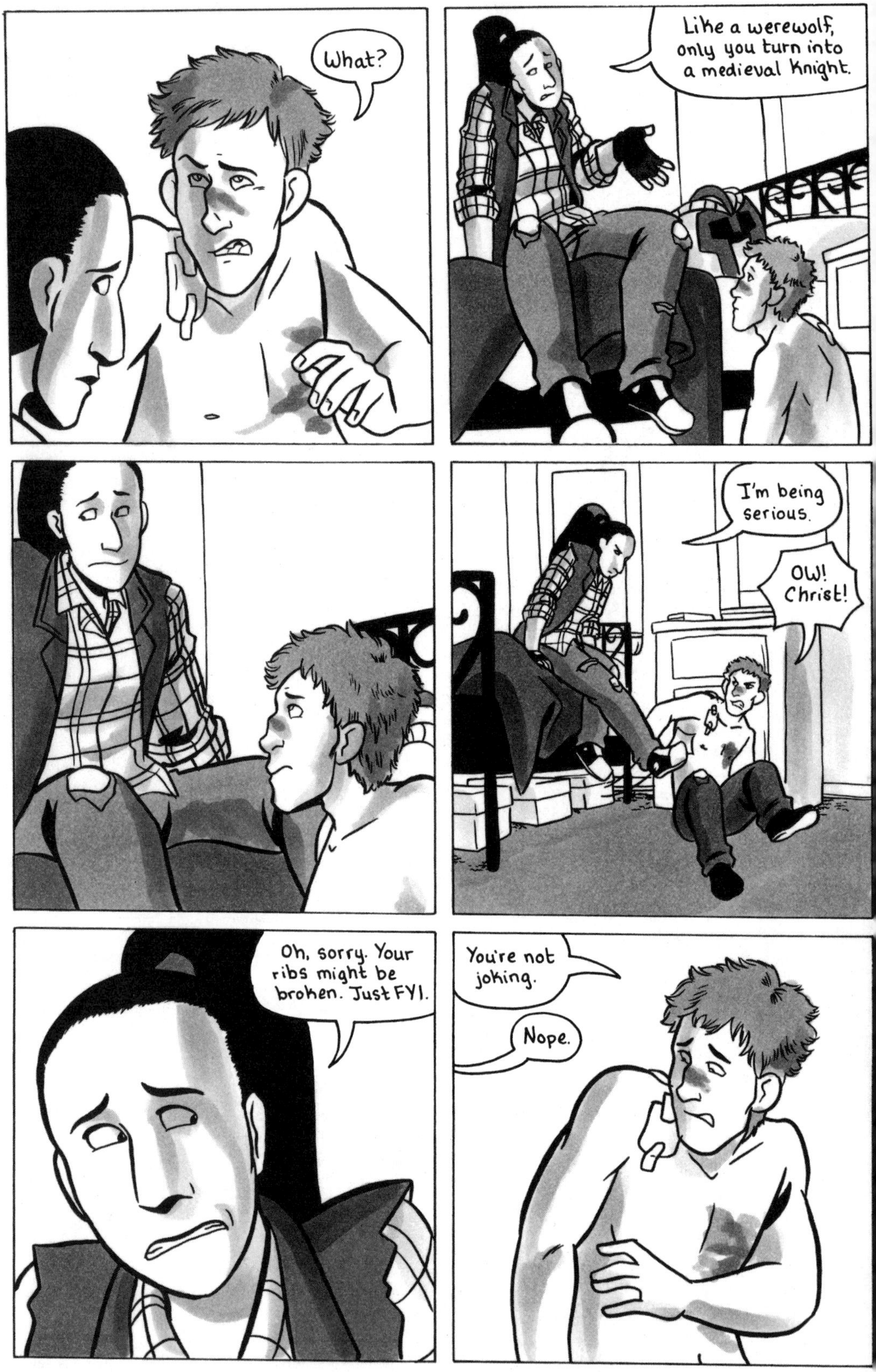
What?
Like a werewolf, only you turn into a medieval Knight.
I'm being serious.
OW! Christ!
Oh, sorry. Your ribs might be broken. Just FYI.
You're not joking.
Nope.

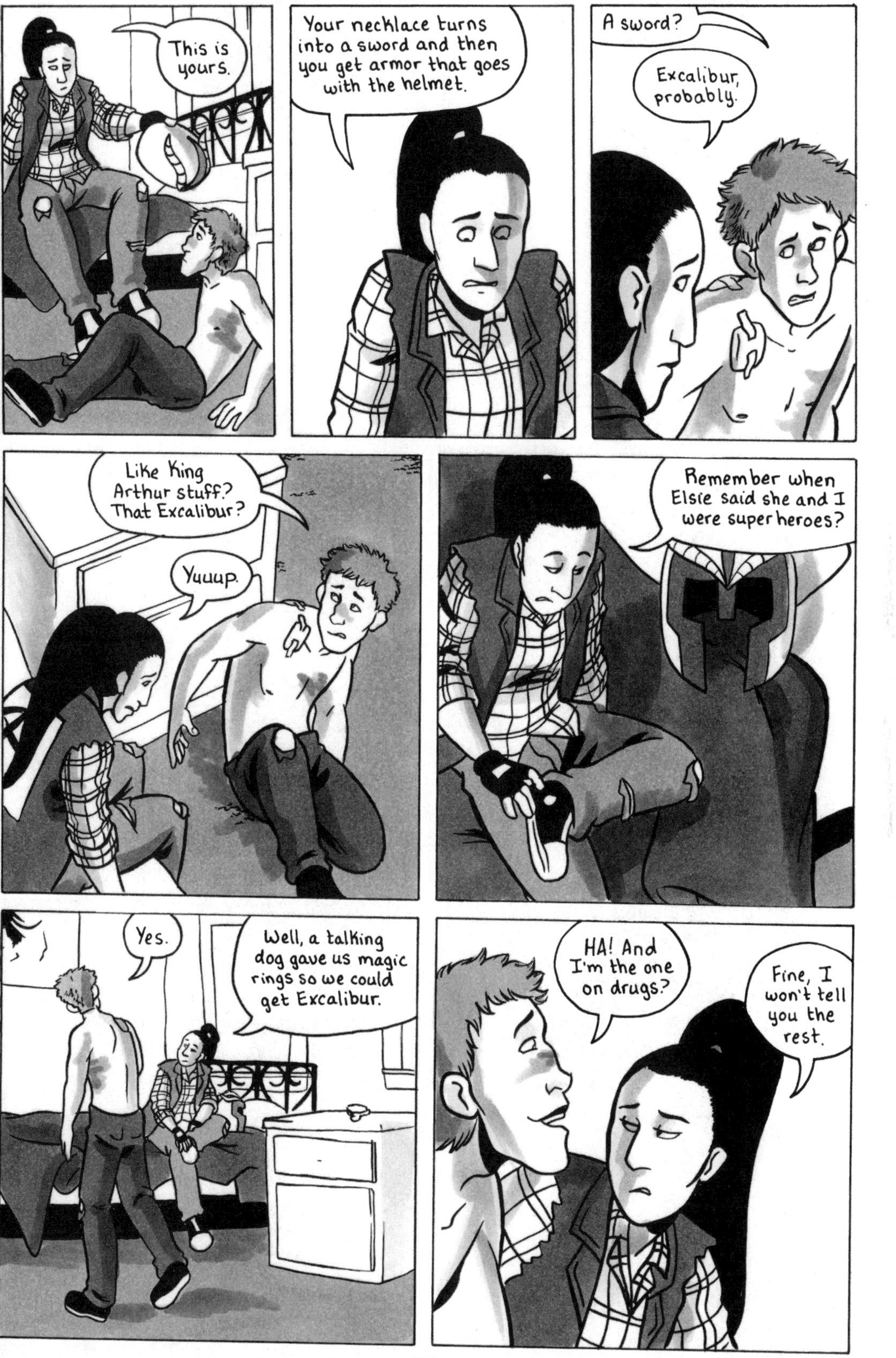
This is yours.
Your necklace turns into a sword and then you get armor that goes with the helmet.
A sword?
Excalibur, probably.
Like King Arthur stuff? That Excalibur?
Yuuup.
Remember when Elsie said she and I were superheroes?
Yes.
Well, a talking dog gave us magic rings so we could get Excalibur.
HA! And I'm the one on drugs?
Fine, I won't tell you the rest.

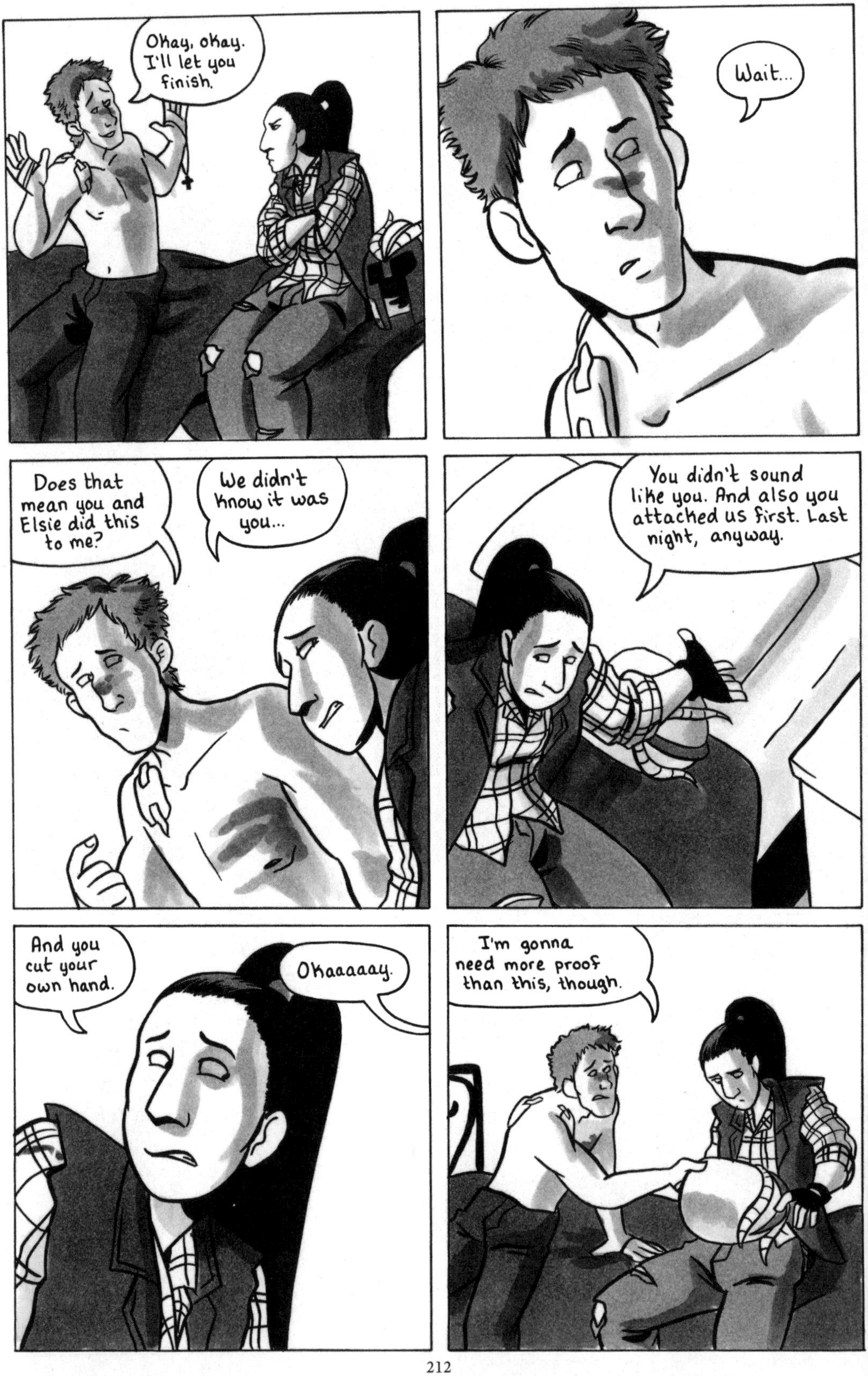
Okay, okay. I'll let you finish.
Wait...
Does that mean you and Elsie did this to me?
We didn't know it was you...
You didn't sound like you. And also you attached us first. Last night, anyway.
And you cut your own hand.
Okaaaaay.
I'm gonna need more proof than this, though.

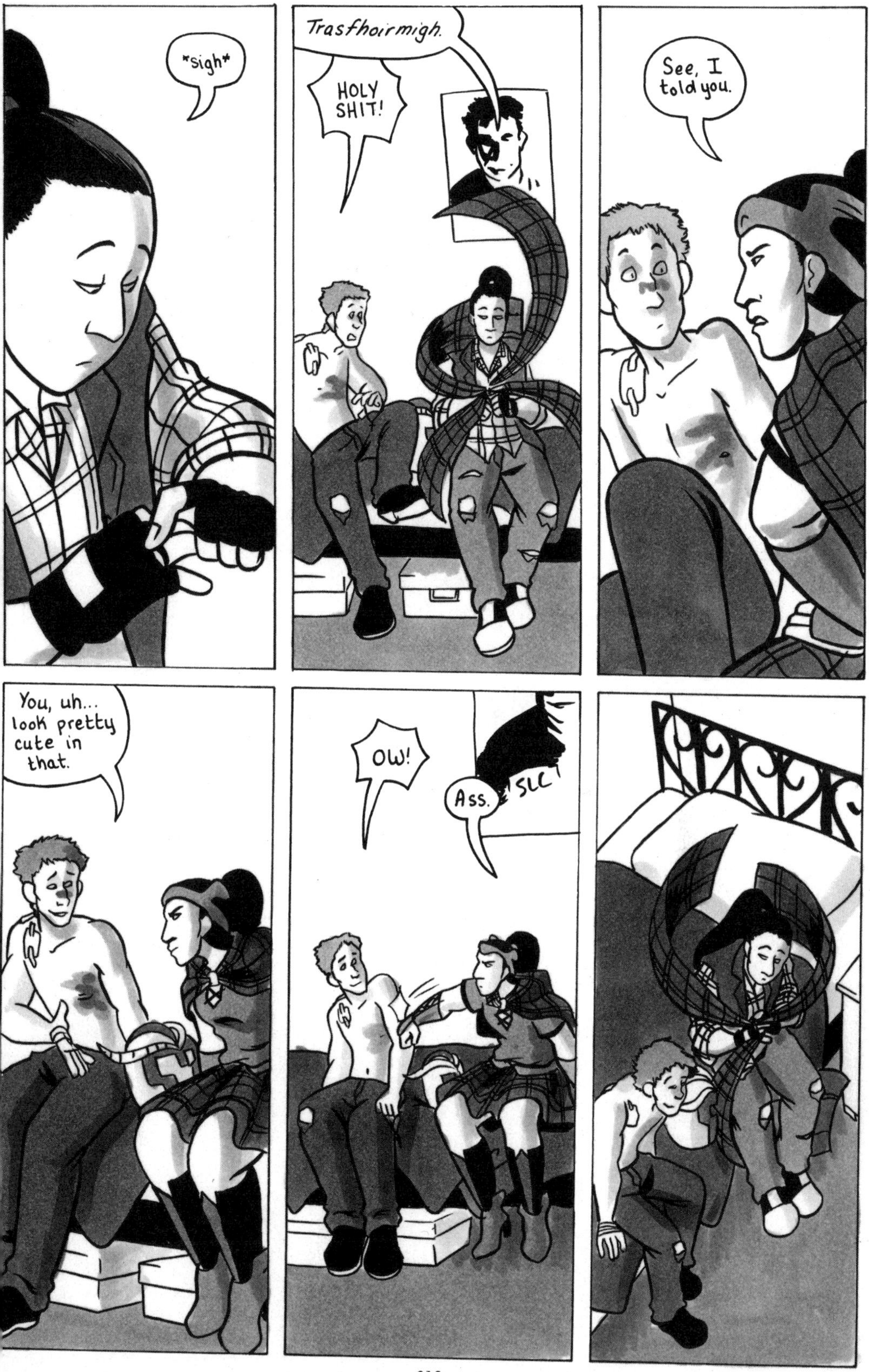
sigh
Trasfhoirmigh.
HOLY SHIT!
See, I told you.
You, uh... look pretty cute in that.
OW!
Ass.
SLC

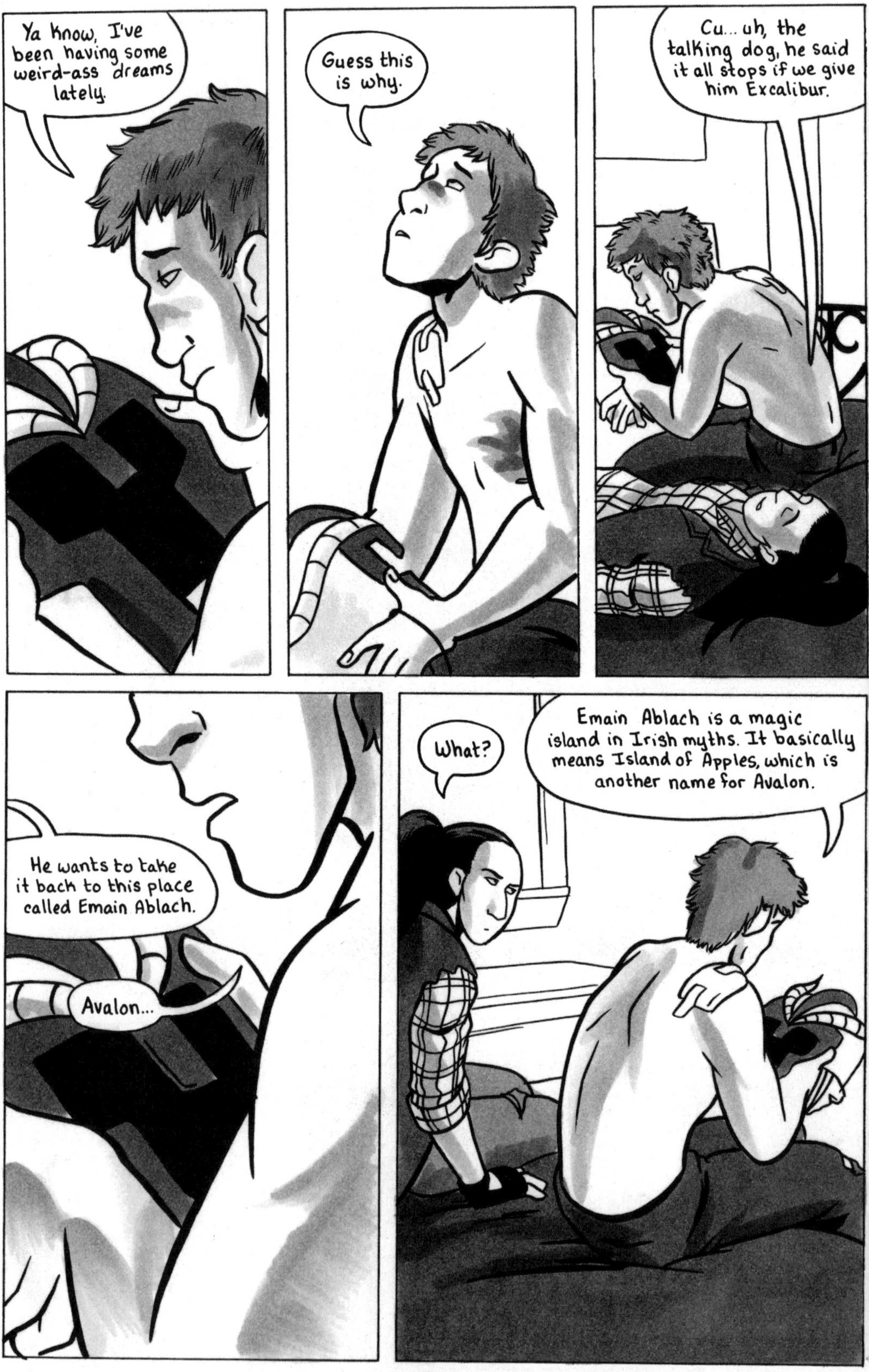
Ya know, I've been having some weird-ass dreams lately.
Guess this is why.
Cu... uh, the talking dog, he said it all stops if we give him Excalibur.
He wants to take it back to this place called Emain Ablach.
Avalon...
What?
Emain Ablach is a magic island in Irish myths. It basically means Island of Apples, which is another name for Avalon.

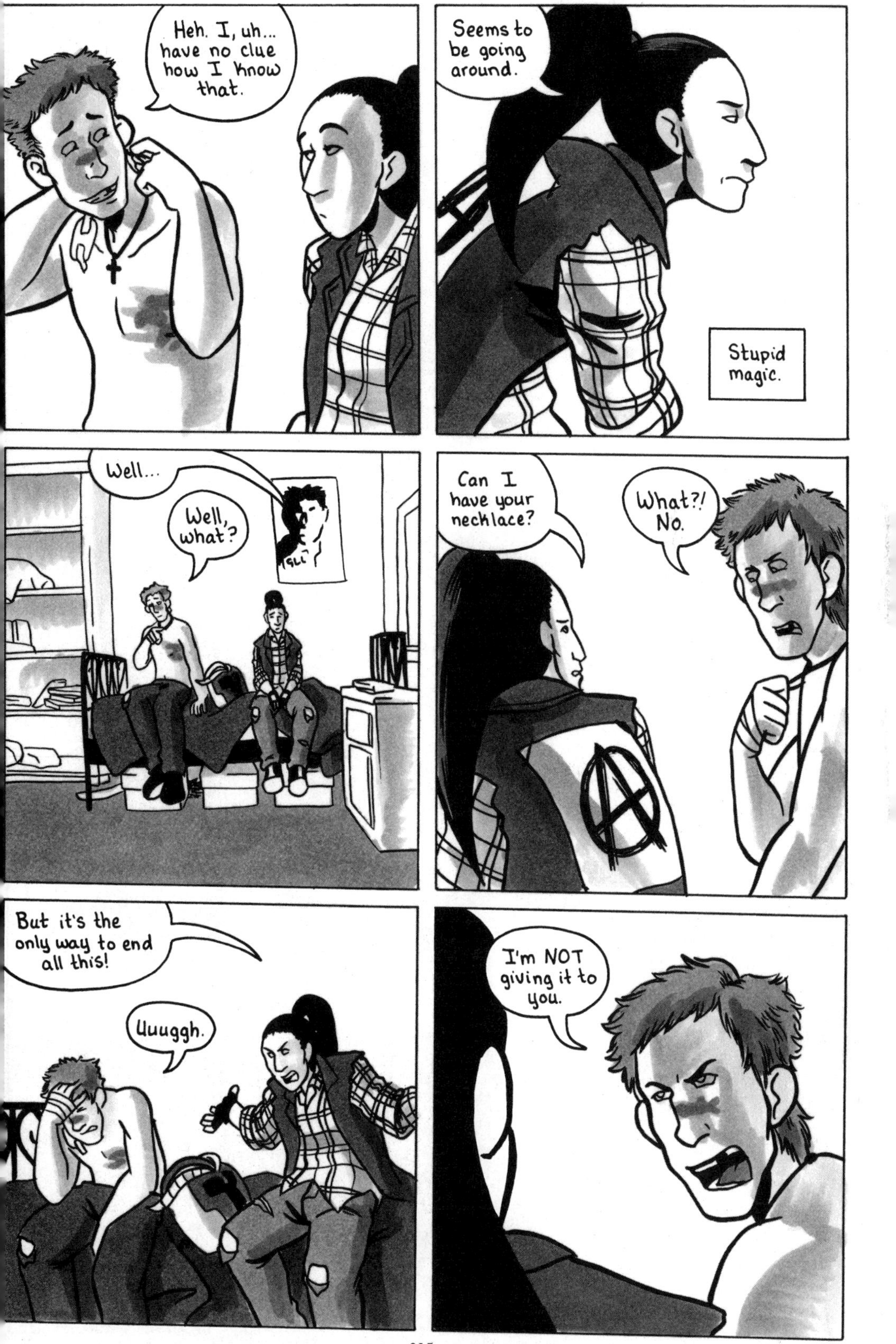
Heh. I, uh... have no clue how I know that.
Seems to be going around.
Stupid magic.
Well...
Well, what?
Can I have your necklace?
What?! No.
But it's the only way to end all this!
Uuuggh.
I'm NOT giving it to you.

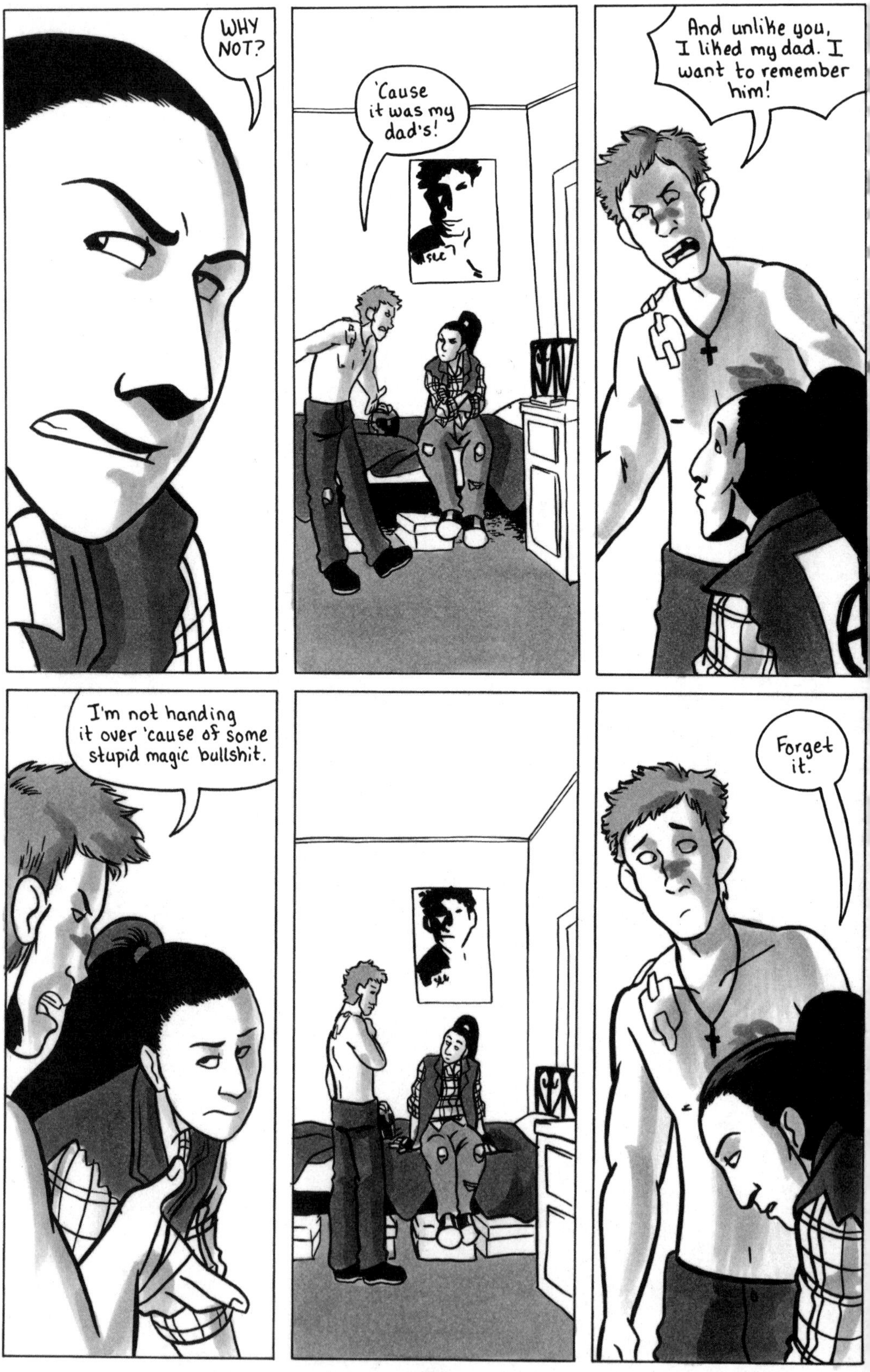
WHY NOT?
'Cause it was my dad's!
And unlike you, I liked my dad. I want to remember him!
I'm not handing it over 'cause of some stupid magic bullshit.
Forget it.

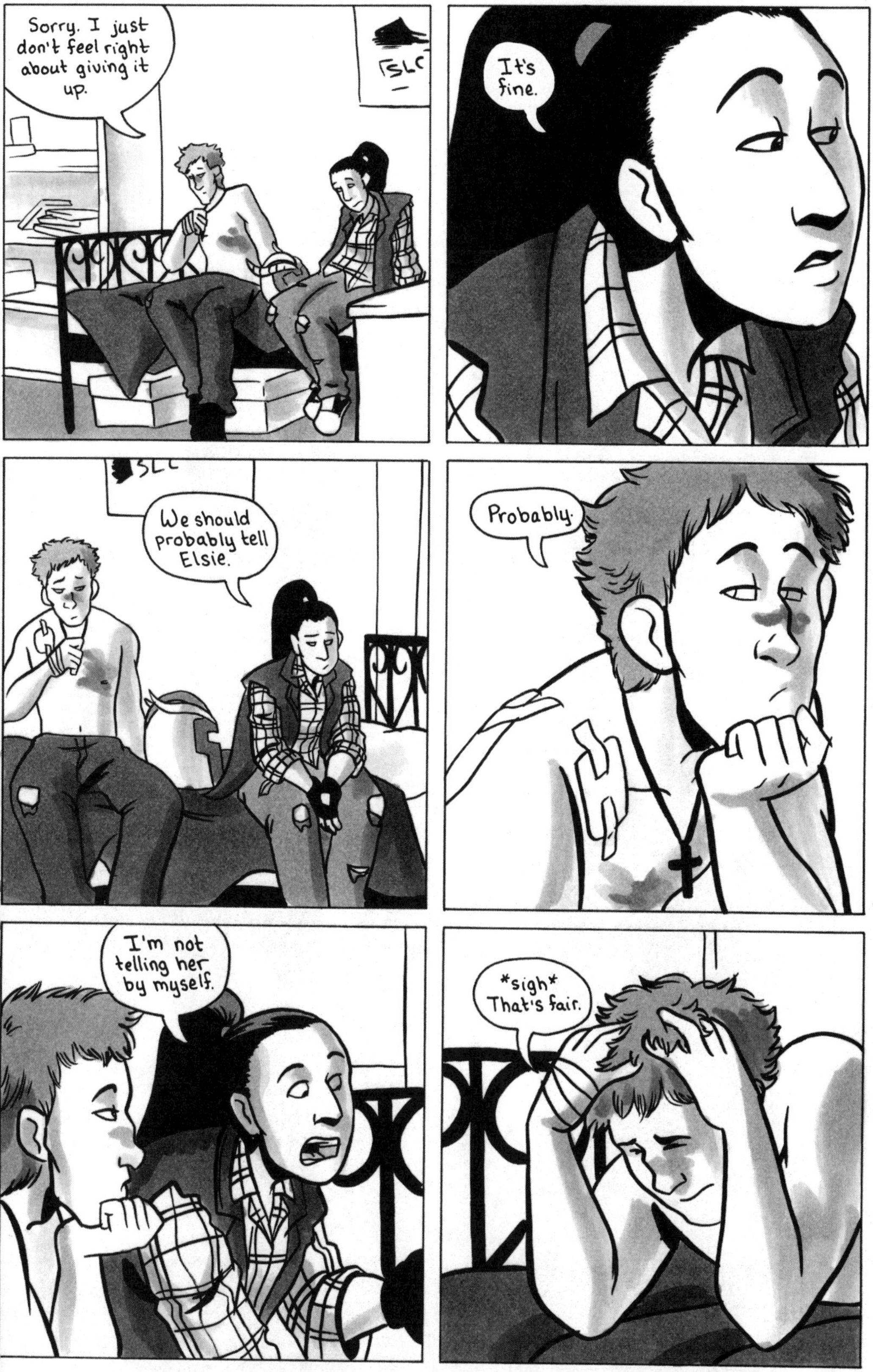
Sorry. I just don't feel right about giving it up.
ISLC
It's fine.
SLC
We should probably tell Elsie.
Probably.
I'm not telling her by myself.
sigh That's fair.

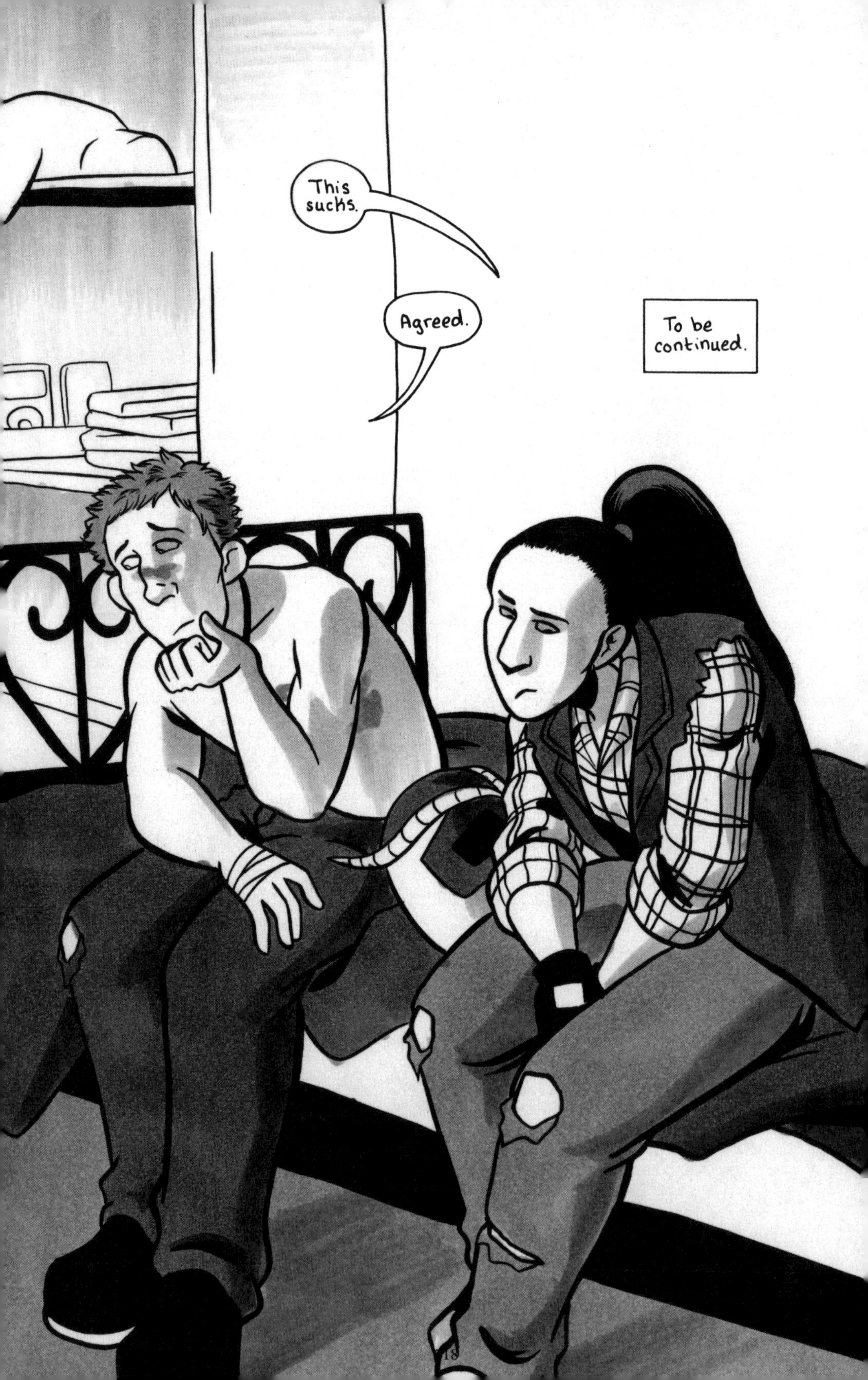
This sucks.
Agreed.
To be continued.

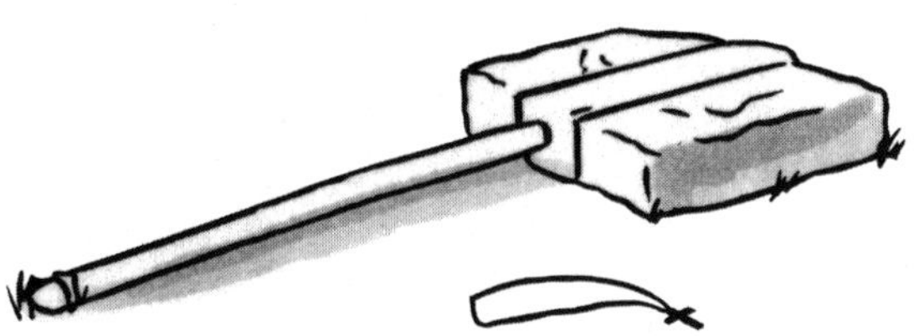

Kel McDonald has been working in comics for over ten years; she spent most of that time on her web comic *Sorcery 101*, which concluded in 2015. More recently, she organized the *Cautionary Fables and Fairy Tales* anthology series while contributing to other anthologies, such as *Dark Horse Presents*, *Smut Peddler*, and *The Sleep of Reason*. She is currently working on the next volume of *Misfits of Avalon* for Dark Horse Comics.

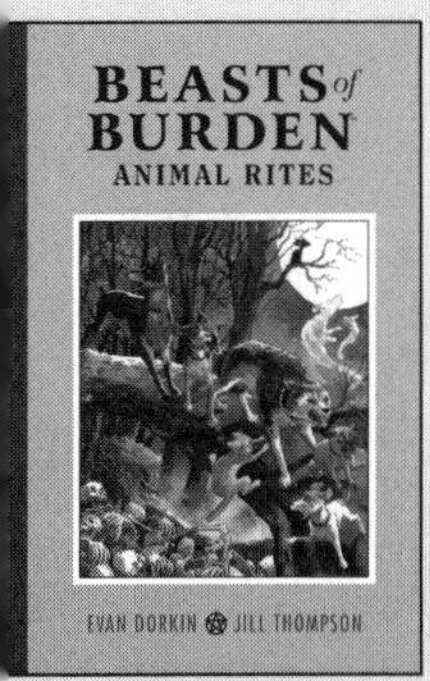
BEASTS of BURDEN
ANIMAL RITES
EVAN DORKIN JILL THOMPSON

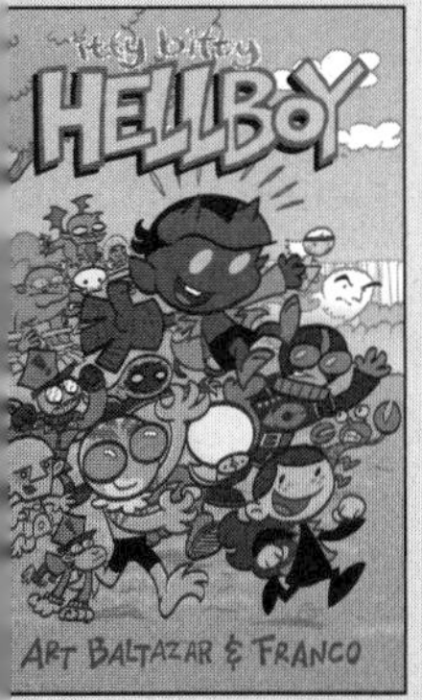
Itty Bitty
HELLBOY
ART BALTAZAR & FRANCO

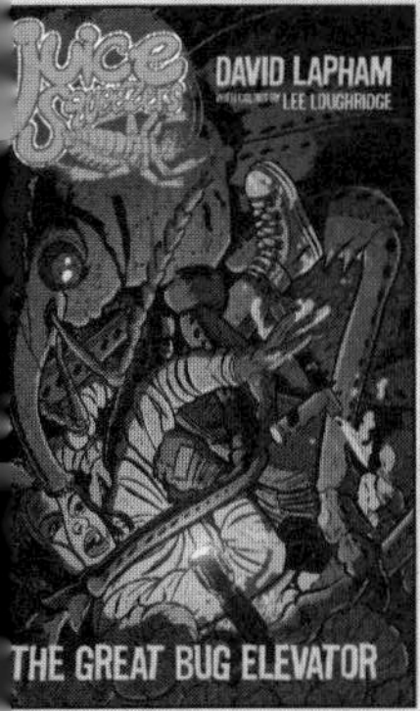
Juice Squeezers
DAVID LAPHAM
LEE LOUGHRIDGE
THE GREAT BUG ELEVATOR

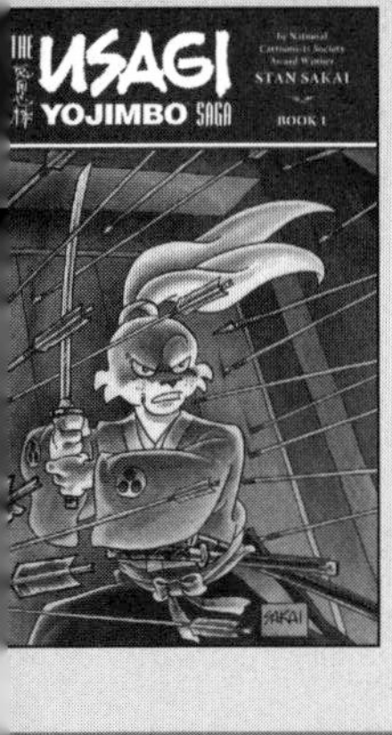
THE USAGI YOJIMBO SAGA
STAN SAKAI
BOOK 1
SAKAI

MORE YOUNG ADULT TITLES FROM

DARK HORSE BOOKS!

BEASTS OF BURDEN: ANIMAL RITES

Written by Evan Dorkin, illustrated by Jill Thompson

Beneath its surface of green lawns and white picket fences, the picturesque little town of Burden Hill harbors dark and sinister secrets. It's up to a heroic gang of dogs—and one cat—to protect the town from the evil forces at work. Adventure, mystery, horror, and humor thrive on every page!

978-1-59582-513-1 | $19.99

ITTY BITTY HELLBOY

Written by Art Baltazar and Franco, illustrated by Art Baltazar

The characters that sprung from Mike Mignola's imagination, with an AW YEAH COMICS twist! This book has ALL the FUN, adventure, and AW YEAHNESS in one itty bitty package!

978-1-61655-414-9 | $9.99

JUICE SQUEEZERS: THE GREAT BUG ELEVATOR

Written and illustrated by David Lapham

Tunnels made by a legion of giant bugs crisscross the fields below the quaint California town of Weeville, and only one thing can stop them from overrunning the place: the Juice Squeezers. A covert group of scrawny tweens, the Squeezers are the only ones who can fit into the cramped subterranean battlefield and fight the insects on the frontlines!

978-1-61655-438-5 | $12.99

THE USAGI YOJIMBO SAGA

Written and illustrated by Stan Sakai

Dark Horse proudly presents Miyamoto Usagi's epic trek along the warrior's path in a new series of deluxe compilations. The rabbit *ronin*'s adventures have won multiple awards and delighted readers for thirty years!

VOLUME 1: 978-1-61655-609-9 | $24.99
VOLUME 2: 978-1-61655-610-5 | $24.99

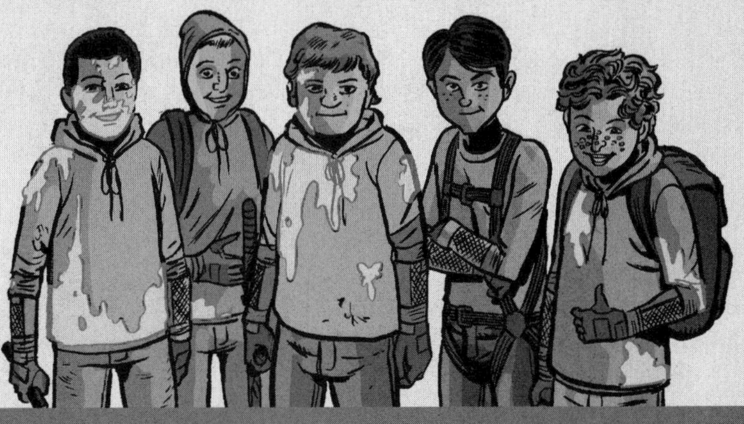

AVAILABLE AT YOUR LOCAL COMICS SHOP OR BOOKSTORE! • To find a comics shop in your area, call 1-888-266-4226.
For more information or to order direct visit DarkHorse.com or call 1-800-862-0052 Mon.–Fri. 9 AM to 5 PM Pacific Time. Prices and availability subject to change without notice.